The Book of
Common Prayer
1559

The Collectes, Epistles,

and Golpels, to be vfed at the celebracion of
the Lordes fupper, and holy Communion through
the yeare.

¶ The fyrft Sundaye in
Aduent.

¶ The Collecte.

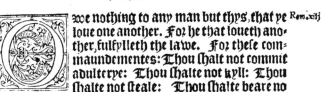

Lmighty God, geue vs grace, that we maye caft away the workes of darkenes, and put vpõ vs the armour of light, now in the time of thys mortal lyfe, (in the whych thy fonne Jefus Chrift came to vifite vs in great humilitie) that in the laft daye, when he fhall come agayne in hys glorious maieftie, to iudge bothe the quicke and the dead: we may ryfe to the life immortal, through him, who lyueth and reygneth with thee and the holy ghoft, nowe and euer. Amen.

The Epiftle.

Ro. xiij

we nothing to any man but thys, that ye loue one another. For he that loueth another, fulfylleth the lawe. For thefe commaundementes: Thou fhalt not commit adulterye: Thou fhalte not kyll: Thou fhalte not fteale: Thou fhalte beare no falfe witnefle: Thou fhalt not luft: and fo forth (yf there be any other commaundemente) it is all comprehended in thys fayinge: namely, loue thy neyghbour as thy felf. Loue hurteth not hys neyghbour: therefore is loue the fulfyllinge of the lawe. Thys alfo, we know the feafon, howe that it is tyme that we fhoulde now awake out of flepe, for now is oure faluation nerer, then when we beleued. The night is paffed, the day is come nye: lette vs therefore caft awaye the dedes of darkenes, and lette vs

A.i.   put

The Book of Common Prayer

1559

The Elizabethan Prayer Book

EDITED BY JOHN E. BOOTY

Published for
The Folger Shakespeare Library
by
The University Press of Virginia
Charlottesville

Publication of this edition of
the 1559 Book of Common Prayer
was made possible by a generous gift from
the Honorable and Mrs. John Clifford Folger.

The University Press of Virginia
Copyright © 1976 by the Folger Shakespeare Library

First published 1976

Frontispiece and ornamental letters are from the
1559 Book of Common Prayer in the Josiah H. Benton
Prayer Book Collection. By courtesy of the Trustees
of the Boston Public Library.

Library of Congress Cataloging in Publication Data

Church of England. Book of common prayer.
    The Book of common prayer, 1559.

    (Folger documents of Tudor and Stuart civilization;
no. 22)
    Bibliography: p. 417.
    Includes index.
    I. Booty, John E.   II.   Series.
BX5145.A4   1559b   264'.03   75-29330
ISBN 0-8139-0503-6

Printed in the United States of America

Editor's Preface

The Book of Common Prayer provides for the Church of England—and for the daughter churches which compose the worldwide Anglican communion—daily, weekly, and seasonal rounds of formal, corporate worship. It came into being in the sixteenth century as a result of the demands of reformers, such as Archbishop Thomas Cranmer, for a simplified, more biblical, and more "modern" order of worship. The Elizabethan Prayer Book which follows was the third and most endurable of the earliest editions and provided the context in which Elizabethans, from Queen Elizabeth and William Shakespeare to the village housewife and yeoman farmer, lived and died.

Most readers of this edition will be thoroughly familiar with the Book of Common Prayer. For the reader less familiar with its contents, it might be advisable to begin by reading carefully the opening essays ("The Preface" and "Of Ceremonies, Why Some Be Abolished and Some Retained"), and then the order of worship for Sunday morning (Morning Prayer, Litany, and Holy Communion), using the tables at the front of the book to locate the Scripture to be read. One might then settle on Easter Day, the chief festival of the Christian year, and suppose that Easter falls on the twenty-first day of the month. In this instance one would read Psalm 105 in Morning Prayer (see p. 24). One would then read Exodus 12 for the first Lesson and Romans 6 for the second (see p. 28). If possible, one should read this Scripture from one of those versions available to Elizabethans, such as the Great Bible, the Bishops' Bible, or the Geneva Bible, although the more accessible Authorized Version (King James Version) of 1611 will suffice. For Holy Communion one would locate Easter Day among the Collects, Epistles, and Gospels (see p. 152). Since Baptism was often the concluding part of the morning sequence of worship, one might wish to read it through after reading Holy Communion.

Having done this, one will have begun to understand not only the Prayer Book but also the Elizabethans, whether they were enthusiastically committed to the Church or not. For all English men and women were required by law to attend their parish church on Sundays. In the parish churches and in the cathedrals the nation was at prayer, the commonwealth was being realized, and God, in whose hands the destinies of all were lodged, was worshiped in spirit and in truth.

The Text of This Edition

The text which follows is that published by Richard Jugge and John Cawode in 1559 (STC 16292). It is the same as that printed in the Parker Society edition,[1] although William Keatinge Clay, the editor of the latter, used a copy of the 1559 Book once belonging to the historian of liturgy William Maskell and now in the British Museum (C.25.m.7.). The copy that I have used is one that once belonged to Aldenham House, Herts., and to Edward Auriol Drummond, and was purchased in 1939 for the Josiah H. Benton Prayer Book Collection now at the Boston Public Library.[2] This edition seems to conform more nearly to the specifications of the 1559 Act of Uniformity than any others supposedly printed in 1559.[3] I have collated this edition, as did Clay, with that of Richard Grafton, using a copy presently in the British Museum (C.25.l.9.). It might be argued that this latter Prayer Book should have been used as my copy text, since in some respects it is more nearly complete; but the fact that the

[1] Clay, *Liturgical Services*, pp. 23–271.

[2] See *The Book of Common Prayer and Books Connected with Its Origin and Growth: Catalogue of the Collection of Josiah Henry Benton*, 2d ed. (Boston, 1914). STC 16292 in entered in the Boston Public Library's copy of the catalog.

[3] See Clay, *Liturgical Services*, pp. xii–xv.

Jugge and Cawode book seems to be more in line with the uniformity act led me to decide that it was the earlier edition and deserved pride of place. The additional prayers set in brackets toward the end of the Litany in this edition were copied from another Jugge and Cawode Prayer Book.[4] Yet another edition published by Jugge and Cawode in 1559 is unique in that it contains the Black Rubric not contained in the copy text for this edition, nor in the 1559 Grafton.[5] It reads:

Although no order can be so perfectly devised, but it may be of some, either for their ignorance and infirmity, or else of malice and obstinacy, misconstrued, depraved, and interpreted in a wrong part: And yet because brotherly charity willeth that so much as conveniently may be, offenses should be taken away: therefore we willing to do the same. Whereas it is ordained in the *Book of Common Prayer*, in the administration of the Lord's Supper, that the communicants kneeling should receive the Holy Communion: which thing being well meant, for a signification of the humble and grateful acknowledging of the benefits of Christ given unto the worthy receiver, and to avoid the prophanation and disorder which about the Holy Communion might else ensue. Lest yet the same kneeling might be thought or taken otherwise, we do declare that it is not meant thereby, that any adoration is done, or ought to be done, either unto the Sacramental bread or wine there bodily received, or unto any real and essential presence there being of Christ's natural flesh and blood. For as concerning the Sacramental bread and wine, they remain still in their very natural substances, and therefore may not be adored, for that where idolatry to be abhorred of all faithful Christians. And as concerning the natural body and blood of our Savior Christ, they are in heaven and not here: for it is against the truth of Christ's true natural body, to be in mo [more] places than in the one at one time.

This copy in the British Museum also contains six leaves of manuscript in front, in what appears to be an early seventeenth-century hand, including prayers and a homily. There is also a prayer dating from the sixteenth century, inserted after B8 and before C1:

---

[4] British Museum C.25.l.19.
[5] British Museum C.112.c.10 (1), sigs. Q8ᵛ–R1ʳ (modernized).

God preserve our Quene Elizabethe, / God destroye all hyr enemyes, God / preserve hyr most honorable Coun- / cellars, god ayde the clergye in set- / tynge forthe of hys truthe, God pre- / serve all the nobility of this realme / and all the comons of the same, God / defende the favorars of the gospell, / God change the hartes of our enemyes and send them a better mynd, / The power of god destroye antichrist / with all hys wyched kyindome, god / send the gospell a ioyfull and free / passage throughout the hole world, / God send unto all degrees such / grace that they may walke wor- / thely in their vocacion And call- / lynge. Amen.

Other editions and copies consulted in the course of research for this text have been, of those published by Jugge and Cawode, British Museum C.25.l.6., which lacks the prayer, "O God, merciful Father, which in the time of Heliseus the prophet . . ." at the end of the Litany and varies in other ways from the copy text; British Museum 6.d.9., which seems to be another copy of C.25.m.7, although imperfect and seemingly with some leaves from another edition; British Museum C.53.c.61; and of those published by Grafton, Cambridge University Library Sel.3.221; and Bodleian (Oxford) Library C.P.1559.d.1. A thorough bibliographical study needs to be done of the sixteenth-century editions of the Book of Common Prayer. Until such a study appears, all statements concerning editions need to be approached with a degree of doubt, including those in the Pollard and Redgrave *Short-Title Catalogue* and those in this essay.

Besides the prayers added in brackets in the Litany, there are other items that are often found included in Elizabethan Prayer Books. Chief among these are the Ordinal, with services for the ordination of deacons and priests, and for the consecration of bishops, and the New Calendar of 1561.[6] The latter is of interest because of the addition of a great number of saints along with national days, such as that of the Accession of Queen Elizabeth, November 17. Of less importance is the collection of "Godly

[6] Both of these are most conveniently found in Clay, *Liturgical Services,* pp. 274–98 (Ordinal), pp. 436–55 (New Calendar).

Prayers" found in some but not all Elizabethan Prayer Books.[7] Other liturgical compositions, official and otherwise, may be found in the Parker Society volumes.[8] Much work needs to be done on these extra–Prayer Book materials.

Marginal notes included in the main body of the text here printed are indicated by a cloister bracket [preceding the note. Exceptions are found in the services of Matrimony and Commination, where some marginal notes are given at the foot of the page. Various silent corrections or alterations have been made. Not all printer's errors have been noted. The spelling has been modernized and in some cases the punctuation has been altered, but I have exercised restraint in this, particularly with regard to the liturgical text itself, in order to preserve the peculiar flavor of the text, which was written to be read aloud. For the convenience of the modern reader, I have modernized names. I have noted original spellings where modern spellings change the pronunciation. This is particularly the case where the names of biblical persons and books of the Bible are concerned. The 1559 Prayer Book adhered by and large to spellings utilized in the Vulgate edition of the Bible, as well as in early English editions. The Authorized Version of 1611 broke away from custom in this regard and used common spellings, which have by and large been followed in subsequent English editions of the Bible. Thus I use "Isaiah" rather than "Esay" and note the original spelling at least on the first use of it in any given portion of the Prayer Book. On the other hand I have modernized "Jhon" and "Chryste" without noting the original spellings since those spellings would not have greatly affected the pronunciation of the names. Roman

---

[7] See *ibid.*, pp. 246–57.

[8] In addition to the two works edited by Clay, *Liturgical Services and Private Prayers*, see such works as Henry Bull's *Christian Prayers and Holy Meditations*, Parker Society Publications, 38 (Cambridge, 1842); and John Norden's *A Progress of Piety*, Parker Society Publications, 31 (Cambridge, 1847). See also, Faye L. Kelly, *Prayer in Sixteenth-Century England*, University of Florida Monographs, Humanities, 22 (Gainesville, Fla., 1966).

numerals have been changed to Arabic. The problem of capitalization is vexing, and I have tried my best to solve it. I beg the reader's indulgence on this as on other matters. When changes have been made, particularly changes in punctuation, I have consulted other sixteenth-century texts, principally the 1559 Grafton Prayer Book and the Great Bible as printed by Richard Harrison in 1562.

In preparing an edition of this nature, it is not always easy to determine how much glossarial annotation is appropriate. My guiding principle has been to include a footnote for each word or usage that might conceivably pose difficulty for a modern reader. I realize that readers familiar with Elizabethan English will find many of these annotations superfluous. I trust, however, that other readers will find them helpful. They are included with the intention of making the 1559 Book of Common Prayer accessible to the widest audience possible.

It is a pleasure to acknowledge the great assistance provided by Megan Lloyd of the Folger Shakespeare Library in preparing this text for the printer.

I also join the Folger in expressing gratitude to the Honorable and Mrs. John Clifford Folger, whose generosity made this publication possible.

Contents

The Book of
Common Prayer

The Book of
Common Prayer and Administration of the Sacraments and other Rites and Ceremonies in the Church of England

Londini, in officina Richardi Jugge & Johannis Cawode

Cum privilegio Regie Majestatis

Anno 1559

The Contents of This Book

An Act for the Uniformity of Common Prayer

and Service in the Church, and the Administration of the Sacraments

HERE at the death of our late sovereign lord King Edward the Sixth there remained one uniform order of common service and prayer and of the administration of sacraments, rites, and ceremonies in the Church of England, which was set forth in one book entitled The Book of Common Prayer and Administration of Sacraments and other Rites and Ceremonies in the Church of England, authorized by Act of Parliament holden[1] in the fifth and sixth years of our said late sovereign lord King Edward the Sixth entitled An Act for the Uniformity of Common Prayer and Administration of the Sacraments; the which was repealed and taken away by Act of Parliament in the first year of the reign of our late sovereign lady Queen Mary, to the great decay of the due honor of God and discomfort to the professors of the truth of Christ's religion.

Be it therefore enacted by the authority of this present Parliament that the said statute[2] of repeal and everything therein contained only concerning the said book and the service, administration of sacraments, rites, and ceremonies contained or appointed in or by the said book shall be void and of none effect from and after the Feast of the Nativity of Saint John Baptist next coming. And that the said book with the order of service and of the administration of sacraments, rites, and ceremonies,

---

[1] *Holden:* held.

[2] Text has "estatute." This obsolete spelling is sometimes used; in this edition it is always changed to the modern spelling.

5

with the alteration and additions therein added and appointed by this statute, shall stand and be from and after the said Feast of the Nativity of Saint John Baptist in full force and effect according to the tenor and effect of this statute; anything in the aforesaid statute of repeal to the contrary notwithstanding.

And further be it enacted by the Queen's Highness, with the assent of the lords and commons in this present Parliament assembled and by authority of the same, that all and singular[3] ministers in any cathedral or parish church or other place within this realm of England, Wales, and the marches of the same, or other the Queen's dominions, shall, from and after the Feast of the Nativity of Saint John Baptist next coming, be bounden to say and use the matins, evensong, celebration of the Lord's Supper, and administration of each of the sacraments, and all their common and open prayer, in such order and form as is mentioned in the said book so authorized by Parliament in the said fifth and sixth year of the reign of King Edward the Sixth, with one alteration or addition of certain Lessons to be used on every Sunday in the year, and the form of the Litany altered and corrected, and two sentences only added in the delivery of the Sacrament to the communicants, and none other or otherwise. And that if any manner of person,[4] vicar, or other whatsoever minister that ought or should sing or say common prayer mentioned in the said book, or minister the sacraments, from and after the Feast of the Nativity of Saint John Baptist next coming, refuse to use the said common prayers or to minister the sacraments in such cathedral or parish church or other places as he should use to minister the same, in such order and form as they be mentioned and set forth in the said book, or shall willfully or obstinately standing in the same use any other rite, ceremony, order, form, or manner of celebrating of the Lord's Supper openly or privily, or matins, evensong, administration of the sacraments, or other

---

[3] *All and singular:* everyone in general and each in particular.

[4] *Person:* parson. In this Act the word *person* often stands for *parson.* The context indicates the meaning.

open prayers than is mentioned and set forth in the said book (open prayer in and throughout this Act is meant that prayer which is for other[5] to come unto or hear, either in common churches or privy chapels or oratories, commonly called the service of the Church) or shall preach, declare, or speak anything in the derogation or depraving of the said book or anything therein contained, or of any part thereof, and shall be thereof lawfully convicted according to the laws of this realm by verdict of twelve men, or by his own confession, or by the notorious evidence of the fact: shall lose and forfeit to the Queen's Highness, her heirs and successors, for his first offense the profit of all his spiritual benefices or promotions coming or arising in one whole year next after this conviction. And also that the person so convicted shall for the same offense suffer imprisonment by the space of six months without bail or mainprise. And if any such person once convict[6] of any offense concerning the premises shall after his first conviction eftsoons[7] offend and be thereof in form aforesaid lawfully convict, that then the same person shall for his second offense suffer imprisonment by the space of one whole year and also shall therefore be deprived, *ipso facto*, of all his spiritual promotions. And that it shall be lawful to all patrons or donors of all and singular the same spiritual promotions, or of any of them, to present or collate to the same as though the person and persons so offending were dead, and that if any such person or persons after he shall be twice convicted in form aforesaid shall offend against any of the premises the third time and shall be thereof in form aforesaid lawfully convicted, that then the person so offending and convicted the third time shall be deprived, *ipso facto*, of all his spiritual promotions and also shall suffer imprisonment during his life.

And if the person that shall offend and be convict in form

---

[5] *Other:* others; the public in contrast to individuals engaging in private devotions.

[6] *Convict:* convicted.

[7] *Eftsoons:* a second time, again.

aforesaid concerning any of the premises shall not be beneficed nor have any spiritual promotion, that then the same person so offending and convict shall for the first offense suffer imprisonment during one whole year next after his said conviction, without bail or mainprise. And if any such person, not having any spiritual promotion, after his first conviction shall eftsoons offend in anything concerning the premises and shall in form aforesaid be thereof lawfully convicted, that then the same person shall for his second offense suffer imprisonment during his life.

And it is ordained and enacted by the authority abovesaid, that if any person or persons whatsoever after the said Feast of the Nativity of Saint John Baptist next coming, shall in any interludes, plays, songs, rhymes, or by other open words, declare or speak anything in the derogation, depraving, or despising of the same book or of anything therein contained or any part thereof, or shall by open fact, deed, or by open threatenings compel or cause or otherwise procure or maintain any parson, vicar, or other minister in any cathedral or parish church or in chapel or in any other place to sing or say any common and open prayer or to minister any sacrament otherwise or in any other manner and form than is mentioned in the said book, or that by any of the said means shall unlawfully interrupt or let[8] any parson, vicar, or other minister in any cathedral or parish church, chapel, or any other place to sing or say common and open prayer or to minister the sacraments or any of them in such manner and form as is mentioned in the said book, that then every such person being thereof lawfully convicted in form abovesaid shall forfeit to the Queen our sovereign lady, her heirs and successors, for the first offense a hundred marks. And if any parson or parsons being once convict of any such offense eftsoons offend against any of the last recited offenses and shall in form aforesaid be thereof lawfully convict, that then the same parson so offending and convict shall for the second offense forfeit to the Queen our sovereign lady, her heirs and successors, four hundred marks.

[8] *Let*: prevent, hinder; sometimes prevention, hindrance.

And if any parson after he in form aforesaid shall have been twice convict of any offense concerning any of the last recited offenses shall offend the third time and be thereof in form abovesaid lawfully convict, that then every parson so offending and convict shall for his third offense forfeit to our sovereign lady the Queen all his goods and catelles[9] and shall suffer imprisonment during his life.

And if any person or persons that for his first offense concerning the premises shall be convict in form aforesaid do not pay the sum to be paid by virtue of his conviction in such manner and form as the same ought to be paid within six weeks next after his conviction, that then every person so convict and so not paying the same shall for the same first offense, instead of the said sum, suffer imprisonment by the space of six months without bail or mainprise. And if any person or persons that for his second offense concerning the premises shall be convict in form aforesaid, do not pay the said sum to be paid by virtue of his conviction and this statute in such manner and form as the same ought to be paid within six weeks next after his said second conviction, that then every person so convicted and not so paying the same, shall for the same second offense, in the stead of the said sum, suffer imprisonment during twelve months without bail or mainprise.

And that from and after the said Feast of the Nativity of Saint John Baptist next coming, all and every person and persons inhabiting within this realm, or any other the Queen's Majesty's dominions, shall diligently and faithfully, having no lawful or reasonable excuse to be absent, endeavor[10] themselves to resort to their parish church or chapel accustomed, or upon reasonable let thereof to some usual place where common prayer and such service of God shall be used in such time of let upon every Sunday and other days ordained and used to be kept as holy days. And then and there to abide orderly and soberly during the time of the common prayer, preachings, or other service of God there to be

[9] *Catelles:* property, chattels.

[10] *Endeavor:* exert.

used and ministered, upon pain of punishment by the censures[11] of the Church. And also upon pain that every person so offending shall forfeit for every such offense twelve pence to be levied by the churchwardens of the parish where such offense shall be done, to the use of the poor of the same parish, of the goods, lands, and tenements of such offender, by way of distress. And for due execution hereof, the Queen's most excellent Majesty, the lords temporal, and all the commons in this present Parliament assembled, doth in God's name earnestly require and charge all the archbishops, bishops, and other ordinaries, that they shall endeavor themselves to the uttermost of their knowledges that the due and true execution hereof may be had throughout their diocese and charges, as they will answer before God for such evils and plagues wherewith Almighty God may justly punish his people for neglecting this good and wholesome law.

And for their authority in this behalf, be it further enacted by the authority aforesaid that all and singular the same archbishops, bishops, and all other their officers exercising ecclesiastical jurisdiction, as well in place exempt as not exempt, within their diocese, shall have full power and authority by this act to reform, correct, and punish by censures of the Church all and singular persons which shall offend within any their jurisdictions or diocese after the said Feast of the Nativity of Saint John Baptist next coming, against this act and statute. Any other law, statute, privilege, liberty, or provision heretofore made, had, or suffered to the contrary notwithstanding.

And it is ordained and enacted by the authority aforesaid that all and every Justices of Oyer and Determiner, or Justices of Assize, shall have full power and authority in every of their open and general sessions to inquire, hear, and determine all, and all manner of offenses that shall be committed or done contrary to any article contained in this present Act, within the limits of the commission to them directed, and to make process for the execu-

---

[11] *Censures:* condemnatory judgment ordinarily administered by church courts.

tion of the same, as they may do against any person being indicted before them of trespass or lawfully convicted thereof.

Provided always, and be it enacted by the authority aforesaid, that all and every archbishop and bishop shall or may at all time and times at his liberty and pleasure join and associate himself by virtue of this Act to the said Justices of Oyer and Determiner, or to the said Justices of Assize, at every of the said open and general sessions to be holden in any place within his diocese, for and to the inquiry, hearing, and determining of the offenses aforesaid.

Provided also, and be it enacted by the authority aforesaid, that the books concerning the said services shall at the costs and charges of the parishioners of every parish and cathedral church be attained and gotten before the said Feast of the Nativity of Saint John Baptist next following, and that all such parishes and cathedral churches or other places, where the said books shall be attained and gotten before the said Feast of the Nativity of Saint John Baptist, shall within three weeks next after the said books so attained and gotten use the said service and put the same in ure[12] according to this Act.

And be it further enacted by the authority aforesaid that no parson or parsons shall be at any time hereafter impeached or otherwise molested of or for any of the offenses above mentioned, hereafter to be committed or done contrary to this Act, unless he or they so offending be thereof indicted at the next general sessions to be holden before any such Justices of Oyer and Determiner, or Justices of Assize, next after any offense committed or done contrary to the tenor of this Act.

Provided always, and be it ordained and enacted by the authority aforesaid, that all and singular lords of the Parliament for the third offense above mentioned shall be tried by their peers.

Provided also, and be it ordained and enacted by the authority

---

[12] *Ure:* use.

aforesaid, that the Mayor of London, and all other mayors, bailiffs, and other head officers of all and singular cities, boroughs, and towns corporate within this realm, Wales, and the marches of the same to the which Justices of Assize do not commonly repair, shall have full power and authority by virtue of this Act to inquire, hear, and determine the offenses abovesaid, and every of them yearly within fifteen days after the Feast of Easter and Saint Michael[13] the Archangel, in like manner and form as Justices of Assize and Oyer and Determiner may do.

Provided always, and be it ordained and enacted by the authority aforesaid, that all and singular archbishops and bishops and every of their chancellors, commissaries, archdeacons and other ordinaries, having any peculiar ecclesiastical jurisdiction, shall have full power and authority by virtue of this Act as well to inquire in their visitation, synods, and elsewhere within their jurisdiction at any other time and place, to take occasions[14] and informations of all and every the things above mentioned, done, committed, or perpetrated within the limits of their jurisdictions and authority, and to punish the same by admonition, excommunication, sequestration, or deprivation and other censures and process in like form as heretofore hath been used in like cases by the Queen's ecclesiastical laws.

Provided always, and be it enacted, that whatsoever person offending in the premises shall for the offense first receive punishment of the ordinary, having a testimonial thereof under the said ordinary's seal, shall not for the same offense eftsoons be convicted before the justices. And likewise receiving for the said first offense punishment by the justices, he shall not for the same offense eftsoons receive punishment of the ordinary. Anything contained in this Act to the contrary notwithstanding.

Provided always, and be it enacted, that such ornaments of the Church and of the ministers thereof shall be retained and be in use as was in this Church of England by authority of Parlia-

---

[13] "Mighel" in text.

[14] *Occasions:* causes, reasons.

ment in the second year of the reign of King Edward the Sixth until other order shall be therein taken by the authority of the Queen's Majesty, with the advice of her commissioners appointed and authorized under the great seal of England for causes ecclesiastical or of the metropolitan of this realm. And also that if there shall happen any contempt or irreverence to be used in the ceremonies or rites of the Church by the misusing of the orders appointed in this book, the Queen's Majesty may, by the like advice of the said commissioners or metropolitan, ordain and publish such farther ceremonies or rites as may be most for the advancement of God's glory, the edifying of his Church, and the due reverence of Christ's holy mysteries and sacraments.

And be it further enacted by the authority aforesaid that all laws, statutes, and ordinances wherein or whereby any other service, administration of sacraments, or common prayer is limited, established, or set forth to be used within this realm or any other the Queen's dominions or countries, shall from henceforth be utterly void and of none effect.

The Preface

HERE was never any thing by the wit[1] of man so well devised, or so sure established, which in continuance of time hath not been corrupted, as (among other things) it may plainly appear by the common prayers in the Church, commonly called divine service. The first original and ground whereof, if a man would search out by the ancient fathers, he shall find that the same was not ordained but of a good purpose and for a great advancement of godliness. For they so ordered the matter that all the whole Bible, or the greatest part thereof, should be read over once in the year, intending thereby that the clergy, and specially such as were ministers of the congregation, should, by often reading and meditation of God's Word, be stirred up to godliness themselves, and be more able to exhort other by wholesome doctrine, and to confute them that were adversaries to the truth. And further, that the people by daily hearing of Holy Scripture read in the Church should continually profit more and more in the knowledge of God and be the more inflamed with the love of his true religion. But these many years past this godly and decent order of the ancient fathers hath been so altered, broken, and neglected by planting in uncertain stories, legends, responds, verses, vain repetitions, commemorations, and synodals that commonly when any book of the Bible was begun, before three or four chapters were read

[1] *Wit:* understanding, intellectual activity.

14

out, all the rest are unread. And in this sort the book of Isaiah[2] was begun in Advent and the book of Genesis in Septuagesima, but they were only begun and never read through. After a like sort were other books of Holy Scripture used. And moreover, whereas Saint Paul would have such language spoken to the people in the Church as they might understand and have profit by hearing the same, the service in this Church of England these many years hath been read in Latin to the people, which they understood not, so that they have heard with their ears only, and their hearts, spirit, and mind have not been edified thereby. And furthermore, notwithstanding that the ancient fathers have divided the Psalms into seven portions whereof every one was called a nocturn, now of late time a few of them have been daily said and oft repeated, and the rest utterly omitted. Moreover, the number and hardness of the rules called the pie and the manifold changings[3] of the service was the cause that to turn the book only was so hard and intricate a matter that many times there was more business to find out what should be read than to read it when it was found out.

These inconveniences therefore considered, here is set forth such an order whereby the same shall be redressed. And for a readiness in this matter, here is drawn out a calendar for that purpose, which is plain and easy to be understanden,[4] wherein, so much as may be, the reading of Holy Scriptures is so set forth that all things shall be done in order without breaking one piece thereof from another. For this cause be cut off anthems, responds, invitatories, and such like things as did break the continual course of the reading of the Scripture. Yet because there is no remedy but that of necessity there must be some rules, therefore certain rules are here set forth, which as they be few in number so they be plain and easy to be understanden. So that here you have an order for prayer, as touching the reading of Holy Scripture,

---

[2] "Esay" in text.

[3] *Changings:* changes.

[4] *Understanden:* understood (understanded in 1596 Book).

15

much agreeable to the mind and purpose of the old fathers, and a great deal more profitable and commodious than that which of late was used. It is more profitable because here are left out many things whereof some be untrue, some uncertain, some vain and superstitious, and is ordained nothing to be read but the very pure Word of God, the Holy Scriptures, or that which is evidently grounded upon the same, and that in such a language and order as is most easy and plain for the understanding, both of the readers and hearers. It is also more commodious, both for the shortness thereof and for the plainness of the order, and for that the rules be few and easy. Furthermore, by this order the curates shall need none other books for their public service but this book and the Bible, by the means whereof the people shall not be at so great charge for books as in time past they have been.

And where[5] heretofore there hath been great diversity in saying and singing in churches within this realm, some following Salisbury use, some Hereford use, some the use of Bangor, some of York, and some of Lincoln, now from henceforth all the whole realm shall have but one use. And if any would judge this way more painful because that all things must be read upon the book whereas before by the reason of so often repetition they could say many things by heart, if those men will weigh their labor with the profit and knowledge which daily they shall obtain by reading upon the book, they will not refuse the pain in consideration of the great profit that shall ensue thereof.

And for as much as nothing can almost be so plainly set forth but doubts may rise in the use and practicing of the same, to appease all such diversity (if any arise) and for the resolution of all doubts concerning the manner how to understand, do, and execute the things contained in this book, the parties that so doubt, or diversely take anything shall alway resort to the bishop of the diocese, who by his discretion shall take order for the quieting and appeasing of the same so that the same order be not con-

---

[5] *Where:* whereas.

trary to anything contained in this book. And if the bishop of the diocese be in any doubt, then may he send for the resolution thereof unto the archbishop.

Though it be appointed in the afore written Preface that all things shall be read and sung in the church in the English tongue, to the end that the congregation may be thereby edified, yet it is not meant but when men say Morning and Evening Prayer privately, they may say the same in any language that they themselves do understand.

And all priests and deacons shall be bound to say daily the Morning and Evening Prayer, either privately or openly, except they be letted[6] by preaching, studying of divinity, or by some other urgent cause.

And the curate that ministereth in every parish church, or chapel, being at home and not being otherwise reasonably letted, shall say the same in the parish church or chapel where he ministereth and shall toll a bell thereto a convenient time before he begin, that such as be disposed may come to hear God's Word and to pray with him.

[6] *Letted:* hindered.

Of Ceremonies, Why
Some Be Abolished and
Some Retained

F such ceremonies as be used in the Church and have had their beginning by the institution of man, some at the first were of godly intent and purpose devised and yet at length turned to vanity and superstition, some entered into the Church by undiscreet devotion and such a zeal as was without knowledge. And forbecause they were winked at in the beginning, they grew daily to more and more abuses, which not only for their unprofitableness but also because they have much blinded the people and obscured the glory of God are worthy to be cut away and clean rejected. Other there be which although they have been devised by man, yet it is thought good to reserve them still, as well for a decent order in the Church, for the which they were first devised, as because they pertain to edification, whereunto all things done in the Church, as the Apostle[1] teacheth, ought to be referred. And although the keeping or omitting of a ceremony in itself considered is but a small thing, yet the willful and contemptuous transgression and breaking of a common order and discipline is no small offense before God.

Let all things be done among you, saith Saint Paul,[2] in a seemly and due order. The appointment of the which order pertaineth not to private men, therefore no man ought to take in hand nor presume to appoint or alter any public or common order in Christ's Church, except he be lawfully called and authorized thereunto.

[1] "Apostles" in text; 1 Cor. 14:26.
[2] 1 Cor. 14:40.

And whereas in this our time the minds of men are so diverse that some think it a great matter of conscience to depart from a piece of the least of their ceremonies, they be so addicted to their old customs, and again on the other side, some be so newfangled that they would innovate all thing, and so do despise the old, that nothing can like[3] them but that is new, it was thought expedient not so much to have respect how to please and satisfy either of these parties, as how to please God and profit them both. And yet lest any man should be offended whom good reason might satisfy, here be certain causes rendered why some of the accustomed ceremonies be put away and some retained and kept still.

Some are put away because the great excess and multitude of them hath so increased in these latter days that the burden of them was intolerable, whereof Saint Augustine in his time complained that they were grown to such a number that the state of Christian people was in worse case concerning that matter than were the Jews. And he counseled that such yoke and burden should be taken away, as time would serve quietly to do it.

But what would Saint Augustine have said if he had seen the ceremonies of late days used among us, whereunto the multitude used in his time was not to be compared? This our excessive multitude of ceremonies was so great and many of them so dark that they did more confound and darken than declare and set forth Christ's benefits unto us.

And besides this, Christ's gospel is not a ceremonial law, as much of Moses' law was, but it is a religion to serve God, not in bondage of the figure or shadow, but in the freedom of spirit, being content only with those ceremonies which do serve to a decent order and godly discipline, and such as be apt to stir up the dull mind of man to the remembrance of his duty to God by some notable and special signification whereby he might be edified.

[3] *Like:* please.

Furthermore, the most weighty cause of the abolishment of certain ceremonies was that they were so far abused, partly by the superstitious blindness of the rude and unlearned and partly by the unsatiable avarice of such as sought more their own lucre than the glory of God, that the abuses could not well be taken away, the thing remaining still. But now, as concerning those persons which peradventure will be offended for that some of the old ceremonies are retained still, if they consider that without some ceremonies it is not possible to keep any order or quiet discipline in the Church, they shall easily perceive just cause to reform their judgments. And if they think much that any of the old do remain and would rather have all devised anew, then such men granting some ceremonies convenient to be had, surely where the old may be well used there they cannot reasonably reprove the old only for their age without bewraying[4] of their own folly. For in such a case they ought rather to have reverence unto them for their antiquity, if they will declare themselves to be more studious of unity and concord than of innovations and newfangleness, which, as much as may be with the true setting forth of Christ's religion, is always to be eschewed. Furthermore, such shall have no just cause with the ceremonies reserved, to be offended. For as those be taken away which were most abused and did burden men's consciences without any cause, so the other that remain are retained for a discipline and order, which upon just causes may be altered and changed, and therefore are not to be esteemed equal with God's law. And moreover, they be neither dark nor dumb ceremonies, but are so set forth that every man may understand what they do mean and to what use they do serve. So that it is not like that they in time to come should be abused as the other have been. And in these our doings, we condemn no other nations, nor prescribe anything but to our own people only. For we think it convenient that every country should use such ceremonies as they shall think best to the setting forth

[4] *Bewraying*: betraying, revealing.

of God's honor or glory and to the reducing of the people to a most perfect and godly living, without error or superstition. And that they should put away other things which from time to time they perceive to be most abused, as in men's ordinances it often chanceth diversely in diverse countries.

The Table and Calendar

Expressing the Order of the Psalms
and Lessons, to Be Said at Morning
and Evening Prayer throughout the
Year, except Certain Proper Feasts, as
the Rules Following More
Plainly Declare

The Order How the Psalter Is
Appointed to Be Read

THE Psalter shall be read through once every month. And because that some months be longer than some other be, it is thought good to make them even by this means.

To every month shall be appointed, as concerning this purpose, just thirty days.

And because January and March hath one day above the said number, and February which is placed between them both hath only twenty-eight days, February shall borrow of either of the months (of January and March) one day. And so the Psalter which shall be read in February must begin the last day of January and end the first day of March.

And whereas May, July, August, October, and December have thirty-one days apiece, it is ordered that the same Psalms shall be read the last day of the said months which were read the day before. So that the Psalter may begin again the first day of the next months[1] ensuing.

[1] *Months:* month, 1559 Grafton.

Now to know what Psalms shall be read every day, look in the Calendar the number that is appointed for the Psalms and then find the same number in this table, and upon that number shall you see what Psalms shall be said at Morning and Evening Prayer.

And where the 119th Psalm is divided into twenty-two portions and is overlong to be read at one time, it is so ordered that at one time shall not be read above four or five of the said portions, as you shall perceive to be noted in this table following.

And here is also to be noted that in this table, and in all other parts of the service, where any Psalms are appointed the number is expressed after the great English Bible, which from the 9th Psalm unto the 148th Psalm, following the division of the Hebrews, doth vary in numbers from the common Latin translation.

The Table for the Order
of the Psalms to Be Said at Morning and Evening Prayer

Days of the Month	Psalms for Morning Prayer	Psalms for Evening Prayer
1	1, 2, 3, 4, 5	6, 7, 8
2	9, 10, 11	12, 13, 14
3	15, 16, 17	18
4	19, 20, 21	22, 23
5	24, 25, 26	27, 28, 29
6	30, 31	32, 33, 34
7	35, 36	37
8	38, 39, 40	41, 42, 43
9	44, 45, 46	47, 48, 49
10	50, 51, 52	53, 54, 55
11	56, 57, 58	59, 60, 61
12	62, 63, 64	65, 66, 67
13	68	69, 70
14	71, 72	73, 74
15	75, 76, 77	78
16	79, 80, 81	82, 83, 84, 85
17	86, 87, 88	89
18	90, 91, 92	93, 94
19	96, 97[1]	98, 99, 100, 101
20	102, 103	104
21	105	106
22	107	108, 109
23	110, 111, 112, 113	114, 115
24	116, 117, 118	119 Inde. 4[2]
25	Inde. 5	Inde. 4
26	Inde. 5	Inde. 4
27	120, 121, 122, 123, 124, 125	126, 127, 128, 129, 130, 131
28	132, 133, 134, 135	136, 137, 138
29	139, 140, 141	142, 143
30	144, 145, 146	147, 148, 149, 150

[1] 1559 Grafton adds 95.

[2] Psalm 119 is divided into twenty-two sections distributed as follows over three days. See *The Holy Bible* [Bishops' Bible] (London: Richard Harrison, [1562]), where the divisions are made and the sections distributed between Evening and Morning Prayer as indicated in the Table.

The Order How
the Rest of Holy Scripture (beside the Psalter) Is Appointed to Be Read

THE Old Testament is appointed for the first Lessons at Morning and Evening Prayer and shall be read through every year once, except certain books and chapters which be least edifying and might best be spared and therefore be left unread.

The New Testament is appointed for the second Lessons at Morning and Evening Prayer and shall be read over orderly every year thrice, beside the Epistles and Gospels, except the Apocalypse,[1] out of the which there be only certain Lessons appointed upon diverse proper feasts.

And to know what Lessons shall be read every day, find the day of the month in the Calendar following and there ye shall perceive the books and chapters that shall be read for the Lessons both at Morning and Evening Prayer.

And here is to be noted that whensoever there be any proper Psalms or Lessons appointed for the Sundays or for any feast, movable or unmovable, then the Psalms and Lessons appointed in the Calendar shall be omitted for that time.

Ye must note also that the Collect, Epistle, and Gospel appointed for the Sunday shall serve all the week after, except there fall some feast that hath his Proper.[2]

This is also to be noted concerning the leap years, that the

---

[1] *Apocalypse:* The Revelation of Saint John the Divine, the last book in the Bible.

[2] *Proper:* the Collect, Epistle, and Gospel for a particular day, as specified in the Prayer Book.

twenty-fifth day of February, which in leap year is counted for two days, shall in those two days alter neither Psalm nor Lesson, but the same Psalms and Lessons which be said the first day shall also serve for the second day.

Also, wheresoever the beginning of any Lesson, Epistle, or Gospel is not expressed, there ye must begin at the beginning of the chapter.

And wheresoever is not expressed how far shall be read, there shall you read to the end of the chapter.

Proper Lessons to Be Read
for the First Lessons Both at Morning Prayer and Evening Prayer on the Sundays throughout the Year, and for Some Also the Second Lessons

	Matins	Evensong
Sundays of Advent		
The first	Isa. 1[1]	Isa. 2
2	5	24
3	25	26
4	30	32
Sundays after Christmas		
The first	37	38
2	41	43
Sundays after the Epiphany		
The first	44	46
2	51	53
3	55	56
4	57	58
5	59	64
Septuagesima	Gen. 1	Gen. 2
Sexagesima	3	6
Quinquagesima	9	12
Lent		
1 Sunday	19	22
2	27	34
3	39	42
4	43	45
5	Exod. 3	Exod. 5
6	9	10

[1] "Esa." in text, here and throughout.

27

	Matins	Evensong
Easter Day		
1 Lesson	12	14
2 Lesson	Rom. 6	Acts 2
Sundays after Easter		
The first	Num. 16	Num. 22
2	23	25
3	Deut. 4	Deut. 5
4	6	7
5	8	9
Sunday after Ascension Day	12	13
Whitsunday		
1 Lesson	17	18
2 Lesson	Acts 10	Acts 19
	Then Peter opened his, etc.	It fortuned when Apollo went to Corinth, etc. *unto* After these things
Trinity Sunday		
1 Lesson	Gen. 18	Josh. 1[2]
2 Lesson	Matt. 3	
Sundays after the Trinity		
The first	Josh. 10	Josh. 23
2	Judg. 4[3]	Judg. 5
3	1 Kings 2	1 Kings 3
4	12	13
5	15	16
6	2 Kings 12	2 Kings 21
7	22	24
8	3 Kings 13	3 Kings 17
9	18	19
10	21	22

[2] "Josue" in text.
[3] "Jud." in text.

	Matins	Evensong
11	4 Kings 5	4 Kings 9[4]
12	10	18
13	19	23
14	Jer. 5	Jer. 22
15	35	36
16	Ezek. 2	Ezek. 14
17	16	18
18	20	24
19	Dan. 3	Dan. 6
20	Joel 2	Mic. 6
21	Hab. 2[5]	Prov. 1
22	Prov. 2	3
23	11	12
24	13	14
25	15	16
26	17	19

Lessons Proper for Holy Days

	Matins	Evensong
Saint Andrew	Prov. 20	Prov. 21
Saint Thomas the Apostle	23	24
Nativity of Christ		
1 Lesson	Isa. 9	Isa. 7 God spake once again to Achas, etc.
2 Lesson	Luke 2, *unto* and unto men of good will	Titus 3 The kindness and love, etc.
Saint Stephen		
1 Lesson	Prov. 28	Eccles. 4
2 Lesson	Acts 6 and 7	Acts 7

[4] Text has "19"; misprint.
[5] "Abacuk" in text.

29

	Matins	Evensong
	Stephen, full of faith and power, etc., *unto* and when forty years, etc.	And when forty years were expired, there appeared unto Moses, etc., *unto* Stephen full of the holy, etc.

Saint John
1 Lesson	Eccles. 5	Eccles. 6
2 Lesson	Apoc. 1[6]	Apoc. 22

Innocents
	Jer. 31 *unto* Moreover I heard Ephraim	Wisd. 1

Circumcision Day
1 Lesson	Gen. 17	Deut. 10, and now Israel, etc.
2 Lesson	Rom. 2	Col. 2

Epiphany Day
1 Lesson	Isa. 60	Isa. 49
2 Lesson	Luke 3, and it fortuned, etc.	John 2, after this he went to Capernaum

Conversion of Saint Paul
1 Lesson	Wisd. 5	Wisd. 6
2 Lesson	Acts 22, *unto,* they heard him	Acts 26[7]

Purification of the Virgin Mary
	Wisd. 9	Wisd. 12

Saint Matthias[8]
	Wisd. 19	Eccles. 1

Annunciation of our Lady
	Eccles. 2	Eccles. 3

[6] *Apoc.:* Apocalypse, the Revelation of Saint John the Divine.
[7] Text has "2"; misprint.
[8] "Matthie" in text.

	Matins	Evensong
Wednesday afore Easter	Hos. 13[9]	Hos. 14
Thursday before Easter	Dan. 9	Jer. 31
Good Friday	Gen. 22	Isa. 53
Easter even	Zech. 9[10]	Exod. 13
Monday in Easter week		
1 Lesson	Exod. 16	17
2 Lesson	Matt. 28	Acts 3
Tuesday in Easter		
1 Lesson	Exod. 20	Exod. 32
2 Lesson	Luke 24, *unto,* And behold two of them	1 Cor. 15
Saint Mark	Eccles. 4	Eccles. 5
Philip and Jacob	7	9
Ascension Day	Deut. 10	Deut. 11
Monday in Whitsun week	30	31
Tuesday in Whitsun week	32	34
Saint Barnabas[11]		
1 Lesson	Eccles. 10	Eccles. 12
2 Lesson	Acts 14	Acts 15, *unto,* After certain days
Saint John Baptist		
1 Lesson	Mal. 3	Mal. 4

[9] "Osee" in text.
[10] "Zach." in text.
[11] "Barnabe" in text.

	Matins	Evensong
2 Lesson	Matt. 3	Matt. 14, *unto*, when Jesus heard
Saint Peter		
1 Lesson	Eccles. 15	Eccles. 19
2 Lesson	Acts. 3	Acts. 4
Saint James	Eccles. 21	Eccles. 23
Saint Bartholomew	25	29
Saint Matthew	35	38
Saint Michael	39	44
Saint Luke	51	Job 1
Saint Simon and Jude		
1 Lesson	24	42
2 Lesson	25[12]	
All Saints	Wisd. 3, *unto*,	Wisd. 5, *unto*, his jealousy
1 Lesson	blessed is rather the barren	also
2 Lesson	Heb. 11, 12 Saints by faith, *unto*, If you endure chastening	Apoc. 19, *unto*, and I saw an angel stand

Proper Psalms on Certain Days

	Matins	Evensong
Christmas Day. Psalm	19	89
	45	110
	85	132

[12] Here both chapters 24 and 25 should be listed as the first Lesson, there being no second Lesson indicated in this place. Cf. *Liber precum publicarum* (1560), in Clay, *Liturgical Services* (Cambridge, 1847), p. 316; and the New Calendar (1561), in *ibid.*, p. 439.

	Matins	Evensong
Easter Day	2	113
	57	114
	111	118
Ascension Day	8	24
	15	68
	21	108
Whitsunday	45[13]	104
	67	145

[13] *Liber precum publicarum* lists Psalms 47 and 66 for Matins; see Clay, *Liturgical Services*, p. 316. The Sarum Calendar lists, after the style of the Great Bible, 48 and 68, which is correct; see Brightman, *The English Rite*, 2 vols. (London, 1915), I, 64. There seems to have been much confusion. Cf. W. Keeling, *Liturgiae Britannicae* (London, 1842), in the Calendar, no pagination.

A Brief Declaration
When Every Term Beginneth and Endeth

BE it known that Easter Term beginneth always the eighteenth day after Easter, reckoning Easter Day for one. And endeth the Monday next after Ascension Day.

Trinity Term beginneth alway the Friday next after Trinity Sunday and endeth the twenty-eighth day of June.

Michaelmas Term beginneth the ninth or tenth day of October and endeth the twenty-eighth or twenty-ninth day of November.

Hilary Term beginneth the twenty-third or twenty-fourth day of January and endeth the twelfth or thirteenth day of February.

In Easter Term on the Ascension Day, in Trinity Term on the Nativity of Saint John Baptist, in Michaelmas Term on the Feast of All Saints, in Hilary Term on the Feast of the Purification of our Lady, the Queen's judges of Westminster do not use to sit in judgment, nor upon any Sundays.

An Almanac
for Thirty Years

The Years of Our Lord	The Golden Number	The Epacta[1]	The Cycle of the Sun	Dominical Letter	Easter Day
1559	2	22	28	A.	26 March
1560	3	3	1	G. F.	14 April
1561	4	14	2	E.	6 April
1562	5	25	3	D.	29 March
1563	6	6	4	C.	11 April
1564	7	17	5	B. A.	2 April
1565	8	28	6	G.	22 April
1566	9	9	7	F.	14 April
1567	10	20	8	E.	30 March
1568	11	1	9	D. C.	18 April
1569	12	12	10	B.	10 April
1570	13	23	11	A.	26 March
1571	14	4	12	G.	15 April
1572	15	15	13	F. E.	6 April
1573	16	26	14	D.	22 March
1574	17	7	15	C.	11 April
1575	18	18	16	B.	3 April
1576	19	119	17	A. G.	22 April
1577	1	11	18	F.	7 April
1578	2	22	19	E.	30 March
1579	3	3	20	D.	29 April
1580	4	14	21	C. B.	3 April
1581	5	25	22	A.	26 March
1582	6	6	23	G.	15 April
1583	7	17	24	F.	31 March
1584	8	28	25	E. D.	19 April
1585	9	9	26	C.	11 April
1586	10	20	27	B.	3 April
1587	11	1	28	A.	16 April
1588	12	12	1	G. F.	7 April

[1] *Epacta:* number of days in the age of the moon on the first day of the year—now January 1, but in 1559, March 22.

35

January Hath Thirty-one Days

				Morning Prayer		Evening Prayer	
			Psalms	The First Lesson	The Second Lesson	The First Lesson	The Second Lesson
2	A	Kalend. Circumcision	1	Gen. 17	Rom. 2	Deut. 10	Col. 2
	b	4 No. Ortus solis	2	Gen. 1	Matt. 1	Gen. 2	Rom. 1
11	c	3 No. Ho. 8. Mi. 3	3	3	2	4	2
	d	Prid. No. Occasus Ho.	4	5	3	6	3
9	e	Nonae. 3 Mi. 57	5	7	4	8	4
8	f	8 Idus. Epiphany	6	Isa.[1] 60	Luke 3	Isa. 49	John 2
	g	7 Idus	7	Gen. 9	Matt. 5	Gen. 11	Rom. 5
6	A	6 Idus	8[2]	12	6	13	6
5	b	5 Idus	9	14	7	15	7
	c	4 Idus	10	16	8	17	8
13	d	3 Idus. Sol in Aquario	11	18	9	19	9
2	e	Prid. Id.	12	20	10	21	10
	f	Idus	13	22	11	23	11
10	g	19 kal. February	14[3]	24	12	25	12
	A	18 kal.	15	26	13	27	13
17	b	17 kal. Term beginneth	16	28	14	29	14
7	c	16 kal.	17	30	15	31	15
	d	15 kal.	18	32	16	33	16
15	e	14 kal.	19	34	17	35	1 Cor. 1
4	f	13 kal.	20	36	18	37	2
	g	12 kal.	21	38[4]	19	39	3
12	A	11 kal.	22	40	20	41	4
1	b	10 kal.	23	42	21	43[5]	5
	c	9 kal.	24	44	22	45	6
9	d	8 kal. Convers. Paul	25	46	Acts 22	47	Acts 26
	e	7 kal.	26	48	Matt. 23[6]	49	1 Cor. 7
17	f	6 kal.[7]	27	50	24	Exod. 1	8
6	g	5 kal.	28	Exod. 2	25	3	9
	A	4 kal.	29	4	26	5	10
14	b	3 kal.	30	6	27	7	11
3	c	Pridie kal.	1	8	28	9	12

[1] "Esay" in text; also in Evening.   [2] Text has "7"; misprint.   [3] Text has "13"; misprint.   [4] Text has "39"; misprint; cf. 1549 Book, in Brightman, *English Rite*, I, 79.   [5] Text has "63"; misprint.   [6] Text has "13"; misprint.   [7] Text has "9"; misprint.

February Hath Twenty-eight Days

				Morning Prayer		Evening Prayer	
			Psalms	The First Lesson	The Second Lesson	The First Lesson	The Second Lesson
	d	Kalend	2	Exod. 10	Mark 1	Exod. 11	1 Cor. 13
11	e	4 No. Puri. Mary	3	12	2	13	14
19	f	3 No. Ortus solis Ho. 7	4	14	3	15	15
8	g	Prid. No. Mi. 14. Occasus	5	16	4	17	16
	A	Nonae. Ho. 4. Mi. 46	6	18	5	19	2 Cor. 1
16	b	8 Idus	7	20	6	21	2
5	c	7 Idus	8	22	7	23[8]	3
	d	6 Idus. Sol in	9	24	8	32	4
13	e	5 Idus. Piscibus[9]	10	33	9	34	5
2	f	4 Idus	11	35	10	40	6
	g	3 Idus	12	Lev. 18	11	Lev. 19	7
10	A	Prid. Id.	13	20	12	Num. 10	8
	b	Idus	14	Num. 11	13	12	9
18	c	16 kal. March	15	13	14	14	10
7	d	15 kal.	16	15	15	16	11
	e	14 kal.	17	17	16	18	12
15	f	13 kal.	18	19	Luke 1	20	13
4	g	12 kal.	19	21	di. 1	22	Gal. 1
	A	11 kal.	20	23	2	24	2
12	b	10 kal.	21	25	3	26	3
1	c	6 kal.	22	27	4	28	4
	d	8 kal.	23	29	5	30	5
9	e	7 kal.	24	31	6	32	6
	f	6 kal. S. Matthias	25	33	7	34	Eph. 1
17	g	5 kal.	26	35	8	36	2
6	A	4 kal.	27	Deut. 1	9	Deut. 2	3
	b[10]	3 kal.	28	3	10	4	4
14	c	Prid. kl.	29	5	11	6	5

[8] Text has "22"; misprint.   [9] 1559 Grafton has this on line with "4 Idus." Text agrees with 1559 Book.   [10] Letter omitted in text.

March Hath Thirty-one Days

| | | | | Morning Prayer | | Evening Prayer | |
			Psalms	The First Lesson	The Second Lesson	The First Lesson	The Second Lesson
3	d	Kalend	30	Deut. 7	Luke 12	Deut. 8	Eph. 6
	e	6 No.	1	9	13	10	Phil. 1
11	f	5 No. Ortus solis	2	11	14	12	2
	g	4 No. Ho. 6. Mi. 18	3	13	15	14	3
19	A	3 No. Occasus	4	15	16	16	4
8	b	Prid. No. Ho. 5. Mi. 42	5	17	17	18	Col. 1
	c	Nonae	6	19	18	20	2
16	d	8 Idus	7	21	19	22	3
5	e	7 Idus	8	23	20	24	4
	f	6 Idus	9	25	21	26	1 Thess. 1
13	g	5 Idus	10	27	22	28	2
2	A	4 Idus. Sol in Ariete	11	29	23	30	3
	b	3 Idus. Equinoctium[11]	12	31	24	32	4
10	c	Prid. Id.[12]	13	33	John 1	34	5
	d	Idus	14	Josh. 1[13]	2	Josh. 2	2 Thess. 1
18	e	17 kl.	15	3	3	4[14]	2
7	f	16 kl. April[15]	16	5[16]	4	6[17]	3
	g	15 kl.	17	7[18]	5	8[19]	1 Tim. 1
15	A	14 kl. Easter term	18	9[20]	6	10[21]	2, 3
4	b	13 kl. beginneth	19	11[22]	7	12[23]	4
	c	12 kl. the 17th	20	13[24]	8	14[25]	5
12	d	11 kl. day after	21	15[26]	9	16[27]	6
1	e	10 kl. Easter Day	22	17[28]	10	18[29]	2 Tim. 1
	f	9 kl.	23	19[30]	11	20	2
9	g	8 kl.	24	21	12	22	3
	A	7 kl. Annun. of Mary[31]	25	23	13	24	4
17	b	6 kl.[32]	26	Judg. 1[33]	14	Judg. 2	Titus 1
6	c	5 kal.	27	3	15	4	2, 3
	d	4 kal.	28	5	16	6	Philem. 1
14	e	3 kal.	29	7	17	8	Heb. 1
3	f	Prid. kl.	30	9[34]	18	10	2

[11] 1552 Book and 1559 Grafton have "*Equinoctium*" two lines above. [12] Text has "Prid. No."; misprint. [13] "Josue" in text; also in Evening. [14] Text has "3"; misprint; corrected by sixteenth-century hand in Boston Public Library copy. [15] 1552 Book and 1559 Grafton have "April" one line above. [16] Text has "4"; misprint; here, and through footnote 30, corrected by sixteenth-century hand in Boston Public Library copy. [17] Text has "4"; misprint. [18] Text has "5"; misprint. [19] Text has "5"; misprint. [20] Text has "6"; misprint. [21] Text has "6"; misprint. [22] Text has "7"; misprint. [23] Text has "7"; misprint. [24] Text has "8";

April Hath Thirty Days

				Morning Prayer		Evening Prayer	
			Psalms	The First Lesson	The Second Lesson	The First Lesson	The Second Lesson
	g	Kalend	1	Judg. 11[35]	John 19	Judg. 12	Heb. 3
11	A	4 No. Ortus solis Ho. 6	2	13	20	14	4
	b	3 No. Mi. 17. Occasus	3	15	21	16	5
19	c	Prid. No. Ho. 6. Mi. 43	4	17	Acts 1	18	6
8	d	Nonae	5	19	2	20	7
16	e	8 Idus	6	21	3	Ruth 1	8
5	f	7 Idus	7	Ruth 2	4	3	9
	g	6 Idus	8	4	5	1 Kings 1[36]	10
13	A	5 Idus	9	1 Kings 2	6	3	11
2	b	4 Idus. Sol in Tauro [37]	10	4	7	5	12
	c	3 Idus	11	6	8	7	13
10	d	Prid. Id.	12	8	9	9	James 1[38]
	e	Idus	13	10	10	11	2
18	f	18 kal. May	14	12	11	13	3
7	g	17 kal.	15	14	12	15	4
	A	16 kal.	16	16	13	17	5
15	b	15 kal.	17	18	14	19	1 Pet. 1
4	c	14 kal.	18	20	15	21	2
	d	13 kal.	19	22	16	23	3
12	e	12 kal.	20	24	17	25	4
1	f	11 kal.	21	26	18	27	5
	g	10 kal.	22	28[39]	19	29	2 Pet. 1
9	A	9 kal. S. George	23	30	20	31	2
	b	8 kal.	24	2 Kings 1	21	2 Kings 2	3
17	c	7 kal. Mark Evan	25	3	22	4	1 John 1
6	d	6 kal.	26	5	23	6	2
	e	5 kal.	27	7	24	8	3
14	f	4 kal.	28	9	25	10	4
3	g	3 kal.	29	11	26	12	5
	A	Prid. kl.	30	13	27	14	2, 3 John

misprint.   [25] Text has "8"; misprint.   [26] Text has "9"; misprint.   [27] Text has "9"; misprint.   [28] Text has "10"; misprint.   [29] Text has "11"; misprint.   [30] Text has "12"; misprint.   [31] 1552 Book and 1559 Grafton have Annunciation one line above.   [32] Text has "9"; misprint.   [33] "Judic." in text; also in Evening.   [34] Text has "10"; misprint.   [35] "Judic." in text; "Judi." in Evening.   [36] "Reg." throughout text.   [37] 1552 Book and 1559 Grafton have this two lines below.   [38] "Jacobi." in text.   [39] Text has "18"; misprint.

May Hath Thirty-one Days

					Morning Prayer		Evening Prayer	
				Psalms	The First Lesson	The Second Lesson	The First Lesson	The Second Lesson
11	b	Kalend. Phil. et Ja.		1	2 Kings 15	Acts 8	2 Kings 16	Jude 1[40]
	c	6 No. Ortus solis		2	17	28	18	Rom. 1
19	d	5 No. Ho. 4. Mi. 23		3	19	Matt. 1	20	2
8	e	4 No. Occasus		4	21	2	22	3
	f	3 No. Ho. 7. Mi. 37		5	23	3	24	4
16	g	Prid. No.		6	3 Kings 1	4	3 Kings 1	5
5	A	Nonae		7	2	5	2	6
	b	8 Idus		8	3	6	4	7
13	c	7 Idus		9	5	7	9	8
2	d	6 Idus		10	9	8	10	9
	e	5 Idus. Sol in Gemini		11	11	9	12	10
10	f	4 Idus		12	13	10	14	11
	g	3 Idus		13	15	11	16	12
18	A	Prid. Id.		14	17	12	18	13
7	b	Idus		15	19	13	20	14
	c	17 kal. June		16	21	14	22	15
15	d	16 kal.		17	4 Kings 1	15	4 Kings 2	16
4	e	15 kal. Term endeth		18	3	16	4	1 Cor. 1
	f	14 kal. the Monday		19	5	17	6	2
12	g	13 kal. after Ascen-		20	7	18	8	3
1	A	12 kal. sion Day		21	9	19	10	4
	b	11 kal.		22	11	20	12	5
9	c	10 kal.		23	13	21	14	6
	d	9 kal.		24	15	22	16	7
17	e	8 kal.		25	17	23	18	8
6	f	7 kal.		26	19[41]	24	20	9
	g	6 kal.		27	21	25	22	10
14	A	5 kal.		28	23	26	24	11
3	b	4 kal.		29	25	27	25[42]	12
	c	3 kal.		30	1 Esd. 1	28	1 Esd. 3	13
11	d	Prid. kl.		30	3	Mark 1	4	14

[40] "Judas" in text. [41] Text has "29"; misprint. [42] 1549 Book and 1559 Grafton have "1 Esdras 1" here and proceed through chap. 5. The text follows the 1552 Book. Cf. Brightman, *English Rite*, I, 95–96.

June Hath Thirty Days

				Morning Prayer		Evening Prayer	
			Psalms	The First Lesson	The Second Lesson	The First Lesson	The Second Lesson
	e	Kalend	1	1 Esd. 5[43]	Mark 2	1 Esd. 6	1 Cor. 15
19	f	4 No. Ortus solis Ho. 3	2	7	3	8	16
8	g	3 No. Mi. 48. Occasus	3	9	4	10	2 Cor. 1
16	A	Prid. No. Ho. 8. Mi. 12	4	2 Esd. 1	5	2 Esd. 2	2
5	b	Nonae. Trinity Term be-	5	3	6	4	3
	c	8 Idus. ginneth 12 days	6	5	7	6	4
13	d	7 Idus. after Whitsun-	7	7	8	8	5
2	e	6 Idus. day and contin-	8	9	9	10	6
	f	5 Idus. ueth 19 days	9	11	10	13	7
10	g	4 Idus	10	Esther 1[44]	11	Esther 2	8
	A	3 Idus. Barnab. Ap.	11	3	Acts 14	4	Acts 15
18	b	Prid. Id. Sol. in Cancro[45]	12	5	Mark 12	6	2 Cor. 9
7	c	Idus. Solstitium Aestivum	13	7	13	8	10
	d	18 kal.	14	9	14	Job 1	11
15	e	17 kal.	15	Job 2	15	3	12
4	f	16 kal.	16	4	16	5	13
	g	15 kal.	17	6	Luke 1	7	Gal. 1
12	A	14 kal.	18	8	2	9	2
1	b	13 kal.	19	10	3	11	3
	c	12 kal.	20	12	4	13	4
9	d	11 kal.	21	14	5	15	5
	e	10 kal.	22	16	6	17, 18	6
17	f	9 kal.	23	19	7	20	Eph. 1
6	g	8 kal. John[46] Baptist	24	Mal. 3	Matt. 3	Mal. 4	Matt. 14
	A	7 kal.	25	Job 21	Luke 8	Job 22	Eph. 2
14	b	6 kal.	26	23	9	24, 25	3
3	c	5 kal.	27	26, 27	10	28	4
	d	4 kal.	28	29	11	30	5
11	e	3 kal. S. Peter Apo.	29	31	Acts 3	32	Acts 4
	f	Prid. kl.	30	33	Luke 12	34	Eph. 6

[43] 1549 Book and 1559 Grafton have "1 Esdras 6" here and proceed in Morning Prayer with chapters 8 and 10, 2 Esdras 2, 4, 6, 8, 10, 12; and in Evening Prayer with 1 Esdras 7 and 9, 2 Esdras 1, 3, 5, 7, 9, 11, 13.   [44] "Hester" in text; "Hest." in Evening.   [45] 1559 Grafton has this one line below. The text probably has it here because the next line is full.   [46] "Joan" in text.

July Hath Thirty-one Days

				Morning Prayer		Evening Prayer	
			Psalms	The First Lesson	The Second Lesson	The First Lesson	The Second Lesson
19	g	Kalend	1	Job 35	Luke 13	Job 36	Phil. 1
8	A	6 No. Ortus solis Ho. 3	2	37	14	38	2
	b	5 No. Mi. 53. Occasus	3	39	15	40	3
16	c	4 No. Ho. 8. Mi. 7	4	41	16	42	4
5	d	3 No.	5	Prov. 1	17	Prov. 2	Col. 1
	e	Prid. No.[47]	6	3	18	4	2
13	f	Nonae. Dog days begin	7	5	19	6	3
2	g	8 Idus	8	7	20	8	4
	A	7 Idus	9	9	21	10	1 Thess. 1[48]
10	b	6 Idus	10	11	22	12	2
	c	5 Idus	11	13	23	14	3
18	d	4 Idus	12	15	24	16	4
7	e	3 Idus. Sol in Leone	13	17	John 1	18	5
	f	Prid. Id.	14	19	2	20	2 Thess. 1
15	g	Idus	15	21	3	22	2
4	A	17 kal. August	16	23	4	24	3
	b	16 kal.	17	25	5	26	1 Tim. 1
12	c	15 kal.	18	27	6	28	2, 3
1	d	14 kal.	19	29	7	30	4
	e	13 kal.	20	31	8	Eccles. 1	5
9	f	12 kal.[49]	21	Eccles. 2	9	3	6
	g	11 kal.	22	4	10	5	2 Tim. 1
17	A	10 kal.	23	6	11	7	2
6	b	9 kal.	24	8	12	9	3
	c	8 kal. James Apo.	25	10	13	11	4
14	d	7 kal.	26	12	14	Jer. 1	Titus 1
3	e	6 kal.	27	Jer. 2	15	3	2, 3
	f	5 kal.	28	4	16	5	Philem. 1
11	g	4 kal.	29	6	17	7	Heb. 1
	A	3 kal.	30	8	18	9	2
19	b	Prid. kl.	30	10	19	11	3

[47] 1559 Grafton has "Term ends." [48] "Tes." in text; also below. [49] Text has "21"; misprint.

August Hath Thirty-one Days

				Morning Prayer		Evening Prayer	
			Psalms	The First Lesson	The Second Lesson	The First Lesson	The Second Lesson
8	c	Kalend. Lammas	1	Jer. 12	John 20	Jer. 13	Heb. 4
16	d	4 No.	2	14	21	15	5
5	e	3 No. Ortus solis	3	16	Acts 1	17	6
	f	Prid. No. Hora. 4. Mi. 37	4	18	2	19	7
13	g	Nonae. Occasus	5	20	3	21	8
2	A	8 Idus. Ho. 7. Mi. 23	6	22	4	23	9
	b	7 Idus	7	24	5	25	10
10	c	6 Idus	8	26	6	27	11
	d	5 Idus	9	28	7	29	12
18	e	4 Idus	10	30	8	31	13
7	f	3 Idus. S. Laurence[50]	11	32	9	33[51]	James 1[52]
	g	Prid. Id.	12	34	10	35	2
15	A	Idus	13	36	11	37	3
4	b	19 kal.[53]	14	38	12	39	4
	c	18 kal. Sol in Virgo[54]	15	40	13	41	5
12	d	17 kal.[55]	16	42	14	43	1 Pet. 1
1	e	16 kal. September[56]	17	44	15	45, 46	2
	f	15 kal.[57] The dog days end[58]	18	47	16	48	3
9	g	14 kal.[59]	19	49	17	50[60]	4
	A	13 kal.	20	51	18	52	5
17	b	12 kal.	21	Lam. 1	19	Lam. 2	2 Pet. 1
6	c	11 kal.	22	3	20	4	2
	d	10 kal.	23	5	21	Ezek. 2[61]	3
14	e	9 kal. Bartho. Apo.	24	Ezek. 3	22	6	1 John 1
3	f	8 kal.	25	7	23	13	2
	g	7 kal.	26	14	24	18	3
11	A	6 kal.	27	33	25	34	4
	b	5 kal.	28	Dan. 1	26	Dan. 2	5
19	c	4 kal.	29	3	27	4	2, 3 John
8	d	3 kal.	30	5	28	6	Jude 1
	e	Prid. kl.	30	7	Matt. 1	8	Rom. 1

[50] 1552 Book and 1559 Grafton have this one line above.   [51] Text has "23"; misprint.   [52] "Jacobi." in text.   [53] Text has "91"; misprint.   [54] "Virgine" in text; 1559 Grafton has "Virgo."   [55] Text has "71"; misprint.   [56] 1552 Book and 1559 Grafton have this three lines above.   [57] Text has "14"; misprint.   [58] This is evidently a misprint. See Sept. 5 and 1559 Grafton.   [59] Text has "15"; misprint.   [60] Number omitted in text.   [61] "Ezech" in text; here and next Morning.

September Hath Thirty Days

				Morning Prayer		Evening Prayer	
			Psalms	The First Lesson	The Second Lesson	The First Lesson	The Second Lesson
16	f	Kalend	1	Dan. 9	Matt. 2	Dan. 10	Rom. 2
5	g	4 No. Ortus solis Ho. 5	2	11	3	12	3
	A	3 No. Mi. 36. Occasus	3	13	4	14	4
13	b	Prid. No. Ho. 6. Mi. 24	4	Hos. 1[62]	5	Hos. 2, 3	5
2	c	Nonae. Dog days end	5	4	6	5, 6	6
	d	8 Idus	6	7	7	8	7
10	e	7 Idus	7	9	8	10	8
	f	6 Idus	8	11	9	12	9
18	g	5 Idus	9	13	10	14	10
7	A	4 Idus	10	Joel 1	11	Joel 2	11
	b	3 Idus	11	3	12	Amos 1	12
15	c	Prid. Id.	12	Amos 2	13	3	13
4	d	Idus. Sol in Libra[63]	13	4	14	5	14
	e	18 kal. October	14	6	15	7	15
12	f	17 kal. Aequinoctium	15	8	16	9	16
1	g	16 kal. autumnale	16	Obad. 1[64]	17	Jon. 1[65]	1 Cor. 1
	A	15 kal.	17	Jon. 2, 3	18	4	2
9	b	14 kal.	18	Mic. 1[66]	19	Mic. 2	3
	c	13 kal.	19	3	20	4	4
17	d	12 kal.	20	5	21	6	5
6	e	11 kal. S. Matthew	21	7	22	Nah. 1[67]	6
	f	10 kal.	22	Nah. 2	23	3	7
14	g	9 kal.	23	Hab. 1[68]	24	Hab. 2	8
3	A	8 kal.	24	3	25	Zeph. 1[69]	9
	b	7 kal.	25	Zeph. 2	26	3	10
11	c	6 kal.	26	Hag. 1[70]	27	Hag. 2	11
	d	5 kal.	27	Zech. 1[71]	28	Zech. 2, 3	12
19	e	4 kal.	28	4, 5	Mark 1	6	13
8	f	3 kal. S. Michael	29	7	2	8	14
	g	Prid. kl.	30	9	3	10	15

[62] "Ozee" in text; "Oze." in Evening. [63] 1552 Book and 1559 Grafton have this two lines below. But see Sarum Calendar, in Brightman, *English Rite*, I, 110. [64] "Abdias" in text. [65] "Jonas" in text. [66] "Miche." in text; also in Evening. [67] "Naum" in text; also next line. [68] "Abacu." in text; also in Evening. [69] "Soph." in text; also next line. [70] "Agge." in text; also in Evening. [71] "Zacha." in text; "Zach." in Evening.

October Hath Thirty-one Days

| | | | | Morning Prayer | | Evening Prayer | |
				The First Lesson	The Second Lesson	The First Lesson	The Second Lesson
			Psalms				
16	A	Kalend	1	Zech. 11[72]	Mark 4	Zech. 12	1 Cor. 16
5	b	6 No. Ortus solis	2	13	5	14	2 Cor. 1
13	c	5 No. Hora. 6. Mi. 35	3	Mal. 1	6	Mal. 2	2
2	d	4 No. Occasus	4	3	7	4	3
	e	3 No. Ho. 5. Mi. 25	5	Tob. 1[73]	8[74]	Tob. 2	4
10	f	Prid. No.	6	3	9	4	5
	g	Nonae	7	5	10	6	6
18	A	8 Idus	8	7	11	8	7
7	b	7 Idus. Term begin	9	9	12	10	8
	c	6 Idus	10	11	13	12	9
15	d	5 Idus	11	13	14	14	10
4	e	4 Idus	12	Jth. 1	15	Jth. 2	11
	f	3 Idus	13	3	16	4	12
12	g	Prid. Id. Sol in Scorpione	14[75]	5	Luke di. 1	6	13
1	A	Idus	15	7	di. 1	8	Gal. 1
	b	17 kal. November	16	9	2	10	2
9	c	16 kal.[76]	17	11	3	12	3
	d	15 kal. Luke Evan.	18	13	4	14	4
17	e	14 kal.	19	15	5	16	5
6	f	13 kal.	20	Wisd. 1[77]	6	Wisd. 2	6
	g	12 kal.	21	3	7	4	Eph. 1
14	A	11 kal.	22	5	8	6	2
3	b	10 kal.	23	7	9	8	3
	c	9 kal.	24	9	10	10	4
11	d	8 kal.	25	11	11	12	5
	e	7 kal.	26	13	12	14	6
19	f	6 kal.	27	15	13	16	Phil. 1
8	g	5 kal. Simon and Jude	28	17	14	18	2
	A	4 kal.	29	19	15	Eccles. 1	3
16	b	3 kal.	30	Eccles. 2	16	3	4
5	c	Prid. kl.	30	4	17	5	Col. 1

[72] "Zacha." in text; also in Evening. [73] "Toby" in text; also in Evening. [74] Text has "7"; misprint. [75] Text has "13"; misprint. [76] Text has "6"; misprint. [77] "Sapie" in text; also in Evening.

45

November Hath Thirty Days

				Morning Prayer		Evening Prayer	
			Psalms	The First Lesson	The Second Lesson	The First Lesson	The Second Lesson
	d	Kalend. All Saints	1	Wisd. 3[78]	Heb. 11, 12	Wisd. 5	Apoc. 19
13[79]	e	4 No. Ortus solis Ho. 7	2	Eccles. 6	Luke 18	Eccles. 7	Col. 2
1[80]	f	3 No. Mi. 34. Occasus	3	8	19	9	3
	g	Prid. No. Ho. 4. Mi. 26	4	10	20	11	4
10	A	Nonae	5	12	21	13	1 Thess. 1
	b	8 Idus	6	14	22	15	2
18	c	7 Idus	7	16	23	17	3
7	d	6 Idus	8	18	24	19	4
	e	5 Idus	9	20	John 1	21	5
15	f	4 Idus	10	22	2	23	2 Thess. 1
4	g	3 Idus	11	24	3	25	2
	A	Prid. Id.	12	26	4	27	3
12	b	Idus. Sol in Sagitario	13	28	5	29	1 Tim. 1
1	c	18 kal. December	14	30	6	31	2, 3
	d	17 kal.	15	32	7	33	4
9	e	16 kal.	16	34	8	35	5
	f	15 kal.	17	36	9	37	6
17	g	14 kal.	18	38	10	39	2 Tim. 1
6	A	13 kal.	19	40	11	41	2
	b	12 kal.	20	42	12	43	3
14	c	11 kal.	21	44	13	45	4
3	d	10 kal.	22	46	14	47	Titus 1
	e	9 kal.[81]	23	48	15	49	2, 3
11	f	8 kal.	24	50	16	51	Philem. 1
	g	7 kal.	25	Bar. 1	17	Bar. 2	Heb. 1
19	A	6 kal.	26	3	18	4	2
8	b	5 kal. Term end.[82]	27	5	19	6	3
	c	4 kal.	28	Isa. 1[83]	20	Isa. 2	4
16	d	3 kal.	29	3	21	4	5
5	e	Prid. kl. Andrew Apo.	30	5	Acts 1	6	6

[78] "Sapi." in text; "Sap." in Evening.　[79] 1559 Grafton has "14"; misprint. [80] 1561 Calendar has "2"; misprint.　[81] 1552 Book and 1559 Grafton have "S. Clement" here.　[82] 1552 Book and 1559 Grafton have this one line below. [83] "Esaye" in text; "Esay." in Evening.

December Hath Thirty-one Days

				Morning Prayer		Evening Prayer	
			Psalms	The First Lesson	The Second Lesson	The First Lesson	The Second Lesson
	f	Kalend	1	Isa. 7[84]	Acts 2	Isa. 8	Heb. 7
14	g	4 No. Sol oritur Ho.	2	9	3	10	8
2	A	3 No. 8 Mi. 12	3	11	4	12	9
10	b	Prid. No. Occ. Ho. 3	4	13	5	14	10
	c	Nonae. Mi. 48	5	15	6	16	11
18	d	8 Idus	6	17	di. 7	18	12
7	e	7 Idus	7	19	di. 7	20, 21	13
	f	6 Idus[85]	8	22	8	23	James 1
15	g	5 Idus	9	24	9	25	2
4	A	4 Idus	10	26	10	27	3
	b	3 Idus	11	28	11	29	4
12	c	Prid. Id. Sol in Capricorno	12	30	12	31	5
1	d	Idus	13	32	13	33	1 Pet. 1
	e	19 kal. January	14	34	14	35	2
9	f	18 kal.	15	36	15	37	3
	g	17 kal.	16	38	16	39	4
17	A	16 kal.	17	40	17	41	5
6	b	15 kal.	18	42	18	43	2 Pet. 1
	c	14 kal.	19	44	19	45	2
14	d	13 kal.	20	46	20	47	3
	e	12 kal.[86] Thomas Apo.	21	48	21	49	1 John 1
	f	11 kal.	22	50	22	51	2
11	g	10 kal.	23	52	23	53	3
	A	9 kal.	24	54	24	55	4
19	b	8 kal. Christmas	25	Isa. 9[87]	Luke 22	Isa. 7	Titus 3
8	c	7 kal. S. Stephen	26	56	Acts 6, 7	57	Acts 7
	d	6 kal. S. John	27[88]	58	Apoc. 1	59	Apoc. 22
16	e	5 kal. Innocents	28	Jer. 31	Acts 25	60	1 John 5
5	f	4 kal.	29	Isa. 61	26	62	2 John 1
	g	3 kal.[89]	30	63	27	64	3 John 1
13	A	Prid. kl.	30	65	28[90]	66	Jude 1

[84] "Esay" in text; also in Evening.   [85] Number omitted in text.   [86] Number omitted in text.   [87] "Esay" in text; also in Evening and below.   [88] Text has "25"; misprint.   [89] Number omitted in text.   [90] Text has "18"; misprint.

47

The Order Where Morning
and Evening Prayer Shall
Be Used and Said

The Morning and Evening Prayer shall be used in the accustomed place of the church, chapel, or chancel, except it shall be otherwise determined by the ordinary of the place; and the chancels shall remain as they have done in times past.

And here is to be noted that the minister at the time of the Communion, and at all other times in his ministration, shall use such ornaments in the church as were in use by authority of Parliament in the second year of the reign of King Edward the Sixth according to the Act of Parliament set in the beginning of this book.

An Order for Morning
Prayer Daily throughout the Year

At the beginning both of Morning Prayer, and likewise of Evening Prayer, the minister shall read with a loud voice some one of these sentences of the Scriptures that follow. And then he shall say that which is written after the said sentences.

AT what time soever a sinner doth repent him of his sin from the bottom of his heart: I will put all his wickedness out of my remembrance, saith the Lord. [Ezek. 18

I do know mine own wickedness, and my sin is alway against me. [Ps. 51

Turn thy face away from our sins, O Lord, and blot out all our offenses. [Ps. 51

A sorrowful spirit is a sacrifice to God: despise not, O Lord, humble and contrite hearts. [Ps. 51

Rent[1] your hearts, and not your garments, and turn to the Lord, your God: because he is gentle and merciful, he is patient and of much mercy, and such a one that is sorry for your afflictions. [Joel 2

To thee, O Lord God, belongeth mercy and forgiveness, for we have gone away from thee, and have not hearkened to thy voice, whereby we might walk in thy laws which thou hast appointed for us. [Dan. 9

Correct us, O Lord, and yet in thy judgment, not in thy fury, lest we should be consumed and brought to nothing. [Jer. 10[2]

Amend your lives, for the kingdom of God is at hand. [Matt. 3

I will go to my father and say to him: Father, I have sinned

---

[1] 1559 Grafton has "Rend," but 1552 and 1661 Books have "Rent"; cf. Brightman, *English Rite*, I, 129. Ordinarily means the result of rending or tearing apart.

[2] Text has "2"; misprint.

against heaven, and against thee, I am no more worthy to be called thy son. [Luke 15

Enter not into judgment with thy servants, O Lord, for no flesh is righteous in thy sight. [Ps. 143³

If we say that we have no sin, we deceive ourselves, and there is no truth in us. [1 John 1

DEARLY beloved brethren, the Scripture moveth us in sundry places, to acknowledge and confess our manifold sins and wickedness, and that we should not dissemble nor cloak them before the face of Almighty God our heavenly Father, but confess them with an humble, lowly, penitent, and obedient heart: to the end that we may obtain forgiveness of the same by his infinite goodness and mercy. And although we ought at all times, humbly to knowledge our sins before God: yet ought we most chiefly so to do, when we assemble and meet together to render thanks for the great benefits that we have received at his hands, to set forth his most worthy praise, to hear his most holy Word, and to ask those things which be requisite and necessary, as well for the body as the soul. Wherefore I pray and beseech you, as many as be here present, to accompany me with a pure heart and humble voice, unto the throne of the heavenly grace, saying after me:

A General Confession

To be said of the whole congregation
after the minister, kneeling.

ALMIGHTY and most merciful Father, we have erred and strayed from thy ways, like lost sheep. We have followed too much the devices and desires of our own hearts. We have offended against thy holy laws. We have left undone those things which we ought to have done, and we have done those things which we ought not to have done, and there is no health in us.

---

³ Text has "142"; misprint.

But thou, O Lord, have mercy upon us miserable offenders. Spare thou them, O God, which confess their faults. Restore thou them that be penitent, according to thy promises declared unto mankind, in Christ Jesu our Lord. And grant, O most merciful Father, for his sake, that we may hereafter live a godly, righteous, and sober life, to the glory of thy holy name.

The Absolution

To be pronounced by the minister alone.

ALMIGHTY God, the Father of our Lord Jesus Christ, which desireth not the death of a sinner, but rather that he may turn from his wickedness and live: and hath given power and commandment to his ministers, to declare and pronounce to his people being penitent, the absolution and remission of their sins: he pardoneth and absolveth all them which truly repent, and unfeignedly believe his holy gospel. Wherefore we beseech him to grant us true repentance and his Holy Spirit, that those things may please him, which we do at this present, and that the rest of our life hereafter, may be pure and holy: so that at the last we may come to his eternal joy: through Jesus Christ our Lord.

The people shall answer. Amen.

Then shall the minister begin the Lord's Prayer with a loud voice.

OUR Father which art in heaven, hallowed be thy name. Thy kingdom come. Thy will be done in earth as it is in heaven. Give us this day our daily bread. And forgive us our trespasses, as we forgive them that trespass against us. And lead us not into temptation. But deliver us from evil. Amen.

Then likewise he shall say.

O Lord open thou our lips.

Answer. And our mouth shall show forth thy praise.

Priest. O God make speed to save us.

Answer. O Lord make haste to help us.

Priest. Glory be to the Father, etc.

As it was in the beginning, etc.

Praise ye the Lord.

Then shall be said or sung this Psalm following.

[*Venite exultemus domino.* 95

O COME let us sing unto the Lord: let us heartily rejoice in the strength of our salvation.

Let us come before his presence with thanksgiving: and show ourself glad in him with psalms.

For the Lord is a great God: and a great king above all gods.

In his hand are all the corners of the earth: and the strength of the hills is his also.

The sea is his, and he made it: and his hands prepared the dry land.

O come, let us worship and fall down: and kneel before the Lord our maker.

For he is the Lord our God: and we are the people of his pasture, and the sheep of his hands.

Today if ye will hear his voice, harden not your hearts: as in the provocation, and as in the day of temptation in the wilderness.

When your fathers tempted me: proved me, and saw my works.

Forty years long was I grieved with this generation, and said: It is a people that do err in their hearts, for they have not known my ways.

Unto whom I sware in my wrath: that they should not enter into my rest.

Glory be to the Father, etc.

Then shall follow certain Psalms in order as they be appointed in a table made for that purpose, except there be proper Psalms

appointed for that day. And at the end of every psalm through-
out the year, and likewise in the end of *Benedictus, Benedicite,
Magnificat,* and *Nunc dimittis,* shall be repeated, **Glory be to the
Father,** etc.

Then shall be read two Lessons distinctly with a loud voice
that the people may hear. The first of the Old Testament, the
second of the New, like as they be appointed by the Calendar,
except there be proper Lessons assigned for that day. The minister that readeth the Lesson standing and turning him so as he
may best be heard of all such as be present. And before every
Lesson, the minister shall say thus. **The first, second, third, or
fourth chapter of Genesis, or Exodus, Matthew, Mark,** or other
like, as is appointed in the Calendar. And in the end of every
chapter he shall say, **Here endeth** such a **chapter** of such a book.

And to the end the people may the better hear, in such places
where they do sing, there shall the Lessons be sung in a plain
tune after the manner of distinct reading, and likewise the Epistle and Gospel.

After the first Lesson shall follow *Te Deum laudamus,* in English, daily through the whole year.

[*Te Deum laudamus*

WE praise thee, O God: we knowledge thee to be the
Lord.

All the earth doth worship thee, the Father everlasting.

To thee all angels cry aloud: the heavens and all the powers
therein.

To thee Cherubin and Seraphin, continually do cry.

Holy, holy, holy, Lord God of Sabaoth.

Heaven and earth are full of the majesty of thy glory.

The glorious company of the apostles, praise thee.

The goodly fellowship of the prophets, praise thee.

The noble army of martyrs, praise thee.

The holy Church throughout all the world, doth knowledge
thee:

The Father of an infinite majesty.

Thy honorable, true, and only Son:

Also the Holy Ghost, the comforter.[4]

Thou art the king of glory, O Christ.

Thou art the everlasting Son of the Father.

When thou tookest upon thee to deliver man, thou didst not abhor the Virgin's womb.

When thou hadst overcome[5] the sharpness of death, thou didst open the kingdom of heaven to all believers.

Thou sittest on the right hand of God, in the glory of the Father.

We believe that thou shalt come to be our judge.

We therefore pray thee, help thy servants, whom thou hast redeemed with thy precious blood.

Make them to be numbered with thy saints, in glory everlasting.

O Lord, save thy people: and bless thine heritage.

Govern them and lift them up forever.

Day by day we magnify thee.

And we worship thy name, ever world without end.

Vouchsafe, O Lord, to keep us this day without sin.

O Lord, have mercy upon us: have mercy upon us.

O Lord, let thy mercy lighten upon us: as our trust is in thee.

O Lord, in thee have I trusted: let me never be confounded.

Or this canticle.

Benedicite omnia opera Domini Domino

O ALL the works of the Lord, bless ye the Lord: praise him and magnify him forever.

O ye angels of the Lord, bless ye the Lord: praise ye him and magnify him forever.

---

[4] *Comforter:* strengthener.

[5] Text has "overcomed," but it is "overcome" in 1559 Grafton.

O ye heavens, bless ye the Lord: praise him and magnify him forever.

O ye waters that be above the firmament, bless ye the Lord: praise him and magnify him forever.

O all ye powers of the Lord, bless ye the Lord: praise him and magnify him forever.

O ye sun and moon, bless ye the Lord: praise him and magnify him forever.

O ye stars of heaven, bless ye the Lord: praise him and magnify him forever.

O ye showers and dew, bless ye the Lord: praise him and magnify him forever.

O ye winds of God, bless ye the Lord: praise him and magnify him forever.

O ye fire and heat, bless ye the Lord: praise him and magnify him forever.

O ye winter and summer, bless ye the Lord: praise him and magnify him forever.

O ye dews and frosts, bless ye the Lord: praise him and magnify him forever.

O ye frost and cold, bless ye the Lord: praise him and magnify him forever.

O ye ice and snow, bless ye the Lord: praise him and magnify him forever.

O ye nights and days, bless ye the Lord: praise him and magnify him forever.

O ye light and darkness,[6] bless ye the Lord: praise him and magnify him forever.

O ye lightnings[7] and clouds, bless ye the Lord: praise him and magnify him forever.

O let the earth bless the Lord: yea, let it praise him and magnify him forever.

[6] Text has "darkedesse," but it is "darkness" in 1559 Grafton.

[7] Text has "lighteninges," and it is "lightcnynges" in 1559 Grafton.

O ye mountains and hills, bless ye the Lord: praise him and magnify him forever.

O all ye green things upon the earth, bless ye the Lord: praise him and magnify him forever.

O ye wells, bless ye the Lord: praise him and magnify him forever.

O ye seas and floods, bless ye the Lord: praise him and magnify him forever.

O ye whales and all that move in the waters, bless ye the Lord: praise him and magnify him forever.

O ye fowls of the air, bless ye the Lord: praise him and magnify him forever.

O all ye beasts and cattle, bless ye the Lord: praise him and magnify him forever.

O ye children of men, bless ye the Lord: praise him and magnify him forever.

O let Israel bless the Lord: praise him and magnify him forever.

O ye priests of the Lord, bless ye the Lord: praise him and magnify him forever.

O ye servants of the Lord, bless ye the Lord: praise him and magnify him forever.

O ye spirits and souls of the righteous, bless ye the Lord: praise him and magnify him forever.

O ye holy and humble men of heart, bless ye the Lord: praise him and magnify him forever.

O Hananiah, Azariah, and Mishael,[8] bless ye the Lord: praise him and magnify him forever.

Glory be to the Father, and to the Son, etc.

And after the second Lesson shall be used and said, *Benedictus,* in English, as followeth.

[8] "Ananias, Azarias, and Misael," in text.

[*Benedictus*

BLESSED be the Lord God of Israel: for he hath visited and redeemed his people.

And hath raised up a mighty salvation for us: in the house of his servant David.

As he spake by the mouth of his holy prophets: which have been since the world began.

That we should be saved from our enemies: and from the hands of all that hate us.

To perform the[9] mercy promised to our forefathers: and to remember his holy covenant.

To perform the oath which he sware to our forefather Abraham: that he would give us.

That we being delivered out of the hands of our enemies: might serve him without fear.

In holiness and righteousness before him: all the days of our life.

And thou child shalt be called the Prophet of the Highest: for thou shalt go before the face of the Lord, to prepare his ways.

To give knowledge of salvation unto his people: for the remission of their sins.

Through the tender mercy of our God: whereby the dayspring from on high hath visited us.

To give light to them that sit in darkness, and in the shadow of death: and to guide our feet into the way of peace.

Glory be to the Father, and to the Son: and to the Holy Ghost.

As it was in the beginning, is now, and ever shall be: world without end. Amen.

Or else this Psalm.

[*Jubilate Deo.* Ps. 100

O BE joyful in the Lord all ye lands: serve the Lord with gladness, and come before his presence with a song.

Be ye sure that the Lord he is God: it is he that hath made us,

[9] Text has "thy," but it is "the" in 1559 Grafton and other editions.

and not we ourselves, we are his people, and the sheep of his pasture.

O go your way into his gates with thanksgiving, and into his courts with praise: be thankful unto him, and speak good of his name.

For the Lord is gracious, his mercy is everlasting: and his truth endureth from generation to generation.

Glory be to the Father, and to the Son, etc.

As it was in the beginning, is now, and ever shall be: world without end. Amen.

Then shall be said the Creed by the minister and the people standing.

I BELIEVE in God the Father Almighty, maker of heaven and earth. And in Jesus Christ his only Son our Lord. Which was conceived by the Holy Ghost, born of the Virgin Mary. Suffered under Pontius[10] Pilate, was crucified, dead, and buried, he descended into hell. The third day he rose again from the dead. He ascended into heaven, and sitteth on the right hand of God the Father Almighty. From thence shall he come to judge the quick[11] and the dead. I believe in the Holy Ghost. The holy catholic Church. The communion of saints. The forgiveness of sins. The resurrection of the body. And the life everlasting. Amen.

And after that, these prayers following, as well at Evening Prayer as at Morning Prayer, all devoutly kneeling.

The minister first pronouncing with a loud voice.

The Lord be with you.
Answer. And with thy spirit.
The minister. Let us pray.

[10] "Ponce" in text; changed to Pontius in 1661.
[11] *Quick:* living.

Lord have mercy upon us.
Christ have mercy upon us.
Lord have mercy upon us.

Then the minister, clerks, and people shall say the Lord's Prayer, in English, with a loud voice.

OUR Father which art, etc.

Then the minister standing up shall say.

O Lord show thy mercy upon us.

Answer. And grant us thy salvation.
Priest. O Lord save the Queen.
Answer. And mercifully hear us, when we call upon thee.
Priest. Endue thy ministers with righteousness.
Answer. And make thy chosen people joyful.
Priest. O Lord save thy people.
Answer. And bless thine inheritance.
Priest. Give peace in our time, O Lord.
Answer. Because there is none other that fighteth for us, but only thou, O God.
Priest. O God make clean our hearts within us.
Answer. And take not thine Holy Spirit from us.

Then shall follow three Collects. The first of the day, which shall be the same that is appointed at the Communion. The second for peace. The third for grace to live well. And the two last Collects shall never alter, but daily be said at Morning Prayer throughout all the year, as followeth.

The Second Collect, for Peace

O GOD, which art author of peace, and lover of concord, in knowledge of whom standeth our eternal life, whose service is perfect freedom: Defend us thy humble servants, in all assaults of our enemies, that we surely trusting in thy defense, may not fear the power of any adversaries; through the might of Jesu Christ our Lord. Amen.

The Third Collect, for Grace

O LORD, our heavenly Father, almighty and everlasting God, which hast safely brought us to the beginning of this day: Defend us in the same with thy mighty power; and grant that this day we fall into no sin, neither run into any kind of danger; but that all our doings may be ordered by thy governance, to do always that is righteous in thy sight; through Jesus Christ our Lord. Amen.

An
Order for Evening Prayer
throughout the Year

The priest shall say.

OUR Father which art, etc.

Then likewise he shall say.

O Lord open thou our lips.

Answer. And our mouth shall show forth thy praise.

Priest. O God make speed to save us.

Answer. Lord make haste to help us.

Priest. Glory be to the Father, and to the Son, and to the Holy Ghost.

As it was in the beginning is now, and ever shall be: world without end. Amen.

Praise ye the Lord.

Then Psalms in order as they be appointed in the table for Psalms, except there be proper Psalms appointed for that day. Then a Lesson of the Old Testament as is appointed likewise in the Calendar, except there be proper Lessons appointed for that day. After that, *Magnificat*, in English, as followeth.

[*Magnificat*. Luke 1

MY soul doth magnify the Lord.
And my spirit hath rejoiced in God my savior.
For he hath regarded the lowliness of his handmaiden.
For behold, from henceforth all generations shall call me blessed.

For he that is mighty, hath magnified me: and holy is his name.

And his mercy is on them that fear him: throughout all generations.

He hath showed strength with his arm: he hath scattered the proud, in the imagination of their hearts.

He hath put down the mighty from their seat: and hath exalted the humble and meek.

He hath filled the hungry with good things: and the rich he hath sent empty away.

He remembering his mercy, hath holpen[1] his servant Israel: as he promised to our forefathers, Abraham and his seed forever.

Glory be to the Father, and to the Son: etc.

As it was in the beginning, is now, and ever, etc.

Or else this Psalm.

[*Cantate domino.* Ps. 98

O SING unto the Lord a new song: for he hath done marvelous things.

With his own right hand, and with his holy arm: hath he gotten himself the victory.

The Lord declared his salvation: his righteousness hath he openly showed in the sight of the heathen.

He hath remembered his mercy and truth toward the house of Israel: and all the ends of the world have seen the salvation of our God.

Show yourselves joyful unto the Lord all ye lands: sing, rejoice, and give thanks.

Praise the Lord upon the harp: sing to the harp with a psalm of thanksgiving.

With trumpets also and shawms:[2] O show yourselves joyful before the Lord the king.

---

[1] *Holpen:* helped.

[2] *Shawms:* medieval instruments of the oboe class, having a double reed enclosed in a globular mouthpiece, used inaccurately here where cornets or horns are intended.

Let the sea make a noise and all that therein is: the round world, and they that dwell therein.

Let the floods clap their hands, and let the hills be joyful together before the Lord: for he is come to judge the earth.

With righteousness shall he judge the world: and the people with equity.

Glory be to the Father, etc.

As it was in the, etc.

Then a Lesson of the New Testament. And after that, *Nunc dimittis*, in English, as followeth.

LORD, now lettest thou thy servant depart in peace: according to thy word.

For mine eyes have seen: thy salvation.

Which thou hast prepared: before the face of all people.

To be a light to lighten the Gentiles: and to be the glory of thy people Israel.

Glory be to the Father, and to the Son, and, etc.

As it was in the beginning, and is now, etc. Amen.

Or else this Psalm.

[*Deus misereatur.* Ps. 67

GOD be merciful unto us, and bless us: and show us the light of his countenance, and be merciful unto us.

That thy way may be known upon earth: thy saving health among all nations.

Let the people praise thee O God: yea let all the people praise thee.

O let the nations rejoice and be glad: for thou shalt judge the folk righteously, and govern the nations upon earth.

Let the people praise thee O God: let all the people praise thee.

Then shall the earth bring forth her increase: and God, even our own God, shall give us his blessing.

God shall bless us: and all the ends of the world shall fear him.

Glory be to the Father, etc.

As it was in the beginning, etc.

Then shall follow the Creed, with other prayers, as is before appointed at Morning Prayer, after *Benedictus*. And with three Collects: first of the day, the second of peace, third for aid against all perils, as hereafter followeth. Which two last Collects shall be daily said at Evening Prayer without alteration.

The Second Collect at Evening Prayer

O GOD, from whom all holy desires, all good counsels, and all just works do proceed: Give unto thy servants that peace which the world cannot give; that both our hearts may be set to obey thy commandments, and also that by thee, we being defended from the fear of our enemies, may pass our time in rest and quietness; through the merits of Jesus Christ our Savior. Amen.

The Third Collect, for Aid against All Perils

LIGHTEN our darkness we beseech thee, O Lord, and by thy great mercy defend us from all perils and dangers of this night, for the love of thy only Son, our Savior Jesus Christ. Amen.

In the feasts of Christmas, the Epiphany, Saint Matthias,[3] Easter, the Ascension, Pentecost, Saint John Baptist, Saint James, Saint Bartholomew, Saint Matthew, Saint Simon and Jude, Saint Andrew, and Trinity Sunday, shall be sung or said, immediately after *Benedictus*, this confession of our Christian faith.

[3] "Mathie" in text.

[*Quicunque vult.*

W HOSOEVER will be saved: before all things it is necessary that he hold the catholic faith.

Which faith except everyone do keep wholly[4] and undefiled:
without doubt he shall perish everlastingly.

And the catholic faith is this: that we worship one God in
Trinity, and Trinity in Unity.

Neither confounding the persons: nor dividing the substance.

For there is one person of the Father, another of the Son: and
another of the Holy Ghost.

But the Godhead of the Father, of the Son, and of the Holy
Ghost is all one: the glory equal, the majesty coeternal.

Such as the Father is, such is the Son: and such is the Holy
Ghost.

The Father uncreate, the Son uncreate: and the Holy Ghost
uncreate.

The Father incomprehensible, the Son incomprehensible: and
the Holy Ghost incomprehensible.

The Father eternal, the Son eternal: and the Holy Ghost
eternal.

And yet they are not three eternals: but one eternal.

As also there be not three incomprehensibles, nor three uncreated: but one uncreated, and one incomprehensible.

So likewise the Father is almighty, the Son almighty: and the
Holy Ghost almighty.

And yet they are not three almighties: but one almighty.

So the Father is God, the Son is God: and the Holy Ghost is
God.

And yet are they not three gods: but one God.

So likewise the Father is Lord, the Son Lord: and the Holy
Ghost Lord.

And yet not three lords: but one Lord.

[4] 1559 Grafton and the 1552 Book have "holy," but it is *integram* that is
being translated here. Cf. Brightman, *English Rite*, I, 168.

65

For like as we be compelled by the Christian verity: to acknowledge every person by himself to be God and Lord;

So are we forbidden by the catholic religion: to say, there be three gods or three lords.

The Father is made of none: neither created nor begotten.

The Son is of the Father alone: not made nor created, but begotten.

The Holy Ghost is of the Father and of the Son: neither made, nor created, nor begotten, but proceeding.

So there is one Father, not three fathers, one Son, not three sons: one Holy Ghost, not three holy ghosts.

And in this Trinity, none is afore or after other: none is greater, nor less than another.

But the whole three persons: be coeternal together and co-equal.

So that in all things, as is aforesaid: the Unity in Trinity, and the Trinity in Unity, is to be worshiped.

He therefore that will be saved: must thus think of the Trinity.

Furthermore, it is necessary to everlasting salvation: that he also believe rightly in the Incarnation of our Lord Jesu Christ.

For the right faith is, that we believe and confess: that our Lord Jesus Christ, the Son of God, is God and man.

God of the substance of the Father, begotten before the worlds: and man of the substance of his mother, born in the world.

Perfect God, and perfect man of a reasonable soul: and human flesh subsisting.

Equal to the Father, as touching his Godhead: and inferior to the Father, touching his manhood.

Who although he be God and man: yet he is not two, but one Christ.

One, not by conversion of the Godhead into flesh: but by taking of the manhood into God.

One altogether, not by confusion of substance: but by unity of person.

For as the reasonable soul and flesh is one man: so God and man is one Christ.

Who suffered for our salvation: descended into hell, rose again the third day from the dead.

He ascended into heaven, he sitteth on the right hand of the Father, God Almighty: from whence he shall come to judge the quick and the dead.

At whose coming all men shall rise again with their bodies: and shall give account for their own works.

And they that have done good, shall go into life everlasting: and they that have done evil, into everlasting fire.

This is the catholic faith: which except a man believe faithfully, he cannot be saved.

Glory be to the Father, and to the Son: and to the Holy Ghost.

As it was in the beginning, is now, and ever shall be: world without end. Amen.

Thus endeth the Order of Morning and Evening Prayer, through the whole year.

Here Followeth the Litany

To be used upon Sundays, Wednesdays,
and Fridays, and at other times, when
it shall be commanded by the ordinary.

O GOD the Father of heaven: have mercy upon us miserable sinners.
O God the Father of heaven: have mercy upon us miserable sinners.

O God the Son, redeemer of the world: have mercy upon us miserable sinners.
O God the Son, redeemer of the world: have mercy upon us miserable sinners.

O God the Holy Ghost, proceeding from the Father and the Son: have mercy upon us miserable sinners.
O God the Holy Ghost, proceeding from the Father and the Son: have mercy upon us miserable sinners.

O holy, blessed, and glorious Trinity, three persons and one God: have mercy upon us miserable sinners.
O holy, blessed, and glorious Trinity, three persons and one God: have mercy upon us miserable sinners.

Remember not, Lord, our offenses, nor the offenses of our forefathers, neither take thou vengeance of our sins: spare us good Lord, spare thy people whom thou hast redeemed with thy most precious blood, and be not angry with us forever.
Spare us good Lord.

From all evil and mischief, from sin, from the crafts and assaults of the devil, from thy wrath, and from everlasting damnation.
Good Lord deliver us.

From all blindness of heart, from pride, vainglory, and hypocrisy, from envy, hatred and malice, and all uncharitableness.

Good Lord deliver us.

From fornication and all other deadly sin, and from all the deceits of the world, the flesh, and the devil.

Good Lord deliver us.

From lightning and tempest, from plague, pestilence, and famine, from battle and murder, and from sudden death.

Good Lord deliver us.

From all sedition and privy[1] conspiracy, from all false doctrine and heresy, from hardness of heart, and contempt of thy Word and commandment.

Good Lord deliver us.

By the mystery of thy holy incarnation, by thy holy nativity and circumcision, by thy baptism, fasting, and temptation.

Good Lord deliver us.

By thine agony and bloody sweat, by thy cross and passion, by thy precious death and burial, by thy glorious resurrection and ascension, and by the coming of the Holy Ghost.

Good Lord deliver us.

In all our time of tribulation, in all time of our wealth, in the hour of death, and in the day of judgment.

Good Lord deliver us.

We sinners do beseech thee to hear us, O Lord God, and that it may please thee to rule and govern thy holy Church universally[2] in the right way.

We beseech thee to hear us good Lord.

That it may please thee to keep and strengthen in the true worshiping of thee, in righteousness and holiness of life thy servant Elizabeth our most gracious Queen and governor.

We beseech thee to hear us good Lord.

That it may please thee to rule her heart in thy faith, fear,

---

[1] *Privy:* secret.

[2] 1549 and 1661 Books have "universal"; 1552 Book and 1559 Grafton have "universally"; cf. Brightman, *English Rite*, I, 176–77.

and love, and that she may evermore have affiance[3] in thee, and ever seek thy honor and glory.

> We beseech thee to hear us good Lord.

That it may please thee to be her defender and keeper, giving her the victory over all her enemies.

> We beseech thee to hear us good Lord.

That it may please thee to illuminate all bishops, pastors, and ministers of the Church, with true knowledge and understanding of thy Word: and that both by their preaching and living, they may set it forth and show it accordingly.

> We beseech thee to hear us good Lord.

That it may please thee to endue the Lords of the Council, and all the nobility, with grace, wisdom, and understanding.

> We beseech thee to hear us good Lord.

That it may please thee to bless and keep the magistrates, giving them grace to execute justice, and to maintain truth.

> We beseech thee to hear us good Lord.

That it may please thee to bless and keep all thy people.

> We beseech thee to hear us good Lord.

That it may please thee to give to all nations unity, peace, and concord.

> We beseech thee to hear us good Lord.

That it may please thee to give us an heart to love and dread thee, and diligently to live after thy commandments.

> We beseech thee to hear us good Lord.

That it may please thee to give all thy people increase of grace, to hear meekly thy Word, and to receive it with pure affection, and to bring forth the fruits of the Spirit.

> We beseech thee to hear us good Lord.

That it may please thee to bring into the way of truth, all such as have erred and are deceived.

> We beseech thee to hear us good Lord.

That it may please thee to strengthen such as do stand, and to

[3] *Affiance:* faith, confidence, assurance.

comfort and help the weakhearted, and to raise them up that fall, and finally to beat down Satan under our feet.

We beseech thee to hear us good Lord.

That it may please thee to succor, help, and comfort all that be in danger, necessity, and tribulation.

We beseech thee to hear us good Lord.

That it may please thee to preserve all that travel[4] by land or by water, all women laboring of child, all sick persons and young children, and to show thy pity upon all prisoners and captives.

We beseech thee to hear us good Lord.

That it may please thee to defend and provide for the fatherless children and widows, and all that be desolate and oppressed.

We beseech thee to hear us good Lord.

That it may please thee to have mercy upon all men.

We beseech thee to hear us good Lord.

That it may please thee to forgive our enemies, persecutors, and slanderers, and to turn their hearts.

We beseech thee to hear us good Lord.

That it may please thee to give and preserve to our use the kindly fruits of the earth, so as in due time we may enjoy them.

We beseech thee to hear us good Lord.

That it may please thee to give us true repentance, to forgive us all our sins, negligences, and ignorances, and to endue us with the grace of thy Holy Spirit to amend our lives according to thy holy Word.

We beseech thee to hear us good Lord.

Son of God: we beseech thee to hear us.

Son of God: we beseech thee to hear us.

O Lamb of God that takest away the sins of the world:

Grant us thy peace.

O Lamb of God that takest away the sins of the world:

Have mercy upon us.

---

[4] Text has "travayle"; alternate spelling of *travel* (OED); in the sixteenth century used interchangeably for both *travel* and *travail*.

O Christ hear us.

  O Christ hear us.

Lord have mercy upon us.

  Lord have mercy upon us.

Christ have mercy upon us.

  Christ have mercy upon us.

Lord have mercy upon us.

  Lord have mercy upon us.

Our Father which art in heaven, etc.

  And lead us not into temptation,

But deliver us from evil.

The versicle. O Lord deal not with us after our sins.

The answer. Neither reward us after our iniquities.

Let us pray.

O GOD, merciful Father, that despisest not the sighing of a contrite heart, nor the desire of such as be sorrowful: Mercifully assist our prayers that we make before thee, in all our troubles and adversities whensoever they oppress us. And graciously hear us, that those evils, which the craft and subtilty of the devil or man worketh against us, be brought to nought, and by the providence of thy goodness, they may be dispersed, that we thy servants being hurt by no persecutions, may evermore give thanks unto thee in thy holy Church; through Jesu Christ our Lord.

  O Lord arise, help us, and deliver us, for thy name's sake.

O God, we have heard with our ears, and our fathers have declared unto us, the noble works that thou didst in their days, and in the old time before them.

  O Lord arise, help us, and deliver us, for thine honor.

Glory be to the Father, and to the Son, and to the Holy Ghost. As it was in the beginning, is now, and ever shall be, world without end. Amen.

From our enemies defend us, O Christ.

    Graciously look upon our afflictions.

Pitifully behold the sorrows of our heart.

    Mercifully forgive the sins of thy people.

Favorably with mercy hear our prayers.

    O Son of David have mercy upon us.

Both now and ever vouchsafe to hear us, O Christ.

    Graciously hear us, O Christ, graciously hear us, O Lord Christ.

The versicle. O Lord let thy mercy be showed upon us.

The answer. As we do put our trust in thee.

Let us pray.

WE humbly beseech thee, O Father, mercifully to look upon our infirmities; and for the glory of thy name's sake, turn from us all those evils that we most righteously have deserved; and grant that in all our troubles we may put our whole trust and confidence in thy mercy, and evermore serve thee in holiness and pureness of living, to thy honor and glory; through our only mediator and advocate, Jesus Christ our Lord. Amen.[5]

[A Prayer for the Queen's Majesty

O LORD, our heavenly father, high and mighty king of kings, Lord of Lords, the only ruler of princes, which doest from thy throne behold all the dwellers upon earth, most heartily we beseech thee with thy favor to behold our most gracious sovereign lady Queen Elizabeth, and so replenish her with the grace of thy Holy Spirit, that she may alway incline to thy will, and walk in thy way; indue her plentifully with heavenly gifts; grant her in health and wealth long to live; strength[6] her that

---

[5] The sequence of prayers which follows within brackets was added in the 1559 Grafton and is copied here from another copy of the 1559 Jugge and Cawode Prayer Book found in the British Museum (C.25.l.19). These prayers appear in all subsequent editions of the 1559 Book.

[6] *Strength:* strengthen.

she may vanquish and overcome all her enemies; and finally after this life, she may attain everlasting joy and felicity, through Jesus Christ our Lord. Amen.

ALMIGHTY and everlasting God, which only workest great marvels, send down upon our bishops and curates, and all congregations committed to their charge, the healthful spirit of thy grace; and that they may truly please thee, pour upon them the continual dew of thy blessing: grant this, O Lord, for the honor of our advocate and mediator, Jesus Christ. Amen.

A Prayer of Chrysostom

ALMIGHTY God, which hast given us grace at this time with one accord to make our common supplications unto thee, and doest promise that when two or three be gathered together in thy name, thou wilt grant their requests: fulfill now, O Lord, the desires and petitions of thy servants as may be most expedient for them, granting us in this world knowledge of thy truth, and in the world to come life everlasting. Amen.

2 Cor. 13

THE grace of our Lord Jesus Christ, and the love of God, and the fellowship of the Holy Ghost, be with us all evermore. Amen.]

For Rain, If the Time Require

O GOD, heavenly Father, which by thy Son Jesu Christ hast promised to all them that seek thy kingdom and the righteousness thereof, all things necessary to their bodily sustenance: Send us we beseech thee in this our necessity, such moderate rain and showers, that we may receive the fruits of the earth to our comfort, and to thy honor; through Jesus Christ our Lord. Amen.

For Fair Weather

O LORD God, which for the sin of man didst once drown all the world, except eight persons, and afterward of thy great mercy didst promise never to destroy it so again: We humbly beseech thee, that although we for our iniquities have worthily deserved this plague of rain and waters, yet upon our true repentance, thou wilt send us such weather whereby we may receive the fruits of the earth in due season, and learn both by thy punishment to amend our lives, and for thy clemency to give thee praise and glory; through Jesus Christ our Lord. Amen.

In the Time of Dearth and Famine

O GOD, heavenly Father, whose gift it is that the rain doth fall, the earth is fruitful, beasts increase, and fishes do multiply: Behold we beseech thee the afflictions of thy people, and grant that the scarcity and dearth (which we do now most justly suffer for our iniquity) may through thy goodness be mercifully turned into cheapness and plenty; for the love of Jesu Christ our Lord, to whom with thee and the Holy Ghost, etc.

Or thus.

O GOD, merciful Father, which in the time of Heliseus[7] the prophet didst suddenly turn in Samaria great scarcity and dearth into plenty and cheapness, and extreme famine into abundance of victual: Have pity upon us, that now be punished for our sins with like adversity; increase the fruits of the earth by thy heavenly benediction; and grant, that we, receiving thy bountiful liberality, may use the same to thy glory, our comfort, and relief of our needy neighbors; through Jesu Christ our Lord. Amen.

[7] *Heliseus:* Elisha.

In the Time of War

O ALMIGHTY God, king of all kings, and governor of all things, whose power no creature is able to resist, to whom it belongeth justly to punish sinners, and to be merciful to them that truly repent: Save and deliver us (we humbly beseech thee) from the hands of our enemies, abate their pride, assuage their malice, and confound their devices, that we, being armed with thy defense, may be preserved evermore from all perils to glorify thee, which art the only giver of all victory; through the merits of thy only Son Jesu Christ our Lord.

In the Time of Any Common Plague or Sickness

O ALMIGHTY God, which in thy wrath in the time of King David didst slay with the plague of pestilence sixty and ten thousand, and yet remembering thy mercy didst save the rest: Have pity upon us miserable sinners, that now are visited with great sickness and mortality, that like as thou didst then command thy angel to cease from punishing, so it may now please thee to withdraw from us this plague and grievous sickness; through Jesu Christ our Lord.

And the Litany shall ever end with this Collect following.[8]

A LMIGHTY God, which hast given us grace at this time with one accord to make our common supplications unto thee, and dost promise that when two or three be gathered in thy name, thou wilt grant their requests: fulfill now, O Lord, the desires and petitions of thy servants, as may be most expedient for them, granting us in this world knowledge of thy truth, and in the world to come, life everlasting. Amen.

[8] 1559 Grafton, and all subsequent editions replace this prayer with the following: "O God, whose nature and property is ever to have mercy, and to forgive, receive our humble petitions: and though we be tied and bound with the chain of our sins: yet let the pitifulness of thy great mercy loose us, for the honor of Jesus Christ's sake, our mediator and advocate. Amen."

The Collects, Epistles,
and Gospels, to Be Used at the Celebration of the Lord's Supper and Holy Communion through the Year

The First Sunday of Advent

The Collect

ALMIGHTY God, give us grace that we may cast away the works of darkness, and put upon us the armor of light, now in the time of this mortal life (in the which thy Son Jesus Christ came to visit us in great humility); that in the last day, when he shall come again in glorious majesty to judge both the quick[1] and the dead, we may rise to the life immortal, through him who liveth and reigneth with thee and the Holy Ghost, now and ever. Amen.

The Epistle [Rom. 13

OWE nothing to any man but this, that ye love one another. For he that loveth another, fulfilleth the law. For these commandments, Thou shalt not commit adultery, Thou shalt not kill, Thou shalt not steal, Thou shalt bear no false witness, Thou shalt not lust, and so forth (if there be any other commandment) it is all comprehended in this saying: namely, Love thy neighbor as thyself. Love hurteth not his neighbor, therefore is love the fulfilling of the law. This also, we know the season how that it is time that we should now awake out of sleep, for now is our salvation nearer than when we believed. The night

[1] *Quick:* living.

is passed, the day is come nigh. Let us therefore cast away the deeds of darkness, and let us put on the armor of light. Let us walk honestly, as it were in the daylight, not in eating and drinking, neither in chambering[2] and wantonness, neither in strife and envying: but put ye on the Lord Jesus Christ and make not provision for the flesh, to fulfill the lusts of it.

The Gospel [Matt. 21

AND when they drew nigh to Jerusalem, and were come to Bethphage unto Mount Olivet, then sent Jesus two of his disciples, saying unto them: Go into the town that lieth over against you, and anon you shall find an ass bound, and a colt with her; loose them and bring them unto me. And if any man say ought unto you, say ye the Lord hath need of them, and straightway he will let you go. All this was done, that it might be fulfilled which was spoken by the Prophet, saying, Tell ye the daughter of Sion: Behold thy king cometh unto thee meek, sitting upon an ass and a colt, the foal of the ass used to the yoke. The disciples went and did as Jesus commanded them, and brought the ass and the colt, and put on them their clothes, and set him thereon. And many of the people spread their garments in the way. Other cut down branches from the trees, and strawed[3] them in the way. Moreover, the people that went before, and they that came after cried, saying, Hosanna to the son of David; Blessed is he that cometh in the name of the Lord; Hosanna in the highest. And when he was come to Jerusalem, all the city was moved, saying, Who is this? And the people said, This is Jesus the Prophet of Nazareth, a city of Galilee. And Jesus went into the temple of God, and cast out all them that sold and bought in the temple, and overthrew the tables of the money-changers, and the seats of them that sold doves, and said unto

[2] *Chambering:* sexual indulgence, lewdness.
[3] *Strawed:* strew.

them, It is written: My house shall be called the house of prayer, but ye have made it a den of thieves.

The Second Sunday

The Collect

BLESSED Lord, which hast caused all Holy Scriptures to be written for our learning: Grant us that we may in such wise hear them, read, mark, learn, and inwardly digest them; that by patience and comfort of thy holy Word, we may embrace and ever hold fast the blessed hope of everlasting life, which thou hast given us in our Savior Jesus Christ.

The Epistle [Rom. 15

WHATSOEVER things are written aforetime, they are written for our learning, that we through patience and comfort of the Scriptures, might have hope. The God of patience and consolation, grant you to be like-minded one toward another, after the ensample[1] of Christ Jesu, that ye all agreeing together, may with one mouth praise God the Father of our Lord Jesu Christ. Wherefore receive ye one another, as Christ received us, to the praise of God. And this I say, that Jesus Christ was a minister of the circumcision for the truth of God, to confirm the promises made unto the fathers, and that the Gentiles might praise God for his mercy; as it is written, For this cause I will praise thee among the Gentiles, and sing unto thy name. And again he saith, Rejoice ye Gentiles, with his people. And again, Praise the Lord all ye Gentiles, and laud him all ye nations together. And again, Isaiah[2] saith, There shall be the root of

[1] *Ensample:* example.
[2] "Esay" in text.

Jesse, and he that shall rise to reign over the Gentiles, in him shall the Gentiles trust. The God of hope, fill you with all joy and peace in believing, that ye may be rich in hope, through the power of the Holy Ghost.

The Gospel [Luke 21

THERE shall be signs in the sun and in the moon, and in the stars, and in the earth the people shall be at their wits' end, through despair. The sea and the water shall roar, and men's hearts shall fail them for fear, and for looking after those things which shall come on the earth. For the powers of heaven shall move. And then shall they see the Son of man come in a cloud, with power and great glory. When these things begin to come to pass, then look up, and lift up your heads, for your redemption draweth nigh. And he showed them a similitude, Behold the fig tree, and all other trees; when they shoot forth their buds, ye see and know of your own selves that summer is then nigh at hand. So likewise ye also (when ye see these things come to pass) be sure that the kingdom of God is nigh. Verily I say unto you, this generation shall not pass, till all be fulfilled. Heaven and earth shall pass, but my words shall not pass.

The Third Sunday

The Collect

LORD, we beseech thee give ear to our prayers, and by thy gracious visitation, lighten the darkness of our heart, by our Lord Jesus Christ.

The Epistle [1 Cor. 4

LET a man this wise esteem us, even as the ministers of Christ, and stewards of the secrets of God. Furthermore it is required of the stewards, that a man be found faithful. With me it is but a very small thing that I should be judged of you, either of man's judgment: no, I judge not mine own self; for I know nought by myself, yet am I not thereby justified. It is the Lord that judgeth me. Therefore judge nothing before the time, until the Lord come, which will lighten things that are hid in darkness, and open the counsels of the hearts; and then shall every man have praise of God.

The Gospel [Matt. 11

WHEN John being in prison heard the works of Christ, he sent two of his disciples, and said unto him, Art thou he that shall come, or do we look for another? Jesus answered and said unto them, Go, and show John again what ye have heard and seen. The blind receive their sight, the lame walk, the lepers are cleansed, and the deaf hear, the dead are raised up, and the poor receive the glad tidings of the gospel. And happy is he that is not offended by me. And as they departed, Jesus began to say unto the people concerning John, What went ye out into the wilderness to see? A reed that is shaken with the wind? Or what went ye out to see? A man clothed in soft raiment? Behold, they that wear soft clothing are in king's houses. But what went ye out for to see? A prophet? Verily I say unto you, and more than a prophet. For this is he of whom it is written, Behold, I send my messenger before thy face, which shall prepare thy way before thee.

The Fourth Sunday

The Collect

LORD, raise up, we pray thee, thy power, and come among us, and with great might succor us; that whereas, through our sins and wickedness, we be sore let[1] and hindered, thy bountiful

---

[1] *Sore let:* severely obstructed.

grace and mercy, through the satisfaction of thy Son our Lord, may speedily deliver us; to whom with thee and the Holy Ghost, be honor and glory world without end.

The Epistle [Phil. 4

REJOICE in the Lord alway, and again I say, Rejoice. Let your softness be known to all men. The Lord is even at hand. Be careful for nothing, but in all prayer and supplication let your petitions be manifest unto God with giving of thanks. And the peace of God, which passeth all understanding, keep your hearts and minds through Christ Jesu.

The Gospel [John 1

THIS is the record of John, when the Jews sent priests and Levites from Jerusalem to ask him, What art thou? And he confessed and denied not, and said plainly, I am not Christ. And they asked him, What then, art thou Elias?[2] And he saith, I am not. Art thou the prophet? And he answered, No. Then said they unto him, What art thou that we may give an answer unto them that sent us? What sayest thou of thyself? He said, I am the voice of a crier in the wilderness: make straight the way of the Lord, as said the Prophet Isaiah.[3] And they which were sent were of the Pharisees. And they asked him, and said unto him, Why baptizest thou then, if thou be not Christ, nor Elias, neither that prophet? John answered them, saying, I baptize with water, but there standeth one among you, whom ye know not. He it is, which though he came after me, was before me, whose shoe-latchet[4] I am not worthy to unloose. These things were done at Bethabara beyond Jordan, where John did baptize.

[2] "Helias" in text, here and below.
[3] "Esay" in text.
[4] *Shoe-latchet:* shoe-lace, thong.

Christmas Day

The Collect

ALMIGHTY God, which hast given us thy only begotten Son to take our nature upon him, and this day to be born of a pure virgin: Grant that we being regenerate and made thy children by adoption and grace, may daily be renewed by thy Holy Spirit; through the same our Lord Jesus Christ who liveth and reigneth with, etc. Amen.

The Epistle [Heb. 1

GOD in times past, diversely and many ways spake unto the fathers by prophets; but in these last days he hath spoken to us by his own Son, whom he hath made heir of all things, by whom also he made the world. Which Son being the brightness of his glory, and the very image of his substance, ruling all things with the word of his power, hath by his own person purged our sins, and sitteth on the right hand of the majesty on high, being so much more excellent than the angels, as he hath by inheritance obtained a more excellent name than they. For unto which of the angels said he at any time, Thou art my Son, this day have I begotten thee? And again, I will be his Father, and he shall be my Son. And again, when he bringeth in the first begotten Son into the world, he saith, And let all the angels of God worship him. And unto the angels he saith, He maketh his angels spirits, and his ministers a flame of fire. But unto the Son he saith, Thy seat, O God, shall be for ever and ever. The scepter of thy kingdom is a right scepter. Thou hast loved righteousness and hated iniquity; wherefore God, even thy God, hath anointed thee with oil of gladness above thy fellows. And thou, Lord, in the beginning hast laid the foundation of the earth, and the heavens are the works of thy hands. They shall perish, but thou endurest. But they all shall wax[1] old as doth a garment, and as a vesture shalt thou change them, and they shall be changed. But thou art even the same, and thy years shall not fail.

The Gospel [John 1

IN the beginning was the Word, and the Word was with God, and God was the Word. The same was in the beginning with God. All things were made by it, and without it was made nothing that was made. In it was life, and the life was the light of men, and the light shineth in the darkness, and the darkness comprehended it not. There was sent from God a man, whose name was John. The same came as a witness, to bear witness of the light, that all men through him might believe. He was not that light, but was sent to bear witness of the light. That light was the true light which lighteth every man that cometh into the world. He was in the world, and the world was made by him, and the world knew him not. He came among his own, and his own received him not. But as many as received him, to them gave he power to be made sons of God, even them that believed on his name, which were born not of blood nor of the will of the flesh, nor yet of the will of man, but of God. And the same Word became flesh and dwelt among us, and we saw the glory of it, as the glory of the only begotten Son of the Father; full of grace and truth.

Saint Stephen's Day

The Collect

GRANT us, O Lord, to learn to love our enemies by the example of thy martyr Saint Stephen, who prayed for his persecutors to thee; which livest, etc.

[1] *Wax:* grow.

Then shall follow a[1] Collect of the Nativity, which shall be said continually unto New Year's Day.

The Epistle [Acts 7

AND Stephen being full of the Holy Ghost, looked up steadfastly with his eyes into heaven, and saw the glory of God, and Jesus standing on the right hand of God, and said, Behold, I see the heavens open, and the Son of man standing on the right hand of God. Then they gave a shout with a loud voice, and stopped their ears, and ran upon him all at once, and cast him out of the city, and stoned him. And the witnesses laid down their clothes at a young man's feet, whose name was Saul. And they stoned Stephen, calling on and saying, Lord Jesu, receive my spirit. And he kneeled down and cried with a loud voice, Lord, lay not this sin to their charge. And when he had thus spoken, he fell asleep.

The Gospel [Matt. 23

BEHOLD, I send unto you prophets, and wise men, and scribes, and some of them ye shall kill and crucify, and some of them shall ye scourge in your synagogues, and persecute them from city to city, that upon you may come all the righteous blood which hath been shed upon the earth, from the blood of righteous Abel, unto the blood of Zacharias the son of Barachias, whom ye slew between the temple and the altar. Verily I say unto you, All these things shall come upon this generation. O Jerusalem, Jerusalem, thou that killest the prophets and stonest them which are sent unto thee, how often would I have gathered thy children together, even as the hen gathereth her chickens under her wings, and ye would not? Behold, your house is left unto you desolate. For I say unto you, Ye shall not see me henceforth, till that ye say, Blessed is he that cometh in the name of the Lord.

[1] 1559 Grafton has "the."

Saint John Evangelist's Day

The Collect

MERCIFUL Lord, we beseech thee to cast thy bright beams of light upon thy Church, that it being lightened by the doctrine of thy blessed Apostle and Evangelist John, may attain to thy everlasting gifts; through Jesus Christ our Lord. Amen.

The Epistle [1 John 1

THAT which was from the beginning, which we have heard, which we have seen with our eyes, which we have looked upon, and our hands have handled, of the word of life: (and the life appeared, and we have seen, and bear witness, and show unto you that eternal life which was with the Father, and appeared unto us;) that which we have seen and heard declare we unto you, that ye also may have fellowship with us, and that our fellowship may be with the Father and his Son Jesus Christ. And this we write unto you, that ye may rejoice, and that your joy may be full. And this is the tidings which we have heard of him, and declare unto you, that God is light, and in him is no darkness at all. If we say we have fellowship with him, and walk in darkness, we lie, and do not the truth. But and if we walk in light, even as he is in light, then have we fellowship with him, and the blood of Jesus Christ his Son cleanseth us from all sin. If we say we have no sin, we deceive ourselves, and the truth is not in us. If we knowledge[1] our sins he is faithful and just to forgive us our sins, and to cleanse us from all unrighteousness. If we say we have not sinned, we make him a liar, and his word is not in us.

---

[1] *Knowledge:* acknowledge.

The Gospel [John 21

JESUS said unto Peter, Follow thou me. Peter turned about, and saw the disciple whom Jesus loved following; which also leaned on his breast at supper, and said, Lord, which is he that betrayeth thee? When Peter therefore saw him, he said to Jesus, Lord, what shall I here do? Jesus said unto him, If I will have him to tarry till I come, what is that to thee? Follow thou me. Then went this saying abroad among the brethren, that that disciple should not die. Yet Jesus said not to him, He shall not die, but, If I will that he tarry till I come, what is that to thee? The same disciple is he which testifieth of these things, and wrote these things. And we know that his testimony is true. There are also many other things which Jesus did, the which if they should be written every one, I suppose the world could not contain the books that should be written.

The Innocents' Day

The Collect

ALMIGHTY God, whose praise this day the young Innocents thy witnesses hath confessed and showed forth, not in speaking, but in dying: Mortify and kill all vices in us, that in our conversation,[1] our life may express thy faith, which with our tongues we do confess; through Jesus Christ our Lord.

The Epistle [Apoc. 14

I LOOKED, and lo, a Lamb stood on the Mount Sion, and with him an hundred and forty-four thousand, having his name and his Father's name written in their foreheads. And I

---

[1] *Conversation:* manner of conducting oneself in the world or in society.

heard a voice from heaven, as the sound of many waters, and as the voice of a great thunder. And I heard the voice of harpers, harping with their harps. And they sung as it were a new song before the seat, and before the four beasts and the elders, and no man could learn the song, but the hundred and forty-four[2] thousand, which were redeemed from the earth. These are they which were not defiled with women, for they are virgins. These follow the Lamb wheresoever he goeth. These were redeemed from men, being the first fruits unto God, and to the Lamb, and in their mouths was found no guile: for they are without spot before the throne of God.

The Gospel [Matt. 2

THE angel of the Lord appeared to Joseph in a sleep, saying, Arise and take the child and his mother, and flee into Egypt, and be thou there till I bring thee word. For it will come to pass that Herod shall seek the child to destroy him. So when he awoke, he took the child and his mother by night, and departed into Egypt, and was there unto the death of Herod, that it might be fulfilled which was spoken of the Lord by the Prophet, saying, Out of Egypt have I called my son. Then Herod when he saw that he was mocked of the Wise men, he was exceeding wroth,[3] and sent forth men of war, and slew all the children that were in Bethlehem,[4] and in all the coasts (as many as were two years old or under) according to the time which he had diligently known out of the Wise men. Then was fulfilled that which was spoken by the prophet Jeremiah,[5] whereas he said, In Rama was there a voice heard, lamentation, weeping, and great mourning: Rachel weeping for her children, and would not be comforted, because they were not.

[2] Text has "forty and four."
[3] *Wroth:* angry.
[4] "Bethleem" in text.
[5] "Jeremie" in text.

88

The Sunday after Christmas Day

The Collect

ALMIGHTY God, which hast given, etc.
As upon Christmas Day.

The Epistle [Gal. 4

AND I say, that the heir, as long as he is a child, differeth not
from a servant, though he be lord of all, but is under tutors
and governors, until the time that the father hath appointed.
Even so we also, when we were children, were in bondage under
the ordinances of the world. But when the time was full come,
God sent his Son made of a woman, and made bond unto the
law,[1] to redeem them which were bond unto the law, that we
through election might receive the inheritance that belongeth
unto the natural sons. Because ye are sons, God hath sent the
Spirit of his Son into our hearts, which crieth, Abba Father.
Wherefore now, thou art not a servant, but a son: If thou be a
son, thou art also an heir of God through Christ.

The Gospel [Matt. 1

THIS is the book of the generation of Jesus Christ, the son
of David, the son of Abraham.[2] Abraham begat[3] Isaac. Isaac
begat Jacob. Jacob begat Judas and his brethren. Judas begat
Phares and Zaram of Thamar. Phares begat Esrom. Esrom
begat Aram. Aram begat Aminadab. Aminadab begat Naasson.
Naasson begat Salmon. Salmon begat Boos of Rahab. Boos begat

---

[1] *Made bond unto the law:* made slave unto the law; "made under the law"
in 1661 Book; Lat., *factum sub lege.* Cf. Brightman, *English Rite,* I, 238–39.

[2] Proper names in this Gospel have been left as found in the text. Otherwise
all proper names have been changed to modern English spellings.

[3] *Begat:* begot.

Obed of Ruth. Obed begat Jesse. Jesse begat David the king. David the king begat Salomon of her that was the wife of Urie. Salomon begat Roboam. Roboam begat Abia. Abia begat Asa. Asa begat Josaphat. Josaphat begat Joram. Joram begat Osias. Osias begat Joatham, Joatham begat Achas. Achas begat Ezechias. Ezechias begat Manasses. Manasses begat Amon. Amon begat Josias. Josias begat Jechonias and his brethren, about the time that they were carried away to Babylon. And after they were brought to Babylon, Jechonias begat Salathiel. Salathiel begat Zorobabell. Zorobabell begat Abiud. Abiud begat Eliachim. Eliachim begat Azor. Azor begat Sadoc. Sadoc begat Achin. Achin begat Eliud. Eliud begat Eleasar. Eleasar begat Matthan. Matthan begat Jacob. Jacob begat Joseph the husband of Mary, of whom was born Jesus, even he that is called Christ. And so all the generations from Abraham to David are fourteen generations. And from David unto the captivity of Babylon are fourteen generations. And from the captivity of Babylon unto Christ are fourteen generations.

The birth of Jesus Christ was on this wise: When his mother Mary was married to Joseph (before they came to dwell together) she was found with child by the Holy Ghost. Then Joseph her husband (because he was a righteous man, and would not put her to shame) was minded privily to depart from her. But while he thus thought, behold, the angel of the Lord appeared unto him in sleep, saying, Joseph, thou son of David, fear not to take unto thee Mary thy wife; for that which is conceived in her cometh of the Holy Ghost. She shall bring forth a son, and thou shalt call his name Jesus, for he shall save his people from their sins.

All this was done, that it might be fulfilled which was spoken of the Lord by the prophet, saying, Behold, a maid shall be with child, and shall bring forth a son, and they shall call his name Emmanuel, which if a man interpret, is as much to say, as God with us. And Joseph, as soon as he awoke out of sleep, did as the angel of the Lord had bidden him, and he took his wife unto

him, and knew[4] her not till she had brought forth her first begotten son, and called his name Jesus.

The Circumcision of Christ

The Collect

ALMIGHTY God, which madest thy blessed Son to be circumcised and obedient to the law for man: Grant us the
true circumcision of the spirit, that our hearts and all our members being mortified from all worldly and carnal lusts, may in
all things obey thy blessed will; through the same thy Son Jesus
Christ our Lord.

The Epistle [Rom. 4

BLESSED is that man to whom the Lord will not impute
sin. Came this blessedness then upon the uncircumcision, or
upon the circumcision also? For we say, that faith was reckoned
to Abraham for righteousness. How was it then reckoned? When
he was in the circumcision, or when he was in the uncircumcision?
Not in time of circumcision, but when he was yet uncircumcised.
And he received the sign of circumcision, as a seal of the righteousness of faith, which he had yet being uncircumcised, that he
should be the father of all them that believe, though they be not
circumcised, that righteousness might be imputed to them also,
and that he might be the father of circumcision, not unto them
only which came of the circumcised, but unto them also that walk
in the steps of the faith that was in our father Abraham before
the time of circumcision. For the promise (that he should be heir
of the world) happened not to Abraham or to his seed through
the law, but through the righteousness of faith. For if they which

---

[4] *Knew:* had sexual intercourse with.

are of the law be heirs, then is faith but vain, and the promise of none effect.

The Gospel [Luke 2

AND it fortuned, as soon as the angels were gone away from the shepherds into heaven, they said one to another, Let us go now even unto Bethlehem,[1] and see this thing that we hear say is happened, which the Lord hath showed unto us. And they came with haste and found Mary and Joseph, and the babe, laid in a manger. And when they had seen it, they published abroad the saying that was told them of that child. And all they that heard it, wondered at those things which were told them of the shepherds. But Mary kept all those sayings and pondered them in her heart. And the shepherds returned, praising and lauding God for all the things that they had heard and seen, even as it was told unto them. And when the eighth day was come that the child should be circumcised, his name was called Jesus, which was named of the angel, before he was conceived in the womb.

If there be a Sunday between the Epiphany and the Circumcision, then shall be used the same Collect, Epistle, and Gospel at the Communion which was used upon the day of Circumcision.

The Epiphany

The Collect

O GOD, which by the leading of a star didst manifest thy only begotten Son to the Gentiles: Mercifully grant, that we which know thee now by faith, may after this life have the fruition of thy glorious Godhead; through Christ our Lord.

[1] "Bethleem" in text.

The Epistle [Eph. 3

FOR this cause I, Paul, am a prisoner of Jesus Christ for you heathen, if ye have heard of the ministration of the grace of God, which is given me to youward.[1] For by revelation showed he the mystery unto me (as I wrote afore in few words, whereby when ye read, ye may understand my knowledge in the mystery of Christ) which mystery in times past was not opened unto the sons of men, as it is now declared unto his holy Apostles and prophets by the Spirit, that the Gentiles should be inheritors also, and of the same body, and partakers of his promise of Christ, by the means of the gospel, whereof I am made a minister according to the gift of the grace of God, which is given unto me after the working of his power. Unto me the least of all saints is this grace given, that I should preach among the Gentiles the unsearchable riches of Christ; and to make all men see what the fellowship of the mystery is, which from the beginning of the world hath been hid in God, which made all things through Jesus Christ; to the intent, that now unto the rulers and powers in heavenly things, might be known by the congregation, the manifold wisdom of God, according to the eternal purpose which he wrought in Christ Jesu our Lord, by whom we have boldness and entrance with the confidence which is by the faith of him.

The Gospel [Matt. 2

WHEN Jesus was born in Bethlehem,[2] a city of Jewry,[3] in the time of Herod the king, behold, there came Wise men from the east to Jerusalem, saying, Where is he that is born King of the Jews? For we have seen his star in the east, and are come to worship him. When Herod the king had heard these

---

[1] *To youward:* for you.

[2] "Bethleem" in text throughout this Gospel.

[3] "Jury," "Jurie," or "Jurye" in text throughout this Gospel.

things, he was troubled and all the city of Jerusalem with him. And when he had gathered all the chief priests and scribes of the people together, he demanded of them where Christ should be born. And they said unto him, At Bethlehem in Jewry. For thus it is written by the prophet, And thou Bethlehem in the land of Jewry art not the least among the princes of Judah, for out of thee there shall come unto me the captain that shall govern my people Israel. Then Herod, when he had privily[4] called the Wise men, he enquired of them diligently what time the star appeared, and he bade them go to Bethlehem, and said, Go your way thither, and search diligently for the child. And when ye have found him, bring me word again, that I may come and worship him also. When they had heard the king, they departed; and lo, the star, which they saw in the east, went before them till it came and stood over the place wherein the child was. When they saw the star, they were exceeding glad, and went into the house, and found the child with Mary his mother, and fell down flat, and worshiped him, and opened their treasures, and offered unto him gifts: gold, frankincense, and myrrh. And after they were warned of God in sleep that they should not go again to Herod, they returned into their own country another way.

The First Sunday after the Epiphany

The Collect

LORD, we beseech thee mercifully to receive the prayers of thy people which call upon thee; and grant that they may both perceive and know what things they ought to do, and also have grace and power, faithfully to fulfill the same; through Jesus Christ our Lord.

[4] *Privily:* secretly.

The Epistle [Rom. 12

I BESEECH you therefore brethren, by the mercifulness of God, that ye make your bodies a quick[1] sacrifice, holy and acceptable unto God, which is your reasonable serving of God. And fashion not yourselves like unto this world but be ye changed in your shape by the renewing of your mind, that ye may prove what thing that good and acceptable and perfect will of God is. For I say, through the grace that unto me given is, to every man among you, that no man stand high in his own conceit, more than it becometh him to esteem of himself: but so judge of himself, that he be gentle and sober, according as God hath dealt to every man the measure of faith. For as we have many members in one body, and all members have not one office, so we being many, are one body in Christ, and every man among ourselves one another's members.

The Gospel [Luke 2

THE father and mother of Jesus went to Jerusalem after the custom of the feast day. And when they had fulfilled the days, as they returned home, the child Jesus abode still in Jerusalem, and his father and mother knew not of it. But they, supposing him to have been in the company, came a day's journey and sought him amongst their kinsfolk and acquaintance. And when they found him not, they went back again to Jerusalem and sought him. And it fortuned, that after three days they found him in the temple, sitting in the midst of the doctors, hearing them and posing[2] them. And all that heard him were astonied[3] at his understanding and answers. And when they saw him, they marveled, and his mother said unto him, Son, why

[1] *Quick:* living.
[2] *Posing:* questioning.
[3] *Astonied:* astonished.

hast thou thus dealt with us? Behold thy father and I have sought thee sorrowing. And he said unto them, How happened that ye sought me? Wist[4] you not that I must go about my Father's business? And they understood not that saying which he spake unto them. And he went down with them, and he came to Nazareth, and was obedient unto them. But his mother kept all these sayings together in her heart. And Jesus prospered in wisdom and age, and in favor with God and men.

The Second Sunday after the Epiphany

The Collect

ALMIGHTY and everlasting God, which dost govern all things in heaven and earth: Mercifully hear the supplications of thy people, and grant us thy peace all the days of our life.

The Epistle [Rom. 12

SEEING that we have divers gifts, according to the grace that is given unto us, if a man have the gift of prophecy, let him have it, that it be agreeing to the faith. Let him that hath an office, wait on his office. Let him that teacheth, take heed to his doctrine. Let him that exhorteth, give attendance to his exhortation. If any man give, let him do it with singleness. Let him that ruleth do it with diligence. If any man show mercy, let him do it with cheerfulness. Let love be without dissimulation. Hate that which is evil, and cleave to that which is good. Be kind one to another with brotherly love. In giving honor, go one before another. Be not slothful in the business which you have in hand. Be fervent in spirit. Apply yourselves to the time. Rejoice in hope. Be patient in tribulation. Continue in prayer.

---

[4] *Wist:* know.

Distribute unto the necessity of the saints. Be ready to harbor.[1]
Bless them which persecute you; bless, I say, and curse not. Be
merry with them that are merry, weep with them that weep. Be
of like affection one toward another. Be not high-minded but
make yourselves equal to them of the lower sort.

The Gospel [John 2

AND the third day was there a marriage in Cana, a city of
Galilee, and the mother of Jesus was there. And Jesus was
called, and his disciples, unto the marriage. And when the wine
failed, the mother of Jesus said unto him, They have no wine.
Jesus said unto her, Woman, what have I to do with thee? Mine
hour is not yet come. His mother said unto the ministers, Whatsoever he saith unto you, do it. And there were standing there
six waterpots of stone, after the manner of purifying of the Jews,
containing two or three firkins[2] apiece. Jesus said unto them, Fill
the waterpots with water. And they filled them up to the brim.
And he said unto them, Draw out now, and bear unto the governor of the feast. And they bare it. When the ruler of the feast
had tasted the water turned into wine, and knew not whence it
was (but the ministers which drew the water knew), he called
the bridegroom, and said unto him, Every man at the beginning
doth set forth good wine, and when men be drunk,[3] then that
which is worse: but thou hast kept the good wine until now. This
beginning of miracles did Jesus in Cana of Galilee, and showed
his glory, and his disciples believed on him.

[1] *Harbor:* show hospitality.
[2] *Two or three firkins:* twenty or thirty gallons.
[3] 1559 Grafton has "drunken."

The Third Sunday

The Collect

ALMIGHTY and everlasting God, mercifully look upon our infirmities, and in all our dangers and necessities, stretch forth thy right hand to help and defend us; through Christ our Lord.

The Epistle [Rom. 12

BE not wise in your own opinions. Recompense to no man evil for evil. Provide aforehand things honest, not only before God, but also in the sight of all men. If it be possible, as much as is in you, live peaceably with all men. Dearly beloved, avenge not yourselves, but rather give place unto wrath. For it is written, Vengeance is mine; I will reward, saith the Lord. Therefore, if thine enemy hunger, feed him; if he thirst, give him drink. For in so doing, thou shalt heap coals of fire on his head. Be not overcome of evil, but overcome evil with goodness.

The Gospel [Matt. 8

WHEN he was come down from the mountain, much people followed him. And behold, there came a leper, and worshiped him, saying, Master, if thou wilt, thou canst make me clean. And Jesus put forth his hand and touched him, saying, I will; be thou clean. And immediately his leprosy was cleansed. And Jesus said unto him, Tell no man, but go and show thyself to the priest, and offer the gift (that Moses commanded to be offered) for a witness unto them. And when Jesus was entered into Capernaum, there came unto him a centurion, and besought him, saying, Master, my servant lieth at home sick of the palsy, and is grievously pained. And Jesus said, When I come unto him, I will heal him. The centurion answered, and said, Sir, I am not worthy that thou shouldest come under my roof, but speak the word only, and my servant shall be healed. For I also am a man subject to the authority of another, and have soldiers under me; and I say to this man, Go, and he goeth, and to another man, Come, and he cometh; and to my servant, Do this, and he doeth it. When Jesus heard these words he marveled, and said to them that followed him, Verily I say unto you, I have not found so great faith in Israel. I say unto you that many shall come from the east, and west, and shall rest with Abraham, Isaac, and Jacob in the kingdom of heaven; but the children of the kingdom shall be cast out into utter darkness, there shall be weeping and gnashing with teeth. And Jesus said unto the centurion, Go thy way; and as thou believest, so be it unto thee. And his servant was healed in the selfsame hour.

The Fourth Sunday

The Collect

GOD, which knowest us to be set in the midst of so many and great dangers, that for man's frailness we cannot always stand uprightly: Grant to us the health of body and soul, that all those things which we suffer for sin, by thy help we may well pass and overcome; through Christ our Lord.

The Epistle [Rom. 13

LET every soul submit himself unto the authority of the higher powers; for there is no power but of God. The powers that be are ordained of God. Whosoever therefore resisteth power, resisteth the ordinance of God. But they that resist, shall receive to themselves damnation. For rulers are not fearful to them that do good, but to them that do evil. Wilt thou be without fear of the power? Do well then, and so shalt thou be praised of the same; for he is the minister of God, for thy wealth. But and if thou do that which is evil, then fear; for he beareth not the sword for nought; for he is the minister of God to take vengeance on them that do evil. Wherefore ye must needs obey, not only for fear of vengeance, but also because of conscience. And even for this cause pay ye tribute, for they are God's ministers, serving for that purpose. Give to every man therefore his duty; tribute, to whom tribute belongeth; custom, to whom custom is due; fear, to whom fear belongeth; honor, to whom honor pertaineth.

The Gospel [Matt. 8

AND when he entered into a ship, his disciples followed him. And behold, there arose a great tempest in the sea, insomuch as the ship was covered with waves, but he was asleep. And his disciples came to him, and awoke him, saying, Master save us; we perish. And he said unto them, Why are ye fearful, O ye of little faith? Then he arose, and rebuked the winds and the sea, and there followed a great calm. But the men marveled, saying, What manner of man is this, that both winds and sea obey him? And when he was come to the other side, into the country of the Gergesenes,[1] there met with him two possessed of devils, which came out of the graves, and were out of measure fierce, so that no man might go by that way. And behold, they cried out, saying, O Jesu, thou Son of God, what have we to do with thee? Art thou come hither to torment us before the time? And there was a good way off from them, a herd of swine, feeding. So the devils besought him, saying, If thou call us out, suffer us to go into the herd of swine. And he said unto them, Go your ways. Then went they out, and departed into the herd of swine. And behold, the whole herd of swine was carried headlong into the sea, and perished in the waters. Then they that kept them, fled, and went their ways into the city and told everything, and what had happened unto the possessed of the devils. And behold, the whole

[1] "Gergesites" in text.

city came out to meet Jesus; and when they saw him, they besought him that he would depart out of their coasts.

The Fifth Sunday

The Collect

LORD, we beseech thee to keep thy Church and household continually in thy true religion; that they which do lean only upon hope of thy heavenly grace, may evermore be defended by thy mighty power; through Christ our Lord.

The Epistle [Col. 3[1]

PUT upon you as the elect of God, tender mercy, kindness, humbleness of mind, meekness, long suffering, forbearing one another, and forgiving one another if any man have a quarrel against another, as Christ forgave you, even so do ye. Above all these things, put on love, which is the bond of perfectness. And the peace of God rule your hearts, to the which peace ye are called in one body. And see that ye be thankful. Let the word of Christ dwell in you plenteously with all wisdom. Teach and exhort your own selves in psalms, and hymns, and spiritual songs, singing with grace in your hearts to the Lord. And whatsoever ye do in word or deed, do all in the name of the Lord Jesu, giving thanks to God the Father by him.

The Gospel [Matt. 13

THE kingdom of heaven is like unto a man which sowed good seed in his field: but while men slept, his enemy came and sowed tares among the wheat, and went his way. But when

---

[1] Text here has "Phil. 2." The printer transposed the marginal citation with that of the Epistle for the Sunday Next before Easter (see p. 118).

the blade was sprung up, and had brought forth fruit, then appeared the tares also. So the servants of the householder came and said unto him, Sir, didst not thou sow good seed in thy field? From whence then hath it tares? He said unto them, The envious man hath done this. The servants said unto him, Wilt thou then that we go and weed them up? But he said, Nay, lest while ye gather up the tares, ye pluck up also the wheat with them. Let both grow together until the harvest, and in the time of harvest, I will say to the reapers, Gather ye first the tares, and bind them together in sheaves to be brent;[2] but gather the wheat into my barn.

The sixth Sunday (if there be so many) shall have the same Collect, Epistle, and Gospel that was upon the fifth Sunday.

The Sunday Called Septuagesima

The Collect

O LORD, we beseech thee favorably to hear the prayers of thy people; that we which are justly punished for our offenses, may be mercifully delivered by thy goodness, for the glory of thy name; through Jesu Christ our Savior, who liveth and reigneth world without end.

The Epistle [1 Cor. 9

PERCEIVE ye not, how that they which run in a course, run all, but one receiveth the reward? So run that ye may obtain. Every man that proveth masteries[1] abstaineth from all things. And they do it to obtain a crown that shall perish, but we to obtain an everlasting crown. I therefore so run, not as at an un-

---

[2] *Brent:* burnt.
[1] *Proveth masteries:* "striveth for the mastery" (AV).

certain thing. So fight I, not as one that beateth the air; but I tame my body, and bring it into subjection, lest by any means it come to pass, that when I have preached to other, I myself should be a castaway.

The Gospel [Matt. 20

THE kingdom of heaven is like unto a man that is an householder, which went out early in the morning to hire laborers into his vincyard. And when the agreement was made with the laborers for a penny a day, he sent them into his vineyard. And he went out about the third hour, and saw other standing idle in the market place, and said unto them, Go ye also into the vineyard, and whatsoever is right, I will give you. And they went their way. Again, he went out about the sixth and ninth hour, and did likewise. And about the eleventh hour he went out, and found other standing idle, and said unto them, Why stand ye here all the day idle? They said unto him, Because no man hath hired us. He saith unto them, Go ye also into the vineyard, and whatsoever is right, that shall ye receive. So when even was come the lord of the vineyard said unto his steward, Call the laborers, and give them their hire, beginning at the last until the first. And when they did come that came about the eleventh hour, they received every man a penny. But when the first came also, they supposed that they should have received more, and they likewise received every man a penny. And when they had received it, they murmured against the good man of the house, saying, These last have wrought but one hour, and thou hast made them equal with us, which have borne the burden and heat of the day. But he answered unto one of them and said, Friend, I do thee no wrong. Didst not thou agree with me for a penny? Take that thine is, and go thy way. I will give unto this last, even as unto thee. Is it not lawful for me to do as me lusteth[2] with mine own goods? Is thine eye evil because I am good? So the last shall be

---

[2] *Lusteth:* desireth; in Great Bible, "listeth."

first, and the first shall be last. For many be called but few be chosen.

The Sunday Called Sexagesima

The Collect

LORD God, which seest that we put not our trust in any thing that we do: Mercifully grant, that by thy power we may be defended against all adversity; through Jesus Christ our Lord.

The Epistle [2 Cor. 11

YE suffer fools gladly, seeing yourselves are wise. For ye suffer if a man bring you into bondage, if a man devour, if a man take, if a man exalt himself, if a man smite you on the face. I speak as concerning rebuke, as though we had been weak in this behalf. Howbeit, whereinsoever any man dare be bold (I speak foolishly), I dare be bold also. They are Hebrews, even so am I. They are Israelites, even so am I. They are the seed of Abraham, even so am I. They are the ministers of Christ (I speak like a fool), I am more: in labors more abundant, in stripes above measure, in prison more plenteously, in death oft. Of the Jews five times received I forty stripes save one. Thrice was I beaten with rods, I was once stoned, I suffered thrice shipwreck, night and day have I been in the deep sea. In journeying often, in perils of waters, in perils of robbers, in jeopardies of mine own nation, in jeopardies among the heathen, in perils in the city, in perils in wilderness, in perils in the sea, in perils among false brethren, in labor and travail, in watchings often, in hunger and thirst, in fastings often, in cold and nakedness. Beside the things which outwardly happen unto me, I am cumbered daily, and do care for all congregations. Who is weak, and I am not weak? Who is offended, and I burn not? If I must needs boast, I will boast of the things that concern mine infirmities. The God and Father of our Lord Jesus Christ, which is blessed for evermore, knoweth that I lie not.

The Gospel [Luke 8

WHEN much people were gathered together, and were come to him out of all cities, he spake by a similitude. The sower went out to sow his seed; and as he sowed, some fell by the wayside, and it was trodden down, and the fowls of the air devoured it up. And some fell on stones, and as soon as it was sprung up, it withered away, because it lacked moistness. And some fell among thorns, and the thorns sprang up with it and choked it. And some fell on good ground, and sprang up and bare fruit an hundred fold. And as he said these things, he cried, He that hath ears to hear, let him hear. And his disciples asked him, saying, What manner of similitude is this? And he said, Unto you it is given to know the secrets of the kingdom of God, but to other by parables; that when they see, they should not see, and when they hear, they should not understand. The parable is this: The seed is the Word of God. Those that are beside the way are they that hear, then cometh the devil and taketh away the Word out of their hearts, lest they should believe and be saved. They on the stones are they, which when they hear, receive the Word with joy, and these have no roots, which for a while believe, and in time of temptation go away. And that which fell among thorns are they, which when they have heard, go forth and are choked with cares and riches, and voluptuous living, and bring forth no fruit. That which fell in the good ground are they, which with a pure and good heart, hear the Word and keep it, and bring forth fruit through patience.

The Sunday Called Quinquagesima

The Collect

O LORD, which dost teach us, that all our doings without charity are nothing worth: Send thy Holy Ghost, and pour in our hearts that most excellent gift of charity, the very bond of peace and all virtues, without the which whosoever liveth, is counted dead before thee. Grant this for thy only Son Jesus Christ's sake.

The Epistle [1 Cor. 13

THOUGH I speak with tongues of men and of angels, and have no love, I am even as sounding brass, or as a tinkling cymbal. And though I could prophesy, and understand all secrets, and all knowledge, yea if I have all faith, so that I could move mountains out of their places, and yet have no love, I am nothing. And though I bestow all my goods to feed the poor, and though I gave my body even that I burned, and yet have no love, it profiteth me nothing. Love suffereth long, and is courteous, love envieth not, love doth not frowardly,[1] swelleth not, dealeth not dishonestly, seeketh not her own, is not provoked to anger, thinketh none evil, rejoiceth not in iniquity. But rejoiceth in the truth, suffereth all things, believeth all things, hopeth all things, endureth all things. Though that prophesying fail, either tongues cease, or knowledge vanish away, yet love falleth never away. For our knowledge is unperfect, and our prophesying is unperfect. But when that which is perfect is come, then that which is unperfect shall be done away. When I was a child, I spake as a child, I understood as a child, I imagined as a child. But as soon as I was a man, I put away childishness. Now

---

[1] *Frowardly:* perversely.

we see in a glass, even in a dark speaking, but then shall we see face to face. Now I know unperfectly, but then shall I know even as I am known. Now abideth faith, hope, and love, even these three, but the chief of these is love.

The Gospel [Luke 18[2]

JESUS took unto him the twelve and said unto them, Behold, we go up to Jerusalem, and all shall be fulfilled that are written by the prophets of the Son of man. For he shall be delivered unto the Gentiles, and shall be mocked, and despitefully intreated, and spitted on. And when they have scourged him, they will put him to death, and the third day he shall rise again. And they understood none of these things. And this saying was hid from them, so that they perceived not the things which were spoken. And it came to pass, that as he was come nigh to Jericho[3] a certain blind man sat by the highway side, begging. And when he heard the people pass by, he asked what it meant. And they said unto him, that Jesus of Nazareth passed by. And he cried saying, Jesu, thou son of David, have mercy on me. And they which went before rebuked him, that he should hold his peace. But he cried so much the more, Thou son of David, have mercy on me. And Jesus stood still, and commanded him to be brought unto him. And when he was come near, he asked him, saying, What wilt thou that I do unto thee? And he said, Lord, that I might receive my sight. And Jesus said unto him, Receive thy sight; thy faith hath saved thee. And immediately he received his sight, and followed him praising God. And all the people when they saw it, gave praise unto God.

[2] Text has "17"; misprint.
[3] "Hiericho" in text.

The First Day of Lent

The Collect

ALMIGHTY and everlasting God, which hatest nothing that thou hast made, and dost forgive the sins of all them that be penitent: Create and make in us new and contrite hearts, that we worthily lamenting our sins, and knowledging our wretchedness, may obtain of thee, the God of all mercy, perfect remission and forgiveness; through Jesus Christ.

The Epistle [Joel 2

TURN you unto me with all your hearts, with fasting, weeping, and mourning. Rent[1] your hearts and not your clothes. Turn you unto the Lord your God, for he is gracious and merciful, long suffering, and of great compassion, and ready to pardon wickedness. Then, no doubt, he also shall turn and forgive: and after his chastening, he shall let your increase remain for meat and drink offerings unto the Lord your God. Blow out with the trumpet in Sion, proclaim a fasting, call the congregation, and gather the people together; warn the congregation, gather the elders, bring the children and sucklings together. Let the bridegroom go forth of his chamber, and the bride out of her closet. Let the priests serve the Lord between the porch and the altar, weeping and saying, Be favorable, O Lord, be favorable unto thy people: let not thine heritage be brought to such confusion, lest the heathen be lords thereof. Wherefore should they say among the heathen, where is now their God?

[1] *Rent:* rend, tear.

The Gospel [Matt. 6

WHEN ye fast, be not sad as the hypocrites are, for they disfigure their faces that it may appear unto men how that they fast. Verily I say unto you, they have their reward. But thou, when thou fastest, anoint thine head, and wash thy face, that it appear not unto men how thou fastest, but unto thy Father which is in secret; and thy Father which seeth in secret, shall reward thee openly. Lay not up for yourselves treasure upon earth, where the rust and moth doth corrupt, and where thieves break through and steal. But lay up for you treasures in heaven, where neither rust nor moth doth corrupt, and where thieves do not break through nor steal. For where your treasure is, there will your hearts be also.

The First Sunday in Lent

The Collect

O LORD, which for our sake didst fast forty days and forty nights: Give us grace to use such abstinence, that our flesh being subdued to the spirit, we may ever obey thy godly motions, in righteousness and true holiness, to thy honor and glory, which livest and reignest, etc.

The Epistle [2 Cor. 6

WE as helpers exhort you, that ye receive not the grace of God in vain. For he saith, I have heard thee in a time accepted, and in the day of salvation have I succored thee. Behold, now is that accepted time; behold, now is that day of salvation. Let us give none occasion of evil, that in our office be found no fault; but in all things let us behave ourselves as the ministers of God, in much patience, in afflictions, in necessities, in anguishes, in stripes, in prisonments, in strifes, in labors, in watchings, in fastings, in pureness, in knowledge, in long-suffering, in kindness, in the Holy Ghost, in love unfained, in the word of truth, in the power of God; by the armor of righteousness of the right hand and of the left, by honor and dishonor, by evil report and good report; as deceivers and yet true, as unknown, and yet known, as dying, and behold we live, as chastened, and not killed, as sorrowing, and yet alway merry, as poor, and yet make many rich, as having nothing, and yet possessing all things.

The Gospel [Matt. 4

THEN was Jesus led away of the spirit into wilderness, to be tempted of the devil. And when he had fasted forty days and forty nights, he was at the last anhungered. And when the tempter came to him, he said, If thou be the Son of God, command that these stones be made bread. But he answered and said, It is written, man shall not live by bread only, but by every word that proceedeth out of the mouth of God. Then the devil taketh him up into the holy city, and setteth him on a pinnacle of the temple, and saith unto him, If thou be the Son of God, cast thyself down headlong. For it is written, he shall give his angels charge over thee, and with their hands they shall hold thee up, lest at any time thou dash thy foot against a stone. And Jesus said unto him: It is written again, Thou shalt not tempt the Lord thy God. Again the devil taketh him up into an exceeding high mountain, and showed him all the kingdoms of the world, and the glory of them,[1] and saith unto him: All these will I give thee, if thou wilt fall down and worship me. Then saith Jesus unto him, Avoid,[2] Satan,[3] for it is written, Thou shalt

[1] Text has "kingdoms of the world, and the world, and the glory of them"; misprint.

[2] *Avoid:* "get thee hence" in 1661 Book and in AV. Cf. Brightman, *English Rite,* I, 297.

[3] "Sathan" in text.

worship the Lord thy God, and him only shalt thou serve. Then the devil leaveth him, and behold, angels came and ministered unto him.

The Second Sunday

The Collect

ALMIGHTY God, which dost see that we have no power of ourselves to help ourselves: Keep thou us both outwardly in our bodies, and inwardly in our souls, that we may be defended from all adversities which may happen to the body, and from all evil thoughts, which may assault and hurt the soul; through Jesus Christ, etc.

The Epistle [1 Thess. 4

WE beseech you brethren, and exhort you by the Lord Jesus, that ye increase more and more, even as ye have received of us, how ye ought to walk, and to please God. For ye know what commandments we gave you by our Lord Jesus Christ. For this is the will of God, even your holiness, that ye should abstain from fornication, and that every one of you should know how to keep his vessel in holiness and honor, and not in the lust of concupiscence, as do the heathen which know not God: that no man oppress and defraud his brother in bargaining, because that the Lord is the avenger of all such things, as we told you before, and testified. For God hath not called us unto uncleanness, but unto holiness. He therefore that despiseth, despiseth not man, but God, which hath sent his Holy Spirit among you.

The Gospel [Matt. 15

JESUS went thence, and departed into the coasts of Tyre and Sidon. And behold, a woman of Canaan (which came out of the same coasts) cried unto him, saying, Have mercy on me, O Lord, thou son of David. My daughter is piteously vexed with a devil. But he answered her nothing at all. And his disciples came and besought him, saying, Send her away, for she crieth after us. But he answered, and said, I am not sent but to the lost sheep of the house of Israel. Then came she and worshiped him, saying, Lord help me. He answered and said, It is not meet to take the children's bread and cast it to dogs. She answered and said, Truth Lord, for the dogs eat of the crumbs which fall from their master's table. Then Jesus answered and said unto her, O woman, great is thy faith: be it unto thee even as thou wilt. And her daughter was made whole, even the same time.

The Third Sunday

The Collect

WE beseech thee Almighty God, look upon the hearty desires of thy humble servants, and stretch forth the right hand of thy majesty, to be our defense against all our enemies; through Jesus Christ our Lord.

The Epistle [Eph. 5

BE you the followers of God as dear children, and walk in love even as Christ loved us, and gave himself for us an offering and a sacrifice of a sweet savor to God. As for fornication, and all uncleanness, or covetousness, let it not be once named among you, as it becometh saints; or filthiness, or foolish talking, or jesting, which are not comely, but rather giving of thanks. For this ye know, that no whoremonger, either unclean person, or covetous person (which is a worshiper of images) hath any inheritance in the kingdom of Christ and of God. Let no man deceive you with vain words; for because of such things cometh the wrath of God upon the children of disobedience. Be not ye therefore companions of them. Ye were sometimes darkness, but now are ye light in the Lord: walk as children of light, for the fruit of the Spirit consisteth in all goodness, and righteousness, and truth. Accept that which is pleasing unto the Lord, and have no fellowship with the unfruitful works of darkness, but rather rebuke them. For it is a shame even to name those things, which are done of them in secret: but all things when they are brought forth by the light are manifest. For whatsoever is manifest, the same is light. Wherefore he saith, Awake thou that sleepest, and stand up from death, and Christ shall give thee light.

The Gospel [Luke 11 [1]

JESUS was casting out a devil that was dumb. And when he had cast out the devil, the dumb spake, and the people wondered. But some of them said, He casteth out devils through Beelzebub the chief of the devils. And other tempted him, and required of him a sign from heaven. But he knowing their thoughts said unto them, Every kingdom divided against itself is desolate; and one house doth fall upon another. If Satan[2] also be divided against himself, how shall his kingdom endure? Because ye say I cast out devils through Beelzebub. If I by the help of Beelzebub cast out devils, by whose help do your children cast them out? Therefore shall they be your judges. But if I with the finger of God cast out devils, no doubt the kingdom of God is come upon you. When a strong man armed watcheth his house, the things that he possesseth are in peace. But when a stronger

---

[1] Text has "12"; misprint.

[2] "Sathan" in text.

than he cometh upon him, and overcometh him, he taketh from him all his harness (wherein he trusted) and divideth his goods. He that is not with me is against me. And he that gathereth not with me, scattereth abroad. When the unclean spirit is gone out of a man, he walketh through dry places seeking rest. And when he findeth none, he saith, I will return again into my house whence I came out. And when he cometh, he findeth it swept and garnished. Then goeth he and taketh to him seven other spirits worse than himself; and they enter in and dwell there. And the end of that man is worse than the beginning. And it fortuned that as he spake these things, a certain woman for the company lift up her voice and said unto him, Happy is the womb that bare thee, and the paps[3] which gave thee suck. But he said, Yea, happy are they that hear the Word of God and keep it.

The Fourth Sunday

The Collect

GRANT, we beseech thee, Almighty God, that we which for our evil deeds are worthily punished, by the comfort of thy grace may mercifully be relieved; through our Lord Jesus Christ.

The Epistle [Gal. 4

TELL me (ye that desire to be under the law) do ye not hear of the law? For it is written that Abraham had two sons, the one by a bondmaid, the other by a freewoman. Yea, and he which was born of the bondwoman was born after the flesh, but he which was born of the freewoman was born by promise, which things are spoken by an allegory. For these are two testaments,

---

[3] *Paps:* nipples, mammillae.

the one from the Mount Sinai,[1] which gendereth[2] unto bondage, which is Agar. For Mount Sinai is Agar in Arabia, and bordereth upon the city which is now called Jerusalem, and is in bondage with her children. But Jerusalem which is above is free, which is the mother of us all. For it is written, Rejoice, thou barren that barest no children; break forth and cry, thou that travailest not; for the desolate hath many mo[3] children than she which hath an husband. Brethren, we are after Isaac the children of promise. But as then he that was born after the flesh persecuted him that was born after the spirit, even so is it now. Nevertheless, what saith the Scripture? Put away the bondwoman and her son. For the son of the bondwoman shall not be heir with the son of the freewoman. So then brethren, we are not children of the bond-woman, but of the freewoman.

The Gospel [John 6

JESUS departed over the Sea of Galilee, which is the Sea of Tiberias, and a great multitude followed him, because they saw his miracles which he did on them that were diseased. And Jesus went up into a mountain, and there he sat with his disciples. And Easter,[4] a feast of the Jews, was nigh. When Jesus then lift up his eyes and saw a great company come unto him, he said unto Philip, Whence shall we buy bread that these may eat? This he said to prove him, for he himself knew what he would do. Philip answered him, Two hundred pennyworth[5] of bread are not sufficient for them, that every man may take a little. One of his disciples, Andrew (Simon Peter's brother), saith unto him,

---

[1] "Sino" in text; "Sina" in next sentence.

[2] *Gendereth:* generates.

[3] *Mo:* more.

[4] *Easter:* Passover.

[5] *Two hundred pennyworth:* two hundred denarii (RSV); approximately forty dollars.

There is a lad which hath five barley loaves and two fishes, but what are they among so many? And Jesus said, Make the people sit down. There was much grass in the place. So the men sat down, in number about five thousand. And Jesus took the bread, and when he had given thanks, he gave to the disciples, and the disciples to them that were sat down, and likewise of the fishes as much as they would. When they had eaten enough, he said unto his disciples, Gather up the broken meat which remaineth, that nothing be lost. And they gathered it together and filled twelve baskets with the broken meat of the five barley loaves, which broken meat remained unto them that had eaten. Then those men (when they had seen the miracle that Jesus did) said, This is of a truth the same prophet that should come into the world.

The Fifth Sunday

The Collect

WE beseech thee Almighty God, mercifully to look upon thy people; that by thy great goodness they may be governed and preserved evermore both in body and soul; through Jesus Christ our Lord.

The Epistle [Heb. 9

CHRIST being an high priest of good things to come, came by a greater and a more perfect tabernacle, not made with hands, that is to say, not of this building; neither by the blood of goats and calves, but by his own blood he entered in once into the holy place, and found eternal redemption. For if the blood of oxen and of goats, and the ashes of a young cow, when it is sprinkled, purifieth the unclean, as touching the purifying of the flesh, how much more shall the blood of Christ (which through the eternal Spirit, offered himself without spot to God) purge your conscience from dead works, for to serve the living God? And for this cause he is the mediator of the new testament, that through death, which chanced for the redemption of those transgressions that were under the first testament, they which are called might receive the promise of eternal inheritance.

The Gospel [John 8

WHICH of you can rebuke me of sin? If I say the truth, why do ye not believe me? He that is of God, heareth God's words. Ye therefore hear them not, because ye are not of God. Then answered the Jews, and said unto him, Say we not well that thou art a Samaritan and hast the devil? Jesus answered, I have not the devil, but I honor my Father, and ye have dishonored me. I seek not mine own praise; there is one that seeketh and judgeth. Verily, verily, I say unto you, if a man keep my saying, he shall never see death. Then said the Jews unto him, Now know we that thou hast the devil. Abraham is dead, and the prophets, and thou sayest, If a man keep my saying he shall never taste of death. Art thou greater than our father Abraham which is dead? And the prophets are dead: whom makest thou thyself? Jesus answered, If I honor my self, mine honor is nothing. It is my Father that honoreth me, which ye say is your God, and yet ye have not known him; but I know him. And if I say I know him not, I shall be a liar like unto you. But I know him and keep his saying. Your father Abraham was glad to see my day, and he saw it and rejoiced. Then said the Jews unto him, Thou art not yet fifty year old, and hast thou seen Abraham? Jesus said unto them, Verily, verily, I say unto you, Ere[1] Abraham was born, I am. Then took they up stones to cast at him, but Jesus hid himself, and went out of the temple.

[1] *Ere:* before.

The Sunday Next before Easter

The Collect

ALMIGHTY and everlasting God, which, of thy tender love toward man, hast sent our Savior Jesus Christ to take upon him our flesh, and to suffer death upon the cross, that all mankind should follow the example of his great humility: Mercifully grant, that we both follow the example of his patience, and be made partakers of his resurrection; through the same Jesus Christ our Lord.

The Epistle [Phil. 2[1]

LET the same mind be in you, that was also in Christ Jesu: which when he was in the shape of God, thought it no robbery to be equal with God. Nevertheless he made himself of no reputation, taking on him the shape of a servant, and became like unto man, and was found in his apparel, as a man. He humbled himself, and became obedient to the death, even the death of the cross. Wherefore God hath also exalted him on high, and given him a name which is above all names, that in the name of Jesus, every knee should bow, both of things in heaven, and things in earth, and things under the earth, and that all tongues should confess, that Jesus Christ is the Lord, unto the praise of God the Father.

The Gospel [Matt. 26

AND it came to pass, when Jesus had finished all these sayings, he said unto his disciples, Ye know that after two days shall be Easter,[2] and the Son of man shall be delivered over to be

---

[1] Text here has "Col. 3." The printer transposed the marginal citation with that for the Fifth Sunday after Epiphany (see p. 101).

[2] *Easter:* Passover.

118

crucified. Then assembled together the chief priests, and the scribes, and the elders of the people, unto the palace of the high priest (which was called Caiaphas) and held a council that they might take Jesus by subtilty, and kill him. But they said, Not on the holy day, lest there be an uproar among the people. When Jesus was in Bethany in the house of Simon the leper, there came unto him a woman having an alabaster box of precious ointment, and poured it on his head as he sat at the board. But when his disciples saw it, they had indignation, saying, Whereto serveth this waste? This ointment might have been well sold, and given to the poor. When Jesus understood that, he said unto them, Why trouble ye the woman? For she hath wrought a good work upon me. For ye have the poor always with you, but me ye shall not have always. And in that she hath cast this ointment on my body, she did it to bury me. Verily I say unto you, Wheresoever this gospel shall be preached in all the world, there shall also this be told that she hath done for a memorial of her. Then one of the twelve (which was called Judas Iscariot)[3] went unto the chief priests, and said unto them, What will ye give me, and I will deliver him unto you? And they appointed unto him thirty pieces of silver. And from that time forth, he sought opportunity to betray him. The first day of sweet bread,[4] the disciples came to Jesus, saying to him, Where wilt thou that we prepare for thee to eat the Passover? And he said, Go into the city to such a man, and say unto him, The Master saith, My time is at hand, I will keep my Easter by thee with my disciples. And the disciples did as Jesus had appointed them and they made ready the Passover. When the even was come, he sat down with the twelve. And as they did eat, he said, Verily I say unto you, that one of you shall betray me. And they were exceeding sorrowful, and began every one of them to say unto him, Lord, is it I? He answered and said, He that dippeth his hand with me in the dish, the same

---

[3] "Iscarioth" in text.
[4] *The first day of sweet bread:* the first day of the Feast of Unleavened Bread.

shall betray me. The Son of man truly goeth, as it is written of him, but woe unto that man by whom the Son of man is betrayed. It had been good for that man if he had not been born. Then Judas, which betrayed him, answered and said, Master, is it I? He said unto him, Thou hast said. And when they were eating, Jesus took bread, and when he had given thanks, he brake it and gave it to the disciples, and said, Take, eat, this is my body. And he took the cup, and thanked, and gave it to them, saying, Drink ye all of this, for this is my blood (which is of the new testament) that is shed for many, for the remission of sins. But I say unto you, I will not drink henceforth of this fruit of the vine tree, until the day when I shall drink it new with you in my Father's kingdom. And when they had said grace, they went out unto Mount Olivet. Then said Jesus unto them, All ye shall be offended because of me this night. For it is written, I will smite the shepherd, and the sheep of the flock shall be scattered abroad: but after I am risen again, I will go before you into Galilee. Peter answered and said unto him, Though all men be offended because of thee, yet will I not be offended. Jesus said unto him, Verily I say unto thee, that in this same night, before the cock crow, thou shalt deny me thrice. Peter said unto him, Yea, though I should die with thee, yet will I not deny thee. Likewise also said all the disciples. Then came Jesus with them unto a farm place (which is called Gethsemane) and said unto the disciples, Sit ye here while I go and pray yonder. And he took with him Peter, and the two sons of Zebedee, and began to wax sorrowful and heavy. Then said Jesus unto them, My soul is heavy even unto the death. Tarry ye here and watch with me. And he went a little farther, and fell flat on his face, and prayed, saying, O my Father, if it be possible, let this cup pass from me; nevertheless, not as I will, but as thou wilt. And he came unto the disciples, and found them asleep, and said unto Peter, What, could ye not watch with me one hour? Watch and pray that ye enter not into temptation. The spirit is willing but the flesh is weak. He went away once again and prayed, saying, O my Father, if this cup may not pass away from me except I drink of it, thy will be fulfilled. And he came and found them asleep again, for their eyes were heavy. And he left them, and went again and prayed the third time, saying the same words. Then cometh he to his disciples, and said unto them, Sleep on now and take your rest. Behold, the hour is at hand, and the Son of man is betrayed into the hands of sinners. Rise, let us be going. Behold, he is at hand that doth betray me. While he yet spake, lo, Judas, one of the number of the twelve, came and with him a great multitude with swords and staves, sent from the chief priests and elders of the people. But he that betrayed him gave them a token, saying, Whomsoever I kiss, the same is he, hold him fast. And forthwith he came to Jesus and said, Hail Master, and kissed him. And Jesus said unto him, Friend, wherefore art thou come? Then came they and laid hands on Jesus, and took him. And behold, one of them that were with Jesus, stretched out his hand and drew his sword, and struck[5] a servant of the high priest, and smote off his ear. Then said Jesus unto him, Put up thy sword into the sheath, for all they that take the sword, shall perish with the sword. Thinkest thou that I came not now to pray to my Father, and he shall give me, even now, more than twelve legions of angels? But how then shall the Scriptures be fulfilled? For thus must it be. In that same hour said Jesus to the multitude, Ye be come out as it were to a thief with swords and staves, for to take me. I sat daily with you teaching in the temple, and ye took me not. But all this is done that the Scriptures of the prophets might be fulfilled. Then all the disciples forsook him and fled. And they took Jesus and led him to Caiaphas[6] the high priest, where the scribes and the elders were assembled. But Peter followed him afar off unto the high priest's palace, and went in, and sat with the servants to see the end. The chief priests and elders, and all the council, sought false witness against Jesus (for to put him to death) but found none; yea, when many false witnesses came,

---

[5] "Stroke" in text.
[6] "Cayphas" in text.

yet found they none. At the last came two false witnesses, and said, This fellow said, I am able to destroy the temple of God, and to build it again in three days. And the chief priest arose, and said unto him, Answerest thou nothing? Why do these bear witness against thee? But Jesus held his peace. And the chief priest answered and said unto him, I charge thee by the living God, that thou tell us whether thou be Christ the Son of God. Jesus said unto him, Thou hast said. Nevertheless I say unto you, hereafter shall ye see the Son of man sitting on the right hand of power, and coming in the clouds of the sky. Then the high priest rent[7] his clothes, saying, He hath spoken blasphemy, what need we of any more witnesses? Behold, now ye have heard his blasphemy, what think ye? They answered and said, He is worthy to die. Then did they spit in his face, and buffeted him with fists. And other smote him on the face with the palm of their hands, saying, Tell us, thou Christ, who is he that smote thee? Peter sat without in the court, and a damsel[8] came to him, saying, Thou also wast with Jesus of Galilee. But he denied before them all, saying, I wot[9] not what thou sayest. When he was gone out into the porch, another wench saw him, and said unto them that were there, This fellow was also with Jesus of Nazareth. And again he denied with an oath, saying, I do not know the man. After a while came unto him they that stood by, and said unto Peter, Surely thou art even one of them, for thy speech bewrayeth[10] thee. Then began he to curse and to swear that he knew not the man. And immediately the cock crew. And Peter remembered the word of Jesu, which said unto him, Before the cock crow, thou shalt deny me thrice; and he went out and wept bitterly. When the morning was come all the chief priests and elders of the people held a council against Jesus, to put him to

[7] *Rent:* tore apart.
[8] "Damosel" in text.
[9] *Wot:* know.
[10] *Bewrayeth:* betrayeth.

death, and brought him bound, and delivered him unto Pontius[11] Pilate the deputy. Then Judas (which had betrayed him) seeing that he was condemned, repented himself, and brought again the thirty plates[12] of silver to the chief priests and elders, saying, I have sinned betraying the innocent blood. And they said, What is that to us? See thou to that. And he cast down the silver plates in the temple, and departed, and went and hanged himself. And the chief priests took the silver plates, and said, It is not lawful for to put them into the treasure, because it is the price of blood. And they took counsel, and bought with them a potter's field to bury strangers in. Wherefore the field is called Acheldema, that is, the field of blood, until this day. Then was fulfilled that which was spoken by Jeremiah[13] the Prophet, saying, And they took thirty silver plates, the price of him that was valued, whom they bought of the children of Israel, and gave them for the potter's field, as the Lord appointed me. Jesus stood before the deputy, and the deputy asked him, saying, Art thou the King of the Jews? Jesus said unto him, Thou sayest. And when he was accused of the chief priests and elders, he answered nothing. Then said Pilate unto him, Hearest thou not how many witnesses they lay against thee? And he answered him to never a word, insomuch that the deputy marveled greatly. At that feast the deputy was wont to deliver unto the people a prisoner whom they would desire. He had then a notable prisoner called Barabbas.[14] Therefore when they were gathered together, Pilate said, Whether will ye that I give loose unto you Barabbas, or Jesus which is called Christ? For he knew that for envy they had delivered him. When he was set down to give judgment, his wife sent unto him, saying, Have thou nothing to do with that just man. For I have suffered this day many things in my sleep, because of him. But

[11] "Poncius" in text.

[12] *Plates:* coins.

[13] "Jeremie" in text.

[14] "Barrabas" in text, here and following.

the chief priests and elders persuaded the people that they should ask Barabbas, and destroy Jesus. The deputy answered, and said unto them, Whether of the twain will ye that I let loose unto you? They said, Barabbas. Pilate said unto them, What shall I do then with Jesus, which is called Christ? They all said unto him, Let him be crucified. The deputy said, What evil hath he done? But they cried more saying, Let him be crucified. When Pilate saw that he could prevail nothing, but that more business was made, he took water, and washed his hands before the people, saying, I am innocent of the blood of this just person, see ye. Then answered all the people, and said, His blood be on us and on our children. Then let he Barabbas loose unto them and scourged Jesus, and delivered him to be crucified. Then the soldiers of the deputy took Jesus into the common hall, and gathered unto him all the company, and they stripped him, and put on him a purple robe, and platted[15] a crown of thorns, and put it upon his head, and a reed in his right hand, and bowed the knee before him, and mocked him, saying, Hail King of the Jews. And when they had spit upon him, they took the reed and smote him on the head. And after that they had mocked him, they took the robe off him again, and put his own raiment on him and led him away to crucify him. And as they came out, they found a man of Cyrene (named Simon), him they compelled to bear his cross. And they came unto the place which is called Golgotha, that is to say, a place of dead men's skulls, and gave him vinegar mingled with gall to drink; and when he had tasted thereof, he would not drink. When they had crucified him, they parted his garments, and did cast lots, that it might be fulfilled which was spoken by the prophet, They parted my garments among them and upon my vesture did they cast lots. And they sat and watched him there, and set up over his head the cause of his death written: This is Jesus the King of the Jews. Then were there two thieves crucified with him, one on the right hand, and another on the left. They that passed by reviled him, wagging their heads and

---

[15] *Platted:* plaited.

saying, Thou that destroyedst the temple of God, and didst build it in three days, save thyself. If thou be the Son of God come down from the cross. Likewise also all the high priests mocking him with the scribes and elders said, He saved other, himself he cannot save. If he be the King of Israel, let him now come down from the cross, and we will believe him. He trusted in God, let him deliver him now, if he will have him: for he said, I am the Son of God. The thieves also which were crucified with him, cast the same in his teeth. From the sixth hour was there darkness over all the land, until the ninth hour. And about the ninth hour, Jesus cried with a loud voice, saying, Ely, Ely lama sabathanye? that is to say, My God, my God, why hast thou forsaken me? Some of them that stood there, when they heard that, said, This man calleth for Elias.[16] And straightway one of them ran and took a sponge, and when he had filled it full of vinegar, he put it on a reed, and gave him to drink. Other said, Let be, let us see whether Elias will come and deliver him. Jesus, when he had cried again with a loud voice, yielded up the ghost. And behold, the veil of the temple[17] did rent in two parts, from the top to the bottom, and the earth did quake and the stones rent, and graves did open and many bodies of saints which slept arose and went out of the graves after his resurrection, and came into the holy city, and appeared unto many. When the centurion, and they that were with him watching Jesus, saw the earth quake, and those things which happened, they feared greatly, saying, Truly this was the Son of God. And many women were there (beholding him afar off) which followed Jesus from Galilee, ministering unto him, emong[18] which was Mary Magdalene, and Mary the mother of James and Joses, and the mother of Zebedee's children.

---

[16] "Helias" in text, here and two sentences hereafter.

[17] *Veil of the temple:* the veil or curtain which separated the Holy of Holies from the Holy Place. The rending signified that the way to the mercy seat is open to all and not reserved to the high priest.

[18] *Emong:* among.

Monday before Easter

The Epistle [Isa. 63[1]

WHAT is he this that cometh from God, with red colored clothes of Bozrah[2] (which is so costly cloth) and cometh in so mightily with all his strength? I am he that teacheth righteousness, and am of power to help. Wherefore then is thy clothing red, and thy raiment like his that treadeth in the wine press? I have trodden the press myself alone, and of all people there is not one with me. Thus will I tread down mine enemies in my wrath, and set my feet upon them in mine indignation, and their blood shall bespring[3] my clothes, and so will I stain all my raiment. For the day of vengeance is assigned in my heart, and the year when my people shall be delivered is come. I looked about me, and there was no man to show me any help. I marveled that no man held me up. Then I held me by mine own arm, and my ferventness sustained me. And thus will I tread down the people in my wrath, and bathe them in my displeasure, and upon the earth will I lay their strength. I will declare the goodness of the Lord, yea, and the praise of the Lord for all that he hath given us, for the great good that he hath done for Israel, which he hath given them of his own favor, and according to the multitude of his loving kindness. For he said these no doubt are my people, and no shrinking children, and so he was their savior. In their troubles he was also troubled with them, and the angel that went forth from his presence, delivered them. Of very love and kindness that he had unto them, he redeemed them. He hath borne them and carried them up, ever since the world began. But after they provoked him to wrath and vexed his holy mind, he was their enemy and fought against them himself; yet remembered Israel the old time of Moses and his people, saying, Where is he

---

[1] "Esa." in text.
[2] "Bosra" in text.
[3] *Bespring:* besprinkle.

that brought them from the water of the sea, with them that feed his sheep? Where is he that hath given his Holy Spirit among them? He led them by the right hand of Moses, with his glorious arm, dividing the water before them (whereby he gat[4] himself an everlasting name). He led them in the deep as an horse is led in the plain, that they should not stumble, as a tame beast goeth in the field, and the breath given of God, giveth him rest. Thus (O God) hast thou led thy people, to make thyself a glorious name withal. Look down then from heaven, and behold the dwelling place of thy sanctuary, and thy glory. How is it that thy jealousy, thy strength, the multitude of thy mercies, and thy loving kindness, will not be intreated of us? Yet art thou our Father. For Abraham knoweth us not, neither is Israel acquainted with us. But thou, Lord, art our Father and redeemer, and thy name is everlasting. O Lord, wherefore hast thou led us out of thy way? Wherefore hast thou hardened our hearts that we fear thee not? Be at one with us again for thy servant's sake, and for the generation of thine heritage. Thy people have had but a little of thy sanctuary in possession, for our enemies have trodden down the holy place. And we were thine from the beginning, when thou wast not their Lord, for they have not called upon thy name.

The Gospel [Mark 14

AFTER two days was Easter,[5] and the days of sweet bread.[6] And the high priests and the scribes sought how they might take him by craft, and put him to death. But they said, Not in the feast day lest any busyness arise among the people. And when he was in Bethany in the house of Simon the leper, even as he sat at meat, there came a woman having an alabaster box of ointment, called nard, that was pure and costly: and she brake the box and poured it upon his head. And there were some that were not

[4] *Gat:* got.

[5] *Easter:* Passover.

[6] *Days of sweet bread:* days of the Feast of Unleavened Bread.

content within themselves, and said, What needed this waste of ointment, for it might have been sold for more than three hundred pence, and have been given unto the poor. And they grudged against her. And Jesus said, Let her alone, why trouble ye her? She hath done a good work on me, for ye have poor with you always, and whensoever ye will ye may do them good, but me have ye not always. She hath done that she could, she came aforehand to anoint my body to the burying. Verily I say unto you, wheresoever this gospel shall be preached throughout the whole world, this also that she hath done shall be rehearsed in remembrance of her. And Judas Iscariot,[7] one of the twelve, went away unto the high priests to betray him unto them. When they heard that, they were glad, and promised that they would give him money. And he sought how he might conveniently betray him. And the first day of sweet bread (when they offered the Passover) his disciples said unto him, Where wilt thou that we go and prepare that thou mayest eat the Passover? And he sent forth two of his disciples, and said unto them: Go ye unto the city, and there shall meet you a man bearing a pitcher of water, follow him. And whethersoever he goeth in, say ye unto the good man of the house, The master saith where is the great chamber where I shall eat the Passover with my disciples? And he will show you a great parlor paved and prepared; there make ready for us. And his disciples went forth, and came into the city, and found as he had said unto them, and they made ready the Passover. And when it was now eventide, he came with the twelve. And as they sat at board and did eat, Jesus said, Verily I say unto you, one of you that eateth with me shall betray me. And they began to be sorry, and to say to him one by one, Is it I? And another said, Is it I? He answered and said unto them, It is one of the twelve, even he that dippeth with me in the platter. The Son of man truly goeth as it is written of him, but woe unto that man by whom the Son of man is betrayed. Good were it for that man, if he had never been born. And as they did eat, Jesus

---

[7] "Iscarioth" in text.

took bread, and when he had given thanks, he brake it, and gave to them, and said, Take, eat, this is my body. And he took the cup, and when he had given thanks, he took it to them, and they all drank of it. And he said unto them, This is my blood of the new testament, which is shed for many. Verily I say unto you, I will drink no more of the fruit of the vine until that day that I drink it new in the kingdom of God. And when they had said grace, they went out to the Mount Olivet. And Jesus saith unto them, All ye shall be offended because of me this night. For it is written, I will smite the shepherd, and the sheep shall be scattered, but after that I am risen again I will go into Galilee before you. Peter said unto him, And though all men be offended, yet will not I. And Jesus saith unto him, Verily I say unto thee that this day, even in this night, before the cock crow twice thou shalt deny me three times. But he spake more vehemently, No, if I should die with thee, I will not deny thee. Likewise also said they all. And they came into a place which was named Gethsemane, and he said to his disciples, Sit ye here while I go aside and pray. And he taketh with him Peter and James and John, and began to wax abashed and to be in an agony, and said unto them, My soul is heavy even unto the death, tarry ye here and watch. And he went forth a little, and fell down flat on the ground and prayed that if it were possible the hour might pass from him. And he said, Abba, Father, all things are possible unto thee, take away this cup from me; nevertheless, not as I will, but that thou wilt be done. And he came and found them sleeping and saith to Peter, Simon, sleepest thou? Couldest not thou watch one hour? Watch ye and pray, lest ye enter into temptation. The spirit truly is ready, but the flesh is weak. And again he went aside and prayed, and spake the same words. And he returned and found them asleep again, for their eyes were heavy, neither wist[8] they what to answer him. And he came the third time and said unto them, Sleep henceforth and take your ease, it is enough. The hour is come, behold the Son of man is betrayed into the

---

[8] *Wist:* know.

hands of sinners. Rise up, let us go. Lo, he that betrayeth me is at hand. And immediately while he yet spake, cometh Judas (which was one of the twelve) and with him a great number of people with swords and staves from the high priests and scribes and elders. And he that betrayed him had given them a general token, saying, Whosoever I do kiss, the same is he; take and lead him away warily. And as soon as he was come, he goeth straightway to him, and saith unto him, Master, Master; and kissed him. And they laid their hands on him, and took him. And one of them that stood by, drew out a sword, and smote a servant of the high priests, and cut off his ear. And Jesus answered, and said unto them, Ye be come out as unto a thief with swords and staves, for to take me. I was daily with you in the temple teaching, and ye took me not; but these things come to pass that the Scripture should be fulfilled. And they all forsook him and ran away. And there followed him a certain young man clothed in linen upon the bare; and the young men caught him, and he left his linen garment, and fled from them naked. And they led Jesus away to the high priest of all, and with him came all the high priests and the elders and the scribes. And Peter followed him a great way off (even till he was come into the palace of the high priest) and he sat with the servants, and warmed himself at the fire. And the high priests and all the council sought for witness against Jesu to put him to death, and found none. For many bear false witness against him, but their witnesses agreed not together. And there arose certain and brought false witness against him, saying, We heard him say, I will destroy this temple that is made with hands, and within three days I will build another made without hands. But yet their witnesses agreed not together. And the high priest stood up among them, and asked Jesus, saying, Answerest thou nothing? How is it that these bear witness against thee? But he held his peace and answered nothing. Again the high priest asked him and said unto him, Art thou Christ, the Son of the blessed? And Jesus said, I am. And ye shall see the Son of man sitting on the right hand of power, and coming in the clouds of heaven. Then the high priest rent[9] his clothes, and said, What need we any further of witnesses? Ye have heard blasphemy, what think ye? And they all condemned him to be worthy of death. And some began to spit at him, and to cover his face, and to beat him with fists, and to say unto him Aread,[10] and the servants buffeted him on the face. And as Peter was beneath in the palace, there came one of the wenches of the high priest. And when she saw Peter warming himself, she looked on him, and said, Wast not thou also with Jesus of Nazareth? And he denied, saying, I know him not, neither wot[11] I what thou sayest. And he went out into the porch, and the cock crew. And a damsel,[12] when she saw him, began again to say to them that stood by, This is one of them. And he denied it again. And anon after they that stood by said again unto Peter, Surely thou art one of them, for thou art of Galilee, and thy speech agreeth thereto. But he began to curse and to swear, saying, I know not this man of whom ye speak. And again the cock crew, and Peter remembered the word that Jesus had said unto him, Before the cock crow twice, thou shalt deny me three times. And he began to weep.

Tuesday before Easter

The Epistle [Isa. 50

THE Lord God hath opened mine ear, therefore can I not say nay, neither withdraw myself, but I offer my back unto the smiters, and my cheeks to the nippers.[1] I turn not my face from shame and spitting, and the Lord God shall help me.

---

[9] *Rent:* tore.
[10] *Aread:* prophesy, explain.
[11] *Wot:* know.
[12] "Damosel" in text.
[1] *Nippers:* those who nip, "those who pull out the beard" (RSV).

Therefore shall I not be confounded. I have hardened my face like a flint stone, for I am sure that I shall not come to confusion. He is at hand that justifieth me; who will then go to law with me? Let us stand one against another. If there be any that will reason with me, let him come hereforth to me. Behold, the Lord God standeth by me; what is he then that can condemn me? Lo, they shall be like as an old cloth; the moth shall eat them up. Therefore, whoso feareth the Lord among you, let him hear the voice of his servant. Whoso walketh in darkness, and no light shineth upon him, let him put his trust in the name of the Lord, and hold him up by his God. But take heed, ye all kindle a fire of the wrath of God, and stir up the coals. Walk on in the glistering[2] of your own fire, and in the coals that ye have kindled. This cometh unto you from my hand, namely that ye shall sleep in sorrow.

The Gospel [Mark 15

AND anon in the dawning, the high priests held a council with the elders and the scribes, and the whole congregation, and bound Jesus and led him away, and delivered him to Pilate. And Pilate asked him, Art thou the King of the Jews? And he answered and said to him, Thou sayest it. And the high priests accused him of many things. So Pilate asked him again, saying, Answerest thou nothing? Behold how many things they lay to thy charge. Jesus answered yet nothing, so that Pilate marveled. At that feast Pilate did deliver unto them a prisoner, whomsoever they would desire. And there was one that was named Barabbas,[3] which lay bound with them that made insurrection; he had committed murder. And the people called unto him, and began to desire him that he would do according as he had ever done unto them. Pilate answered them, saying, Will ye that I let loose unto you the King of the Jews? For he knew that the high priests

[2] *Glistering:* glittering, sparkling.
[3] "Barrabas" in text, here and following.

had delivered him of envy. But the high priests moved the people that he should rather deliver Barabbas unto them. Pilate answered again, and said unto them, What will ye that I then do unto him, whom ye call the King of the Jews? And they cried again, Crucify him. Pilate said unto them, What evil hath he done? And they cried the more fervently, Crucify him. And so Pilate willing to content the people, let loose Barabbas unto them, and delivered up Jesus (when he had scourged him) for to be crucified. And the soldiers led him away into the common hall, and called together the whole multitude, and they clothed him with purple, and they platted[4] a crown of thorns, and crowned him withal, and began to salute him, Hail, King of the Jews. And they smote him on the head with a reed, and did spit upon him, and bowed their knees and worshiped him. And when they had mocked him, they took the purple off him, and put his own clothes on him, and led him out to crucify him. And they compelled one that passed by, called Simon of Cyrene[5] (the father of Alexander and Rufus) which came out of the field, to bear his cross. And they brought him to a place named Golgotha (which if a man interpret, is the place of dead men's skulls) and they gave him to drink wine mingled with myrrh, but he received it not. And when they had crucified him, they parted his garments, casting lots upon them what every man should take. And it was about the third hour, and they crucified him. And the title of his cause was written, The King of the Jews. And they crucified with him two thieves, the one on his right hand, and the other on his left. And the Scripture was fulfilled which saith, He was counted among the wicked. And they that went by railed on him, wagging their heads, and saying, Ah[6] wretch, thou that destroyest the temple, and buildest it again in three days, save thyself and come down from the cross. Likewise also mocked him

[4] *Platted:* plaited.

[5] "Sirene" in text.

[6] "A" in text, and in 1549 and 1552 Books. Cf. Brightman, *English Rite,* I, 346–47.

the high priests among themselves, with the scribes, and said, He saved other men, himself he cannot save. Let Christ the King of Israel descend now from the cross, that we may see and believe. And they that were crucified with him, checked[7] him also. And when the sixth hour was come, darkness arose over all the earth, until the ninth hour. And at the ninth hour, Jesus cried with a loud voice, saying, Eloy, Eloy, lama sabathany? Which is (if one interpret it) My God, my God, why hast thou forsaken me? And some of them that stood by, when they heard that, said, Behold, he calleth for Elias.[8] And one ran and filled a sponge full of vinegar, and put it on a reed, and gave him to drink, saying, Let him alone. Let us see whether Elias will come and take him down. But Jesus cried with a loud voice and gave up the ghost. And the veil of the temple[9] rent[10] in two pieces, from the top to the bottom. And when the centurion (which stood before him) saw that he so cried and gave up the ghost, he said, Truly this man was the Son of God. There were also women a good way off, beholding him, among whom was Mary Magdalene, and Mary[11] the mother of James the little, and of Joses, and Mary Salome (which also when he was in Galilee had followed him and ministered unto him) and many other women, which came up with him to Jerusalem. And now when the even was come (because it was the day of preparing that goeth before the Sabbath) Joseph of the city of Arimathea, a noble counselor, which also looked for the kingdom of God, came and went in boldly unto Pilate, and begged of him the body of Jesu. And Pilate marveled that he was already dead, and called unto him the centurion, and asked of him whether he had been any while dead. And when he knew the truth of the centurion, he gave the body to Joseph, and he bought a linen cloth, and took him down, and

---

[7] *Checked:* rebuked.

[8] "Helias" in text, here and below.

[9] See p. 125, n. 17, above.

[10] *Rent:* split.

[11] "Marie" in text.

wrapped him in the linen cloth, and laid him in a sepulcher that was hewn out of a rock, and rolled a stone before the door of the sepulcher. And Mary Magdalene, and Mary Joses beheld where he was laid.

Wednesday before Easter

The Epistle [Heb. 9

WHERE as is a testament, there must also of necessity be the death of him that maketh the testament. For the testament taketh authority when men are dead. For it is yet of no value as long as he that maketh the testament is alive. For which cause also, neither the first testament was ordained without blood. For when Moses had declared all the commandment to all the people, according to the law, he took the blood of calves and of goats, with water and purple wool, and hyssop,[1] and sprinkled both the book and all the people, saying, This is the blood of the testament which God hath appointed unto you. Moreover he sprinkled the tabernacle with blood also and all the ministering vessels. And almost all things are by the law purged with blood, and without shedding of blood is no remission. It is need then, that the similitudes of heavenly things be purified with such things, but that the heavenly things themselves be purified with better sacrifices than are those. For Christ is not entered into the holy places that are made with hands (which are similitudes of true things), but is entered into very heaven for to appear now in the sight of God for us, not to offer himself often, as the high priest entereth into the holy place every year with strange blood; for then must he have often suffered since the world began. But now in the end of the world hath he appeared once, to put sin to flight by the offering up of himself. And as it is appointed unto all men that they shall once die, and

[1] Text has "ysope."

then cometh the judgment, even so Christ was once offered to take away the sins of many, and unto them that look for him shall he appear again without sin unto salvation.

The Gospel [Luke 22

THE feast of sweet bread[2] drew nigh, which is called Easter,[3] and the high priests and scribes sought how they might kill him, for they feared the people. Then entered Satan into Judas, whose surname was Iscariot[4] (which was of the number of the twelve) and he went his way and commoned[5] with the high priests and officers, how he might betray him unto them. And they were glad, and promised to give him money. And he consented, and sought opportunity to betray him unto them, when the people were away. Then came the day of sweet bread,[6] when of necessity the Passover must be offered. And he sent Peter and John, saying, Go and prepare us the Passover, that we may eat. They said unto him, Where wilt thou that we prepare? And he said unto them, Behold, when ye enter into the city, there shall a man meet you bearing a pitcher of water, him follow into the same house that he entereth in and ye shall say unto the good man of the house, The Master saith unto thee, where is the guest chamber where I shall eat the Passover with my disciples? And he shall show you a great parlor paved;[7] there make ready. And they went and found as he had said unto them, and they made ready the Passover. And when the hour was come, he sat down and the twelve Apostles with him. And he said unto them, I have inwardly desired to eat this Passover with you before that I suffer. For I say unto you, Henceforth will I not eat of it any

[2] *Feast of sweet bread:* Feast of Unleavened Bread.

[3] *Easter:* Passover.

[4] "Iscariothe" in text.

[5] *Commoned:* conferred.

[6] *Sweet bread:* unleavened bread.

[7] *Paved:* "furnished" (AV).

more, until it be fulfilled in the kingdom of God. And he took the cup, and gave thanks, and said, Take this and divide it among you. For I say unto you, I will not drink of the fruit of this vine, until the kingdom of God come. And he took bread, and when he had given thanks, he brake it, and gave unto them, saying, This is my body which is given for you; this do in the remembrance of me. Likewise also when he had supped, he took the cup, saying, This cup is the new testament in my blood, which is shed for you. Yet behold the hand of him that betrayeth me is with me on the table. And truly the Son of man goeth as it is appointed, but woe unto that man by whom he is betrayed. And they began to inquire among themselves, which of them it was that should do it. And there was a strife among them, which of them should seem to be the greatest. And he said unto them, The kings of nations reign over them, and they that have authority upon them are called gracious. But ye shall not so be. But he that is greatest among you shall be as the younger, and he that is chief shall be as he that doth minister. For whether is greater, he that sitteth at meat, or he that serveth? Is it not he that sitteth at meat? But I am among you as he that ministereth. Ye are they which have bidden[8] with me in my temptations. And I appoint unto you a kingdom, as my Father hath appointed to me, that ye may eat and drink at my table in my kingdom, and sit on seats judging the twelve tribes of Israel. And the Lord said, Simon, Simon, behold, Satan hath desired to sift you, as it were wheat. But I have prayed for thee, that thy faith fail not. And when thou art converted strength[9] thy brethren. And he said unto him, Lord, I am ready to go with thee into prison, and to death. And he said, I tell thee Peter, the cock shall not crow this day, till thou have denied me thrice that thou knewest me. And he said unto them, When I sent you without wallet, and scrip,[10] and shoes, lacked ye anything? And they said, No. Then said he unto them, But

---

[8] *Bidden:* remained.

[9] *Strength:* strengthen.

[10] *Scrip:* a small bag or satchel.

now he that hath a wallet, let him take it up, and likewise his scrip. And he that hath no sword, let him sell his coat and buy one. For I say unto you, that yet the same which is written must be performed in me, Even among the wicked was he reputed. For those things which are written of me have an end. And they said, Lord, behold, here are two swords. And he said unto them, It is enough. And he came out, and went (as he was wont) to Mount Olivet. And the disciples followed him. And when he came to the place, he said unto them, Pray, lest ye fall into temptation. And he gat[11] himself from them about a stone's cast, and kneeled down and prayed, saying, Father, if thou wilt, remove this cup from me. Nevertheless, not my will, but thine be fulfilled. And there appeared an angel unto him from heaven, comforting him. And he was in an agony, and prayed the longer, and his sweat was like drops of blood trickling down to the ground. And when he arose from prayer, and was come to his disciples, he found them sleeping for heaviness, and he said unto them, Why sleep ye? Rise and pray, lest ye fall into temptation. While he yet spake, behold, there came a company, and he that was called Judas, one of the twelve, went before them, and pressed nigh to Jesus, to kiss him. But Jesus said unto him, Judas, betrayest thou the Son of man with a kiss? When they which were about him saw what would follow, they said unto him, Lord, shall we smite with the sword? And one of them smote a servant of the high priests, and stroke off his right ear. Jesus answered and said, Suffer ye thus far forth. And when he touched his ear he healed him. Then Jesus said unto the high priests, and rulers of the temple, and the elders which were come to him, Ye be come out as unto a thief with swords and staves. When I was daily with you in the temple, ye stretched forth no hands against me; but this is even your very hour, and the power of darkness. Then took they him and led him, and brought him to the high priest's house. But Peter followed afar off. And when they had kindled

[11] *Gat:* got.

a fire in the mids[12] of the palace, and were set down together, Peter also sat down among them. But when one of the wenches beheld him as he sat by the fire (and looked upon him) she said, This same fellow was also with him. And he denied him, saying, Woman, I know him not. And after a little while another saw him, and said, Thou art also of them. And Peter said, Man, I am not. And about the space of an hour after, another affirmed, saying, Verily this fellow was with him also, for he is of Galilee. And Peter said, Man, I wot[13] not what thou sayest. And immediately while he yet spake, the cock crew. And the Lord turned back and looked upon Peter. And Peter remembered the word of the Lord, how he had said unto him, Before the cock crow, thou shalt deny me thrice. And Peter went out and wept bitterly. And the men that took Jesus mocked him, and smote him, and when they had blindfolded him they stroke him on the face, and asked him, saying, Aread,[14] who is he that smote thee? And many other things despitefully said they against him. And as soon as it was day, the elders of the people, and the high priests and scribes, came together and led him into their council, saying, Art thou very Christ? Tell us. And he said unto them, If I tell you, ye will not believe me, and if I ask you, you will not answer, nor let me go. Hereafter shall the Son of man sit on the right hand of the power of God. Then said they all, Art thou then the Son of God? He said, Ye say that I am. And they said, What need we of any further witness? For we ourselves have heard of his own mouth.

[12] *Mids:* middle.
[13] *Wot:* know.
[14] *Aread:* prophesy, explain.

Thursday before Easter

The Epistle [1 Cor. 11

THIS I warn you of, and commend not, that ye come not together after a better manner, but after a worse. For first of
all, when ye come together in the congregation, I hear that there
is dissension among you, and I partly believe it. For there must
be sects among you, that they which are perfect among you may
be known. When ye come together therefore into one place, the
Lord's Supper cannot be eaten for every man beginneth afore to
eat his own supper. And one is hungry, and another is drunken.
Have ye not houses to eat and drink in? Despise ye the congregation of God, and shame them that have not? What shall I say
unto you? Shall I praise you? In this I praise you not. That which
I delivered unto you, I received of the Lord. For the Lord Jesus,
the same night in which he was betrayed, took bread, and when
he had given thanks, he brake it, and said, Take ye and eat, this
is my body which is broken for you. This do ye in the remembrance of me. After the same manner also, he took the cup when
supper was done, saying, This cup is the new testament in my
blood. This do, as oft as ye drink it, in remembrance of me. For
as often as ye shall eat this bread, and drink of this cup, ye shall
show the Lord's death till he come. Wherefore, whosoever shall
eat of this bread, and drink of this cup of the Lord unworthily,
shall be guilty of the body and blood of the Lord. But let a man
examine himself, and so let him eat of the bread, and drink of
the cup. For he that eateth and drinketh unworthily, eateth and
drinketh his own damnation, because he maketh no difference of
the Lord's body. For this cause many are weak and sick among
you, and many sleep. For if we had judged ourselves, we should
not have been judged. But when we are judged of the Lord, we
are chastened, that we should not be damned with the world.
Wherefore my brethren, when ye come together to eat, tarry
one for another. If any man hunger, let him eat at home, that ye

come not together unto condemnation. Other things will I set in order when I come.

The Gospel [Luke 23[1]

THE whole multitude of them arose, and led him unto Pilate. And they began to accuse him, saying, We found this fellow perverting the people, and forbidding to pay tribute to Caesar, saying that he is Christ, a king. And Pilate apposed[2] him, saying, Art thou the King of the Jews? He answered him and said, Thou sayest it. Then said Pilate to the high priests and to the people, I find no fault in this man. And they were the more fierce, saying, He moveth the people, teaching throughout all Jewry,[3] and began at Galilee, even to this place. When Pilate heard mention of Galilee, he asked whether the man were of Galilee. And as soon as he knew that he belonged unto Herod's jurisdiction, he sent him to Herod, which was also at Jerusalem at that time. And when Herod saw Jesus, he was exceeding glad, for he was desirous to see him of a long season, because he had heard many things of him, and he trusted to have seen some miracles done by him. Then he questioned with him many words. But he answered him nothing. The high priests and scribes stood forth and accused him straightly. And Herod with his men of war despised him. And when he had mocked him, he arrayed him in white clothing, and sent him again to Pilate. And the same day Pilate and Herod were made friends together. For before they were at variance. And Pilate called together the high priests, and the rulers, and the people, and said unto them, Ye have brought this man unto me as one that perverteth the people, and behold, I examine him before you and find no fault in this man of those things whereof ye accuse him, no nor yet Herod. For I sent you unto him, and lo, nothing worthy of death is done unto him. I

---

[1] Text has "22"; misprint.

[2] *Apposed:* examined, questioned.

[3] "Juri" in text.

will therefore chasten him and let him loose. For of necessity he must have let one loose to them at that feast. And all the people cried at once, saying, Away with him, and deliver us Barabbas:[4] which for a certain insurrection made in the city, and for a murder, was cast into prison. Pilate spake again unto them, willing to let Jesus loose. But they cried, saying, Crucify him, crucify him. He said unto them the third time, What evil hath he done? I find no cause of death in him. I will therefore chasten him and let him go. And they cried with loud voices, requiring that he might be crucified. And the voices of them and of the high priests prevailed. And Pilate gave sentence that it should be as they required, and he let loose unto them him that (for insurrection and murder) was cast into prison, whom they had desired. And he delivered to them Jesus to do with him what they would. And as they led him away, they caught one Simon of Cyrene coming out of the field, and on him laid they the cross, that he might bear it after Jesus. And there followed him a great company of people, and of women, which bewailed and lamented him. But Jesus turned back unto them and said, Ye daughters of Jerusalem, weep not for me, but weep for yourselves, and for your children. For behold the days will come in the which they shall say, Happy are the barren, and the wombs that never bare, and the paps[5] which never gave suck. Then shall they begin to say to the mountains, Fall on us, and to the hills, Cover us. For if they do this in a green tree, what shall be done in the dry? And there were two evildoers led with him to be slain. And after that they were come to the place (which is called Calvary) there they crucified him and the evildoers, one on the right hand, and the other on the left. Then said Jesus, Father forgive them, for they wot[6] not what they do. And they parted his raiment, and cast lots. And the people stood and beheld. And the rulers mocked him with them, saying, He saved other men, let him save himself if he be

---

[4] "Barrabas" in text, here and following.

[5] *Paps:* nipples, mammillae.

[6] *Wot:* know.

very Christ the chosen of God. The soldiers also mocked him, and came and offered him vinegar, and said, If thou be the King of the Jews, save thyself. And a superscription[7] was written over him, with letters of Greek, and Latin, and Hebrew: This is the King of the Jews. And one of the evildoers which were hanged, railed on him, saying, If thou be Christ, save thyself and us. But the other answered and rebuked him, saying, Fearest thou not God, seeing thou art in the same damnation? We are righteously punished, for we receive according to our deeds, but this man hath done nothing amiss. And he said unto Jesus, Lord, remember me when thou comest into thy kingdom. And Jesus said unto him, Verily I say unto thee, today shalt thou be with me in paradise. And it was about the sixth hour, and there was a darkness over all the earth, until the ninth hour; and the sun was darkened. And the veil of the temple[8] did rent,[9] even through the mids.[10] And when Jesus had cried with a loud voice, he said, Father, into thy hands I commend my spirit. And when he thus had said, he gave up the ghost. When the centurion saw what had happened, he glorified God, saying, Verily this was a righteous man. And all the people that came together to that sight, and saw the things which had happened, smote their breasts and returned. And all his acquaintance, and the women that followed him from Galilee, stood afar off beholding these things. And behold, there was a man named Joseph, a counselor, and he was a good man and a just (the same had not consented to the counsel and deed of them), which was of Arimathea, a city of the Jews, which same also waiteth for the kingdom of God. He went unto Pilate and begged the body of Jesus, and took it down, and wrapped it in a linen cloth, and laid it in a sepulcher that was hewn in stone, wherein never man before had been laid. And that day was the preparing of the Sabbath, and the Sabbath drew on.

---

[7] *Superscription:* a piece of writing on or above.
[8] See p. 125, n. 17, above.
[9] *Rent:* split.
[10] *Mids:* middle.

The women that followed after, which had come with him from Galilee, beheld the sepulcher, and how his body was laid. And they returned, and prepared sweet odors and ointments, but rested on the Sabbath day, according to the commandments.

On Good Friday

The Collects

ALMIGHTY God, we beseech thee graciously to behold this thy family, for the which our Lord Jesus Christ was contented to be betrayed and given up into the hands of wicked men, and to suffer death upon the cross; who liveth and reigneth, etc.

ALMIGHTY and everlasting God, by whose Spirit the whole body of the church is governed and sanctified: Receive our supplications and prayers, which we offer before thee for all estates of men in thy holy congregation, that every member of the same in his vocation and ministry, may truly and godly serve thee; through our Lord Jesus Christ.

MERCIFUL God, who hast made all men, and hatest nothing that thou hast made, nor wouldest the death of a sinner, but rather that he should be converted and live: Have mercy upon all Jews, Turks, infidels, and heretics, and take from them all ignorance, hardness of heart, and contempt of thy Word: And so fetch them home blessed Lord, to thy flock, that they may be saved among the remnant of the true Israelites, and be made one fold, under one shepherd Jesus Christ our Lord; who liveth and reigneth, etc.

The Epistle [Heb. 10

THE law (which hath but a shadow of good things to come, and not the very fashion of things themselves) can never with those sacrifices which they offer year by year continually, make the comers thereunto perfect. For would not then those sacrifices have ceased to have been offered, because that the offerers once purged should have had no more conscience of sins? Nevertheless, in those sacrifices is there mention made of sins every year. For the blood of oxen and goats cannot take away sins. Wherefore, when he cometh into the world, he saith, Sacrifice and offering thou wouldest not have, but a body hast thou ordained me. Burnt offerings also for sin hast thou not allowed. Then said I, Lo, I am here. In the beginning of the book it is written of me, that I should do thy will, O God. Above, when he saith, Sacrifice and offering, and burnt sacrifices, and sin offerings thou wouldest not have, neither hast thou allowed them (which yet are offered by the law); then said he, Lo, I am here to do thy will, O God: he taketh away the first to establish the latter. By the which will, we are made holy, even by the offering of the body of Jesu Christ once for all. And every priest is ready daily ministering and offering oftentimes one manner of oblation, which can never take away sins. But this man, after he hath offered one sacrifice for sins, is set down forever on the right hand of God, and from henceforth tarrieth till his foes be made his footstool. For with one offering hath he made perfect forever them that are sanctified. The Holy Ghost himself also beareth us record, even when he told before, This is the testament that I will make unto them. After those days (saith the Lord) I will put my laws in their hearts, and in their minds will I write them, and their sins and iniquities will I remember no more. And where remission of these things is, there is no more offering for sins. Seeing therefore brethren, that by the means of the blood of Jesu, we have liberty to enter into the holy place by the new and living way which he hath prepared for us, through the veil (that is to say, by his flesh), and seeing also that we have an high priest which is ruler over the house of God, let us draw nigh with a true heart and a sure faith, sprinkled in our hearts from an evil conscience, and washed in our bodies with pure water. Let us keep the profession of our hope, without wavering (for he is faithful that promised) and let us consider one another, to the intent that we may provoke unto love, and to good works, not forsaking the fellowship that we have among ourselves, as the manner of some is; but let us exhort one another, and that so much the more, because ye see that the day draweth nigh.

The Gospel [John 18

WHEN Jesus had spoken these words, he went forth with his disciples over the brook Cedron, where was a garden, into the which he then entered with his disciples. Judas, which also betrayed him, knew the place, for Jesus ofttimes resorted thither with his disciples. Judas then after he had received a bond[1] of men (and ministers of the high priests and Pharisees) came thither with lanterns, and firebrands, and weapons. And Jesus knowing all things that should come on him went forth and said unto them, Whom seek ye? They answered him, Jesus of Nazareth. Jesus said unto them, I am he. Judas also which betrayed him stood with them. As soon then as he had said unto them, I am he, they went backward and fell to the ground. Then asked he them again, Whom seek ye? They said, Jesus of Nazareth. Jesus answered, I have told you that I am he; if ye seek me therefore, let these go their way, that the saying might be fulfilled which he spake, Of them which thou gavest me, have I not lost one. Then Simon Peter having a sword, drew it, and smote the high priest's servant, and cut off his right ear. The servant's name was Malchus. Therefore saith Jesus unto Peter, Put up thy sword into thy sheath. Shall I not drink of the cup which my Father hath given me? Then the company and the captain, and the ministers of the Jews took Jesus and bound him, and led him away to Annas first, for he was father-in-law to Caiaphas,[2] which was the high priest the same year. Caiaphas was he that gave counsel to the Jews that it was expedient that one man should

---

[1] *Bond:* band.

[2] "Cayphas" or "Caiaphas" throughout this Gospel.

die for the people. And Simon Peter followed Jesus, and so did another disciple. That disciple was known to the high priest, and went in with Jesus unto the palace of the high priest. But Peter stood at the door without. Then went out that other disciple (which was known to the high priest) and spake to the damsel[3] that kept the door, and brought in Peter. Then said the damsel that kept the door unto Peter, Art not thou also one of this man's disciples? He said, I am not. The servants and ministers stood there, which had made a fire of coals, for it was cold, and they warmed themselves. Peter also stood among them and warmed himself. The high priest then asked Jesus of his disciples, and of his doctrine. Jesus answered him, I spake openly in the world. I ever taught in the synagogue and in the temple whither all the Jews have resorted, and in secret have I said nothing. Why askest thou me? Ask them which heard me, what I said unto them. Behold, they can tell what I said. When he had thus spoken, one of the ministers which stood by, smote Jesus on the face, saying, Answerest thou the high priest so? Jesus answered him, If I have evil spoken, bear witness of the evil. But if I have well spoken, why smitest thou me? And Annas sent him bound unto Caiaphas the high priest. Simon Peter stood and warmed himself. Then said they unto him, Art not thou also one of his disciples? He denied it, and said, I am not. One of the servants of the high priests (his cousin, whose ear Peter smote off) said unto him, Did not I see thee in the garden with him? Peter therefore denied again; and immediately the cock crew. Then led they Jesus from Caiaphas into the hall of judgment. It was in the morning, and they themselves went not into the judgment hall, lest they should be defiled, but that they might eat the Passover. Pilate then went out to them, and said, What accusation bring you against this man? They answered, and said unto him, If he were not an evildoer, we would not have delivered him unto thee. Then said Pilate unto them, Take ye him and judge him after your own law. The Jews therefore said unto him, It is not lawfull

---

[3] Text has "damosell"; "damosel" in next line.

for us to put any man to death that the words of Jesus might be fulfilled, which he spake signifying what death he should die. Then Pilate entered into the judgment hall again, and called Jesus, and said unto him, Art thou the King of the Jews? Jesus answered, Sayest thou that of thyself, or did other tell it thee of me? Pilate answered, Am I a Jew? Thine own nation and high priests have delivered thee unto me: what hast thou done? Jesus answered, My kingdom is not of this world. If my kingdom were of this world, then would my ministers surely fight, that I should not be delivered to the Jews, but now is my kingdom not from hence. Pilate therefore said unto him, Art thou a king then? Jesus answered, Thou sayest that I am a king. For this cause was I born and for this cause came into the world, that I should bear witness unto the truth. And all that are of the truth hear my voice. Pilate said unto him, What thing is truth? And when he had said this, he went out again unto the Jews, and saith unto them, I find in him no cause at all. Ye have a custom that I should deliver you one loose at Easter.[4] Will ye that I loose unto you the King of the Jews? Then cried they all again, saying, Not him, but Barabbas;[5] the same Barabbas was a murderer. Then Pilate took Jesus therefore, and scourged him. And the soldiers wound a crown of thorns and put it on his head. And they did on him a purple garment, and came unto him, and said, Hail King of the Jews. And they smote him on the face. Pilate went forth again, and said unto them, Behold, I bring him forth to you that ye may know that I find no fault in him. Then came Jesus forth, wearing a crown of thorn and a robe of purple. And he saith unto them, Behold the man. When the priests therefore and the ministers saw him, they cried, Crucify him, crucify him. Pilate saith unto them, Take ye him and crucify him, for I find no cause in him. The Jews answered him, We have a law, and by our law he ought to die, because he made himself the Son of God. When Pilate heard that saying, he was the more afraid, and went

[4] *Easter:* Passover.
[5] "Barrabas" in text, here and following.

again into the judgment hall, and said unto Jesus, Whence art thou? But Jesus gave him none answer. Then said Pilate unto him, Speakest thou not unto me? Knowest thou not that I have power to crucify thee, and have power to loose thee? Jesus answered, Thou couldest have no power at all against me, except it were given thee from above. Therefore he that delivered me unto thee hath the more sin. And from thenceforth sought Pilate means to loose him. But the Jews cried, saying, If thou let him go, thou art not Caesar's friend, for whosoever maketh himself a king, is against Caesar. When Pilate heard that saying, he brought Jesus forth, and sat down to give sentence in a place that is called the Pavement, but in the Hebrew tongue, Gabbatha. It was the preparing day of Easter, about the sixth hour. And he saith unto the Jews, Behold your king. They cried, saying, Away with him, away with him, crucify him. Pilate saith unto them, Shall I crucify your king? The high priests answered, We have no king but Caesar. Then delivered he him to them to be crucified. And they took Jesus and led him away, and he bare his cross, and went forth into a place which is called the place of dead men's skulls, but in Hebrew, Golgotha, where they crucified him, and two other with him, on either side one, and Jesus in the midst. And Pilate wrote a title and put it upon the cross. The writing was, Jesus of Nazareth King of the Jews. This title read many of the Jews, for the place where Jesus was crucified was near to the city. And it was written in Hebrew, Greek, and Latin. Then said the high priests of the Jews to Pilate, write not King of the Jews, but that he said, I am King of the Jews. Pilate answered, What I have written that I have written. Then the soldiers when they had crucified Jesus, took his garments, and made four parts, to every soldier a part, and also his coat. The coat was without seam, wrought[6] upon throughout. They said therefore among themselves, Let us not divide it, but cast lots for it who shall have it; that the Scripture might be fulfilled, saying, They have parted my raiment among them, and for my coat did they cast lots. And

---

[6] *Wrought:* finished from rough or crude material.

the soldiers did such things in deed. There stood by the cross of Jesus his mother, and his mother's sister, Mary the wife of Cleophas, and Mary Magdalene. When Jesus therefore saw his mother and the disciple whom he loved, standing, he saith unto his mother, Woman, behold thy son. Then said he to the disciple, Behold thy mother. And from that hour the disciple took her for his own. After these things, Jesus knowing that all things were now performed, that the Scripture might be fulfilled, he saith, I thirst. So there stood a vessel by, full of vinegar; therefore they filled a sponge with vinegar, and wound it about with hyssop,[7] and put it to his mouth. As soon as Jesus then received of the vinegar, he said, It is finished, and bowed his head, and gave up the ghost. The Jews therefore, because it was the preparing of the Sabbath, that the bodies should not remain upon the cross on the Sabbath day (for that Sabbath day was an high day), besought Pilate that their legs might be broken, and that they might be taken down. Then came the soldiers and brake[8] the legs of the first, and of the other which was crucified with him. But when they came to Jesus, and saw that he was dead already, they brake not his legs, but one of the soldiers with a spear thrust him into the side, and forthwith there came out blood and water. And he that saw it bare record, and his record is true. And he knoweth that he saith true, that ye might believe also. For these things were done that the Scripture should be fulfilled, Ye shall not break a bone of him. And again another Scripture saith, They shall look upon him whom they have pierced. After this, Joseph of Arimathea (which was a disciple of Jesus, but secretly for fear of the Jews) besought Pilate that he might take down the body of Jesus. And Pilate gave him license. He came therefore and took the body of Jesus. And there came also Nicodemus[9] (which at the beginning came to Jesus by night) and brought of myrrh and aloes mingled together about an hundred pound weight.

---

[7] Text has "ysope."

[8] *Brake:* broke.

[9] "Nichodemus" in text.

Then took they the body of Jesus, and wound it in linen clothes with the odors, as the manner of the Jews is to bury. And in the place where he was crucified, there was a garden, and in the garden a new sepulcher, wherein was never man laid. There laid they Jesus therefore because of the preparing of the Sabbath of the Jews, for the sepulcher was nigh at hand.

Easter Even

The Epistle [1 Pet. 3

IT is better (if the will of God be so) that ye suffer for well doing than for evil doing. Forasmuch as Christ hath once suffered for sins, the just for the unjust, to bring us to God, and was killed as pertaining to the flesh, but was quickened in the Spirit. In which Spirit he also went and preached to the spirits that were in prison, which sometime had been disobedient, when the long suffering of God was once looked for, in the days of Noah,[1] while the ark was a preparing, wherein a few, that is to say, eight souls were saved by the water, like as baptism also now saveth us: not the putting away of the filth of the flesh, but in that a good conscience consenteth to God by the resurrection of Jesus Christ, which is on the right hand of God, and is gone into heaven; angels, powers, and might, subdued unto him.

The Gospel [Matt. 27

WHEN the even was come, there came a rich man of Arimathea, named Joseph, which also was Jesus' disciple. He went unto Pilate and begged the body of Jesus. Then Pilate commanded the body to be delivered. And when Joseph had taken the body, he wrapped it in a clean linen cloth, and laid it in his new tomb, which he had hewn out, even in the rock, and

---

[1] "Noe" in text.

rolled a great stone to the door of the sepulcher, and departed. And there was Mary Magdalene, and the other Mary, sitting over against the sepulcher. The next day that followeth the day of preparing, the high priests and Pharisees came together unto Pilate, saying, Sir, we remember that this deceiver said while he was yet alive, After three days I will rise again. Command therefore that the sepulcher be made sure until the third day, lest his disciples come and steal him away, and say unto the people, he is risen from the dead; and the last error shall be worse than the first. Pilate said unto them, Ye have a watch, go your way, make it as sure as ye can. So they went and made the sepulcher sure with the watchmen, and sealed the stone.

Easter Day

At Morning Prayer, instead of the Psalm, O come let us, etc., these anthems shall be sung or said.

CHRIST rising again from the dead, now dieth not. Death from henceforth hath no power upon him. For in that he died, he died but once to put away sin: but in that he liveth, he liveth unto God. And so likewise, count yourselves dead unto sin, but living unto God in Christ Jesus our Lord.[1]

CHRIST is risen again, the first fruits of them that sleep: for seeing that by man came death, by man also cometh the resurrection of the dead. For as by Adam all men do die, so by Christ, all men shall be restored to life.[2]

The Collect

ALMIGHTY God, which through thy only begotten Son Jesus Christ, hast overcome death, and opened unto us the gate of everlasting life: We humbly beseech thee, that as by thy

[1] Rom. 6:9–11.
[2] 1 Cor. 15:20–22.

special grace preventing us,[3] thou dost put in our minds good desires, so by thy continual help, we may bring the same to good effect; through Jesus Christ our Lord, who liveth and reigneth, etc.

The Epistle [Col. 3

IF ye be risen again with Christ, seek those things which are above, where Christ sitteth on the right hand of God. Set your affection on heavenly things, and not on earthly things. For ye are dead, and your life is hid with Christ in God. Whensoever Christ (which is our life) shall show himself, then shall ye also appear with him in glory. Mortify therefore your earthly members, fornication, uncleanness, unnatural lust, evil concupiscence, and covetousness, which is worshiping of idols, for which things' sake, the wrath of God useth to come on the children of unbelief, among whom ye walked sometime when ye lived in them.

The Gospel [John 20

THE first day of the Sabbaths,[4] came Mary Magdalene early (when it was yet dark) unto the sepulcher, and saw the stone taken away from the grave. Then she ran and came to Simon Peter, and to the other disciple whom Jesus loved, and saith unto them, They have taken away the Lord out of the grave, and we cannot tell where they have laid him. Peter therefore went forth, and that other disciple, and came unto the sepulcher. They ran both together and that other disciple did outrun Peter, and came first to the sepulcher. And when he had stooped down, he saw the linen clothes lying, yet went he not in. Then came Simon Peter following him, and went into the sepulcher, and saw the linen clothes lie, and the napkin that was about his head not lying with the linen clothes, but wrapped together in

[3] *Preventing us:* predisposing us, going before.
[4] *The first day of the Sabbaths:* "the first day of the week" (RSV).

a place by itself. Then went in also that other disciple which came first to the sepulcher, and he saw and believed. For as yet they knew not the Scripture that he should rise again from death. Then the disciples went away again to their own home.

Monday in Easter Week

The Collect

ALMIGHTY God, which through thy only begotten Son Jesus Christ, hath[1] overcome death and opened unto us the gate of everlasting life: We humbly beseech thee, that as by thy special grace preventing us,[2] thou dost put in our minds good desires, so by thy continual help, we may bring the same to good effect; through Jesus Christ our Lord, who liveth and reigneth, etc.

The Epistle [Acts 10

PETER opened his mouth and said, Of a truth I perceive that there is no respect of persons with God, but in all people, he that feareth him and worketh righteousness, is accepted with him. Ye know the preaching that God sent unto the children of Israel, preaching peace by Jesus Christ which is Lord over all things; which preaching was published throughout all Jewry (and began in Galilee, after the baptism which John preached) how God anointed Jesus of Nazareth with the Holy Ghost, and with power. Which Jesus went about doing good and healing all that were oppressed of the devil, for God was with him. And we are witnesses of all things which he did in the land of the Jews, and at Jerusalem,[3] whom they slew and hanged on tree.

[1] *Hath:* "hast" in Collect for Easter.
[2] *Preventing us:* predisposing us, going before.
[3] "Jherusalem" in text.

Him God raised up the third day and showed him openly, not to all the people, but to us witnesses (chosen before of God for the same intent) which did eat and drink with him after he arose from death. And he commanded us to preach unto the people, and to testify that it is he which was ordained of God to be the judge of the quick[4] and the dead. To him give all the prophets witness, that through his name, whosoever believeth in him, shall receive remission of sins.

The Gospel [Luke 24[5]

BEHOLD, two of the disciples went that same day to a town called Emmaus, which was from Jerusalem about sixty furlongs. And they talked together of all the things that had happened. And it chanced while they commoned[6] together and reasoned, Jesus himself drew near, and went with them. But their eyes were holden[7] that they should not know him. And he said unto them, What manner of communications are these that ye have one to another as ye walk, and are sad? And the one of them (whose name was Cleophas) answered and said unto him, Art thou only a stranger in Jerusalem, and hast not known the things which have chanced there in these days? He said unto them, What things? And they said unto him, Of Jesus of Nazareth, which was a prophet, mighty in deed and word before God and all the people; and how the high priests and our rulers delivered him to be condemned to death, and have crucified him. But we trusted that it had been he which should have redeemed Israel. And as touching all these things, today is even the third day that they were done. Yea and certain women also of our company made us astonied,[8] which came early unto the sepulcher,

---

[4] *Quick:* living.

[5] Text has "23"; misprint.

[6] *Commoned:* conferred, conversed.

[7] *Holden:* held, "kept from recognizing him" (RSV).

[8] *Astonied:* astonished.

and found not his body; and came, saying, that they had seen a vision of angels, which said that he was alive. And certain of them which were with us went to the sepulcher, and found it even so as the women had said, but him they saw not. And he said unto them, O fools and slow of heart to believe all that the prophets have spoken. Ought not Christ to have suffered these things, and to enter into his glory? And he began at Moses[9] and all the prophets, and interpreted unto them in all Scriptures which were written of him. And they drew nigh unto the town, which they went unto. And he made as though he would have gone further. And they constrained him, saying, Abide with us, for it draweth toward night, and the day is far passed. And he went in to tarry with them. And it came to pass as he sat at meat with them, he took bread and blessed it, and brake,[10] and gave to them. And their eyes were opened, and they knew him, and he vanished out of their sight. And they said between themselves, Did not our hearts burn within us while he talked with us by the way, and opened to us the Scriptures? And they rose up the same hour, and returned to Jerusalem, and found the eleven gathered together, and them that were with them, saying, The Lord is risen indeed, and hath appeared to Simon. And they told what things were done in the way, and how they knew him in breaking of bread.

Tuesday in Easter Week

The Collect

ALMIGHTY Father, which hast given thy only Son to die for our sins, and to rise again for our justification: Grant us so to put away the leaven of malice and wickedness, that we

---

[9] "Moises" in text.

[10] *Brake:* broke.

may alway serve thee in pureness of living and truth; through Jesus Christ our Lord.

The Epistle [Acts 13

YE men and brethren, children of the generation of Abraham, and whosoever among you feareth God: to you is this word of salvation sent. For the inhabiters of Jerusalem and their rulers, because they knew him not, nor yet the voices of the Prophets, which are read every Sabbath day, they have fulfilled them in condemning him. And when they found no cause of death in him, yet desired they Pilate to kill him. And when they had fulfilled all that were written of him, they took him down from the tree, and put him in a sepulcher. But God raised him again from death the third day, and he was seen many days of them which went with him from Galilee to Jerusalem, which are witnesses unto the people. And we declare unto you, how that the promise (which was made unto the fathers) God hath fulfilled unto their children (even unto us), in that he raised up Jesus again. Even as it is written in the second Psalm: Thou art my Son, this day have I begotten thee.[1] As concerning that he raised him up from death, now no more to return to corruption, he said on this wise, The holy promises made to David, will I give faithfully unto you.[2] Wherefore he saith also in another place, Thou shalt not suffer thine Holy[3] to see corruption.[4] For David (after that he had in his time fulfilled the will of God) fell on sleep, and was laid unto his fathers, and saw corruption. But he whom God raised again, saw no corruption. Be it known unto you therefore (ye men and brethren) that through this man is preached unto you forgiveness of sins, and that by him all that believe are justi-

[1] Ps. 2:7.
[2] Isa. 55:3.
[3] *Holy:* "Holy One" (RSV).
[4] Ps. 16:10.

fied from all things, from which ye could not be justified by the law of Moses. Beware therefore, lest that fall on you which is spoken of in the Prophets, Behold ye despisers and wonder, and perish ye, for I do a work in your days, which ye shall not believe though a man declare it unto you.[5]

The Gospel [Luke 24

JESUS stood in the mids[6] of his disciples, and said unto them, Peace be unto you. It is I, fear not. But they were abashed and afraid, and supposed that they had seen a spirit. And he said unto them, Why are ye troubled, and why do thoughts arise in your hearts? Behold my hands and my feet, that it is even I myself. Handle me and see, for a spirit hath no flesh and bones, as ye see me have. And when he had thus spoken, he showed them his hands and his feet. And while they yet believed not for joy, and wondered, he said unto them, Have ye here any meat? And they offered him a piece of a broiled fish, and of an honeycomb. And he took it, and did eat before them. And he said unto them, These are the words which I spake unto you, while I was yet with you, that all must needs be fulfilled which were written of me in the law of Moses, and in the Prophets, and in the Psalms. Then opened he their wits[7] that they might understand the Scriptures and said unto them, Thus it is written, and thus it behooved Christ to suffer, and to rise again from death the third day, and that repentance and remission of sins should be preached in his name among all nations, and must begin at Jerusalem. And ye are witnesses of these things.

[5] Hab. 1:5.
[6] *Mids:* middle.
[7] *Wits:* minds.

The First Sunday after Easter

The Collect

ALMIGHTY God, etc. As at the Communion on Easter Day.

The Epistle [1 John 5

ALL that is born of God, overcometh the world. And this is the victory that overcometh the world, even our faith. Who is he that overcometh the world, but he that believeth that Jesus is the Son of God? This Jesus Christ is he that came by water and blood, not by water only, but by water and blood. And it is the Spirit that beareth witness, because the Spirit is truth. For there are three which bear record in heaven: the Father, the Word, and the Holy Ghost, and these three are one. And there are three which bear record in earth: the Spirit, and water, and blood, and these three are one. If we receive the witness of men, the witness of God is greater. For this is the witness of God that is greater, which he testified of his Son. He that believeth on the Son of God, hath the witness in himself. He that believeth not God, hath made him a liar, because he believeth not the record that God gave his Son. And this is the record, how that God hath given unto us eternal life, and this life is in his Son. He that hath the Son, hath life; and he that hath not the Son of God, hath not life.

The Gospel [John 20

THE same day at night, which was the first day of the Sabbaths,[1] when the doors were shut (where the disciples were assembled together for fear of the Jews) came Jesus and stood

---

[1] *The first day of the Sabbaths:* "the first day of the week" (RSV).

in the mids,[2] and said unto them, Peace be unto you. And when he had so said, he showed unto them his hands and his side. Then were the disciples glad when they saw the Lord. Then said Jesus to them again, Peace be unto you. As my Father sent me, even so send I you also. And when he had said these words, he breathed on them, and said unto them, Receive ye the Holy Ghost. Whosoever's sins ye remit, they are remitted unto them. And whosoever's sins ye retain, they are retained.

The Second Sunday after Easter

The Collect

ALMIGHTY God, which hast given thy holy[1] Son to be unto us, both a sacrifice for sin, and also an example of godly life: Give us the grace that we may always most thankfully receive that his inestimable benefit, and also daily endeavor ourselves to follow the blessed steps of his most holy life.

The Epistle [1 Pet. 2

THIS is thankworthy, if a man for conscience toward God endure grief, and suffer wrong undeserved. For what praise is it, if when ye be buffeted for your faults, ye take it patiently? But and if when ye do well, ye suffer wrong and take it patiently, then is there thank with God. For hereunto verily were ye called. For Christ also suffered for us, leaving us an ensample[2] that ye should follow his steps, which did no sin, neither was there guile

---

[2] *Mids:* middle.

[1] *Holy:* This would seem to be an error, since the author of the prayer was using the opening Collect for Easter Tuesday, where the word is *unigentum*, that is to say, "only" or "only begotten"; 1596 Prayer Book has "thine only."

[2] *Ensample:* example.

found in his mouth; which when he was reviled, reviled not again, when he suffered, he threatened not, but committed the vengeance to him that judgeth righteously; which his own self bore our sins in his body on the tree, that we being delivered from sin, should live unto righteousness. By whose stripes ye were healed. For ye were as sheep going astray, but are now turned unto the shepherd, and bishop of your souls.

The Gospel [John 10

CHRIST said unto his disciples, I am the good shepherd: a good shepherd giveth his life for the sheep. An hired servant, and he which is not the shepherd (neither the sheep are his own) seeth the wolf coming and leaveth the sheep and fleeth, and the wolf catcheth and scattereth the sheep. The hired servant fleeth because he is an hired servant and careth not for the sheep. I am the good shepherd, and know my sheep, and am known of mine. As my Father knoweth me, even so know I also my Father. And I give my life for the sheep. And other sheep I have which are not of this fold: them also must I bring, and they shall hear my voice, and there shall be one fold and one shepherd.

The Third Sunday

The Collect

ALMIGHTY God, which showeth to all men that be in error the light of thy truth, to the intent that they may return into the way of righteousness: Grant unto all them that be admitted into the fellowship of Christ's religion, that they may eschew those things that be contrary to their profession, and follow all such things as be agreeable to the same; through our Lord Jesus Christ.

The Epistle [1 Pet. 2

DEARLY beloved, I beseech you as strangers and pilgrims, abstain from fleshly lusts which fight against the soul, and see that ye have honest conversation among the Gentiles, that whereas they backbite you as evildoers, they may see your good works, and praise God in the day of visitation. Submit yourselves therefore to every man for the Lord's sake, whether it be unto the king as unto the chief head, either unto rulers, as unto them that are sent of him for the punishment of evildoers, but for the laud of them that do well. For so is the will of God, that with well doing, ye may stop the mouths of foolish and ignorant men: as free, and not as having the liberty for a cloak of maliciousness, but even as the servants of God. Honor all men. Love brotherly fellowship. Fear God. Honor the king.

The Gospel [John 16

JESUS said to his disciples, After a while ye shall not see me, and again after a while ye shall see me, for I go to the Father. Then said some of his disciples between themselves, What is this that he saith unto us, After a while ye shall not see me, and again after a while ye shall see me, and that I go to the Father? They said therefore, What is this that he saith, After a while? We cannot tell what he saith. Jesus perceived that they would ask him, and said unto them, Ye inquire of this between yourselves, because I said, After a while ye shall not see me, and again after a while ye shall see me. Verily, verily, I say unto you, ye shall weep and lament, but contrariwise the world shall rejoice. Ye shall sorrow, but your sorrow shall be turned to joy. A woman when she travaileth hath sorrow, because her hour is come. But as soon as she is delivered of the child, she remembereth no more the anguish for joy that a man is born into the world. And ye now therefore have sorrow, but I will see you again, and your hearts shall rejoice, and your joy shall no man take from you.

The Fourth Sunday

The Collect

ALMIGHTY God, which dost make the minds of all faithful men to be of one will: Grant unto thy people, that they may love the thing which thou commandest, and desire that which thou dost promise; that among the sundry and manifold changes of the world, our hearts may surely there be fixed, where as true joys are to be found; through Jesus Christ our Lord.

The Epistle [James 1

EVERY good gift, and every perfect gift, is from above, and cometh down from the Father of lights, with whom is no variableness, neither shadow of change. Of his own will begat[1] he us with the word of truth, that we should be the first fruits of his creatures. Wherefore (dear brethren) let every man be swift to hear, slow to speak, slow to wrath. For the wrath of man worketh not that which is righteous before God. Wherefore lay apart all filthiness and superfluity of maliciousness, and receive with meekness the word that is grafted in you, which is able to save your souls.

The Gospel [John 16

JESUS said unto his disciples, Now I go my way to him that sent me, and none of you asketh me whether[2] I go. But because I have said such things unto you, your hearts are full of sorrow. Nevertheless I tell you the truth, it is expedient for you that I go away. For if I go not away, that Comforter[3] will not

[1] *Begat:* begot.
[2] Great Bible and 1549 and 1552 Books have "whither," but it is "whether" in 1559 Grafton.
[3] *Comforter:* Παράκλητος, Paraclete, Holy Spirit, Strengthener.

163

come unto you. But if I depart, I will send him unto you. And when he is come, he will rebuke the world of sin, and of righteousness, and of judgment. Of sin, because they believe not on me. Of righteousness, because I go to my Father, and ye shall see me no more. Of judgment, because the prince of this world is judged already. I have yet many things to say unto you, but ye cannot bear them away now. Howbeit when he is come (which is the Spirit of truth), he will lead you into all truth. He shall not speak of himself, but whatsoever he shall hear, that shall he speak; and he will show you things to come. He shall glorify me, for he shall receive of mine, and shall show unto you. All things that the Father hath are mine; therefore said I unto you, that he shall take of mine, and show unto you.

The Fifth Sunday

The Collect

LORD, from whom all good things do come: Grant us thy humble servants, that by thy holy inspiration we may think those things that be good, and by thy merciful guiding may perform the same; through our Lord Jesus Christ.

The Epistle [James 1

SEE that ye be doers of the word, and not hearers only, deceiving your own selves. For if any man hear the word, and declareth not the same by his works, he is like unto a man beholding his bodily face in a glass. For as soon as he hath looked on himself he goeth his way, and forgetteth immediately what his fashion was. But whoso looketh in the perfect law of liberty, and continueth therein (if he be not a forgetful hearer, but a doer of the work) the same shall be happy in his deed. If any man emong[1] you seem to be devout, and refraineth not his tongue, but deceiveth his own heart, this man's devotion is in vain. Pure devotion, and undefiled before God the Father is this: to visit the fatherless and widows in their adversity, and to keep himself unspotted of the world.

The Gospel [John 16

VERILY, verily, I say unto you, whatsoever ye ask the Father in my name, he will give it you. Hitherto have ye asked nothing in my name. Ask and ye shall receive, that your joy may be full. These things have I spoken unto you by proverbs. The time will come, when I shall no more speak unto you by proverbs, but I shall show you plainly from my Father. At that day shall ye ask in my name, and I say not unto you that I will speak unto my Father for you, for the Father himself loveth you, because ye have loved me, and have believed that I came out from God. I went out from the Father, and came into the world. Again, I leave the world, and go to the Father. His disciples said unto him, Lo, now thou talkest plainly, and speakest no proverb. Now are we sure that thou knowest all things, and needest not that any man should ask thee any question; therefore believe we that thou camest from God. Jesus answered them, Now ye do believe. Behold, the hour draweth nigh and is already come, that ye shall be scattered every man to his own, and shall leave me alone. And yet am I not alone, for the Father is with me. These words have I spoken unto you, that in me ye might have peace, for in the world shall ye have tribulation: but be of good cheer, I have overcome the world.

[1] *Emong:* among.

The Ascension Day

The Collect

GRANT, we beseech thee Almighty God, that like as we do believe thy only begotten Son our Lord to have ascended into the heavens; so we may also in heart and mind thither ascend, and with him continually dwell.

The Epistle [Acts 1

IN the former treatise (dear Theophilus) we have spoken of all that Jesus began to do and teach, until the day in which he was taken up, after that he through the Holy Ghost had given commandments unto the Apostles, whom he had chosen; to whom also he showed himself alive after his passion (and that by many tokens) appearing unto them forty days, and speaking of the kingdom of God; and gathered them together, and commanded them that they should not depart from Jerusalem, but to wait for the promise of the Father, whereof (saith he) ye have heard of me. For John truly baptized with water, but ye shall be baptized with the Holy Ghost, after these few days. When they therefore were come together, they asked of him, saying, Lord, wilt thou at this time restore again the kingdom of Israel? And he said unto them, It is not for you to know the times or the seasons which the Father hath put in his own power. But ye shall receive power after the Holy Ghost is come upon you. And ye shall be witnesses unto me, not only in Jerusalem, but also in all Jewry, and in all Samaria, and even unto the world's end. And when he had spoken these things, while they beheld, he was taken up on high, and a cloud received him up out of their sight. And while they looked steadfastly up toward heaven as he went, behold, two men stood by them in white apparel, which also said, Ye men of Galilee, why stand ye gazing up into heaven? This same Jesus which is taken up from you into heaven, shall so come, even as ye have seen him go into heaven.

The Gospel [Mark 16

JESUS appeared unto the eleven as they sat at meat, and cast in their teeth their unbelief and hardness of heart, because they believed not them which had seen that he was risen again from the dead. And he said unto them, Go ye into all the world, and preach the gospel to all creatures: he that believeth and is baptized, shall be saved. But he that believeth not shall be damned. And these tokens shall follow them that believe. In my name they shall cast out devils, they shall speak with new tongues, they shall drive away serpents. And if they drink any deadly thing it shall not hurt them. They shall lay their hand on the sick and they shall recover. So then when the Lord had spoken unto them, he was received into heaven, and is on the right hand of God. And they went forth, and preached everywhere, the Lord working with them, and confirming the word with miracles following.

The Sunday after the Ascension Day

The Collect

O GOD, the king of glory, which hast exalted thine only Son Jesus Christ, with great triumph unto thy kingdom in heaven: We beseech thee leave us not comfortless, but send to us thine Holy Ghost to comfort[1] us, and exalt us unto the same place whether[2] our Savior Christ is gone before; who liveth and reigneth, etc.

---

[1] *Comfortless . . . comfort:* without strength . . . strengthen.

[2] 1549 and 1552 Books have "whither." Cf. Brightman, *English Rite,* I, 438–39.

The Epistle [1 Pet. 4

THE end of all things is at hand. Be ye therefore sober, and watch unto prayer. But above all things have fervent love among yourselves, for love shall cover the multitude of sins. Be ye harborous[3] one to another without grudging. As every man hath received the gift, even so minister the same one to another, as good ministers of the manifold graces of God. If any man speak, let him talk as the words of God. If any man minister, let him do it as of the ability which God ministereth to him, that God in all things may be glorified through Jesus Christ, to whom be praise and dominion for ever and ever. Amen.

The Gospel [John 15

WHEN the Comforter[4] is come whom I will send unto you from the Father (even the Spirit of truth, which proceedeth of the Father) he shall testify of me. And ye shall bear witness also, because ye have been with me from the beginning. These things have I said unto you, because ye should not be offended. They shall excommunicate you; yea, the time shall come, that whosoever killeth you, will think that he doth God service. And such things will they do unto you, because they have not known the Father, neither yet me. But these things I have told you, that when the time is come, ye may remember then that I told you.

Whitsunday

The Collect

GOD which as upon this day has taught the hearts of thy faithful people, by the sending to them the light of thy Holy Spirit: Grant us by the same Spirit to have a right judg-

---

[3] *Harborous:* hospitable.

[4] *Comforter:* Παράκλητος, Paraclete, Holy Spirit, Strengthener.

ment in all things, and evermore to rejoice in his holy comfort;[1] through the merits of Christ Jesu our Savior, who liveth and reigneth with thee in the unity of the same Spirit, one God, world without end.

The Epistle [Acts 2

WHEN the fifty days were come to an end, they were all with one accord together in one place. And suddenly there came a sound from heaven, as it had been the coming of a mighty wind, and it filled all the house where they sat. And there appeared unto them cloven tongues, like as they had been of fire, and it sat upon each one of them. And they were all filled with the Holy Ghost, and began to speak with other tongues, even as the same Spirit gave them utterance. Then were dwelling at Jerusalem Jews, devout men out of every nation of them that are under heaven. When this was noised about, the multitude came together and were astonied,[2] because that every man heard them speak with his own language. They wondered all and marveled, saying among themselves, Behold, are not all these which speak of Galilee? And how hear we every man his own tongue wherein we were born? Parthians, and Medes, and Elamites, and the inhabiters of Mesopotamia, and of Jewry, and of Cappadocia, of Pontus and Asia, Phrygia and Pamphylia, of Egypt, and of the parties[3] of Libya, which is beside Cyrene,[4] and strangers of Rome, Jews and proselytes, Greeks and Arabians, we have heard them speak in our own tongues the great works of God.

[1] *Comfort:* strength.
[2] *Astonied:* astonished.
[3] *Parties:* parts.
[4] "Syren" in text.

The Gospel [John 14⁵

JESUS said unto his disciples, If ye love me, keep my commandments. And I will pray the Father, and he shall give you
another Comforter,⁶ that he may abide with you forever, even
the Spirit of truth, whom the world cannot receive, because the
world seeth him not, neither knoweth him. But ye know him,
for he dwelleth with you, and shall be in you. I will not leave
you comfortless, but will come to you. Yet a little while, and the
world seeth me no more, but ye see me. For I live, and ye shall
live. That day shall ye know that I am in my Father, and you
in me, and I in you. He that hath my commandments, and
keepeth them, the same is he that loveth me. And he that loveth
me, shall be loved of my Father, and I will love him, and will
show mine own self unto him. Judas saith unto him (not Judas
Iscariot),⁷ Lord, what is done that thou wilt show thyself unto
us, and not unto the world? Jesus answered, and said unto them,
If a man love me, he will keep my sayings, and my Father will
love him, and we will come unto him, and dwell with him. He
that loveth me not, keepeth not my sayings. And the word which
ye hear, is not mine, but the Father's which sent me. These things
have I spoken unto you, being yet present with you. But the
Comforter, which is the Holy Ghost whom my Father will send
in my name, he shall teach you all things, and bring all things to
your remembrance, whatsoever I have said unto you. Peace I
leave with you, my peace I give unto you. Not as the world
giveth, give I unto you. Let not your hearts be grieved, neither
fear. Ye have heard how I said unto you, I go, and come again
unto you. If ye loved me, ye would verily rejoice, because I
said, I go unto the Father. For the Father is greater than I. And
now have I showed you before it come, that when it is come to
pass, ye might believe. Hereafter will I not talk many words

---

⁵ Text has "13"; misprint.
⁶ *Comforter:* Παράκλητος, Paraclete, Holy Spirit, Strengthener.
⁷ "Iscarioth" in text.

unto you. For the prince of this world cometh, and hath nought in me. But that the world may know that I love the Father. And as the Father gave me commandment, even so do I.

Monday in Whitsun Week

The Collect

GOD which, etc. (As upon Whitsunday.)

The Epistle [Acts 10

THEN Peter opened his mouth and said, Of a truth I perceive that there is no respect of persons with God, but in all people, he that feareth him, and worketh righteousness, is accepted with him. Ye know the preaching that God sent unto the children of Israel, preaching peace by Jesus Christ which is Lord over all things. Which preaching was published throughout all Jewry (and began in Galilee after the baptism which John preached) how God anointed Jesus of Nazareth with the Holy Ghost and with power. Which Jesus went about doing good, and healing all that were oppressed of the devil. For God was with him. And we are witnesses of all things which he did in the land of the Jews, and at Jerusalem; whom they slew and hanged on a tree. Him God raised up the third day, and showed him openly, not to all the people, but unto us witnesses (chosen before of God for the same intent) which did eat and drink with him after he arose from death. And he commanded us to preach unto the people, and to testify that it is he which was ordained of God to be the judge of quick[1] and dead. To him give all the prophets witness, that through his name whosoever believeth in him, shall receive remission of sins. While Peter yet spake these words, the Holy Ghost fell on all them which heard the preach-

---

[1] *Quick:* living.

ing. And they of the circumcision which believed, were astonied,[2] as many as came with Peter, because that on the Gentiles also was shed out the gift of the Holy Ghost. For they heard them speak with tongues, and magnify God. Then answered Peter, Can any man forbid water that these should not be baptized which have received the Holy Ghost as well as we? And he commanded them to be baptized in the name of the Lord. Then prayed they him to tarry a few days.

The Gospel [John 3

SO God loved the world, that he gave his only begotten Son, that whosoever believeth in him, should not perish, but have everlasting life. For God sent not his Son into the world to condemn the world, but that the world through him might be saved. But he that believeth on him, is not condemned. But he that believeth not, is condemned already, because he hath not believed in the name of the only begotten Son of God. And this is the condemnation, that light is come into the world, and men loved darkness more than light, because their deeds were evil. For every one that evil doeth, hateth the light, neither cometh to the light, lest his deeds should be reproved. But he that doth the truth, cometh to the light, that his deeds may be known, how that they are wrought[3] in God.

The Tuesday after Whitsunday

The Collect

GOD which, etc. (As upon Whitsunday.)

[2] *Astonied:* astonished.

[3] *Wrought:* done; Lat., *quia in deo sunt facta.* Cf. Brightman, *English Rite,* I, 450.

The Epistle [Acts 8

WHEN the Apostles which were at Jerusalem heard say, that Samaria had received the Word of God, they sent unto them Peter and John. Which when they were come down, prayed for them that they might receive the Holy Ghost. For as yet he was come on none of them, but they were baptized only in the name of Christ Jesu. Then laid they their hands on them, and they received the Holy Ghost.

The Gospel [John 10

VERILY, verily, I say unto you, he that entereth not in by the door into the sheepfold, but climbeth up some other way, the same is a thief and a murderer. But he that entereth in by the door, is the shepherd of the sheep. To him the porter openeth, and the sheep hear his voice, and he calleth his own sheep by name, and leadeth them out. And when he hath sent forth his own sheep, he goeth before them, and the sheep follow him, for they know his voice. A stranger will they not follow, but will flee from him, for they know not the voice of strangers. This proverb spake Jesus unto them, but they understood not what things they were which he spake unto them. Then said Jesus unto them again, Verily, verily, I say unto you, I am the door of the sheep. All (even as many as came before me) are thieves and murderers, but the sheep did not hear them. I am the door; by me if any enter in, he shall be safe, and shall go in and out, and find pasture. A thief cometh not but for to steal, kill, and destroy. I am come that they might have life, and that they might have it more abundantly.

Trinity Sunday

The Collect

ALMIGHTY and everlasting God, which hast given unto us thy servants grace, by the confession of a true faith, to acknowledge the glory of the eternal Trinity, and in the power of the divine majesty to worship the unity: We beseech thee, that through the steadfastness of this faith we may evermore be defended from all adversity, which livest and reignest, one God, world without end. Amen.

The Epistle [Apoc. 4

AFTER this I looked, and behold, a door was open in heaven, and the first voice which I heard, was as it were of a trumpet, talking with me, which said, Come up hither, and I will show thee things which must be fulfilled hereafter. And immediately I was in the Spirit. And behold, a seat was set in heaven, and one sat on the seat. And he that sat was to look upon like unto a jasper stone, and a sardine stone.[1] And there was a rainbow about the seat, in sight like unto an emerald. And about the seat were twenty-four seats. And upon the seats twenty-four elders, sitting clothed in white raiment, and had on their heads crowns of gold. And out of the seat proceeded lightnings, and thunderings, and voices. And there were seven lamps of fire burning before the seat, which are the seven Spirits of God. And before the seat there was a sea of glass like unto crystal, and in the mids[2] of the seat, and round about the seat, were four beasts full of eyes, before and behind. And the first beast was like a lion, and the second beast like a calf, and the third beast had a face as a man, and the fourth beast was like a flying eagle. And the four beasts had each of them six wings about him, and they were full of eyes within.

[1] *Sardine stone:* "carnelian" (RSV).
[2] *Mids:* middle, midst.

And they did not rest day, neither night, saying, Holy, holy, holy, Lord God Almighty, which was, and is, and is to come. And when those beasts gave glory and honor, and thanks to him that sat on the seat (which liveth for ever and ever) the twenty-four elders fell down before him,[3] that sat on the throne, and worshiped him that liveth forever, and cast their crowns before the throne, saying, Thou art worthy O Lord (our God) to receive glory and honor, and power, for thou hast created all things, and for thy will's sake they are and were created.

The Gospel [John 3

THERE was a man of the Pharisees named Nicodemus,[4] a ruler of the Jews. The same came to Jesus by night, and said unto him, Rabbi, we know that thou art a teacher come from God, for no man could do such miracles as thou doest, except God were with him. Jesus answered and said unto him, Verily, verily, I say unto thee, Except a man be born from above, he cannot see the kingdom of God. Nicodemus said unto him, How can a man be born when he is old? Can he enter into his mother's womb and be born again? Jesus answered, Verily, verily, I say unto thee, Except a man be born of water, and of the Spirit, he cannot enter into the kingdom of God. That which is born of the flesh, is flesh, and that which is born of the Spirit, is spirit. Marvel not thou that I said to thee, Ye must be born from above. The wind bloweth where it lusteth,[5] and thou hearest the sound thereof, but thou canst not tell whence it cometh, nor whether[6] he goeth. So is every one that is born of the Spirit. Nicodemus answered and said unto him, How can these things be? Jesus answered and said unto him, Art thou a master in Israel, and knowest not these things? Verily, verily, I say unto thee, We

---

[3] Text has "on"; misprint.

[4] "Nichodemus" in text.

[5] *Lusteth:* chooseth.

[6] 1549 and 1552 Books have "whither." Cf. p. 167, n. 2 above.

speak that we know, and testify that we have seen, and ye receive not our witness. If I have told you earthly things, and ye believe not, how shall ye believe if I tell you of heavenly things? And no man ascendeth up to heaven, but he that came down from heaven, even the Son of man which is in heaven. And as Moses⁷ lift up the serpent in the wilderness, even so must the Son of man be lift up, that whosoever believeth in him perish not, but have everlasting life.

The First Sunday after Trinity Sunday

The Collect

GOD the strength of all them that trust in thee: Mercifully accept our prayers; and because the weakness of our mortal nature can do no good thing without thee, grant us the help of thy grace, that in keeping of thy commandments, we may please thee both in will and deed; through Jesus Christ our Lord.

The Epistle [1 John 4

DEARLY beloved, let us love one another, for love cometh of God. And everyone that loveth, is born of God, and knoweth God. He that loveth not, knoweth not God, for God is love. In this appeareth the love of God to usward,¹ because that God sent his only begotten Son into the world, that we might live through him. Herein is love, not that we loved God, but that he loved us, and sent his Son to be the agreement² for our sins. Dearly beloved, if God so loved us, we ought also one to love another. No man hath seen God at any time. If we love one another, God dwelleth in us, and his love is perfect in us. Hereby know

---

⁷ "Moyses" in text.

¹ 1661 Book has "towards us." Cf. Brightman, *English Rite*, II, 463.

² *Agreement:* "expiation" (RSV).

we that we dwell in him and he in us, because he hath given us of his Spirit. And we have seen and do testify that the Father sent the Son to be the Savior of the world. Whosoever confesseth that Jesus is the Son of God, in him dwelleth God, and he in God. And we have known and believed the love that God hath to us. God is love, and he that dwelleth in love dwelleth in God, and God in him. Herein is the love perfect in us, that we should trust in the day of judgment. For as he is, even so are we in this world. There is no fear in love, but perfect love casteth out fear, for fear hath painfulness. He that feareth, is not perfect in love. We love him, for he loved us first. If a man say, I love God, and yet hate his brother, he is a liar. For how can he that loveth not his brother whom he hath seen, love God whom he hath not seen? And this commandment have we of him, that he which loveth God, should love his brother also.

The Gospel [Luke 16

THERE was a certain rich man, which was clothed in purple and fine white,[3] and fared deliciously every day. And there was a certain beggar named Lazarus, which lay at his gate full of sores, desiring to be refreshed with the crumbs which fell from the rich man's board, and no man gave unto him. The dogs came also and licked his sores. And it fortuned that the beggar died, and was carried by the angels into Abraham's bosom. The rich man also died and was buried. And being in hell in torments, he lift up his eyes and saw Abraham afar off, and Lazarus in his bosom, and he cried and said, Father Abraham, have mercy on me, and send Lazarus, that he may dip the tip of his finger in water, and cool my tongue, for I am tormented in this flame. But Abraham said, Son, remember that thou in thy life-time receivedst thy pleasure, and contrariwise Lazarus received pain.

---

[3] *Fine White:* Lat., *bysso*; a fine kind of flax and the linen made from it. Cf. Brightman, *English Rite*, II, 464. On the Greek βύσσος, cf. H. B. Liddell and R. Scott, *A Greek-English Lexicon*, new ed. (Oxford, 1966), p. 334.

But now he is comforted, and thou art punished. Beyond all this, between us and you there is a great space set, so that they which would go from hence to you, cannot, neither may come from thence to us. Then he said, I pray thee therefore Father, send him to my father's house (for I have five brethren) for to warn them, lest they come also into this place of torment. Abraham said unto him, They have Moses[4] and the prophets; let them hear them. And he said, Nay, Father Abraham, but if one come unto them from the dead, they will repent. He said unto him, If they hear not Moses and the prophets, neither will they believe though one rose from death again.

The Second Sunday

The Collect

LORD, make us to have a perpetual fear and love of thy holy name, for thou never failest to help and govern them, whom thou dost bring up in thy steadfast love; grant this, etc.

The Epistle [1 John 3

MARVEL not my brethren, though the world hate you. We know that we are translated from death unto life, because we love the brethren. He that loveth not his brother, abideth in death. Whosoever hateth his brother is a manslayer.[1] And ye know that no manslayer hath eternal life abiding in him. Hereby perceive we love, because he gave his life for us, and we ought to give our lives for the brethren. But whoso hath this world's good, and seeth his brother have need, and shutteth up his compassion from him, how dwelleth the love of God in him? My babes, let us not love in word, neither in tongue, but in deed

---

[4] "Moyses" in text, here and in last sentence.
[1] Text has "manslear."

and in verity.[2] Hereby we know that we are of the verity, and can quiet our hearts before him. For if our heart condemn us, God is greater than our heart, and knoweth all things. Dearly beloved, if our heart condemn us not, then have we trust to God-ward.[3] And whatsoever we ask, we receive of him, because we keep his commandments, and do those things which are pleasant in his sight. And this is his commandment, that we believe on the name of his Son Jesus Christ, and love one another as he gave commandment. And he that keepeth his commandments dwell-eth in him, and he in him. And hereby we know that he abideth in us, even by the Spirit which he hath given us.

The Gospel [Luke 14

A CERTAIN man ordained a great supper, and bade many, and sent his servant at suppertime, to say to them that were bidden, Come, for all things are now ready. And they all at once began to make excuse. The first said unto him, I have bought a farm, and I must needs go and see it. I pray thee have me excused. And another said, I have bought five yoke of oxen, and I go to prove them. I pray thee have me excused. And an-other said, I have married a wife, and therefore I cannot come. And the servant returned and brought his master word again thereof. Then was the good man of the house displeased and said unto his servant, Go out quickly into the streets and quarters of the city and bring in hither the poor and feeble, and the halt and blind. And the servant said, Lord, it is done as thou hast commanded and yet there is room. And the lord said unto the servant, Go out unto the highways and hedges, and compel them to come in that my house may be filled. For I say unto you, that none of these men which were bidden shall taste of my supper.

[2] *Verity:* truth.
[3] *To Godward:* toward God.

The Third Sunday

The Collect

LORD, we beseech thee mercifully to hear us, and unto whom thou hast given an hearty desire to pray: Grant that by thy mighty aid we may be defended; through Jesus Christ our Lord.

The Epistle [1 Pet. 5

SUBMIT yourselves every man one to another, knit yourselves together in lowliness of mind. For God resisteth the proud, and giveth grace to the humble. Submit yourselves therefore under the mighty hand of God, that he may exalt you when the time is come. Cast all your care upon him, for he careth for you. Be sober, and watch, for your adversary the devil, as a roaring lion, walketh about, seeking whom he may devour; whom resist steadfast in the faith, knowing that the same afflictions are appointed unto your brethren that are in the world. But the God of all grace which hath called us unto his eternal glory by Christ Jesu, shall his own self (after that ye have suffered a little affliction) make you perfect, settle, strength[1] and stablish you. To him be glory and dominion for ever and ever. Amen.

The Gospel [Luke 15

THEN resorted unto him all the publicans and sinners for to hear him. And the Pharisees and scribes murmured, saying, He receiveth sinners, and eateth with them. But he put forth this parable unto them, saying, What man among you having an hundred sheep, if he lose one of them, doth not leave ninety and nine in the wilderness, and goeth after that which is lost, until he find it? And when he hath found it, he layeth it on his shoulders

[1] *Strength*: strengthen.

with joy. And as soon as he cometh home, he calleth together his lovers[2] and neighbors, saying unto them, Rejoice with me, for I have found my sheep which was lost. I say unto you, that likewise joy shall be in heaven over one sinner that repenteth, more than over ninety and nine just persons which need no repentance. Either what woman having ten groats,[3] if she lose one, doth not light a candle and sweep the house, and seek diligently till she find it? And when she hath found it, she calleth her lovers and her neighbors together, saying, Rejoice with me, for I have found the groat which I lost. Likewise, I say unto you, shall there be joy in the presence of the angels of God over one sinner that repenteth.

The Fourth Sunday

The Collect

GOD, the protector of all that trust in thee, without whom nothing is strong, nothing is holy: Increase and multiply upon us thy mercy, that thou being our ruler and guide, we may so pass through things temporal, that we finally lose not the things eternal; grant this heavenly Father, for Jesus Christ's sake our Lord.

The Epistle [Rom. 8

I SUPPOSE that the afflictions of this life are not worthy of the glory which shall be showed upon us.[1] For the fervent desire of the creature abideth, looking when the sons of God

---

[2] *Lovers:* friends; Lat., *amicos*, friend; Gk., φίλους, beloved, dear one. Cf. Liddell and Scott, *Greek-English Lexicon*, p. 1939.

[3] *Groats:* coins, each equal to four pence; not issued after 1662 (OED).

[1] 1661 Book has "revealed in us." Cf. Brightman, *English Rite*, II, 475.

shall appear, because the creature is subdued to vanity against the will thereof, but for his will, which hath subdued the same in hope. For the same creature shall be delivered from the bondage of corruption, into the glorious liberty of the sons of God. For we know that every creature groaneth with us also, and travaileth in pain, even unto this time. Not only it, but we also which have the first fruits of the Spirit, mourn in ourselves also, and wait for the adoption of the children of God, even the deliverance of our bodies.

The Gospel [Luke 6

BE ye merciful as your Father also is merciful. Judge not, and ye shall not be judged. Condemn not, and ye shall not be condemned. Forgive, and ye shall be forgiven. Give, and it shall be given unto you; good measure, and pressed down, and shaken together, and running over, shall men give into your bosoms. For with the same measure that ye mete[2] withal, shall other men mete to you again. And he put forth a similitude unto them. Can the blind lead the blind? Do they not both fall into the ditch? The disciple is not above his master. Every man shall be perfect, even as his master is. Why seest thou a mote in thy brother's eye, but considerest not the beam that is in thine own eye? Either how canst thou say to thy brother, Brother, let me pull out the mote that is in thine eye, when thou seest not the beam that is in thine own eye? First thou hypocrite, cast out the beam out of thine own eye, then shalt thou see perfectly to pull out the mote that is in thy brother's eye.

[2] *Mete:* measure.

The Fifth Sunday

The Collect

GRANT Lord, we beseech thee, that the course of this world may be so peaceably ordered by thy governance, that thy congregation may joyfully serve thee in all godly quietness; through Jesus Christ our Lord.

The Epistle [1 Pet. 3

BE you all of one mind, and of one heart, love as brethren, be pitiful, be courteous, meek, not rendering evil for evil, or rebuke for rebuke, but contrariwise bless, knowing that ye are thereunto called, even that ye should be heirs of the blessing. For he that doth long after life, and loveth to see good days, let him refrain his tongue from evil, and his lips that they speak no guile. Let him eschew evil and do good. Let him seek peace and ensue[1] it. For the eyes of the Lord are over the righteous, and his ears are open unto their prayers. Again, the face of the Lord is over them that do evil. Moreover, who is he that will harm you, if ye follow that which is good? Yea, happy are ye if any trouble happen unto you for righteousness' sake. Be not ye afraid for any terror of them, neither be ye troubled, but sanctify the Lord God in your hearts.

The Gospel [Luke 5

IT came to pass, that when the people pressed upon him to hear the Word of God, he stood by the lake of Gennesaret, and saw two ships stand by the lake's side, but the fishermen were gone out of them, and were washing their nets. And he entered into one of the ships (which pertained to Simon) and prayed him that he would thrust out a little from the land. And

---

[1] *Ensue:* pursue.

he sat down, and taught the people out of the ship. When he had left speaking, he said unto Simon, Launch out into the deep and let slip your nets to make a draught.[2] And Simon answered and said unto him, Master, we have labored all night, and have taken nothing. Nevertheless at thy commandment I will loose forth the net. And when they had so done, they enclosed a great multitude of fishes. But their net brake,[3] and they beckoned to their fellows (which were in the other ship) that they should come and help them. And they came and filled both ships, that they sunk again. When Simon Peter saw this, he fell down at Jesus' knees, saying, Lord, go from me, for I am a sinful man. For he was astonied[4] and all that were with him at the draught of fishes which they had taken. And so was also James and John the sons of Zebedee which were partners with Simon. And Jesus said unto Simon, Fear not, from henceforth thou shalt catch men. And they brought the ships to land, and forsook all and followed him.

The Sixth Sunday

The Collect

GOD which hast prepared to them that love thee such good things as pass all man's understanding: Pour into our hearts such love toward thee, that we, loving thee in all things, may obtain thy promises, which exceed all that we can desire, through Jesus Christ our Lord.

---

[2] *Draught:* action of drawing a net for fish.
[3] *Brake:* broke.
[4] *Astonied:* astonished.

The Epistle [Rom. 6

KNOW ye not, that all we which are baptized in Jesus Christ, are baptized to die with him? We are buried then with him by baptism for to die, that likewise as Christ was raised from death by the glory of the Father, even so we also should walk in a new life. For if we be graft[1] in death like unto him, even so shall we be partakers of the holy resurrection. Knowing this, that your old man is crucified with him also, that the body of sin might utterly be destroyed, that henceforth we should not be servants unto sin. For he that is dead is justified from sin. Wherefore, if we be dead with Christ, we believe that we shall also live with him, knowing that Christ being raised from death, dieth no more. Death hath no more power over him. For as touching that he died, he died concerning sin once. And as touching that he liveth, he liveth unto God. Likewise consider ye also, that ye are dead as touching sin, but are alive unto God, through Jesus Christ our Lord.

The Gospel [Matt. 5

JESUS said unto his disciples, Except your righteousness exceed the righteousness of the scribes and Pharisees, ye cannot enter into the kingdom of heaven. Ye have heard that it was said unto them of old time, Thou shalt not kill; whosoever killeth, shall be in danger of judgment. But I say unto you, that whosoever is angry with his brother (unadvisedly) shall be in danger of judgment. And whosoever say unto his brother, Raca,[2] shall be in danger of a council.[3] But whosoever saith, Thou fool, shall be in danger of hell fire. Therefore, if thou offerest thy gift at the altar, and there rememberest that thy brother hath ought against thee, leave there thine offering before the altar,

---

[1] *Graft:* planted; cf. Lat., *complantati*, planted together.
[2] *Raca:* empty, worthless, good-for-nothing; text has "Racha."
[3] Text has "counsel."

and go thy way first and be reconciled to thy brother, and then come and offer thy gift. Agree with thine adversary quickly, whiles thou art in the way with him, lest at any time the adversary deliver thee to the judge, and the judge deliver thee to the minister, and then thou be cast into prison. Verily I say unto thee, Thou shalt not come out thence, till thou have paid the uttermost farthing.

The Seventh Sunday

The Collect

LORD of all power and might, which art the author and giver of all good things: Graft in our hearts the love of thy name, increase in us true religion, nourish us with all goodness, and of thy great mercy keep us in the same; through Jesus Christ our Lord.

The Epistle [Rom. 6

I SPEAK grossly[1] because of the infirmity of your flesh. As ye have given your members servants to uncleanness, and to iniquity (from one iniquity to another) even so now give over your members servants unto righteousness, that ye may be sanctified. For when ye were servants of sin, ye were void of righteousness. What fruit had you then in those things whereof ye are now ashamed? For the end of those things are death. But now are ye delivered from sin, and made the servants of God, and have your fruit to be sanctified, and the end everlasting life. For the reward of sin is death, but eternal life is the gift of God, through Jesus Christ our Lord.

---

[1] 1661 Book has "I speak after the manner of men"; Lat., *Human dico propter.* Cf. Brightman, *English Rite*, II, 484–85.

The Gospel [Mark 8[2]

IN those days, when there was a very great company, and had nothing to eat, Jesus called his disciples unto him, and said unto them, I have compassion on the people, because they have been now with me three days, and have nothing to eat. And if I send them away fasting to their own houses, they shall faint by the way, for divers of them came from far. And his disciples answered him, Where should a man have bread here in the wilderness to satisfy these? And he asked them, How many loaves have ye? They said, Seven. And he commanded the people to sit down on the ground. And he took the seven loaves. And when he had given thanks, he brake[3] and gave to his disciples to set before them. And they did set them before the people. And they had a few small fishes. And when he had blessed, he commanded them also to be set before them. And they did eat and were sufficed. And they took up of the broken meat that was left seven basketsful. And they that did eat were above four thousand. And he sent them away.

The Eighth Sunday

The Collect

GOD, whose providence is never deceived: We humbly beseech thee, that thou wilt put away from us all hurtful things, and give those things which be profitable for us; through Jesus Christ our Lord.

The Epistle [Rom. 8

BRETHREN, we are debtors, not to the flesh, to live after the flesh. For if ye live after the flesh, ye shall die. But if ye through the Spirit do mortify the deeds of the body, ye shall

---

[2] Text has "Math. 8"; misprint.

[3] *Brake:* broke.

live. For as many as are led by the Spirit of God, they are the
sons of God. For ye have not received the spirit of bondage to
fear any more; but ye have received the Spirit of adoption,
whereby ye cry, Abba, Father. The same Spirit certifieth our
spirit, that we are the sons of God. If we be sons, then are we
also heirs: the heirs I mean of God, and heirs annexed with
Christ; if so be that we suffer with him, that we may be also
glorified together with him.

The Gospel [Matt. 7

BEWARE of false prophets, which come to you in sheep's
clothing, but inwardly they are ravening wolves. Ye shall
know them by their fruits. Do men gather grapes of thorns?
Or figs of thistles? Even so every good tree bringeth forth good
fruits. But a corrupt tree bringeth forth evil fruits. A good tree
cannot bring forth bad fruits, neither can a bad tree bring forth
good fruits. Every tree that bringeth not forth good fruit is
hewn down, and cast into the fire. Wherefore by their fruits ye
shall know them. Not every one that saith unto me, Lord, Lord,
shall enter into the kingdom of heaven: but he that doth the will
of my Father which is in heaven, he shall enter into the kingdom
of heaven.

The Ninth Sunday

The Collect

GRANT to us Lord we beseech thee, the Spirit to think and
do always such things as be rightful; that we which cannot
be without thee, may by thee be able to live according to thy
will; through Jesu Christ our Lord.

The Epistle [1 Cor. 10

BRETHREN, I would not that ye should be ignorant, how that our fathers were all under the cloud, and all passed through the sea, and were all baptized under Moses[1] in the cloud, and in the sea, and did all eat of one spiritual meat, and did all drink of one spiritual drink. And they drank of the spiritual rock that followed them, which rock was Christ. But in many of them had God no delight. For they were overthrown in the wilderness. These are ensamples[2] to us, that we should not lust after evil things, as they lusted. And that ye should not be worshipers of images, as were some of them, according as it is written, The people sat down to eat and drink, and rose up to play. Neither let us be defiled with fornication, as some of them were defiled with fornication, and fell in one day three and twenty thousand. Neither let us tempt Christ, as some of them tempted, and were destroyed of serpents. Neither murmur ye, as some of them murmured, and were destroyed of the destroyer. All these things happened unto them for ensamples, but are written to put us in remembrance, whom the ends of the world are come upon. Wherefore, let him that thinketh he standeth, take heed lest he fall. There hath none other temptation taken you, but such as followed the nature of man. But God is faithful, which shall not suffer you to be tempted above your strength; but shall in the mids[3] of temptation, make a way, that ye may be able to bear it.

The Gospel [Luke 16

JESUS said to his disciples, There was a certain rich man, which had a steward, and the same was accused unto him, that he had wasted his goods. And he called him, and said unto him, How is it that I hear this of thee? Give accounts of

---

[1] "Moyses" in text.
[2] *Ensamples:* examples.
[3] *Mids:* middle.

thy stewardship, for thou mayest be no longer steward. The steward said within himself, What shall I do, for my master taketh away from me the stewardship? I cannot dig, and to beg I am ashamed. I wot[4] what to do, that when I am put out of the stewardship they may receive me into their houses. So when he had called all his master's debtors together, he said unto the first, How much owest thou unto my master? And he said, An hundred tons of oil. And he said unto him, Take thy bill and sit down quickly, and write fifty. Then said he to another, How much owest thou? And he said, An hundred quarters of wheat. He said unto him, Take thy bill and write fourscore. And the Lord commended the unjust steward, because he had done wisely. For the children of this world are in their nation wiser than the children of light. And I say unto you, Make you friends of the unrighteous Mammon, that when ye shall have need, they may receive you into everlasting habitations.

The Tenth Sunday

The Collect

LET thy merciful ears, O Lord, be open to the prayers of thy humble servants; and that they may obtain their petitions, make them to ask such things as shall please thee; through Jesus Christ our Lord.

The Epistle [1 Cor. 12

CONCERNING spiritual things (brethren) I would not have you ignorant. Ye know that ye were Gentiles, and went your ways unto dumb images, even as ye were led. Wherefore I declare unto you, that no man speaking by the Spirit of God defieth Jesus. Also no man can say that Jesus is the Lord,

---

[4] *Wot:* know.

but by the Holy Ghost. There are diversities of gifts, yet but one Spirit. And there are differences of administrations, and yet but one Lord. And there are diverse manners of operations, and yet but one God, which worketh all in all. The gift of the Spirit is given to every man, to edify withal. For to one is given through the Spirit, the utterance of wisdom. To another is given the utterance of knowledge, by the same Spirit. To another is given faith by the same Spirit. To another the gift of healing by the same Spirit. To another power to do miracles. To another to prophesy. To another judgment to discern spirits. To another diverse tongues. To another the interpretation of tongues. But these all worketh the selfsame Spirit, dividing to every man a several gift, even as he will.

The Gospel [Luke 19

AND when he was come near to Jerusalem,[1] he beheld the city, and wept on it, saying, If thou hadst known those things which belong unto thy peace, even in this thy day thou wouldest take heed. But now are they hid from thine eyes. For the days shall come unto thee, that thy enemies shall cast a bank[2] about thee, and compass thee round, and keep thee in on every side, and make thee even with the ground, and the children which are in thee. And they shall not leave in thee one stone upon another, because thou knowest not the time of thy visitation. And he went into the temple, and began to cast out them that sold therein, and them that bought, saying unto them, It is written, My house is the house of prayer, but ye have made it a den of thieves. And he taught daily in the temple.

[1] "Hierusalem" in text.
[2] *Bank:* a rampart; Lat., *vallo,* an earthen wall or rampart set with palisades.

The Eleventh Sunday

The Collect

GOD which declarest thy almighty power most chiefly in showing mercy and pity: Give unto us abundantly thy grace, that we, running to thy promises, may be partakers of thy heavenly treasure; through Jesus Christ our Lord.

The Epistle [1 Cor. 15

BRETHREN, as pertaining to the gospel which I preached unto you, which ye have also accepted, and in the which ye continue, by the which ye are also saved, I do you to weet[1] after what manner I preached unto you, if ye keep it, except ye have believed in vain. For first of all I delivered unto you that which I received, how that Christ died for our sins, agreeing to the Scriptures. And that he was buried, and that he rose again the third day, according to the Scriptures. And that he was seen of Cephas, then of the twelve. After that he was seen of mo[2] than five hundred brethren at once, of which many remain unto this day, and many are fallen asleep. After that appeared he to James, then to all the Apostles. And last of all he was seen of me, as of one that was born out of due time. For I am the least of the Apostles, which am not worthy to be called an apostle, because I have persecuted the congregation of God. But by the grace of God, I am that I am. And his grace which is in me, was not in vain. But I labored more abundantly than they all, yet not I, but the grace of God which is with me. Therefore, whether it were I or they, so we preached, and so ye have believed.

[1] *Weet:* know.
[2] *Mo:* more.

The Gospel [Luke 18

CHRIST told this parable unto certain which trusted in themselves that they were perfect, and despised other. Two men went up into the temple to pray, the one a Pharisee, and the other a publican. The Pharisee stood and prayed thus with himself. God, I thank thee that I am not as other men are, extortioners, unjust, adulterers, or as this publican. I fast twice in the week. I give tithe[3] of all that I possess. And the publican standing afar off, would not lift up his eyes to heaven, but smote his breast, saying, God be merciful to me a sinner. I tell you, this man departed home to his house justified more than the other. For every man that exalteth himself shall be brought low. And he that humbleth himself shall be exalted.

The Twelfth Sunday

The Collect

ALMIGHTY and everlasting God, which art always more ready to hear than we to pray, and art wont to give more than either we desire or deserve: Pour down upon us the abundance of thy mercy, forgiving us those things whereof our conscience is afraid, and giving unto us that, that our prayer dare not presume to ask; through Jesus Christ our Lord.

The Epistle [2 Cor. 3

SUCH trust have we through Christ to Godward,[1] not that we are sufficient of ourselves to think anything as of ourselves, but if we be able unto anything, the same cometh of God,

---

[3] *I give tithe:* I give a tenth; Lat., *decimas do.* Brightman, *English Rite*, II, 500.
[1] *To Godward:* toward God.

which hath made us able to minister the new testament, not of the letter, but of the Spirit. For the letter killeth, but the Spirit giveth life. If the ministration of death through the letters figured in stones was glorious, so that the children of Israel could not behold the face of Moses for the glory of his countenance (which glory is done away), why shall not the ministration of the Spirit be much more glorious? For if the ministration of condemnation be glorious, much more doth the ministration of righteousness exceed in glory.

The Gospel [Mark 7

JESUS departed from the coasts of Tyre and Sidon, and came unto the Sea of Galilee through the mids[2] of the coasts of the ten cities.[3] And they brought unto him one that was deaf and had an impediment in his speech, and they prayed him to put his hand upon him. And when he had taken him aside from the people, he put his fingers into his ears and did spit, and touched his tongue, and looked up to heaven and sighed, and said unto him, Ephata,[4] that is to say, Be opened. And straightway his ears were opened, and the string of his tongue was loosed, and he spake plain. And he commanded them that they should tell no man. But the more he forbade them, so much the more a great deal they published, saying, He hath done all things well, he hath made both the deaf to hear, and the dumb to speak.

[2] *Mids:* middle.
[3] *Ten Cities:* Decapolis.
[4] *Ephata:* Ephphatha.

The Thirteenth Sunday

The Collect

ALMIGHTY and merciful God, of whose only gift it cometh, that thy faithful people do unto thee true and laudable service: Grant we beseech thee, that we may so run to thy heavenly promises, that we fail not finally to attain the same; through Jesus Christ our Lord.

The Epistle [Gal. 3

TO Abraham and his seed were the promises made. He saith not in his seeds, as many, but in thy seed, as of one, which is Christ. This I say, that the law which began afterward, beyond four hundred thirty years, doth not disannul the testament that was confirmed afore[1] of God unto Christward,[2] to make the promise of none effect. For if the inheritance come of the law, it cometh not now of promise. But God gave it to Abraham by promise. Wherefore then serveth the law? The law was added because of transgression (till the seed came, to whom the promise was made) and it was ordained by angels in the hand of a mediator. A mediator is not a mediator of one, but God is one. Is the law then against the promise of God? God forbid. For if there had been a law given which could have given life, then no doubt righteousness should have come by the law. But the Scripture concludeth all things under sin, that the promise by the faith of Jesus Christ, should be given to them that believe.

The Gospel [Luke 10

HAPPY are the eyes which see the things that ye see. For I tell you that many prophets and kings have desired to see those things which ye see, and have not seen them, and to hear

[1] *Afore:* before.
[2] *Unto Christward:* in Christ.

those things which ye hear, and have not heard them. And behold, a certain lawyer stood up and tempted him, saying, Master, what shall I do to inherit eternal life? He said unto him, What is written in the law? How readest thou? And he answered, and said, Love the Lord thy God with all thy heart, and with all thy soul, and with all thy strength, and with all thy mind, and thy neighbor as thyself. And he said unto him, Thou hast answered right. This do, and thou shalt live. But he, willing to justify himself, said unto Jesus, And who is my neighbor? Jesus answered, and said, A certain man descended from Jerusalem to Jericho,[3] and fell among thieves, which robbed him of his raiment, and wounded him, and departed, leaving him half dead. And it chanced that there came down a certain priest that same way, and when he saw him, he passed by. And likewise a Levite, when he went nigh to the place, came and looked on him and passed by. But a certain Samaritan as he journeyed came unto him, and when he saw him, he had compassion on him, and went to, and bound up his wounds, and poured in oil and wine, and set him on his own beast, and brought him to a common inn, and made provision for him. And on the morrow, when he departed, he took out two pence, and gave them to the host, and said unto him, Take cure[4] of him, and whatsoever thou spendest more, when I come again, I will recompense thee. Which now of these three thinkest thou was neighbor unto him that fell among the thieves? And he said unto him, He that showed mercy on him. Then said Jesus to him, Go, and do thou likewise.

[3] "Hiericho" in text.
[4] *Cure:* care.

The Fourteenth Sunday

The Collect

ALMIGHTY and everlasting God, give unto us the increase of faith, hope, and charity, and that we may obtain that which thou dost promise, make us to love that which thou dost command; through Jesus Christ our Lord.

The Epistle [Gal. 5

I SAY, Walk in the Spirit, and fulfill not the lust of the flesh. For the flesh lusteth contrary to the Spirit, and the Spirit contrary to the flesh. These are contrary one to another, so that ye cannot do whatsoever ye would. But and if ye be led of the Spirit, then are ye not under the law. The deeds of the flesh are manifest, which are these: adultery, fornication, uncleanness, wantonness, worshiping of images, witchcraft, hatred, variance, zeal, wrath, strife, seditions, sects, envying, murder, drunkenness, gluttony, and suchlike. Of the which I tell you before, as I have told you in times past, that they which commit such things shall not be inheritors of the kingdom of God. Contrarily, the fruit of the Spirit is love, joy, peace, long-suffering, gentleness, goodness, faithfulness, meekness, temperance. Against such there is no law. They truly that are Christ's have crucified the flesh with the affections and lusts.

The Gospel [Luke 17

AND it chanced as Jesus went to Jerusalem, that he passed through Samaria and Galilee. And as he entered into a certain town, there met him ten men that were lepers, which stood afar off and put forth their voices, and said, Jesus, Master, have mercy upon us. When he saw them, he said unto them, Go show yourselves unto the priests. And it came to pass that as they went they were cleansed. And one of them, when he saw that he was cleansed, turned back again, and with a loud voice praised God, and fell down on his face at his feet, and gave him thanks. And the same was a Samaritan. And Jesus answered, and said, Are there not ten cleansed? But where are those nine? There are not found that returned again to give God praise, save only this stranger. And he said unto him, Arise, go thy way, thy faith hath made thee whole.

The Fifteenth Sunday

The Collect

KEEP, we beseech thee, O Lord, the[1] Church with thy perpetual mercy; and because the frailty of man, without thee, cannot but fall, keep us ever by thy help, and lead us to all things profitable to our salvation; through Jesus Christ our Lord. Amen.

The Epistle [Gal. 6

YE see how large a letter I have written to you with mine own hand. As many as desire with outward appearance to please carnally, the same constrain you to be circumcised, only lest they should suffer persecution for the cross of Christ. For they themselves which are circumcised, keep not the law, but desire to have you circumcised, that they might rejoice in your flesh. God forbid that I should rejoice, but in the cross of our Lord Jesu Christ, whereby the world is crucified unto me, and I unto the world. For in Christ Jesu, neither circumcision availeth anything at all, nor uncircumcision, but a new creature. And as many as walk according unto this rule, peace be on them, and mercy, and upon

---

[1] "The" makes sense here, but it is "thy" in the 1549 and 1552 Books (see Brightman, *English Rite*, II, 512–13) and in 1559 Grafton.

Israel that pertaineth to God. From henceforth, let no man put me to business. For I bear in my body the marks of the Lord Jesu. Brethren, the grace of our Lord Jesu Christ be with your spirit. Amen.

The Gospel [Matt. 6

N O man can serve two masters, for either he shall hate the one, and love the other, or else lean to the one, and despise the other. Ye cannot serve God and Mammon. Therefore I say unto you, Be not careful for your life, what ye shall eat or drink, or yet for your body, what raiment you shall put on. Is not the life more worth than meat? And the body more of value than raiment? Behold the fowls of the air, for they sow not, neither do they reap, nor carry into the barns, and your heavenly Father feedeth them. Are ye not much better than they? Which of you (by taking careful thought) can add one cubit[2] unto his stature? And why care ye for raiment? Consider the lilies of the field how they grow. They labor not, neither do they spin. And yet I say unto you, that even Solomon[3] in all his royalty was not clothed like one of these. Wherefore, if God so clothe the grass of the field (which though it stand today, is tomorrow cast into the furnace), shall he not much more do the same for you, O ye of little faith? Therefore take no thought, saying, What shall we eat, or what shall we drink, or wherewith shall we be clothed? After all these things do the Gentiles seek. For your heavenly Father knoweth that ye have need of all these things. But rather seek ye first the kingdom of God, and the righteousness thereof, and all these things shall be ministered unto you. Care not then for tomorrow, for tomorrow day shall care for itself. Sufficient unto the day is the travail thereof.

[2] *Cubit:* an ancient measure based on the length of the forearm, usually eighteen to twenty-two inches.

[3] "Salomon" in text.

The Sixteenth Sunday

The Collect

LORD, we beseech thee, let thy continual pity cleanse and defend thy congregation;[1] and because it cannot continue in safety without thy succor, preserve it evermore by thy help and goodness; through Jesus Christ our Lord.

The Epistle [Eph. 3

I DESIRE that you faint not because of my tribulations that I suffer for your sakes, which is your praise. For this cause I bow my knees unto the Father of our Lord Jesus Christ, which is Father of all, that is called Father in heaven and in earth, that he would grant you, according to the riches of his glory, that ye may be strengthed with might by his Spirit in the inner man, that Christ may dwell in your hearts by faith, that ye, being rooted and grounded in love, might be able to comprehend with all saints what is the breadth, length, depth, and height, and to know the excellent love of the knowledge of Christ, that ye might be fulfilled with all fullness, which cometh of God. Unto him that is able to do exceeding abundantly above all that we ask or think, according to the power that worketh in us, be praise in the congregation by Christ Jesus, throughout all generations from time to time. Amen.

The Gospel [Luke 7

AND it fortuned that Jesus went into a city called Nain,[2] and many of his disciples went with him, and much people. When he came nigh to the gate of the city, behold there was a

---

[1] 1661 Book has "Church"; Lat., *Ecclesiam*. Brightman, *English Rite*, II, 516–17.

[2] "Naim" in text.

dead man carried out, which was the only son of his mother, and she was a widow, and much people of the city was with her. And when the Lord saw her, he had compassion on her, and said unto her, Weep not. And he came nigh and touched the coffin, and they that bare him stood still. And he said, Young man, I say unto thee, Arise. And he that was dead, sat up, and began to speak. And he delivered him to his mother. And there came a fear on them all. And they gave the glory unto God, saying, A great prophet is risen up among us, and God hath visited his people. And this rumor of him went forth throughout all Jewry, and throughout all the regions which lie round about.

The Seventeenth Sunday

The Collect

LORD, we pray thee that thy grace may always prevent[1] and follow us, and make us continually to be given to all good works; through Jesu Christ our Lord.

The Epistle [Eph. 4

I (WHICH am a prisoner of the Lord's) exhort you, that ye walk worthy of the vocation wherewith ye are called, with all lowliness and meekness, with humbleness of mind, forbearing one another, through love. And be diligent to keep the unity of the Spirit, through the bond of peace, being one body and one Spirit, even as ye are called in one hope of your calling. Let there be but one Lord, one faith, one baptism, one God and Father of all, which is above all, and through all, and in you all.

[1] *Prevent:* go before.

The Gospel [Luke 14

I T chanced that Jesus went into the house of one of the chief Pharisees, to eat bread on the Sabbath day, and they watched him. And behold, there was a certain man before him which had the dropsy. And Jesus answered and spake unto the lawyers and Pharisees, saying, Is it lawful to heal on the Sabbath day? And they held their peace. And he took him and healed him, and let him go, and answered them, saying, Which of you shall have an ass or an ox fallen into a pit, and will not straightway pull him out on the Sabbath day? And they could not answer him again to these things. He put forth also a similitude to the guests, when he marked how they pressed to be in the highest rooms, and said unto them, When thou are bidden to a wedding of any man, sit not down in the highest room, lest a more honorable man than thou be bidden of him; and he (that bade him and thee) come and say to thee, Give this man room; and thou begin with shame to take the lowest room. But rather when thou art bidden, go and sit in the lowest room, that when he that bade thee cometh, he may say unto thee, Friend, sit up higher. Then shalt thou have worship in the presence of them that sit at meat with thee. For whosoever exalteth himself, shall be brought low, and he that humbleth himself, shall be exalted.

The Eighteenth Sunday

The Collect

L ORD we beseech thee, grant thy people grace to avoid the infections of the devil, and with pure heart and mind to follow thee, the only God, through Jesus Christ our Lord.

The Epistle [1 Cor. 1

I THANK my God always on your behalf, for the grace of God, which is given you by Jesus Christ, that in all things ye are made rich by him, in all utterance, and in all knowledge; by the which things the testimony of Jesus Christ was confirmed in you: so that ye are behind in no gift, waiting for the appearing of our Lord Jesus Christ, which shall also strength[1] you to the end, that you may be blameless in the day of the coming of our Lord Jesus Christ.

The Gospel [Matt. 22[2]

WHEN the Pharisees had heard that Jesus did put the Sadducees to silence, they came together, and one of them (which was a doctor of law) asked him a question, tempting him and saying, Master, which is the greatest commandment in the law? Jesus said unto him, Thou shalt love the Lord thy God with all thy heart, and with all thy soul, and with all thy mind. This is the first and greatest commandment. And the second is like unto it. Thou shall love thy neighbor as thy self. In these two commandments hang all the law and the prophets. While the Pharisees were gathered together, Jesus asked them saying, What think ye of Christ? Whose son is he? They said unto him, the son of David. He said unto them, How then doth David in spirit call him Lord, saying, The Lord said unto my Lord, Sit thou on my right hand till I make thine enemies thy footstool? If David then call him Lord, how is he then his son? And no man was able to answer him anything, neither durst[3] any man (from that day forth) and ask him any mo[4] questions.

---

[1] 1661 Book has "confirm"; Lat., *confirmabit*. Brightman, *English Rite*, II, 524.

[2] Text has "21"; misprint.

[3] *Durst:* darest.

[4] *Mo:* more.

The Nineteenth Sunday

The Collect

O GOD, forasmuch as without thee, we are not able to please thee; Grant that the working of thy mercy may in all things direct and rule our hearts; through Jesus Christ our Lord.

The Epistle [Eph. 4

THIS I say and testify through the Lord, that ye henceforth walk not as other Gentiles walk, in vanity of their mind, while they are blinded in their understanding, being far from a godly life, by the means of the ignorance that is in them, and because of the blindness of their hearts, which being past repentance have given themselves over unto wantonness, to work all manner of uncleanness, even with greediness. But ye have not so learned Christ. If so be that ye have heard of him, and have taught in him, as the truth is in Jesu (as concerning the conversation[1] in times past) to lay from you the old man, which is corrupt according to the deceivable lusts. To be renewed also in the spirit of your mind, and to put on that new man, which after God is shapen in righteousness and true holiness. Wherefore put away lying, and speak every man truth unto his neighbor, forasmuch as we are members one of another. Be angry and sin not. Let not the sun go down upon your wrath, neither give place to the backbiter.[2] Let him that stole, steal no more, but let him rather labor with his hands the thing which is good, that he may give him that needeth. Let not filthy communication proceed out of your mouth, but that which is good to edify withal, as oft as need is, that it may minister grace unto the hearers. And grieve not the Holy Spirit of God, by whom ye are sealed unto the day of re-

[1] *Conversation:* "manner of life" (RSV).

[2] 1661 Book has "neither give place to the devil"; Lat., *Nolite locum dare diabolo*. Brightman, *English Rite*, II, 528–29.

demption. Let all bitterness and fierceness, and wrath, and roaring, and cursed speaking, be put away from you, with all maliciousness. Be ye courteous one to another, merciful, forgiving one another, even as God for Christ's sake hath forgiven you.

The Gospel [Matt. 9

JESUS entered into a ship, and passed over, and came into his own city. And behold they brought to him a man sick of the palsy, lying in a bed. And when Jesus saw the faith of them, he said to the sick of the palsy, Son be of good cheer; thy sins be forgiven thee. And behold, certain of the scribes said within themselves, This man blasphemeth. And when Jesus saw their thoughts he said, Wherefore think ye evil in your hearts? Whether is it easier to say, Thy sins be forgiven thee, or to say, Arise and walk? But that ye may know that the Son of man hath power to forgive sins in earth, then saith he to the sick of the palsy, Arise, take up thy bed, and go unto thine house. And he arose and departed to his house. But the people that saw it marveled and glorified God, which hath given such power unto men.

The Twentieth Sunday

The Collect

ALMIGHTY and merciful God, of thy bountiful goodness keep us from all things that may hurt us; that we being ready both in body and soul, may with free hearts accomplish those things that thou wouldest have done; through Jesus Christ our Lord.

The Epistle [Eph. 5

TAKE heed therefore, how ye walk circumspectly, not as unwise, but as wise men, redeeming the time, because the days are evil. Wherefore be ye not unwise, but understand what the will of the Lord is. And be not drunken with wine, wherein is excess, but be filled with the Spirit, speaking unto yourselves in psalms and hymns, and spiritual songs, singing and making melody to the Lord in your hearts, giving thanks always for all things unto God the Father, in the name of our Lord Jesus Christ, submitting yourselves one to another in the fear of God.

The Gospel [Matt. 22[1]

JESUS said to his disciples, The kingdom of heaven is like unto a man that was a king, which made a marriage for his son, and sent forth his servants to call them that were bidden to the wedding, and they would not come. Again he sent forth other servants saying, Tell them which are bidden, Behold, I have prepared my dinner, mine oxen and my fatlings are killed, and all things are ready: come unto the marriage. But they made light of it, and went their ways, one to his farm place, another to his merchandise, and the remnant took his servants and entreated them shamefully and slew them. But when the king heard thereof, he was wroth[2] and sent forth his men of war, and destroyed those murderers, and brent[3] up their city. Then said he to his servants, The marriage indeed is prepared, but they which were bidden were not worthy. Go ye therefore out into the highways, and as many as ye find, bid them to the marriage. And the servants went forth into the highways and gathered together all, as many as they could find, both good and bad, and the wedding was furnished with guests. Then the king came in to see the

---

[1] Text has "20"; misprint.
[2] *Wroth:* angry.
[3] *Brent:* burnt.

guests, and when he spied there a man which had not on a wedding garment, he said unto him, Friend, how camest thou in hither, not having a wedding garment? And he was even speechless. Then said the king to the ministers, Take and bind him hand and foot, and cast him into utter darkness; there shall be weeping and gnashing of teeth. For many be called, but few are chosen.

The Twenty-first Sunday

The Collect

GRANT we beseech thee, merciful Lord, to thy faithful people, pardon and peace, that they may be cleansed from all their sins, and serve thee with a quiet mind; through Jesus Christ our Lord.

The Epistle [Eph. 6

MY brethren, be strong through the Lord, and through the power of his might. Put on all the armor of God, that ye may stand against all the assaults of the devil. For we wrestle not against blood and flesh, but against rule,[1] against power, against worldly rulers, even governors of the darkness of this world, against spiritual craftiness in heavenly things. Wherefore take unto you the whole armor of God, that ye may be able to resist in the evil day, and stand perfect in all things. Stand therefore, and your loins gird with the truth, having on the breastplate of righteousness, and having shoes on your feet, that ye may be prepared for the gospel of peace. Above all, take to you the shield of faith, wherewith ye may quench all the fiery darts of the wicked. And take the helmet of salvation, and the sword

---

[1] *Rule:* "principalities" (RSV); "authorities" (New English Bible); Lat., *principes.*

of the Spirit, which is the Word of God. And pray always with all manner of prayer and supplication in the Spirit, and watch thereunto with all instance and supplication, for all saints and for me, that utterance may be given unto me, that I may open my mouth freely, to utter the secrets of my gospel (whereof I am a messenger in bonds) that therein I may speak freely, as I ought to speak.

The Gospel [John 4

THERE was a certain ruler, whose son was sick at Capernaum. As soon as the same heard that Jesus was come out of Jewry into Galilee, he went unto him, and besought him that he would come down and heal his son. For he was even at the point of death. Then said Jesus unto him, Except ye sees signs and wonders, ye will not believe. The ruler said unto him, Sir, come down, or ever that[2] my son die. Jesus saith unto him, Go thy way; thy son liveth. The man believed the word that Jesus had spoken unto him. And he went his way. And as he was going down the servants met him, and told him, saying, Thy son liveth. Then inquired he of them the hour, when he began to amend. And they said unto him, Yesterday at the seventh hour the fever left him. So the father knew that it was the same hour, in the which Jesus said unto him, Thy son liveth. And he believed, and all his household. This is again the second miracle that Jesus did, when he was come out of Jewry into Gallilee.

[2] *Or ever that:* "ere" in 1661 Book.

The Twenty-second Sunday

The Collect

LORD, we beseech thee to keep thy household the Church in continual godliness; that through thy protection it may be free from all adversities, and devoutly given[1] to serve thee in good works, to the glory of thy name; through Jesus Christ our Lord.

The Epistle [Phil. 1

I THANK my God with all remembrance of you, always in all my prayers for you, and pray with gladness, because ye are come into the fellowship of the gospel, from the first day until now. And am surely certified of this, that he which hath begun a good work in you, shall perform it until the day of Jesus Christ: as it becometh me that I should so judge of you all,[2] because I have you in my heart, forasmuch as ye are all companions of grace with me, even in my bonds, and in the defending and establishing of the gospel. For God is my record how greatly I long after you all, from the very heart root[3] in Jesus Christ. And this I pray, that your love may increase yet more and more in knowledge, and in all understanding, that ye may accept the things that are most excellent; that ye may be pure, and such as offend no man, until the day of Christ; being filled with the fruit of righteousness, which cometh by Jesus Christ, unto the glory and praise of God.

[1] Text has "give."

[2] *As it becometh me that I should so judge of you all:* "As it becometh me, so judge I you all" (Great Bible).

[3] *Heart root:* affection; Lat., *visceribus*, internal organ, viscera; Gk., σπλάγχνοις, metaph, the seat of the feelings, affections. Cf. Liddell and Scott, *Greek-English Lexicon*, p. 1628.

The Gospel [Matt. 18

PETER said unto Jesus, Lord how oft shall I forgive my brother, if he sin against me, till seven times? Jesus said unto him, I say not unto thee, until seven times, but seventy times seven times. Therefore is the kingdom of heaven likened unto a certain man that was a king, which would take accounts of his servants. And when he had begun to reckon, one was brought unto him, which ought[4] him ten thousand talents.[5] But forasmuch as he was not able to pay, his Lord commanded him to be sold, and his wife and children, and all that he had, and payment to be made. The servant fell down and besought him, saying, Sir, have patience with me, and I will pay thee all. Then had the Lord pity on that servant, and loosed him, and forgave him the debt. So the same servant went out and found one of his fellows which ought him an hundred pence, and he laid hands on him, and took him by the throat, saying, Pay that thou owest. And his fellow fell down and besought him, saying, Have patience with me, and I will pay thee all. And he would not, but went and cast him into prison, till he should pay the debt. So when his fellows saw what was done, they were very sorry, and came and told unto their lord all that had happened. Then his lord called him, and said unto him, O thou ungracious servant. I forgave thee all that debt when thou desiredst me. Shouldest not thou also have had compassion on thy fellow, even as I had pity on thee? And his lord was wroth,[6] and delivered him to the jailers, till he should pay all that was due unto him. So likewise shall my heavenly Father do also unto you, if ye from your hearts forgive not (every one his brother) their trepasses.

[4] *Ought:* owed.

[5] *Talents:* ancient coins valued at various amounts depending upon time and place.

[6] *Wroth:* angry.

The Twenty-third Sunday

The Collect

GOD our refuge and strength, which art the author of all godliness: Be ready to hear the devout prayers of thy[1] Church; and grant that those things which we ask faithfully, we may obtain effectually; through Jesu Christ our Lord.

The Epistle [Phil. 3

BRETHREN, be followers together of me, and look on them which walk even so as ye have us for an ensample.[2] For many walk (of whom I have told you often, and now tell you weeping) that they are the enemies of the cross of Christ, whose end is damnation, whose belly is their god, and glory to their shame, which are worldly minded. But our conversation[3] is in heaven, from whence we look for the Savior, even the Lord Jesus Christ, which shall change our vile body, that he may make it like unto his glorious body, according to the working whereby he is able also to subdue all things unto himself.

The Gospel [Matt. 22

THEN the Pharisees went out, and took counsel how they might tangle him in his words. And they sent out unto him their disciples with Herod's servants, saying, Master, we know that thou art true, and teachest the way of God truly, neither carest thou for any man: for thou regardest not the outward appearance of men. Tell us therefore, how thinkest thou? Is it lawful that tribute be given unto Caesar, or not? But Jesus perceiv-

---

[1] Text has "the"; misprint.

[2] *Ensample:* example.

[3] *Conversation:* manner of conducting oneself in society (OED); "commonwealth" (RSV).

ing their wickedness, said, Why tempt ye me ye hypocrites? Show me the tribute money. And they took him a penny. And he said unto them, Whose is this image and superscription?[4] They said unto him, Caesar's. Then said he unto them, Give therefore unto Caesar, the things which are Caesar's, and unto God, those things which are God's. When they heard these words, they marveled, and left him, and went their way.

The Twenty-fourth Sunday

The Collect

LORD, we beseech thee, assoil[1] thy people from their offenses; that through thy bountiful goodness, we may be delivered from the bands[2] of all those sins, which by our frailty we have committed; grant this, etc.

The Epistle [Col. 1

WE give thanks to God, the Father of our Lord Jesus Christ, always for you in our prayers. For we have heard of your faith in Christ Jesu, and of the love which ye bear to all saints, for the hope's sake which is laid up in store for you in heaven. Of which hope ye heard before by the true word of the gospel, which is come unto you even as it is, fruitful, and groweth as it is also among you, from the day in the which ye heard of it, and had experience in the grace of God through the truth, as ye learned of Epaphras,[3] our dear fellow servant, which is for you a faithful minister of Christ, which also declared unto us your love which ye have in the Spirit. For this cause we also, ever

---

[4] *Superscription:* a piece of writing on or above.

[1] *Assoil:* absolve.

[2] *Bands:* shackles.

[3] "Epaphra" in text.

since the day we heard of it, have not ceased to pray for you, and to desire that ye might be fulfilled with the knowledge of his will, in all wisdom and spiritual understanding; that ye might walk worthy of the Lord, that in all things ye may please, being fruitful in all good works, and increasing in the knowledge of God, strengthed with all might, through his glorious power, unto all patience and long-suffering, with joyfulness, giving thanks unto the Father, which hath made us meet[4] to be partakers of the inheritance of saints in light.

The Gospel [Matt. 9

WHILE Jesus spake unto the people, behold there came a certain ruler, and worshiped him, saying, My daughter is even now deceased, but come and lay thy hand upon her, and she shall live. And Jesus arose and followed him, and so did his disciples. And behold, a woman which was diseased with an issue of blood twelve years came behind him and touched the hem of his vesture. For she said within herself, If I may touch but even his vesture only, I shall be safe.[5] But Jesus turned him about, and when he saw her, he said, Daughter, be of good comfort, thy faith hath made thee safe. And the woman was made whole even the same time. And when Jesus came into the ruler's house, and saw the minstrels, and people making a noise, he said unto them, Get you hence, for the maid is not dead but sleepeth. And they laughed him to scorn. But when the people were put forth, he went in, and took her by the hand, and said, Damsel,[6] arise. And the damsel arose. And this noise was abroad in all that land.

[4] *Meet:* suitable, fit.

[5] *Safe:* saved; Lat., *salvus erit*; Gk., σωθήσῃ. D. E. Nestle, *Novum testamentum Graeca et Latina* (Stuttgart, 1951), pp. 412–13.

[6] Text has "damosell"; "damosel" in next sentence.

The Twenty-fifth Sunday

The Collect

STIR up, we beseech thee, O Lord, the wills of thy faithful people; that they plenteously bringing forth the fruit of good works, may of thee be plenteously rewarded; through Jesus Christ our Lord.

The Epistle [Jer. 23[1]

BEHOLD, the time cometh, saith the Lord, that I will raise up the righteous branch of David, which king shall bear rule, and he[2] shall prosper with wisdom, and shall set up equity and righteousness again in earth. In his time shall Judah be saved, and Israel shall dwell without fear. And this is the name that they shall call him, even the Lord our righteousness. And therefore behold, the time cometh, saith the Lord, that it shall be no more said, The Lord liveth which brought the children of Israel out of the land of Egypt: but, The Lord liveth which brought forth and led the seed of the house of Israel out of the north land, and from all countries where I have scattered them, and they shall dwell in their own land again.

The Gospel [John 6

WHEN Jesus lift up his eyes, and saw a great company come unto him, he saith unto Philip, Whence shall we buy bread that these may eat? This he said to prove him, for he himself knew what he would do. Philip answered him, Two hundred pennyworth[3] of bread are not sufficient for them, that every man

---

[1] This citation is not in the text, but is in 1559 Grafton.

[2] *Of . . . he:* these words are transposed in text.

[3] *Two hundred pennyworth:* "two hundred denarii" (RSV); approximately forty dollars.

may take a little. One of his disciples (Andrew, Simon Peter's brother) said unto him, There is a lad here, which hath five barley loaves and two fishes, but what are they among so many? And Jesus said, Make the people sit down. There was much grass in the place. So the men sat down, in number about five thousand. And Jesus took the bread, and when he had given thanks, he gave to the disciples, and the disciples to them that were set down. And likewise of the fishes as much as they would. When they had eaten enough, he saith unto his disciples, Gather up the broken meat which remaineth, that nothing be lost. And they gathered it together, and filled twelve baskets with the broken meat of the five barley loaves, which broken meat remained unto them that had eaten. Then those men (when they had seen the miracle that Jesus did) said, This is of a truth the same prophet that should come into the world.

If there be any mo[4] Sundays before Advent Sunday, to supply the same shall be taken the service of some of those Sundays that were omitted between the Epiphany and Septuagesima.

Saint Andrew's Day

The Collect

ALMIGHTY God, which didst give such grace unto thy holy Apostle Saint Andrew, that he readily obeyed the calling of thy Son Jesus Christ, and followed him without delay: Grant unto us all, that we being called by the holy Word, may forwith give over ourselves obediently to follow thy holy commandments; through the same Jesus Christ our Lord.

[4] *Mo:* more.

The Epistle [Rom. 10

IF thou knowledge[1] with thy mouth that Jesus is the Lord, and believe in thy heart that God raised him up from death, thou shalt be safe.[2] For to believe with the heart justifieth, and to knowledge with the mouth, maketh a man safe. For the Scripture saith, Whosoever believeth on him, shall not be confounded. There is no difference between the Jew and the Gentile. For one is Lord of all, which is rich unto all that call upon him. For whosoever doth call on the name of the Lord, shall be safe. How then shall they call on him on whom they have not believed? How shall they believe on him on whom they have not heard? How shall they hear without a preacher? And how shall they preach without they be sent? As it is written, How beautiful are the feet of them which bring tidings of peace, and bring tidings of good things? But they have not all obeyed to the gospel. For Isaiah[3] saith, Lord, who hath believed our sayings? So then faith cometh by hearing, and hearing cometh by the Word of God. But I ask, Have they not heard? No doubt their sound went out into all lands, and their words into the ends of the world. But I demand whether Israel did know or not? First Moses saith, I will provoke you to envy by them that are no people, by a foolish nation I will anger you. Isaiah after that is bold, and saith, I am found of them that sought me not. I am manifest unto them that asked not after me. But against Israel he saith, All day long have I stretched forth my hands unto a people that believeth not, but speaketh against me.

The Gospel [Matt. 4

AS Jesus walked by the Sea of Galilee, he saw two brethren, Simon, which was called Peter, and Andrew his brother, casting a net into the sea, for they were fishers. And he saith

---

[1] *Knowledge:* acknowledge.
[2] *Safe:* saved.
[3] "Esay" in text, here and below.

unto them, Follow me, and I will make you to become fishers of men. And they straightway left their nets, and followed him. And when he was gone forth from thence, he saw other two brethren, James the son of Zebedee, and John his brother, in the ship with Zebedee their father, mending their nets; and he called them. And they immediately left the ship and their father, and followed him.

Saint Thomas the Apostle

The Collect

ALMIGHTY and everliving God, which for the more confirmation of the faith, didst suffer thy holy Apostle Thomas to be doubtful in thy Son's resurrection: Grant us so perfectly, and without all doubt, to believe in thy Son Jesus Christ, that our faith in thy sight never be reproved; hear us, O Lord, through the same Jesus Christ, to whom with thee and the Holy Ghost be all honor, etc.

The Epistle [Eph. 2

NOW are ye not strangers nor foreigners, but citizens with the saints, and of the household of God, and are built upon the foundation of the Apostles and prophets, Jesus Christ himself being the head cornerstone: in whom what building soever is coupled together, it groweth unto an holy temple of the Lord; in whom also ye are built together, to be an habitation of God through the Holy Ghost.

The Gospel [John 20

THOMAS one of the twelve, which is called Didymus, was not with them when Jesus came. The other disciples therefore said unto him, We have seen the Lord. But he said unto them, Except I see in his hands the print of the nails, and put my finger into the print of the nails, and thrust my hand into his side, I will not believe. And after eight days, again his disciples were within, and Thomas with them. Then came Jesus when the doors were shut, and stood in the mids,[1] and said, Peace be unto you. And after that, he said to Thomas, Bring thy finger hither, and see my hands, and reach hither thy hand, and thrust it into my side, and be not faithless, but believing. Thomas answered and said unto him, My Lord and my God. Jesus said unto him, Thomas, because thou hast seen me, thou hast believed. Blessed are they that have not seen, and yet have believed. And many other signs truly did Jesus in the presence of his disciples, which are not written in this book. These are written that ye might believe that Jesus Christ is the Son of God, and that in believing ye might have life through his name.

The Conversion of Saint Paul

The Collect

GOD, which hast taught all the world through the preaching of thy blessed Apostle Saint Paul: Grant we beseech thee, that we which have his wonderful conversion in remembrance, may follow and fulfill thy holy doctrine that he taught; through Jesu Christ our Lord.

The Epistle [Acts 9

AND Saul, yet breathing out threatenings and slaughter against the disciples of the Lord, went unto the high priest, and desired of him letters to carry to Damascus[1] to the synagogues, that if he found any of this way (were they men or

---

[1] *Mids:* midst, middle.

[1] "Damasco" in text, here and throughout.

women) he might bring them bound to Jerusalem. And when he journeyed, it fortuned that as he was come nigh to Damascus, suddenly there shined round about him a light from heaven, and he fell to the earth, and heard a voice saying to him, Saul, Saul, why persecutest thou me? And he said, What art thou Lord? And the Lord said, I am Jesus whom thou persecutest. It is hard for thee to kick against the prick.[2] And he, both trembling and astonied,[3] said, Lord what wilt thou have me to do? And the Lord said unto him, Arise and go into the city, and it shall be told thee what thou must do. The men which journeyed with him, stood amazed, hearing a voice, but seeing no man. And Saul arose from the earth, and when he opened his eyes, he saw no man. But they led him by the hand and brought him into Damascus. And he was three days without sight, and neither did eat nor drink. And there was a certain disciple at Damascus, named Ananias, and to him said the Lord in a vision, Ananias? And he said, Behold, I am here, Lord. And the Lord said unto him, Arise and go into the street (which is called straight) and seek in the house of Judas, after one called Saul of Tarsus.[4] For behold, he prayeth and hath seen in a vision a man named Ananias coming in to him, and putting his hands on him, that he might receive his sight. Then Ananias answered, Lord, I have heard by many of this man how much evil he hath done to thy saints at Jerusalem: and here he hath authority of the high priests to bind all that call on thy name. The Lord said unto him, Go thy way, for he is a chosen vessel unto me, to bear my name before the Gentiles, and kings, and the children of Israel. For I will show him how great things he must suffer for my name's

---

[2] *It is hard for thee to kick against the prick:* It hurts you to spurn the goad (that is, the growing conviction that the Christian case is true). Cf. F. J. Foakes-Jackson and K. Lake, *The Beginnings of Christianity*, IV (London, 1933), 101, 318–19; F. F. Bruce, *Commentary on the Book of the Acts* (Grand Rapids, 1960), pp. 192, 491; and J. Munck, *The Acts of the Apostles*, Anchor Bible (New York, 1967), p. 242.

[3] *Astonied:* astonished.

[4] "Tharsus" in text.

sake. And Ananias went his way, and entered into the house, and put his hands on him, and said, Brother Saul, the Lord that appeared unto thee in the way as thou camest, hath sent me, that thou mightest receive thy sight, and be filled with the Holy Ghost. And immediately there fell from his eyes as it had been scales, and he received sight, and arose, and was baptized, and received meat, and was comforted. Then was Saul a certain days with the disciples which were at Damascus. And straightway he preached Christ in the synagogues, how that he was the Son of God. But all that heard him were amazed, and said, is not this he that spoiled[5] them which called on this name in Jerusalem, and came hither for that intent, that he might bring them bound unto the high priests? But Saul increased the more in strength, and confounded the Jews which dwelt at Damascus, affirming that this was very Christ.

The Gospel [Matt. 19

PETER answered, and said unto Jesus, Behold we have forsaken all and followed thee. What shall we have therefore? Jesus said unto them, Verily I say unto you, that when the Son of man shall sit in the seat of his majesty, ye that have followed me in the regeneration shall sit also upon twelve seats, and judge the twelve tribes of Israel. And everyone that forsaketh house, or brethren, or sisters, or father, or mother, or wife, or children, or lands for my name's sake, shall receive an hundredfold, and shall inherit everlasting life. But many that are first shall be last, and the last shall be first.

[5] *Spoiled:* seized, took by force; Lat., *qui expugnabat.* Brightman, *English Rite,* II, 564.

The Purification of Saint Mary the Virgin

The Collect

ALMIGHTY and everlasting God, we humbly beseech thy majesty, that as thy only begotten Son was this day presented in the temple, in substance of our flesh, so grant that we may be presented unto thee with pure and clear minds, by Jesus Christ our Lord.

The Epistle

The same that is appointed for the Sunday.

The Gospel [Luke 2

WHEN the time of their purification (after the law of Moses) was come, they brought him to Jerusalem, to present him to the Lord (as it is written in the law of the Lord, Every man child that first openeth the matrix[1] shall be called holy to the Lord) and to offer (as it is said in the law of the Lord) a pair of turtledoves, or two young pigeons. And behold, there was a man in Jerusalem,[2] whose name was Simeon. And the same man was just and godly, and looked for the consolation of Israel; and the Holy Ghost was in him. And an answer had he received of the Holy Ghost that he should not see death, except he first saw the Lord Christ. And he came by inspiration[3] into the temple.

[1] *Matrix:* womb.

[2] "Hierusalem" in text.

[3] 1661 Book has "by the Spirit"; Lat., *Et venit in spiritu in templum* (Brightman, *English Rite*, II, 568); Gk., ἐν τῷ πνεύματι (A. Merk, *Novum testamentum* [Rome, 1957], p. 196).

Saint Matthias's[1] Day

The Collect

ALMIGHTY God, which in the place of the traitor Judas, didst choose thy faithful servant Matthias[2] to be of the number of thy twelve Apostles: Grant that thy Church being alway preserved from false apostles, may be ordered and guided by faithful and true pastors; through Jesus Christ our Lord.

The Epistle [Acts 1

IN those days Peter stood up in the mids[3] of the disciples and said (the number of names that were together were about an hundred and twenty), Ye men and brethren, this Scripture must needs have been fulfilled, which the Holy Ghost through the mouth of David spake before of Judas, which was guide to them that took Jesus. For he was numbered with us, and had obtained fellowship in his administration.[4] And the same hath now possessed a plat[5] of ground, with the reward of iniquity, and when he was hanged burst asunder in the mids, and all his bowels gushed out. And it was known unto all the inhabiters of Jerusalem,[6] insomuch that the same field is called in their mother tongue Aceldama,[7] that is to say, the bloody field. For it is written in the book of Psalms, His habitation be void, and no man be dwelling therein, and his bishopric[8] let another take. Wherefore,

---

[1] "Mathies" in text.

[2] "Mathie" in text.

[3] *Mids:* midst.

[4] *Administration:* ministry.

[5] *Plat:* a patch of ground.

[6] "Hierusalem" in text.

[7] "Acheldama" in text.

[8] *Bishopric:* office; Gk., ἐπισκοπεία. Liddell and Scott, *Greek-English Lexicon*, p. 657.

of these men which have companied with us (all the time that the Lord Jesus had all his conversation[9] among us, beginning at the baptism of John unto that same day that he was taken up from us) must one be ordained to be a witness with us of his resurrection. And they appointed two, Joseph which is called Barsabas (whose surname was Justus) and Matthias.[10] And when they prayed, they said, Thou Lord knowest the hearts of all men, show whether of these two thou hast chosen, that he may take the room of this ministration and apostleship, from which Judas by transgression fell, that he might go to his own place. And they gave forth their lots, and the lot fell on Matthias, and he was counted with the eleven Apostles.

The Gospel [Matt. 11

I N that time Jesus answered and said, I thank thee, O Father, Lord of heaven and earth, because thou hast hid these things from the wise and prudent, and hast showed them unto babes. Verily, Father, even so was it thy good pleasure. All things are given unto me of my Father. And no man knoweth the Son, but the Father. Neither knoweth any man the Father, save the Son, and he to whomsoever the Son will open him. Come unto me all ye that labor and are laden, and I will ease you. Take my yoke upon you and learn of me, for I am meek and lowly in heart, and ye shall find rest unto your souls: for my yoke is easy, and my burden is light.

[9] *Conversation:* society, commerce; Lat., *quo intravit et exuit into nos.* Brightman, *English Rite,* II, 572.

[10] "Mathias" in text, here and following.

The Annunciation of the Virgin Mary

The Collect

WE beseech thee, Lord, pour thy grace into our hearts, that as we have known Christ thy Son's incarnation, by the message of an angel, so by his cross and passion we may be brought unto the glory of his resurrection; through the same Christ our Lord.

The Epistle [Isa. 7[1]

GOD spake once again unto Ahaz, saying, Require a token of the Lord thy God, whether it be toward the depth beneath, or toward the height above. Then said Ahaz, I will require none, neither will I tempt the Lord. And he said, Hearken to,[2] ye of the house of David: is it not enough for you, that ye be grievous unto men, but ye must grieve my God also? And therefore the Lord shall give you a token: Behold, a virgin shall conceive and bear a son, and thou his mother shall call his name Immanuel.[3] Butter and honey shall he eat, that he may know to refuse the evil, and choose the good.

The Gospel [Luke 1

AND in the sixth month, the angel Gabriel was sent from God unto a city of Galilee, named Nazareth, to a virgin spoused to a man whose name was Joseph, of the house of David, and the virgin's name was Mary. And the angel went unto her, and said, Hail, full of grace, the Lord is with thee. Blessed art thou among women. When she saw him, she was abashed at his saying, and cast in her mind what manner of salvation that should

---

[1] "Esai" in text.
[2] *Hearken to:* listen.
[3] "Emanuel" in text.

be. And the angel said unto her, Fear not Mary, for thou hast found grace with God. Behold, thou shalt conceive in thy womb, and bear a son, and shalt call his name Jesus. He shall be great, and shall be called the Son of the Highest. And the Lord God shall give unto him the seat of his father David, and he shall reign over the house of Jacob forever, and of his kingdom there shall be none end. Then said Mary to the angel, How shall this be, seeing I know not[4] a man? And the angel answered and said unto her, The Holy Ghost shall come upon thee, and the power of the highest shall overshadow thee. Therefore also that holy thing which shall be born, shall be called the Son of God. And behold thy cousin Elizabeth, she hath also conceived a son in her age. And this is the sixth month, which was called barren, for with God nothing shall be unpossible. And Mary said, Behold the handmaid of the Lord, be it unto me according to thy word. And the angel departed from her.

Saint Mark's Day

The Collect

ALMIGHTY God, which hast instructed thy holy Church with the heavenly doctrine of thy evangelist Saint Mark: Give us grace so to be established by thy holy gospel that we be not, like children, carried away with every blast of vain doctrine; through Jesus Christ our Lord.

The Epistle [Eph. 4

UNTO every one of us is given grace, according to the measure of the gift of Christ. Wherefore he saith, When he went up on high, he led captivity captive, and gave gifts unto men. That he ascended, what meaneth it, but that he also de-

---

[4] *I know not:* I do not have sexual intercourse with.

scended first into the lowest parts of the earth? He that descended is even the same also that ascended up above all heavens, to fulfill all things. And the very same made some apostles, some prophets, some evangelists, some shepherds, and teachers, to the edifying of the saints, to the work and administration,[1] even to the edifying of the body of Christ till we all come to the unity of the faith, and knowledge of the Son of God, unto a perfect man, unto the measure of the full perfect age of Christ. That we henceforth should be no more children, wavering and carried about with every wind of doctrine, by the wiliness of men, through craftiness whereby they lay await for us to deceive us. But let us follow the truth in love, and in all things grow in him which is the head, even Christ, in whom if all the body be coupled and knit together, throughout every joint, wherewith one ministereth to another (according to the operation, as every part hath his measure), he increaseth the body, unto the edifying of itself through love.

The Gospel [John 15

I AM the true vine, and my Father is a husbandman. Every branch that beareth not fruit in me he will take away. And every branch that beareth fruit will he purge, that it may bring forth more fruit. Now are ye clean through the words which I have spoken unto you. Bide in me, and I in you. As the branch cannot bear fruit of itself, except it bide in the vine, no more can ye, except ye abide in me. I am the vine, ye are the branches. He that abideth in me and I in him, the same bringeth forth much fruit. For without me, can ye do nothing. If a man bide not in me, he is cast forth as a branch, and is withered. And men gather them, and cast them into the fire, and they burn. If ye abide in me, and my words abide in you, ask what ye will, and it shall be done for you. Herein is my Father glorified, that ye bear much fruit, and become my disciples. As the Father hath loved me,

---

[1] *Administration:* ministry.

even so also have I loved you. Continue you in my love. If ye keep my commandments, ye shall bide in my love, even as I have kept my Father's commandments, and abide in his love. These things have I spoken unto you, that my joy might remain in you, and that your joy might be full.

Saint Philip and James

The Collect

ALMIGHTY God, whom truly to know is everlasting life: Grant us perfectly to know thy Son Jesus Christ to be the way, the truth, and the life, as thou hast taught Saint Philip, and other the Apostles; through Jesus Christ our Lord.

The Epistle [James 1

JAMES the servant of God, and of the Lord Jesus Christ, sendeth greeting to the twelve tribes which are scattered abroad. My brethren, count it for an exceeding joy when ye fall into diverse temptations, knowing this, that the trying of your faith gendereth patience. And let patience have her perfect work, that ye may be perfect, and sound, lacking nothing. If any of you lack wisdom, let him ask of him that giveth it, even God, which giveth to all men indifferently, and casteth no man in the teeth,[1] and it shall be given him. But let him ask in faith, and waver not, for he that doubteth is like a wave on the sea, which is tossed of the winds, and carried with violence. Neither let that man think that he shall receive anything of the Lord. A wavering minded man is unstable in all his ways. Let the brother which is of low degree rejoice when he is exalted. Again, let him that is rich rejoice when he is made low. For even as the flower of the

---

[1] *And casteth no man in the teeth:* Lat., *et non improperat*, and does not reproach, taunt. Nestle, *Novum testamentum Graeca et Latina*, p. 574.

grass, shall he pass away. For as the sun riseth with heat, and the grass withereth, and his flower falleth away, and the beauty of the fashion of it perisheth, even so shall the rich man perish in his ways. Happy is the man that endureth temptation. For when he is tried, he shall receive the crown of life, which the Lord hath promised to them that love him.

The Gospel [John 14

AND Jesus said unto his disciples, Let not your hearts be troubled. Ye believe in God, believe also in me. In my Father's house are many mansions. If it were not so, I would have told you. I go to prepare a place for you. And if I go to prepare a place for you, I will come again and receive you even unto myself, that where I am, there may ye be also. And whither I go, you know, and the way ye know. Thomas saith unto him, Lord, we know not whither thou goest. And how is it possible for us to know the way? Jesus saith unto him, I am the way, and the truth, and the life. No man cometh to the Father but by me. If ye had known me, ye had known my Father also. And now ye know him and have seen him. Philip saith unto him, Lord, show us the Father, and it sufficeth us. Jesus saith unto him, Have I been so long time with you, and yet hast thou not known me? Philip, he that hath seen me, hath seen my Father, and how sayest thou then, show us the Father? Believest not thou that I am in the Father, and the Father in me? The words that I spake unto you, I spake not of myself. But the Father that dwelleth in me, is he that doeth the works. Believe me that I am in the Father, and the Father in me. Or else believe me for the work's sake. Verily, verily, I say unto you, He that believeth on me, the works that I do, the same shall he do also, and greater works than these shall he do, because I go unto my Father. And whatsoever ye ask in my name, that will I do, that the Father may be glorified by the Son. If ye shall ask anything in my name, I will do it.

Saint Barnabas[1] Apostle

The Collect

LORD Almighty, which hast endued thy holy Apostle Barnabas with singular gifts of thy Holy Ghost: Let us not be destitute of thy manifold gifts, nor yet of grace to use them alway to thy honor and glory; through Jesus Christ our Lord.

The Epistle [Acts 11

TIDINGS of these things came unto the ears of the congregation, which was in Jerusalem. And they sent forth Barnabas, that he should go unto Antioch. Which when he came, and had seen the grace of God, was glad and exhorted them all, that with purpose of heart they would continually cleave unto the Lord. For he was a good man, and full of the Holy Ghost and of faith, and much people was added unto the Lord. Then departed Barnabas to Tarsus[2] to seek Saul. And when he had found him, he brought him unto Antioch. And it chanced, that a whole year they had their conversation[3] with the congregation[4] there, and taught much people, insomuch that the disciples of Antioch were the first that were called Christian.[5] In those days came prophets from the city of Jerusalem unto Antioch. And there stood[6] up one of them named Agabus, and signified by the Spirit that there should be great dearth throughout all the world, which came to pass in the Emperor Claudius's days. Then the disciples,

---

[1] "Barnabe" in text.

[2] "Tharsus" in text.

[3] *Conversation:* society, commerce; 1661 Book has "assembled themselves with." Brightman, *English Rite*, II, 589.

[4] 1661 Book has "Church" (Brightman, II, 589); Lat., *ecclesia*; Gk. ἐκκλησία. Merk, *Novum testamentum*, p. 437.

[5] "Christen" in text.

[6] Text has "stody."

every man according to his ability, purposed to send succor unto the brethren which dwelt in Jewry, which thing they also did, and sent it to the elders by the hands of Barnabas and Saul.

The Gospel [John 15

THIS is my commandment, that ye love together as I have loved you. Greater love hath no man than this, that a man bestow his life for his friends. Ye are my friends, if ye do whatsoever I command you. Henceforth call I not you servants, for the servant knoweth not what his lord doeth. But you have I called friends, for all things that I have heard of my Father, have I opened to you. Ye have not chosen me, but I have chosen you, and ordained you to go and bring forth fruit, and that your fruit should remain, that whatsoever ye ask of the Father in my name, he may give it you.

Saint John Baptist

The Collect

ALMIGHTY God, by whose providence thy servant John Baptist was wonderfully born, and sent to prepare the way of thy Son our Savior by preaching of penance:[1] Make us so to follow his doctrine and holy life, that we may truly repent according to his preaching, and after his example constantly speak the truth, boldly rebuke vice, and patiently suffer for the truth's sake; through Jesus Christ our Lord.

[1] 1661 Book has "repentance" (Brightman, *English Rite*, II, 593). See Cosin, *Works*, V (Oxford, 1855), 512, for suggestion as to source of change.

The Epistle [Isa. 40

BE of good cheer my people. O ye prophets comfort my people, saith your God, comfort Jerusalem at the heart, and tell her that her travail is at an end, that her offense is pardoned, that she hath received of the Lord's hand sufficient correction for all her sins. A voice cried in the wilderness, Prepare the way of the Lord in the wilderness, make straight the path for our God in the desert. Let all valleys be exalted, and every mountain and hill be laid low. What so is crooked, let it be made straight, and let the rough be made plain fields. For the glory of the Lord shall appear, and all flesh shall at once see it; for why? the mouth of the Lord hath spoken it. The same voice spake, Now cry. And the prophet answered, What shall I cry? That all flesh is grass, and that all the goodliness thereof is as the flower of the field. The grass is withered, the flower falleth away. Even so is the people as grass, when the breath of the Lord bloweth upon them. Nevertheless, whether the grass wither, or that the flower fade away, yet the word of our God endureth forever. Go up unto the high hill (O Sion) thou that bringest good tidings, lift up thy voice with power. O thou preacher Jerusalem, lift it up without fear, and say unto the cities of Judah, Behold your God, behold, the Lord God shall come with power, and bear rule with his arm. Behold, he bringeth his treasure with him, and his works go before him. He shall feed his flock like an herdman.[2] He shall gather the lambs together with his arm, and carry them in his bosom, and shall kindly entreat[3] those that bear young.

The Gospel [Luke 1

ELIZABETH'S time came that she should be delivered, and she brought forth a son. And her neighbors and her cousins heard how the Lord had showed great mercy upon her, and re-

[2] *Herdman:* shepherd; text has "heardman."
[3] *Entreat:* "lead" (RSV).

joiced with her. And it fortuned that in the eighth day they came to circumcise the child, and called his name Zacharias[4] after the name of his father. And his mother answered and said, Not so, but his name shall be called John. And they said unto her, There is none in thy kindred that is named with this name. And they made signs to his father, how he would have him called. And he asked for writing tables,[5] and wrote, saying, His name is John. And they marveled all. And his mouth was opened immediately, and his tongue also, and he spake and praised God. And fear came on all them that dwelt nigh unto him. And all these sayings was noised abroad throughout all the high country of Jewry, and they that heard them laid them up in their hearts, saying, What manner of child shall this be? And the hand of the Lord was with him. And his father Zacharias was filled with the Holy Ghost, and prophesied, saying, Praised be the Lord God of Israel, for he hath visited and redeemed his people. And hath raised up an horn of salvation[6] unto us, in the house of his servant David. Even as he promised by the mouth of his holy prophets, which were since the world began. That we should be saved from our enemies, and from the hand of all that hate us. That he would deal mercifully with our fathers, and remember his holy covenant. And he would perform the oath which he sware to our father Abraham for to forgive us. That we being delivered out of the hands of our enemies, might serve him without fear, all the days of our life, in such holiness and righteousness as are acceptable for him. And thou child shalt be called the Prophet of the Highest, for thou shalt go before the face of the Lord to prepare his ways. To give knowledge of salvation unto his people for the remission of sins. Through the tender mercy of our God, whereby the dayspring from on high hath visited us. To give

---

[4] "Zachary" in text.

[5] *Tables:* tablets.

[6] *Horn of salvation:* means of defense or resistance, thus used of God or Christ (OED). See *Benedictus*, Morning Prayer, p. 57, where it is "a mighty salvation."

light to them that sat in darkness and in the shadow of death, to guide our feet into the way of peace. And the child grew and waxed strong in spirit and was in wilderness til the day came, when he should show himself unto the Israelites.

Saint Peter's Day

The Collect

ALMIGHTY God, which by thy Son Jesus Christ hast given to thy Apostle Saint Peter many excellent gifts and commandest him earnestly to feed thy flock: Make, we beseech thee, all bishops and pastors diligently to preach thy holy Word, and the people obediently to follow the same, that they may receive the crown of everlasting glory; through Jesus Christ our Lord.

The Epistle [Acts 12[1]

AT the same time Herod the king stretched forth his hands to vex certain of the congregation. And he killed James the brother of John with the sword. And because he saw it pleased the Jews, he proceeded further and took Peter also. Then were the days of sweet bread.[2] And when he had caught him, he put him in prison also and delivered him to four quaternions[3] of soldiers to be kept, intending after Easter[4] to bring him forth to the people. And Peter was kept in prison; but prayer was made without ceasing of the congregation unto God for him. And when Herod would have brought him out unto the people, the same night slept Peter between two soldiers, bound with two chains.

---

[1] This citation is not in the text, but is in 1559 Grafton.

[2] *Days of sweet bread:* days of the Feast of Unleavened Bread.

[3] *Four quaternions:* four squads, or four squads of four soldiers each (RSV, OED).

[4] *Easter:* Passover.

And the keepers before the door kept the prison. And behold the angel of the Lord was there present, and a light shined in the habitation. And he smote Peter on the side, and stirred him up, saying, Arise up quickly. And his chains fell from his hands. And the angel said unto him, Gird thyself, and bind on thy sandals. And he so did. And he saith unto him: Cast thy garment about thee and follow me. And he came out and followed him, and wist[5] not that it was truth which was done by the angel, but thought he had seen a vision. When they were past the first and second watch, they came unto the iron gate that leadeth unto the city, which opened to them by the own accord. And they went out and passed through one street, and forthwith the angel departed from him. And when Peter was come to himself, he said, Now I know of a surety that the Lord hath sent his angel, and hath delivered me out of the hand of Herod, and from all waiting of the people of the Jews.

The Gospel [Matt. 16[6]

WHEN Jesus came into the coasts of the city which is called Caesarea Philippi, he asked his disciples saying, Whom do men say that I, the Son of man, am? They said, Some say that thou art John Baptist, some Elias,[7] some Jeremiah,[8] or one of the prophets. He saith unto them, But whom say ye that I am? Simon Peter answered, and said, Thou art Christ, the Son of the living God. And Jesus answered, and said unto him, Happy art thou, Simon the son of Jonas, for flesh and blood hath not opened that unto thee, but my Father which is in heaven. And I say unto thee, that thou art Peter and upon this rock I will build my congregation.[9] And the gates of hell shall not prevail against it. And

[5] *Wist:* knew.

[6] Text has "15"; misprint.

[7] "Helias" in text.

[8] "Jeremias" in text.

[9] 1661 Book has "Church"; Lat., *ecclesiam*; Gk., ἐκκλησίαν. Brightman, *English Rite*, II, 602.

I will give unto thee the keys of the kingdom of heaven. And whatsoever thou bindest in earth, shall be bound in heaven: and whatsoever thou loosest in earth, shall be loosed in heaven.

Saint James the Apostle

The Collect

GRANT, O merciful God, that as thy holy Apostle Saint James, leaving his father and all that he had, without delay, was obedient unto the calling of thy Son Jesus Christ, and followed him; so we, forsaking all worldly and carnal affections, may be evermore ready to follow thy commandments; through Jesu Christ our Lord.

The Epistle [Acts 11

IN those days came prophets from the city of Jerusalem unto Antioch. And there stood up one of them named Agabus, and signified by the spirit that there should be great dearth throughout all the world, which came to pass in the Emperor Claudius's days. Then the disciples, every man according to his ability, purposed to send succor unto the brethren which dwelt in Jewry, which thing they also did, and sent it to the elders, by the hands of Barnabas and Saul. At the same time Herod the king stretched forth his hands to vex certain of the congregation.[1] And he killed James the brother of John with the sword. And because he saw it pleased the Jews, he proceeded farther and took Peter also.

The Gospel [Matt. 20

THEN came to him the mother of Zebedee's children, with her sons, worshiping him, and desiring a certain thing of him. And he said unto her, What wilt thou? She said unto

---

[1] 1661 Book has "Church."

him, Grant that these my two sons may sit, the one on thy right hand, and the other on thy left, in thy kingdom. But Jesus answered and said, Ye wot[2] not what ye ask. Are ye able to drink of the cup that I shall drink of, and to be baptized with the baptism that I am baptized with? They said unto him, We are. He said unto them, Ye shall drink indeed of my cup, and be baptized with the baptism that I am baptized with, but to sit on my right hand, and on my left, is not mine to give, but it shall chance unto them that it is prepared for of my Father. And when the ten heard this, they disdained at[3] the two brethren. But Jesus called them unto him, and said, Ye know that the princes of the nations have dominion over them, and they that are great men exercise authority upon them. It shall not be so among you. But whosoever will be great among you, let him be your minister, and whosoever will be chief among you, let him be your servant. Even as the Son of man came not to be ministered unto, but to minister, and to give his life a redemption for many.

Saint Bartholomew

The Collect

O ALMIGHTY and everlasting God, which hast given grace to thy Apostle Bartholomew truly to believe and to preach thy word: Grant, we beseech thee unto thy Church, both to love that he believed, and to preach that he taught; through Christ our Lord.

[2] *Wot:* know.
[3] *They disdained at:* they treat with contempt and scorn.

The Epistle [Acts 5 [1]

BY the hands of the Apostles were many signs and wonders showed among the people. And they were altogether with one accord in Solomon's[2] porch. And of other durst no man join himself to them, nevertheless the people magnified them. The number of them that believed in the Lord, both of men and women, grew more and more, insomuch that they brought the sick into the streets, and laid them on beds and couches, that at the least way the shadow of Peter, when he came by, might shadow some of them. There came also a multitude out of the cities round about, unto Jerusalem, bringing sick folks, and them which were vexed with unclean spirits. And they were healed every one.

The Gospel [Luke 22

AND there was a strife among them, which of them should seem to be the greatest. And he said unto them, The kings of nations reign over them, and they that have authority upon them, are called gracious lords. But ye shall not so be. But he that is greatest among you, shall be as the younger, and he that is chief, shall be as he that doth minister. For whether is greater, he that sitteth at meat, or he that serveth? Is not he that sitteth at meat? But I am among you as he that ministereth. Ye are they which have bidden with me in my temptations. And I appoint unto you a kingdom, as my Father hath appointed unto me, that ye may eat and drink at my table in my kingdom, and sit on seats judging the twelve tribes of Israel.

[1] This citation is not in the text, but is in 1559 Grafton.
[2] "Salomons" in text.

Saint Matthew

The Collect

ALMIGHTY God, which by thy blessed Son didst call Matthew from the receipt of custom[1] to be an Apostle and evangelist: Grant us grace to forsake all covetous desires, and inordinate love of riches, and to follow thy said Son Jesus Christ, who liveth and reigneth, etc.

The Epistle [2 Cor. 4

SEEING that we have such an office, even as God hath had mercy on us, we go not out of kind,[2] but have cast from us the cloaks of unhonesty, and walk not in craftiness, neither handle we the Word of God deceitfully, but open the truth, and report ourselves to every man's conscience in the sight of God. If our gospel be yet hid, it is hid among them that are lost, in whom the God of this world hath blinded the minds of them which believe not, lest the light of the gospel of the glory of Christ (which is the image of God) should shine unto them. For we preach not ourselves, but Christ Jesus to be the Lord, and ourselves your servants, for Jesus' sake. For it is God that commandeth the light to shine out of darkness, which hath shined in our hearts, for to give the light of the knowledge of the glory of God, in the face of Jesus Christ.

The Gospel [Matt. 9

AND as Jesus passed forth from thence, he saw a man (named Matthew) sitting at the receipt of custom, and he said unto him, Follow me. And he arose and followed him. And it

---

[1] *Receipt of custom:* tax office.

[2] *We go not out of kind:* we do not swerve, lose the character appropriate to one's birth and family (OED).

came to pass as Jesus sat at meat in his house, behold many publicans also and sinners that came, sat down with Jesus and his disciples. And when the Pharisees saw it, they said unto his disciples, Why eateth your master with publicans and sinners? But when Jesus heard that, he said unto them, They that be strong need not the physician, but they that are sick. Go ye rather and learn what that meaneth, I will have mercy, and not sacrifice: for I am not come to call the righteous but sinners to repentance.

Saint Michael and All Angels

The Collect

EVERLASTING God, which hast ordained and constituted the services of all angels and men in a wonderful order: Mercifully grant, that they which always do thee service in heaven, may by thy appointment succor and defend us in earth; through Jesus Christ our Lord, etc.

The Epistle [Apoc. 12

THERE was a great battle in heaven. Michael and his angels fought with the dragon, and the dragon fought with his angels, and prevailed not, neither was there place found any more in heaven. And the great dragon, that old serpent, called the devil and Satan,[1] was cast out, which deceiveth all the world. And he was cast into the earth, and his angels were cast out also with him. And I heard a loud voice, saying, In heaven is now made salvation and strength, and the kingdom of our God, and the power of his Christ. For the accuser of our brethren is cast down, which accused them before God day and night. And they overcame him by the blood of the Lamb, and by the word of their testimony, and they loved not their lives unto the death.

[1] "Sathanas" in text.

239

Therefore rejoice heavens, and ye that dwell in them. Woe unto the inhabiters of the earth, and of the sea, for the devil is come down unto you, which hath greath wrath, because he knoweth that he hath but a short time.

The Gospel [Matt. 18

AT the same time came the disciples unto Jesus, saying, Who is the greatest in the kingdom of heaven? Jesus called a child unto him, and set him in the midst of them, and said, Verily I say unto you, except ye turn and become as children, ye shall not enter into the kingdom of heaven. Whosoever therefore humbleth himself as this child, that same is the greatest in the kingdom of heaven. And whosoever receiveth such a child in my name, receiveth me. But whoso doth offend one of these little ones which believe in me, it were better for him that a millstone were hanged about his neck, and that he were drowned in the depth of the sea. Woe unto the world, because of offenses. Necessary it is that offenses come, but woe unto the man by whom the offense cometh. Wherefore, if thy hand or thy foot hinder thee, cut him off, and cast it from thee. It is better for thee to enter into life halt or maimed, rather than thou shouldest (having two hands or two feet) be cast into everlasting fire. And if thine eye offend thee, pluck it out, and cast it from thee. It is better for thee to enter into life with one eye, rather than (having two eyes) to be cast into hell-fire. Take heed that ye despise not one of these little ones. For I say unto you, that in heaven their angels do always behold the face of my Father, which is in heaven.

Saint Luke the Evangelist

The Collect

ALMIGHTY God, which calledst Luke the physician, whose praise is in the gospel, to be a physician of the soul: It may please thee by the wholesome medicines of his doctrine, to heal all the diseases of our souls; through thy Son Jesu Christ our Lord.

The Epistle [2 Tim. 4 [1]

WATCH thou in all things, suffer afflictions, do the work thoroughly of an evangelist, fulfill thine office unto the uttermost: be sober. For I am now ready to be offered, and the time of my departing is at hand. I have fought a good fight, I have fulfilled my course, I have kept the faith. From henceforth there is laid up for me a crown of righteousness, which the Lord (that is a righteous judge) shall give me at that day: not to me only, but to all them that love his coming. Do thy diligence that thou mayest come shortly unto me. For Demas hath forsaken me, and loveth this present world, and is departed unto Thessalonica. Crescens is gone to Galatia,[2] Titus unto Dalmatia,[3] only Luke[4] is with me. Take Mark and bring him with thee, for he is profitable unto me for the ministration. And Tychicus[5] have I sent to Ephesus. The cloak that I left at Troas[6] with Carpus, when thou comest bring with thee, and the books, but specially the parchment. Alexander the coppersmith did me much evil:

---

[1] Text has "2 Tim. 3"; misprint.
[2] "Galacia" in text.
[3] "Dalmacia" in text.
[4] "Lucas" in text.
[5] "Tichicus" in text.
[6] "Troada" in text.

the Lord reward him according to his deeds, of whom be thou ware[7] also, for he hath greatly withstand our words.

The Gospel [Luke 10

THE Lord appointed other seventy, and two also, and sent them two and two before him into every city and place, whither he himself would come. Therefore he said unto them, The harvest is great, but the laborers are few. Pray ye therefore the Lord of the harvest, to send forth laborers into the harvest. Go your ways: behold, I send you forth as lambs among wolves. Bear no wallet, neither scrip,[8] nor shoes, and salute no man by the way. Into whatsoever house ye enter, first say, Peace be to this house. And if the son of peace be there, your peace shall rest upon him: if not, it shall return to you again. And in the same house tarry still, eating and drinking such as they give. For the laborer is worthy of his reward.

Simon and Jude Apostles

The Collect

ALMIGHTY God, which hast builded thy congregation[1] upon the foundation of the Apostles and prophets, Jesu Christ himself being the head cornerstone: Grant us so to be joined together in unity of spirit by their doctrine, that we may be made an holy temple acceptable to thee; through Jesu Christ our Lord.

[7] *Ware:* wary.
[8] *Scrip:* a small bag or satchel.
[1] 1661 Book has "Church"; Matthew Wren's suggestion (see Brightman, *English Rite*, II, 629).

The Epistle [Jude 1

JUDAS the servant of Jesu Christ, the brother of James: to them which are called and sanctified in God the Father, and preserved in Jesu Christ. Mercy unto you, and peace and love be multiplied. Beloved, when I gave all diligence to write unto you of the common salvation, it was needful for me to write unto you, to exhort you that ye should continually labor in the faith, which was once given unto the saints. For there are certain ungodly men craftily crept in, of which it was written afore time unto such judgment. They turn the grace of our God unto wantonness, and deny God (which is the only Lord) and our Lord Jesu Christ. My mind is therefore to put you in remembrance forasmuch as ye once know this, how that the Lord (after that he had delivered the people out of Egypt) destroyed them which after believed not. The angels also which kept not their first state, but left their own habitation, he hath reserved in everlasting chains under darkness, unto the judgment of the great day, even as Sodom and Gomorrah,[2] and the cities about them, which in like manner defiled themselves with fornication and followed strange flesh, are set forth for an example, and suffer the pain of eternal fire. Likewise these being deceived by dreams, defile the flesh, despise rulers, and speak evil of them that are in authority.

The Gospel [John 15

THIS command I you, that ye love together. If the world hate you, ye know it hated me before it hated you. If ye were of the world, the world would love his own. Howbeit, because ye are not of the world, but I have chosen you out of the world, therefore the world hateth you. Remember the word that I say unto you, The servant is not greater than the lord. If they

---

[2] "Gomor" in text.

have persecuted me, they will also persecute you. If they have kept my saying, they will keep yours also. But all these things will they do unto you for my name's sake, because they have not known him that sent me. If I had not come and spoken unto them, they should have had no sin: but now have they nothing to cloak their sin withal. He that hateth me, hateth my Father also. If I had not done among them the works which none other man did, they should have had no sin. But now have they both seen and hated not only me, but also my Father. But this happeneth, that the saying might be fulfilled that is written in their law, They hated me without a cause. But when the Comforter is come, whom I will send unto you from the Father, even the Spirit of truth (which proceedeth of the Father) he shall testify of me. And ye shall bear witness also, because ye have been with me from the beginning.

All Saints

The Collect

ALMIGHTY God, which hast knit together thy elect in one communion and fellowship, in the mystical body of thy Son Christ our Lord: grant us grace so to follow thy holy saints in all virtues and godly living, that we may come to those inspeakable[1] joys, which thou hast prepared for them that unfainedly love thee; through Jesus Christ our Lord.

The Epistle [Apoc. 7

BEHOLD, I, John, saw another angel ascend from the rising of the sun, which had the seal of the living God, and he cried with a loud voice to the four angels (to whom power was

---

[1] 1549 and 1661 Books have "unspeakable." Brightman, *English Rite*, II, 632–33.

given to hurt the earth and the sea) saying, Hurt not the earth, neither the sea, neither the trees, till we have sealed the servants of our God in their foreheads. And I heard the number of them which were sealed, and there were sealed an hundred and forty-four thousand of all the tribes of the children of Israel.

Of the tribe of Juda[2] were sealed twelve thousand.
Of the tribe of Ruben were sealed twelve thousand.
Of the tribe of Gad were sealed twelve thousand.
Of the tribe of Aser were sealed twelve thousand.
Of the tribe of Neptalim were sealed twelve thousand.
Of the tribe of Manasses were sealed twelve thousand.
Of the tribe of Symeon were sealed twelve thousand.
Of the tribe of Levi were sealed twelve thousand.
Of the tribe of Isachar were sealed twelve thousand.
Of the tribe of Zabulon were sealed twelve thousand.
Of the tribe of Joseph were sealed twelve thousand.
Of the tribe of Benjamin were sealed twelve thousand.

After this I beheld, and lo, a great multitude (which no man can number) of all nations and people, and tongues, stood before the seat, and before the Lamb, clothed with long white garments, and palms in their hands, and cried with a loud voice, saying, Salvation be ascribed to him that sitteth upon the seat of our God, and unto the Lamb. And all the angels stood in the compass of the seat, and of the elders, and the four beasts, and fell before the seat on their faces, and worshiped God, saying, Amen. Blessing, and glory, and wisdom, and thank,[3] and honor, and power, and might, be unto our God forevermore. Amen.

The Gospel [Matt. 5

JESUS, seeing the people, went up into the mountain, and when he was set, his disciples came to him, and after that he had opened his mouth, he taught them, saying, Blessed are the poor in spirit, for theirs is the kingdom of heaven. Blessed

---

[2] The proper names here have been left as found in text.
[3] 1661 Book has "thanksgiving." Brightman, *English Rite*, II, 635.

are they that mourn, for they shall receive comfort. Blessed are the meek, for they shall receive the inheritance of the earth. Blessed are they which hunger and thirst after righteousness, for they shall be satisfied. Blessed are the merciful, for they shall obtain mercy. Blessed are the pure in heart, for they shall see God. Blessed are the peacemakers, for they shall be called the children of God. Blessed are they which suffer persecution for righteousness sake, for theirs is the kingdom of heaven. Blessed are ye when men revile you and persecute you, and shall falsely say all manner of evil sayings against you for my sake: rejoice and be glad, for great is your reward in heaven. For so persecuted they the prophets which were before you.

The Order for the Administration

of the Lord's Supper, or Holy Communion

So many as do intend to be partakers of the Holy Communion, shall signify their names to the curate overnight, or else in the morning, afore[1] the beginning of Morning Prayer, or immediately after.

And if any of those be an open and notorious evil liver, so that the congregation by him is offended, or have done any wrong to his neighbors by word or deed: the curate having knowledge thereof, shall call him, and advertise him, in any wise not to presume to the Lord's Table, until he have openly declared himself to have truly repented and amended his former naughty[2] life, that the congregation may thereby be satisfied, which afore were offended; and that he have recompensed the parties whom he hath done wrong unto, or at the least declare himself to be in full purpose so to do, as soon as he conveniently may.

The same order shall the curate use with those betwixt whom he preceiveth malice and hatred to reign, not suffering them to be partakers of the Lord's Table until he know them to be reconciled. And if one of the parties so at variance be content to forgive from the bottom of his heart all that the other hath trespassed against him, and to make amends for that he himself hath offended, and the other party will not be persuaded to a godly unity, but remain still in his frowardness[3] and malice: the minis-

[1] *Afore:* before.
[2] *Naughty:* morally bad, wicked.
[3] *Frowardness:* perversity.

ter in that case ought to admit the penitent person to the Holy Communion, and not him that is obstinate.

The Table having at the Communion time a fair white linen cloth upon it, shall stand in the body of the church, or in the chancel, where Morning Prayer and Evening Prayer be appointed to be said. And the priest standing at the north side of the Table shall say the Lord's Prayer with this Collect following.

ALMIGHTY God, unto whom all hearts be open, all desires known, and from whom no secrets are hid: Cleanse the thoughts of our hearts by the inspiration of thy Holy Spirit, that we may perfectly love thee, and worthily magnify thy holy name; through Christ our Lord. Amen.

Then shall the priest rehearse distinctly all the Ten Commandments, and the people, kneeling, shall after every commandment ask God's mercy for their transgression of the same, after this sort.

Minister. God spake these words and said, I am the Lord thy God, Thou shalt have none other gods but me.

People. Lord have mercy upon us, and incline our hearts to keep this law.

Minister. Thou shalt not make to thyself any graven image, nor the likeness of anything that is in heaven above, or in the earth beneath, nor in the water under the earth. Thou shalt not bow down to them, nor worship them: For I the Lord thy God am a jealous God, and visit the sin of the fathers upon the children, unto the third and fourth generation of them that hate me, and show mercy unto thousands in them that love me, and keep my commandments.

People. Lord have mercy upon us, and incline our hearts to keep this law.

Minister. Thou shalt not take the name of the Lord thy God in vain: for the Lord will not hold him guiltless that taketh his name in vain.

People. Lord have mercy upon us, and incline our hearts to keep this law.

Minister. Remember that thou keep holy the Sabbath day: six days shalt thou labor and do all that thou hast to do, but the seventh day is the Sabbath of the Lord thy God. In it thou shalt do no manner of work, thou and thy son and thy daughter, thy manservant, and thy maidservant, thy cattle, and the stranger that is within thy gates: For in six days the Lord made heaven and earth, the sea, and all that in them is, and rested the seventh day: wherefore the Lord blessed the seventh day and hallowed it.

People. Lord have mercy upon us, and incline our, etc.

Minister. Honor thy father and thy mother, that thy days may be long in the land which the Lord thy God giveth thee.

People. Lord have mercy upon us, and incline our, etc.

Minister. Thou shalt do no murder.

People. Lord have mercy upon us, and incline our, etc.

Minister. Thou shalt not commit adultery.

People. Lord have mercy upon us, and incline our, etc.

Minister. Thou shalt not steal.

People. Lord have mercy upon us, and incline our, etc.

Minister. Thou shalt not bear false witness against thy neighbor.

People. Lord have mercy upon us, and incline our hearts to keep this law.

Minister. Thou shalt not covet thy neighbor's house. Thou shalt not covet thy neighbor's wife, nor his servant, nor his maid, nor his ox, nor his ass, nor anything that is his.

People. Lord have mercy upon us, and write all these thy laws in our hearts, we beseech thee.

Then shall follow the Collect of the day, with one of these two Collects following for the Queen, the priest standing up and saying.

Let us pray.   Priest.

ALMIGHTY God, whose kingdom is everlasting, and power
infinite: Have mercy upon the whole congregation, and so
rule the heart of thy chosen servant Elizabeth, our queen and
governor, that she (knowing whose minister she is) may above
all things seek thy honor and glory; and that we her subjects
(duly considering whose authority she hath) may faithfully
serve, honor, and humbly obey her, in thee, and for thee, according to thy blessed Word and ordinance; through Jesus Christ
our Lord, who with thee and the Holy Ghost liveth and reigneth
ever one God, world without end. Amen.

ALMIGHTY and everlasting God, we be taught by thy holy
Word, that the hearts of kings are in thy rule and governance, and that thou dost dispose and turn them, as it seemeth
best to thy godly wisdom: We humbly beseech thee, so to dispose and govern the heart of Elizabeth, thy servant, our queen
and governor, that in all her thoughts, words, and works, she
may ever seek thy honor and glory, and study to preserve thy
people committed to her charge, in wealth, peace, and godliness.
Grant this, O merciful Father, for thy dear Son's sake, Jesus
Christ our Lord. Amen.

Immediately after the Collects, the priest shall read the Epistle beginning thus.

The Epistle written in the   Chapter of   . And the
Epistle ended, he shall say the Gospel, beginning thus.

The Gospel, written in the   Chapter of   . And the
Epistle and Gospel being ended shall be said the Creed.

I BELIEVE in one God, the Father Almighty, maker of heav-
en and earth, and of all things visible and invisible. And in
one Lord Jesu Christ, the only begotten Son of God, begotten
of his Father before all worlds: God of God, light of light, very
God of very God: begotten, not made, being of one substance
with the Father, by whom all things were made: who for us men
and for our salvation, came down from heaven, and was incarnate
by the Holy Ghost, of the Virgin Mary, and was made man: and

was crucified also for us, under Pontius[4] Pilate. He suffered and was buried, and the third day he rose again according to the Scriptures, and ascended into heaven, and sitteth at the right hand of the Father. And he shall come again with glory, to judge both the quick[5] and the dead, whose kingdom shall have none end. And I believe in the Holy Ghost, the Lord and giver of life, who proceedeth from the Father and the Son, who with the Father and the Son together is worshiped and glorified, who spake by the prophets. And I believe one catholic and apostolic Church. I acknowledge one baptism, for the remission of sins. And I look for the resurrection of the dead, and the life of the world to come. Amen.

After the Creed, if there be no sermon, shall follow one of the homilies already set forth or hereafter to be set forth by common authority.

After such sermon, homily, or exhortation, the curate shall declare unto the people whether there be any holy days or fasting days the week following, and earnestly exhort them to remember the poor, saying one or mo[6] of these sentences following, as he thinketh most convenient by his discretion.

LET your light so shine before men, that they may see your good works, and glorify your Father which is in heaven. [Matt. 5

Lay not up for yourselves treasure upon the earth where the rust and moth doth corrupt, and where thieves break through and steal. But lay up for yourselves treasures in heaven, where neither rust nor moth doth corrupt, and where thieves do not break through and steal. [Matt. 6

Whatsoever you would that men should do unto you, even so do unto them: for this is the law and the Prophets. [Matt. 7

Not everyone that saith unto me, Lord, Lord, shall enter into

---

[4] "Poncius" in text.
[5] *Quick:* living.
[6] *Mo:* more.

the kingdom of heaven: but he that doeth the will of my Father which is in heaven. [Matt. 7

Zaccheus[7] stood forth, and said unto the Lord, Behold Lord, the half of my goods I give to the poor, and if I have done any wrong to any man, I restore fourfold. [Luke 19

Who goeth a warfare at any time of his own cost? Who planteth a vineyard, and eateth not of the fruit thereof? Or who feedeth a flock, and eateth not of the milk of the flock? [1 Cor. 9

If we have sown unto you spiritual things, is it a great matter, if we shall reap your worldly things? [1 Cor. 9

Do ye not know, that they which minister about holy things, live of the sacrifice? They which wait of the altar, are partakers with the altar. Even so hath the Lord also ordained, that they which preach the gospel, should live of the gospel. [1 Cor. 9

He which soweth little, shall reap little: and he that soweth plenteously, shall reap plenteously. Let every man do according as he is disposed in his heart, not grudging, or of necessity: for God loveth a cheerful giver. [2 Cor. 9[8]

Let him that is taught in the Word, minister unto him that teacheth, in all good things. Be not deceived, God is not mocked: for whatsoever a man soweth, that shall he reap. [Gal. 6

While we have time, let us do good unto all men, and specially unto them which are of the household of faith. [Gal. 6

Godliness is great riches, if a man be contented with that he hath: for we brought nothing into the world, neither may we carry anything out. [1 Tim. 6

Charge them which are rich in this world, that they be ready to give, and glad to distribute: laying up in store for themselves a good foundation against the time to come, that they may attain eternal life. [1 Tim. 6

God is not unrighteous that he will forget your works and labor that proceedeth of love: which love ye have showed for his

---

[7] "Zache" in text.

[8] Text has "1 Cor. 9"; misprint.

name's sake, which have ministered unto saints, and yet do minister. [Heb. 6

To do good and to distribute, forget not: for with such sacrifices God is pleased. [Heb. 13

Whoso hath this world's good, and seeth his brother have need, and shutteth up his compassion from him, how dwelleth the love of God in him? [1 John 3

Give almose[9] of thy goods, and turn never thy face from any poor man, and then the face of the Lord shall not be turned away from thee. [Tob. 4

Be merciful after thy power. If thou hast much, give plenteously. If thou hast little, do thy diligence gladly to give of that little: for so gatherest thou thyself a good reward in the day of necessity. [Tob. 4

He that hath pity upon the poor, lendeth unto the Lord: and look what he layeth out, it shall be paid him again. [Prov. 19

Blessed be the man that provideth for the sick and needy, the Lord shall deliver him in the time of trouble. [Ps. 41

Then shall the churchwardens, or some other by them appointed, gather the devotion[10] of the people, and put the same into the poor men's box. And upon the offering days appointed, every man and woman shall pay to the curate the due and accustomed offerings. After which done, the priest shall say.

Let us pray for the whole state of Christ's Church militant here in earth.

ALMIGHTY and everliving God, which by thy holy Apostle hast taught us to make prayers and supplications, and to give thanks for all men: We humbly beseech thee most

---

[9] *Almose:* alms. See Frere, *Visitation Articles,* 3 vols. (London, 1910), III, 236, 260.

[10] *Devotion:* an offering made as an act of worship, alms.

mercifully to accept our almose,[11] and to receive these our prayers which we offer unto thy divine majesty; beseeching thee to inspire continually, the universal Church with the spirit of truth, unity, and concord: And grant that all they that do confess thy holy name, may agree in the truth of thy holy Word, and live in unity and godly love. We beseech thee also to save and defend all Christian kings, princes, and governors, and specially thy servant Elizabeth our queen, that under her we may be godly and quietly governed: And grant unto her whole Council, and to all that be put in authority under her, that they may truly and indifferently minister justice, to the punishment of wickedness and vice, and to the maintenance of God's true religion and virtue. Give grace (O heavenly Father) to all bishops, pastors, and curates, that they may both by their life and doctrine set forth thy true and lively Word, and rightly and duly administer thy holy sacraments: And to all thy people give thy heavenly grace, and especially to this congregation here present, that with meek heart and due reverence, they may hear and receive thy holy Word, truly serving thee in holiness and righteousness all the days of their life. And we most humbly beseech thee of thy goodness (O Lord) to comfort and succor all them which in this transitory life be in trouble, sorrow, need, sickness, or any other adversity. Grant this, O Father, for Jesus Christ's sake, our only mediator and advocate. Amen.

Then shall follow this exhortation at certain times when the curate shall see the people negligent to come to the Holy Communion.

WE be come together at this time, dearly beloved brethren, to feed at the Lord's Supper, unto the which in God's behalf I bid you all that be here present, and beseech you for the Lord Jesus Christ's sake, that ye will not refuse to come thereto, being so lovingly called and bidden of God himself. Ye know

[11] Margin note: "If there be none alms given unto the poor, then shall the words of accepting our alms be left out unsaid."

how grievous and unkind a thing it is, when a man hath prepared a rich feast, decked his table with all kind of provision, so
that there lacketh nothing but the guests to sit down; and yet
they which be called without any cause most unthankfully refuse
to come. Which of you in such a case would not be moved? Who
would not think a great injury and wrong done unto him?
Wherefore most dearly beloved in Christ, take ye good heed
lest ye, withdrawing yourselves from this holy supper, provoke
God's indignation against you. It is an easy matter for a man
to say, I will not communicate, because I am otherwise letted[12]
with worldly business, but such excuses be not so easily accepted
and allowed before God. If any man say, I am a grievous sinner,
and therefore am afraid to come: wherefore then do you not repent and amend? When God calleth you, be you not ashamed
to say you will not come? When you should return to God, will
you excuse yourself and say that you be not ready? Consider
earnestly with yourselves how little such fained excuses shall
avail before God. They that refused the feast in the Gospel, because they had bought a farm, or would try their yokes of oxen,
or because they were married, were not so excused but counted
unworthy of the heavenly feast. I for my part am here present,
and according unto mine office, I bid you in the name of God. I
call you in Christ's behalf, I exhort you, as you love your own
salvation, that ye will be partakers of this Holy Communion.
And as the Son of God did vouchsafe to yield up his soul by death
upon the cross for your health;[13] even so it is your duty to receive
the communion together in the remembrance of his death, as he
himself commanded. Now if you will in no wise thus do, consider
with yourselves how great injury you do unto God, and how
sore[14] punishment hangeth over your heads for the same. And
whereas you offend God so sore in refusing this holy banquet, I
admonish, exhort, and beseech you that unto this unkindness ye

[12] *Letted:* hindered.
[13] *Health:* salvation.
[14] *Sore:* harsh, harshly.

will not add any more. Which thing ye shall do, if ye stand by as gazers and lookers on them that do communicate, and be no partakers of the same yourselves. For what thing can this be accounted else, than a further contempt and unkindness unto God? Truly it is a great unthankfulness to say nay when ye be called; but the fault is much greater when men stand by, and yet will neither eat nor drink this Holy Communion with other. I pray you what can this be else, but even to have the mysteries of Christ in derision? It is said unto all, Take ye and eat. Take and drink ye all of this: do this in remembrance of me. With what face then, or with what countenance shall ye hear these words? What will this be else but a neglecting, a despising, and mocking of the testament of Christ? Wherefore, rather than you should so do, depart you hence, and give place to them that be godly disposed. But when you depart, I beseech you, ponder with yourselves from whom you depart: ye depart from the Lord's Table, ye depart from your brethren, and from the banquet of most heavenly food. These things if ye earnestly consider, ye shall by God's grace return to a better mind, for the obtaining whereof we shall make our humble petitions, while we shall receive the Holy Communion.

And some time shall be said this also at the discretion of the curate.

D EARLY beloved, forasmuch as our duty is to render to Almighty God our heavenly Father most hearty thanks, for that he hath given his Son our Savior Jesus Christ, not only to die for us, but also to be our spiritual food and sustenance, as it is declared unto us, as well by God's Word, as by the holy sacraments of his blessed body and blood, the which being so comfortable[15] a thing to them which receive it worthily, and so dangerous to them that will presume to receive it unworthily: My duty is to exhort you to consider the dignity of the holy mystery, and the great peril of the unworthy receiving thereof,

[15] *Comfortable:* strengthening.

and so to search and examine your own consciences, as you should come holy and clean to a most godly and heavenly feast, so that in no wise you come but in the marriage garment, required of God in Holy Scripture, and so come and be received as worthy partakers of such a heavenly table. The way and the means thereto is: First to examine your lives and conversation[16] by the rule of God's commandments, and whereinsoever ye shall perceive yourselves to have offended, either by will, word, or deed, there bewail your own sinful lives, confess yourselves to Almighty God with full purpose of amendment of life. And if ye shall perceive your offenses to be such as be not only against God but also against your neighbors, then ye shall reconcile yourselves unto them, ready to make restitution and satisfaction according to the uttermost of your powers, for all injuries and wrongs done by you to any other, and likewise being ready to forgive other that have offended you, as you would have forgiveness of your offenses at God's hand. For otherwise the receiving of the Holy Communion doth nothing else but increase your damnation. And because it is requisite that no man should come to the Holy Communion but with a full trust in God's mercy, and with a quiet conscience, therefore if there be any of you which by the means aforesaid,[17] cannot quiet his own conscience, but requireth further comfort[18] or counsel, then let him come to me, or some other discreet and learned minister of God's Word, and open his grief that he may receive such ghostly[19] counsel, advice, and comfort as his conscience may be relieved, and that by the ministry of God's Word he may receive comfort and the benefit of absolution, to the quieting of his conscience, and avoiding of all scruple and doubtfulness.

Then shall the priest say this exhortation.

[16] *Conversation:* manner of conducting oneself in the world and society.
[17] *Aforesaid:* before mentioned.
[18] *Comfort:* strengthening.
[19] *Ghostly:* spiritual.

DEARLY beloved in the Lord, ye that mind to come to the Holy Communion of the Body and Blood of our Savior Christ, must consider what Saint Paul writeth to the Corinthians, how he exhorteth all persons diligently to try and examine themselves, before they presume to eat of that bread, and drink of that cup. For as the benefit is great, if with a truly penitent heart and lively faith we receive that holy Sacrament (for then we spiritually eat the flesh of Christ, and drink his blood, then we dwell in Christ and Christ in us, we be one with Christ, and Christ with us), so is the danger great if we receive the same unworthily. For then we be guilty of the body and blood of Christ our Savior. We eat and drink our own damnation, not considering the Lord's body. We kindle God's wrath against us. We provoke him to plague us with divers diseases, and sundry kinds of death. Therefore, if any of you be a blasphemer of God, an hinderer or slanderer of his Word, an adulterer, or be in malice or envy, or in any other grievous crime, bewail your sins, and come not to this holy table, lest after the taking of that holy Sacrament, the devil enter into you, as he entered into Judas, and fill you full of all iniquities, and bring you to destruction, both of body and soul. Judge therefore yourselves (brethren) that ye be not judged of the Lord. Repent you truly for your sins past, have a lively and steadfast faith in Christ our Savior. Amend your lives, and be in perfect charity with all men, so shall ye be meet[20] partakers of those holy mysteries. And above all things ye must give most humble and hearty thanks to God the Father, the Son, and the Holy Ghost, for the redemption of the world by the death and passion of our Savior Christ both God and man; who did humble himself, even to the death upon the cross for us miserable sinners, which lay in darkness and shadow of death, that he might make us the children of God, and exalt us to everlasting life. And to the end that we should alway remember the exceeding great love of our master and only Savior Jesus Christ, thus dying for us, and the innumerable benefits which by his pre-

[20] *Meet:* suitable.

cious bloodshedding he hath obtained to us, he hath instituted and ordained holy mysteries, as pledges of his love, and continual remembrance of his death, to our great and endless comfort.[21] To him therefore, with the Father and the Holy Ghost, let us give (as we are most bounden) continual thanks, submitting ourselves wholly to his holy will and pleasure, and studying to serve him in true holiness and righteousness all the days of our life. Amen.

Then shall the priest say to them that come to receive the Holy Communion.

YOU that do truly and earnestly repent you of your sins, and be in love and charity with your neighbors, and intend to lead a new life, following the commandments of God, and walking from henceforth in his holy ways: Draw near, and take this holy Sacrament to your comfort; make your humble confession to Almighty God before this congregation here gathered together in his holy name, meekly[22] kneeling upon your knees.

Then shall this general confession be made in the name of all those that are minded to receive the Holy Communion, either by one of them, or else by one of the ministers, or by the priest himself, all kneeling humbly upon their knees.

ALMIGHTY God, Father of our Lord Jesus Christ, maker of all things, judge of all men, we knowledge[23] and bewail our manifold sins and wickedness, which we from time to time most grievously have committed, by thought, word, and deed, against thy divine majesty, provoking most justly thy wrath and indignation against us. We do earnestly repent, and be heartily sorry for these our misdoings. The remembrance of them is grievous unto us, the burden of them is intolerable. Have mercy upon us, have mercy upon us most merciful Father, for thy Son our Lord Jesus Christ's sake; forgive us all that is past, and grant

[21] *Comfort:* strengthening.

[22] *Meekly:* not haughty, not vain, but submissively; "devoutly" in 1928 American Book; see "humbly upon their knees" in the rubric following.

[23] *Knowledge:* acknowledge.

that we may ever hereafter serve and please thee, in newness of life, to the honor and glory of thy name, through Jesus Christ our Lord. Amen.

Then shall the priest, or the bishop being present, stand up, and turning himself to the people, say thus.

ALMIGHTY God our heavenly Father, who of his great mercy hath promised forgiveness of sins to all them which with hearty repentance and true faith turn unto him: Have mercy upon you, pardon and deliver you from all your sins, confirm and strength[24] you in all goodness, and bring you to everlasting life, through Jesus Christ our Lord. Amen.

Then shall the priest also say.

Hear what comfortable words our Savior Christ saith, to all that truly turn to him.

COME unto me all that travail and be heavy laden and I shall refresh you.[25] So God loved the world, that he gave his only begotten Son, to the end that all that believe in him should not perish but have life everlasting.[26]
Hear also what Saint Paul saith.
This is a true saying, and worthy of all men to be received, that Jesus Christ came into the world to save sinners.[27]
Hear also what Saint John saith.
If any man sin, we have an advocate with the Father, Jesus Christ the righteous, and he is the propitiation for our sins.[28]

After the which the priest shall proceed, saying.

Lift up your hearts.
Answer. We lift them up unto the Lord.

[24] 1559 Grafton has "strengthen."
[25] Matt. 11:28.
[26] John 3:16.
[27] 1 Tim. 1:15.
[28] 1 John 2:1–2.

Priest. Let us give thanks unto our Lord God.

Answer. It is meet[29] and right so to do.

Priest. It is very meet, right, and our bounden duty that we should at all times, and in all places, give thanks unto thee, O Lord, holy Father, almighty, everlasting God.

Here shall follow the proper preface, according to the time, if there be any specially appointed, or else immediately shall follow: Therefore with angels, etc.

Proper Prefaces

Upon Christmas Day, and Seven Days After

BECAUSE thou didst give Jesus Christ, thine only Son, to be born as this day for us, who by the operation of the Holy Ghost, was made very man of the substance of the Virgin Mary his mother, and that without spot of sin, to make us clean from all sin. Therefore, etc.

Upon Easter Day, and Seven Days After

BUT chiefly are we bound to praise thee, for the glorious resurrection of thy Son Jesus Christ our Lord: for he is the very Paschal Lamb, which was offered for us, and hath taken away the sin of the world, who by his death hath destroyed death, and by his rising to life again, hath restored to us everlasting life. Therefore with, etc.

Upon the Ascension Day, and Seven Days After

THROUGH thy most dear beloved Son, Jesus Christ our Lord: who after his most glorious resurrection, manifestly appeared to all his Apostles, and in their sight ascended up into

[29] *Meet:* proper, suitable.

heaven, to prepare a place for us, that where he is, thither might we also ascend, and reign with him in glory. Therefore with, etc.

Upon Whitsunday, and Six Days After

THROUGH Jesus Christ our Lord, according to whose most true promise, the Holy Ghost came down this day from heaven, with a sudden great sound, as it had been a mighty wind, in the likeness of fiery tongues, lighting upon the Apostles to teach them, and to lead them to all truth, giving them both the gift of diverse languages, and also boldness, with fervent zeal, constantly to preach the gospel unto all nations, whereby we are brought out of darkness and error, into the clear light and true knowledge of thee, and of thy Son Jesus Christ. Therefore with, etc.

Upon the Feast of Trinity Only

IT is very meet, right, and our bounden duty, that we should at all times, and in all places, give thanks to thee, O Lord, almighty and everlasting God, which art one God, one Lord, not one only person, but three persons in one substance: for that which we believe of the glory of the Father, the same we believe of the Son, and of the Holy Ghost, without any difference or inequality. Therefore with, etc.

After which preface, shall follow immediately.

THEREFORE with angels and archangels, and with all the company of heaven, we laud and magnify thy glorious name, evermore praising thee, and saying: Holy, holy, holy, Lord God of hosts; heaven and earth are full of thy glory; glory be to thee, O Lord most high.

Then shall the priest kneeling down at God's board, say in the name of all them that shall receive the communion, this prayer following.

WE do not presume to come to this[30] thy table (O merciful Lord) trusting in our own righteousness, but in thy manifold and great mercies. We be not worthy so much as to gather the crumbs under thy table, but thou art the same Lord, whose property is always to have mercy. Grant us therefore (gracious Lord) so to eat the flesh of thy dear Son Jesus Christ, and to drink his blood, that our sinful bodies may be made clean by his body, and our souls washed through his most precious blood, and that we may evermore dwell in him, and he in us. Amen.

Then the priest standing up shall say as followeth.

ALMIGHTY God our heavenly Father, which of thy tender mercy didst give thine only Son Jesus Christ, to suffer death upon the cross for our redemption; who made there (by his one oblation of himself once offered) a full, perfect, and sufficient sacrifice, oblation, and satisfaction for the sins of the whole world; and did institute, and in his holy gospel command us to continue, a perpetual memory of that his precious death, until his coming again. Hear us, O merciful Father, we beseech thee; and grant that we receiving these thy creatures of bread and wine, according to thy Son our Savior Jesu Christ's holy institution, in remembrance of his death and passion, may be partakers of his most blessed Body and Blood: who in the same night that he was betrayed, took bread, and when he had given thanks, he brake[31] it, and gave it to his disciples, saying, Take, eat, this is my body which is given for you. Do this in remembrance of me. Likewise after supper he took the cup, and when he had given thanks, he gave it to them, saying, Drink ye all of this, for this is my blood of the new testament, which is shed for you and for many, for remission of sins: do this as oft as ye shall drink it in remembrance of me.

Then shall the minister first receive the communion in both kinds himself, and next deliver it to other ministers, if any be

[30] *To come to this:* "to come" not in text, but in 1559 Grafton.
[31] *Brake:* broke.

there present (that they may help the chief minister) and after to the people in their hands kneeling. And when he delivereth the bread, he shall say.

THE body of our Lord Jesus Christ which was given for thee, preserve thy body and soul into everlasting life: and take and eat this, in remembrance that Christ died for thee, and feed on him in thy heart by faith, with thanksgiving.

And the minister that delivereth the cup, shall say.

THE blood of our Lord Jesus Christ which was shed for thee, preserve thy body and soul into everlasting life: and drink this in remembrance that Christ's blood was shed for thee, and be thankful.

Then shall the priest say the Lord's Prayer, the people repeating after him every petition.

After shall be said as followeth.

O LORD and heavenly Father, we thy humble servants, entirely desire thy fatherly goodness, mercifully to accept this our sacrifice of praise and thanksgiving, most humbly beseeching thee to grant that by the merits and death of thy Son Jesus Christ, and through faith in his blood, we and all thy whole Church may obtain remission of our sins, and all other benefits of his passion. And here we offer and present unto thee, O Lord, ourselves, our souls and bodies, to be a reasonable, holy, and lively sacrifice unto thee, humbly beseeching thee, that all we which be partakers of this Holy Communion, may be fulfilled with thy grace, and heavenly benediction. And although we be unworthy, through our manifold sins, to offer unto thee any sacrifice, yet we beseech thee to accept this our bounden duty and service, not weighing our merits, but pardoning our offenses, through Jesus Christ our Lord, by whom and with whom, in the unity of the Holy Ghost, all honor and glory be unto thee, O Father Almighty, world without end. Amen.

Or this.

ALMIGHTY and everliving God, we most heartily thank thee, for that thou dost vouchsafe to feed us, which have duly received these holy mysteries, with the spiritual food of the most precious body and blood of thy Son our Savior Jesus Christ, and dost assure us thereby of thy favor and goodness toward us, and that we be very members incorporate in thy mystical body, which is the blessed company of all faithful people, and be also heirs through hope of thy everlasting kingdom, by the merits of the most precious death and passion of thy dear Son. We now most humbly beseech thee, O heavenly Father, so to assist us with thy grace, that we may continue in that holy fellowship, and do all such good works as thou hast prepared for us to walk in; through Jesus Christ our Lord, to whom with thee and the Holy Ghost, be all honor and glory, world without end. Amen.

Then shall be said or sung.

GLORY be to God on high. And in earth peace, good will toward men. We praise thee, we bless thee, we worship thee, we glorify thee, we give thanks to thee for thy great glory. O Lord God heavenly king, God the Father Almighty. O Lord, the only begotten Son Jesu Christ: O Lord God, Lamb of God, Son of the Father, that takest away the sins of the world, have mercy upon us. Thou that takest away the sins of the world, have mercy upon us. Thou that takest away the sins of the world, receive our prayer. Thou that sittest at the right hand of God the Father, have mercy upon us. For thou only art holy: Thou only art the Lord: Thou only, (O Christ) with the Holy Ghost, art most high in the glory of God the Father. Amen.

Then the priest or the bishop, if he be present, shall let them depart with this blessing.

THE peace of God which passeth all understanding, keep your hearts and minds in the knowledge and love of God, and of his Son Jesu Christ our Lord: And the blessing of God Almighty, the Father, the Son, and the Holy Ghost, be amongst you, and remain with you always. Amen.

Collects to be said after the offertory when there is no Communion, every such day one. And the same may be said also as often as occasion shall serve after the Collects, either of Morning and Evening Prayer, Communion, or Litany, by the discretion of the minister.

ASSIST us mercifully, O Lord, in these our supplications, and prayers, and dispose the way of thy servants toward the attainment of everlasting salvation; that among all the changes and chances of this mortal life, they may ever be defended by thy most gracious and ready help; through Christ our Lord. Amen.

O ALMIGHTY Lord and everliving God, vouchsafe we beseech thee to direct, sanctify, and govern both our hearts and bodies, in the ways of thy laws, and in the works of thy commandments; that through thy most mighty protection, both here and ever, we may be preserved in body and soul; through our Lord and Savior Jesus Christ. Amen.

GRANT we beseech thee Almighty God, that the words which we have heard this day with our outward ears, may through thy grace be so grafted inwardly in our hearts, that they may bring forth in us the fruit of good living, to the honor and praise of thy name; through Jesus Christ our Lord. Amen.

PREVENT[32] us, O Lord, in all our doings, with thy most gracious favor, and further us with thy continual help; that in all our works begun, continued, and ended in thee, we may glorify thy holy name, and finally by thy mercy obtain everlasting life; through Jesus Christ our Lord. Amen.

ALMIGHTY God, the fountain of all wisdom, which knowest our necessities before we ask, and our ignorance in asking: We beseech thee to have compassion upon our infirmities, and those things which for our unworthiness we dare not, and

[32] *Prevent:* go before.

for our blindness we cannot ask, vouchsafe to give us for the worthiness of thy Son Jesus Christ our Lord. Amen.

ALMIGHTY God, which hast promised to hear the petitions of them that ask in thy Son's name: We beseech thee mercifully to incline thine ears to us, that have made now our prayers and supplications unto thee; and grant that those things which we have faithfully asked according to thy will, may effectually be obtained, to the relief of our necessity, and to the setting forth of thy glory; through Jesus Christ our Lord. Amen.

Upon the holy days, if there be no Communion, shall be said all that is appointed at the Communion, until the end of the homily, concluding with the general prayer for the whole estate of Christ's Church militant here in earth, and one or mo[33] of these Collects before rehearsed, as occasion shall serve.

And there shall be no celebration of the Lord's Supper except there be a good number to communicate with the priest, according to his discretion.

And if there be not above twenty persons in the parish of discretion to receive the communion, yet there shall be no Communion, except four, or three at the least, communicate with the priest. And in cathedral and collegiate churches where be many priests and deacons, they shall all receive the communion with the minister every Sunday at the least, except they have a reasonable cause to the contrary.

And to take away the superstition, which any person hath or might have in the bread and wine, it shall suffice that the bread be such as is usual to be eaten at the table with other meats, but the best and purest wheat bread that conveniently may be gotten. And if any of the bread or wine remain, the curate shall have it to his own use.

The bread and wine for the Communion shall be provided by the curate and the churchwardens at the charges of the parish,

[33] *Mo:* more.

and the parish shall be discharged of such sums of money, or other duties, which hitherto they have paid for the same, by order of their houses every Sunday.

And note, that every parishioner shall communicate at the least three times in the year, of which Easter to be one, and shall also receive the sacraments and other rites, according to the order in this book appointed. And yearly at Easter, every parishioner shall reckon with his parson, vicar, or curate, or his, or their deputy or deputies, and pay to them or him all ecclesiastical duties,[34] accustomably due, then and at that time to be paid.

[34] *Duties:* money or goods due in payment to the church.

The Ministration of Baptism
to Be Used in the Church

It appeareth by ancient writers that the sacrament of Baptism in the old time was not commonly ministered but at two times in the year: at Easter and Whitsuntide. At which times it was openly ministered in the presence of all the congregation: which custom (now being grown out of use) although it cannot for many considerations be well restored again, yet it is thought good to follow the same as near as conveniently may be. Wherefore the people are to be admonished that it is most convenient that Baptism should not be ministered but upon Sundays and other holy days when the most number of people may come together, as well for that the congregation there present may testify the receiving of them that be newly baptized into the number of Christ's Church, as also because in the baptism of infants every man present may be put in remembrance of his own profession made to God in his baptism. For which cause also, it is expedient that baptism be ministered in the English tongue. Nevertheless (if necessity so require) children may at all times be baptized at home.

Public Baptism

When there are children to be baptized upon the Sunday or holy day, the parents shall give knowledge overnight, or in the morning afore[1] the beginning of Morning Prayer, to the curate. And then the godfathers, godmothers, and people with the children must be ready at the font either immediately after the last Lesson at Morning Prayer, or else immediately after the last Lesson at Evening Prayer, as the curate by his discretion shall appoint. And then standing there, the priest shall ask whether the children be baptized or no. If they answer, No: then shall the priest say thus.

DEARLY beloved, forasmuch as all men be conceived and born in sin, and that our Savior Christ saith, None can enter into the kingdom of God, except he be regenerate and born anew of water and the Holy Ghost: I beseech you to call upon God the Father, through our Lord Jesus Christ, that of his bounteous mercy he will grant to these children that thing which by nature they cannot have, that they may be baptized with water and the Holy Ghost, and received into Christ's holy Church, and be made lively members of the same.

Then the priest shall say.

Let us pray.

ALMIGHTY and everlasting God, which of thy great mercy didst save Noah[2] and his family in the ark from perishing by water, and also didst safely lead the children of Israel thy people through the Red Sea, figuring thereby thy holy Baptism, and by the baptism of thy well-beloved Son Jesus Christ, didst sanctify the flood Jordan and all other waters to the mystical

---

[1] *Afore:* before.
[2] "Noe" in text.

washing away of sin: We beseech thee for thy infinite mercies, that thou wilt mercifully look upon these children, sanctify them and wash them with thy Holy Ghost, that they being delivered from thy wrath may be received into the ark of Christ's Church, and being steadfast in faith, joyful through hope, and rooted in charity, may so pass the waves of this troublesome world, that finally they may come to the land of everlasting life, there to reign with thee, world without end; through Jesus Christ our Lord. Amen.

ALMIGHTY and immortal God, the aid of all that need, the helper of all that flee to thee for succor, the life of them that believe, and the resurrection of the dead: We call upon thee for these infants, that they coming to thy holy Baptism may receive remission of their sins by spiritual regeneration. Receive them (O Lord) as thou hast promised by thy well-beloved Son, saying, Ask and you shall have; seek and you shall find; knock and it shall be opened unto you. So give now unto us that ask. Let us that seek find. Open the gate unto us that knock; that these infants may enjoy the everlasting benediction of thy heavenly washing, and may come to the eternal kingdom which thou hast promised by Christ our Lord. Amen.

Then shall the priest say. Hear the words of the Gospel written by Saint Mark in the tenth chapter.

[Mark 10

AT a certain time they brought children to Christ that he should touch them, and his disciples rebuked those that brought them. But when Jesus saw it, he was displeased, and said unto them, Suffer little children to come unto me, and forbid them not, for to such belongeth the kingdom of God. Verily I say unto you, whosoever doth not receive the kingdom of God as a little child, he shall not enter therein. And when he had taken them up in his arms, he put his hands upon them and blessed them.

After the Gospel is read, the minister shall make this brief exhortation upon the words of the Gospel.

FRIENDS, you hear in this Gospel the words of our Savior Christ, that he commanded the children to be brought unto him; how he blamed those that would have kept them from him; how he exhorteth all men to follow their innocency. You perceive how by his outward gesture and deed he declared his good will toward them. For he embraced them in his arms, he laid his hands upon them, and blessed them. Doubt not ye therefore, but earnestly believe, that he will likewise favorably receive these present infants, that he will embrace them with the arms of his mercy, that he will give unto them the blessing of eternal life, and make them partakers of his everlasting kingdom. Wherefore we being thus persuaded of the good will of our heavenly Father toward these infants, declared by his Son Jesus Christ, and nothing doubting but that he favorably alloweth this charitable work of ours, in bringing these children to his holy Baptism: Let us faithfully and devoutly give thanks unto him, and say.

ALMIGHTY and everlasting God, heavenly Father, we give thee humble thanks, that thou hast vouchsafed to call us to the knowledge of thy grace and faith in thee: Increase this knowledge, and confirm this faith in us evermore. Give thy Holy Spirit to these infants, that they may be born again, and be made heirs of everlasting salvation; through our Lord Jesus Christ, who liveth and reigneth with thee and the Holy Spirit, now and forever. Amen.

Then the priest shall speak unto the godfathers and godmothers on this wise.

WELL-BELOVED friends, ye have brought these children here to be baptized; ye have prayed that our Lord Jesus Christ would vouchsafe to receive them, to lay his hands upon them, to bless them, to release them of their sins, to give them the kingdom of heaven, and everlasting life. Ye have heard also that our Lord Jesus Christ hath promised in his gospel to grant all these things that ye have prayed for; which promise he for his part will most surely keep and perform. Wherefore after this promise made by Christ, these infants must also faithfully for their part promise by you that be their sureties, that they will forsake the devil and all his works, and constantly believe God's holy Word, and obediently keep his commandments.

Then shall the priest demand of the godfathers and god-mothers these questions following.

D OST thou forsake the devil and all his works, the vain pomp, and glory of the world, with all covetous desires of the same, the carnal desires of the flesh, so that thou wilt not follow, nor be led by them?

Answer. I forsake them all.

Minister. Dost thou believe in God the Father Almighty, maker of heaven and earth? And in Jesus Christ his only begotten Son our Lord, and that he was conceived by the Holy Ghost, born of the Virgin Mary, that he suffered under Pontius[3] Pilate, was crucified, dead, and buried, that he went down into hell, and also did rise again the third day, that he ascended into heaven and sitteth at the right hand of God the Father Almighty, and from thence shall come again at the end of the world, to judge the quick[4] and the dead?

And dost thou believe in the Holy Ghost, the holy catholic Church, the communion of saints, the remission of sins, the resurrection of the flesh, and everlasting life after death?

Answer. All this I steadfastly believe.

Minister. Wilt thou be baptized in this faith?

Answer. That is my desire.

Then shall the priest say.

[3] "Poncius" in text.
[4] *Quick:* living.

O MERCIFUL God, grant that the old Adam in these children may be so buried, that the new man may be raised up in them. Amen.

Grant that all carnal affections may die in them, and that all things belonging to the Spirit may live and grow in them. Amen.

Grant that they may have power and strength to have victory, and to triumph against the devil, the world, and the flesh. Amen.

Grant that whosoever is here dedicated to thee by our office and ministry, may also be endued with heavenly virtues, and everlastingly rewarded through thy mercy, O blessed Lord God, who dost live and govern all things world without end. Amen.

ALMIGHTY everliving God, whose most dearly beloved Son Jesus Christ, for the forgiveness of our sins, did shed out of his most precious side both water and blood,[5] and gave commandment to his disciples that they should go teach all nations, and baptize them in the name of the Father, the Son, and the Holy Ghost: Regard, we beseech thee, the supplications of thy congregation, and grant that all thy servants which shall be baptized in this water, may receive the fullness of thy grace, and ever remain in the number of thy faithful and elect children; through Jesus Christ our Lord.

Then the priest shall take the child in his hands, and ask the name, and naming the child, shall dip it in the water, so it be discreetly and warely[6] done, saying.

N. I baptize thee in the name of the Father, and of the Son, and of the Holy Ghost. Amen.

And if the child be weak, it shall suffice to pour water upon it, saying the foresaid words.

N. I baptize thee in the name of the Father, and of the Son, and of the Holy Ghost. Amen.

[5] Text has "bould"; misprint.
[6] *Warely*: warily.

274

Then the priest shall make a cross upon the child's forehead, saying.

WE receive this child into the congregation of Christ's flock, and do sign him with the sign of the cross, in token that hereafter he shall not be ashamed to confess the faith of Christ crucified, and manfully to fight under his banner against sin, the world, and the devil, and to continue Christ's faithful soldier and servant unto his life's end. Amen.

Then shall the priest say.

SEEING now, dearly beloved brethren, that these children be regenerate and grafted into the body of Christ's congregation: let us give thanks unto God for these benefits, and with one accord make our prayers unto Almighty God, that they may lead the rest of their life according to this beginning.

Then shall be said.

OUR Father which art in heaven, etc.

Then shall the priest say.

WE yield thee hearty thanks, most merciful Father, that it hath pleased thee to regenerate this infant with thy Holy Spirit, to receive him for thy own child by adoption, and to incorporate him into thy holy congregation. And humbly we beseech thee to grant that he being dead unto sin, and living unto righteousness, and being buried with Christ in his death, may crucify the old man, and utterly abolish the whole body of sin, that as he is made partaker of the death of thy Son, so he may be partaker of his resurrection. So that finally with the residue of thy holy congregation, he may be inheritor of thine everlasting kingdom, through Christ our Lord. Amen.

At the last end, the priest calling the godfathers and godmothers together, shall say this short exhortation following.

FORASMUCH as these children have promised by you to forsake the devil and all his works, to believe in God, and to serve him: you must remember that it is your parts[7] and duties to see that these infants be taught so soon as they shall be able to learn what a solemn vow, promise, and profession they have made by you. And that they may know these things the better, ye shall call upon them to hear sermons. And chiefly ye shall provide that they may learn the Creed, the Lord's Prayer, and the Ten Commandments in the English tongue, and all other things which a Christian man ought to know and believe to his soul's health; and that these children may be virtuously brought up to lead a godly and a Christian life, remembering alway that baptism doth represent unto us our profession, which is to follow the example of our Savior Christ, and to be made like unto him, that as he died and rose again for us, so should we which are baptized die from sin, and rise again unto righteousness, continually mortifying all our evil and corrupt affections, and daily proceeding in all virtue and godliness of living.

The minister shall command that the children be brought to the bishop to be confirmed of him, so soon as they can say in their vulgar tongue the articles of the faith, the Lord's Prayer, and the Ten Commandments, and be further instructed in the Catechism set forth for that purpose, accordingly as it is there expressed.

[7] *Parts:* the part or portion of all godparents.

Of Them That Be Baptized
in Private Houses, in Time of Necessity

The pastors and curates shall oft admonish the people that they defer not the baptism of infants any longer than the Sunday or other holy day next after the child be born, unless upon a great and reasonable cause declared to the curate, and by him approved.

And also they shall warn them, that without great cause and necessity they baptize not children at home in their houses. And when great need shall compel them so to do, that then they minister it on this fashion.

First let them that be present call upon God for his grace and say the Lord's Prayer, if the time will suffer. And then one of them shall name the child, and dip him in the water, or pour water upon him, saying these words.

N. I baptize thee in the name of the Father, and of the Son, and of the Holy Ghost. Amen.

And let them not doubt but that the child so baptized is lawfully and sufficiently baptized, and ought not to be baptized again in the church. But yet nevertheless, if the child which is after this sort baptized do afterward live, it is expedient that he be brought into the church to the intent the priest may examine and try whether the child be lawfully baptized or no. And if those that bring any child to the church do answer that he is already baptized, then shall the priest examine them further.

By whom the child was baptized?
Who was present when the child was baptized?
Whether they called upon God for grace and succor in that necessity?
With what thing, or what matter they did baptize the child?
With what words the child was baptized?

Whether they think the child to be lawfully and perfectly baptized?

And if the minister shall prove by the answers of such as brought the child that all things were done as they ought to be, then shall not he christen the child again, but shall receive him as one of the flock of the true Christian people, saying thus.

I CERTIFY you, that in this case ye have done well and according unto due order concerning the baptizing of this child, which being born in original sin and in the wrath of God, is now by the laver[1] of regeneration in Baptism, received into the number of the children of God, and heirs of everlasting life: for our Lord Jesus Christ doth not deny his grace and mercy unto such infants, but most lovingly doth call them unto him, as the holy gospel doth witness to our comfort[2] on this wise.[3]

AT a certain time they brought children unto Christ that he should touch them, and his disciples rebuked those that brought them. But when Jesus saw it, he was displeased, and said unto them, Suffer little children to come unto me, and forbid them not, for to such belongeth the kingdom of God. Verily I say unto you, whosoever doth not receive the kingdom of God as a little child, he shall not enter therein. And when he had taken them up in his arms, he put his hands upon them and blessed them.

After the Gospel is read, the minister shall make this brief exhortation upon the words of the Gospel.

FRIENDS, you hear in this Gospel the words of our Savior Christ, that he commanded the children to be brought unto him; how he blamed those that would have kept them from him; how he exhorted all men to follow their innocency. Ye perceive

---

[1] *Laver:* water.

[2] *Comfort:* strengthening.

[3] The marginal reference, Mark 10, given before (p. 271), is omitted here.

how by his outward gesture and deed he declared his good will toward them. For he embraced them in his arms, he laid his hands upon them, and blessed them. Doubt ye not therefore, but earnestly believe that he hath likewise favorably received this present infant, that he hath embraced him with the arms of his mercy, that he hath given unto him the blessing of eternal life, and made him partaker of his everlasting kingdom. Wherefore we being thus persuaded of the good will of our heavenly Father, declared by his Son Jesus Christ toward this infant: Let us faithfully and devoutly give thanks unto him, and say the prayer which the Lord himself taught, and in declaration of our faith, let us recite the articles contained in our Creed.

Here the minister with the godfathers and godmothers shall say.

OUR Father which art in heaven, etc.

Then shall the priest demand the name of the child, which being by the godfathers and godmothers pronounced, the minister shall say.

DOST thou in the name of this child forsake the devil and all his works, the vain pomp and glory of the world, with all the covetous desires of the same, the carnal desires of the flesh, and not to follow and be led by them?

Answer. I forsake them all.

Minister. Dost thou in the name of this child profess this faith, to believe in God the Father Almighty, maker of heaven and earth. And in Jesus Christ his only begotten Son our Lord, and that he was conceived by the Holy Ghost, born of the Virgin Mary, that he suffered under Pontius[4] Pilate, was crucified, dead, and buried, that he went down into hell, and also did rise again the third day, that he ascended into heaven, and sitteth at the

---

[4] "Poncius" in text.

right hand of God the Father Almighty, and from thence he shall come again at the end of the world to judge the quick[5] and the dead?

And do you in his name believe in the Holy Ghost, the holy catholic Church, the communion of saints, the remission of sins, resurrection, and everlasting life after death?

Answer. All this I steadfastly believe.

Let us pray.

ALMIGHTY and everlasting God, heavenly Father, we give thee humble thanks, for that thou hast vouchsafed to call us to the knowledge of thy grace and faith in thee: Increase this knowledge, and confirm this faith in us evermore. Give thy Holy Spirit to this infant, that he being born again, and being made heir of everlasting salvation, through our Lord Jesus Christ, may continue thy servant, and attain thy promise; through the same our Lord Jesus Christ thy Son, who liveth and reigneth with thee in the unity of the same Holy Spirit everlastingly. Amen.

Then shall the minister make this exhortation to the god-fathers and godmothers.

FORASMUCH as this child hath promised by you to forsake the devil and all his works, to believe in God, and to serve him: you must remember that it is your part[6] and duty to see that this infant be taught, so soon as he shall be able to learn, what a solemn vow, promise, and profession he hath made by you. And that he may know these things the better, ye shall call upon him to hear sermons. And chiefly ye shall provide that he may learn the Creed, the Lord's Prayer, and the Ten Commandments in the English tongue, and all other things which a Christian man ought to know and believe to his soul's health. And that this child may be virtuously brought up, to lead a godly and

[5] *Quick:* living.
[6] *Part:* the part or portion of all godparents.

a Christian life, remembering alway that baptism doth represent unto us our profession, which is to follow the example of our Savior Christ, and be made like unto him, that as he died and rose again for us, so should we which are baptized die from sin, and rise again unto righteousness, continually mortifying all our evil and corrupt affections, and daily proceeding in all virtue and godliness of living.

And so forth, as in Public Baptism.

But if they which bring the infants to the church do make an uncertain answer to the priest's questions, and say that they cannot tell what they thought, did, or said in that great fear and trouble of mind (as oftentimes it chanceth) then let the priest baptize him in form above written, concerning Public Baptism, saving that at the dipping of the child in the font, he shall use this form of words.

I F thou be not baptized already.   N.   I baptize thee in the name of the Father, and of the Son, and of the Holy Ghost. Amen.

Confirmation, Wherein
Is Contained a Catechism
for Children

To the end that Confirmation may be ministered to the more edifying of such as shall receive it (according unto Saint Paul's doctrine, who teacheth that all things should be done in the Church to the edification of the same) it is thought good that none hereafter shall be confirmed, but such as can say in their mother tongue the articles of the faith, the Lord's Prayer, and the Ten Commandments, and can also answer to such questions of this short catechism as the bishop (or such as he shall appoint) shall by his discretion appose[1] them in. And this order is most convenient to be observed for divers considerations.

First, because that when children come to the years of discretion and have learned what their godfathers and godmothers promised for them in Baptism, they may then themselves with their own mouth, and with their own consent, openly before the church ratify and confirm the same, and also promise that by the grace of God, they will evermore endeavor themselves faithfully to observe and keep such things as they by their own mouth and confession have assented unto.

Secondly, forasmuch as Confirmation is ministered to them that be baptized, that by imposition of hands and prayer they may receive strength and defense against all temptations to sin, and the assaults of the world and the devil: it is most meet[2] to be ministered when children come to that age that partly by the frailty of their own flesh, partly by the assaults of the world and the devil, they begin to be in danger to fall into sundry kinds of sin.

[1] *Appose:* examine.
[2] *Meet:* proper, suitable.

Thirdly, for that it is agreeable with the usage of the Church in times past, whereby it was ordained that Confirmation should be ministered to them that were of perfect[3] age, that they being instructed in Christ's religion, should openly profess their own faith, and promise to be obedient unto the will of God.

And that no man shall think that any detriment shall come to children by deferring of their confirmation, he shall know for truth that it is certain by God's Word, that children being baptized have all things necessary for their salvation, and be undoubtedly saved.

A Catechism, That Is to Say, an Instruction to Be Learned of Every Child before He Be Brought to Be Confirmed of the Bishop

Question. What is your name?

Answer. N. or M.

Question. Who gave you this name?

Answer. My godfathers and godmothers in my Baptism, wherein I was made a member of Christ, the child of God, and an inheritor of the kingdom of heaven.

Question. What did your godfathers and godmothers then for you?

Answer. They did promise and vow three things in my name. First, that I should forsake the devil and all his works and pomps, the vanities of the wicked world, and all the sinful lusts of the flesh. Secondly, that I should believe all the articles of the Christian[4] faith. And thirdly, that I should keep God's holy will and commandments, and walk in the same all the days of my life.

Question. Dost thou not think that thou art bound to believe and to do as they have promised for thee?

---

[3] *Perfect:* of full age, grown up; see note.
[4] Text has "christen."

Answer. Yes, verily. And by God's help so I will. And I heartily thank our heavenly Father, that he hath called me to this state of salvation, through Jesus Christ our Savior. And I pray God to give me his grace, that I may continue in the same unto my life's end.

Question. Rehearse the articles of thy belief.

Answer. I believe in God the Father Almighty, maker of heaven and of earth. And in Jesus Christ his only Son our Lord. Which was conceived of the Holy Ghost, born of the Virgin Mary. Suffered under Pontius[5] Pilate, was crucified, dead, and buried, he descended into hell. The third day he rose again from the dead. He ascended into heaven, and sitteth at the right hand of God the Father Almighty. From thence he shall come to judge the quick[6] and the dead. I believe in the Holy Ghost, the holy catholic Church, the communion of saints, the forgiveness of sins, the resurrection of the body, and the life everlasting. Amen.

Question. What dost thou chiefly learn in these articles of thy belief?

Answer. First, I learn to believe in God the Father, who hath made me and all the world.

Secondly, in God the Son, who hath redeemed me and all mankind.

Thirdly, in God the Holy Ghost, who sanctifieth me and all the elect people of God.

Question. You said that your godfathers and godmothers did promise for you that you should keep God's commandments. Tell me how many there be?

Answer. Ten.

Question. Which be they?

Answer. The same which God spake in the twentieth chapter[7]

---

[5] "Ponce" in text.

[6] *Quick:* living.

[7] "Chapiter" in text.

of Exodus, saying, I am the Lord thy God which have brought thee out of the land of Egypt,[8] out of the house of bondage.

I. Thou shalt have none other Gods but me.

II. Thou shalt not make to thyself any graven image, nor the likeness of anything that is in heaven above, or in the earth beneath, nor in the water under the earth: thou shalt not bow down to them nor worship them. For I the Lord thy God am a jealous God, and visit the sins of the fathers upon the children, unto the third and fourth generation of them that hate me, and show mercy unto thousands in them that love me, and keep my commandments.

III. Thou shalt not take the name of the Lord thy God in vain: for the Lord will not hold him guiltless that taketh his name in vain.

IV. Remember thou keep holy the Sabbath day. Six days shalt thou labor and do all that thou hast to do: but the seventh day is the Sabbath of the Lord thy God. In it thou shalt do no manner of work, thou, and thy son and thy daughter, thy manservant, and thy maidservant, thy cattle, and the stranger that is within thy gates: for in six days the Lord made heaven and earth, the sea, and all that in them is, and rested the seventh day. Wherefore the Lord blessed the seventh day, and hallowed it.

V. Honor thy father and thy mother, that thy days may be long in the land which the Lord thy God giveth thee.

VI. Thou shalt do no murder.

VII. Thou shalt not commit adultery.

VIII. Thou shalt not steal.

IX. Thou shalt not bear false witness against thy neighbor.

X. Thou shalt not covet thy neighbor's house, thou shalt not covet thy neighbor's wife, nor his servant, nor his maid, nor his ox, nor his ass, nor anything that is his.

Question. What dost thou chiefly learn by these commandments?

---

[8] "Egipte" in text.

Answer. I learn two things. My duty toward God, and my duty toward my neighbor.

Question. What is thy duty toward God?

Answer. My duty toward God is, to believe in him, to fear him, and to love him with all my heart, with all my mind, with all my soul, and with all my strength. To worship him. To give him thanks. To put my whole trust in him. To call upon him. To honor his holy name and his Word, and to serve him truly all the days of my life.

Question. What is thy duty toward thy neighbor?

Answer. My duty toward my neighbor is, to love him as myself. And to do to all men as I would they should do unto me. To love, honor, and succor my father and mother. To honor and obey the king and his ministers. To submit myself to all my governors, teachers, spiritual pastors, and masters. To order myself lowly and reverently to all my betters. To hurt nobody by word nor deed. To be true and just in all my dealing. To bear no malice nor hatred in my heart. To keep my hands from picking and stealing, and my tongue from evil speaking, lying, and slandering. To keep my body in temperance, soberness, and chastity. Not to covet nor desire other men's goods. But learn and labor truly to get mine own living, and to do my duty in that state of life, unto which it shall please God to call me.

Question. My good child know this, that thou art not able to do these things of thyself, nor to walk in the commandments of God, and to serve him, without his special grace, which thou must learn at all times to call for by diligent prayer. Let me hear therefore if thou canst say the Lord's Prayer.

Answer. Our Father, which art in heaven, hallowed be thy name. Thy kingdom come. Thy will be done in earth as it is in heaven. Give us this day our daily bread. And forgive us our trespasses, as we forgive them that trespass against us. And lead us not into temptation. But deliver us from evil. Amen.

Question. What desirest thou of God in this prayer?

Answer. I desire my Lord God our heavenly Father, who is

the giver of all goodness, to send his grace unto me and to all people, that we may worship him, serve him, and obey him as we ought to do. And I pray unto God that he will send us all things that be needful both for our souls and bodies. And that he will be merciful unto us, and forgive us our sins: and that it will please him to save and defend us in all dangers ghostly[9] and bodily. And that he will keep us from all sin and wickedness, and from our ghostly enemy, and from everlasting death. And this I trust he will do of his mercy and goodness, through our Lord Jesu Christ. And therefore I say. Amen. So be it.

So soon as the children can say in their mother tongue the articles of the faith, the Lord's Prayer, the Ten Commandments, and also can answer to such questions of this short catechism as the bishop (or such as he shall appoint) shall by his discretion appose them in: then shall they be brought to the bishop by one that shall be his godfather or godmother, that every child may have a witness of his Confirmation.

And the bishop shall confirm them on this wise.

Confirmation

OUR help is in the name of the Lord.

Answer. Which hath made both heaven and earth.
Minister. Blessed is the name of the Lord.
Answer. Henceforth world without end.
Minister. Lord hear our prayer.
Answer. And let our cry come to thee.

Let us pray.

ALMIGHTY and everliving God, who hast vouchsafed to regenerate these thy servants by water and the Holy Ghost, and hast given unto them forgiveness of all their sins: Strength-

[9] *Ghostly:* spiritual.

en them we beseech thee (O Lord) with the Holy Ghost, the comforter, and daily increase in them thy manifold gifts of grace: the spirit of wisdom and understanding, the spirit of counsel and ghostly strength, the spirit of knowledge and true godliness; and fulfill them (O Lord) with the spirit of thy holy fear. Amen.

Then the bishop shall lay his hand upon every child severally, saying.

DEFEND, O Lord, this child with thy heavenly grace, that he may continue thine forever, and daily increase in thy Holy Spirit more and more, until he come unto thy everlasting kingdom. Amen.

Then shall the bishop say.

ALMIGHTY everliving God, which makest us both to will and to do those things that be good and acceptable unto thy majesty: We make our humble supplications unto thee for these children, upon whom (after the example of thy holy Apostles) we have laid our hands, to certify them (by this sign) of thy favor and gracious goodness toward them. Let thy fatherly hand, we beseech thee, ever be over them. Let thy Holy Spirit ever be with them, and so lead them in the knowledge and obedience of thy Word, that in the end they may obtain the everlasting life; through our Lord Jesus Christ, who with thee and the Holy Ghost liveth and reigneth one God, world without end. Amen.

Then the bishop shall bless the children, thus saying.

THE blessing of God Almighty, the Father, the Son, and the Holy Ghost, be upon you, and remain with you forever. Amen.

The curate of every parish, or some other at his appointment, shall diligently upon Sundays and holy days, half an hour before Evensong, openly in the church instruct and examine so many children of his parish sent unto him as the time will serve, and as he shall think convenient, in some part of this Catechism.

And all fathers and mothers, masters and dames, shall cause their children, servants, and prentices[10] (which have not learned their catechism) to come to the church at the time appointed, and obediently to hear, and be ordered by the curate, until such time as they have learned all that is here appointed for them to learn. And whensoever the bishop shall give knowledge for children to be brought afore[11] him to any convenient place for their confirmation, then shall the curate of every parish either bring or send in writing the names of all those children of his parish which can say the articles of their faith, the Lord's Prayer, and the Ten Commandments, and also how many of them can answer to the other questions contained in this catechism.

And there shall none be admitted to the Holy Communion, until such time as he can say the catechism, and be confirmed.

[10] *Prentices:* apprentices.
[11] *Afore:* before.

The Form of Solemnization
of Matrimony

First the banns must be asked three several Sundays or holy days, in the time of service, the people being present after the accustomed manner.

And if the persons that would be married dwell in divers parishes, the banns must be asked in both parishes, and the curate of the one parish shall not solemnize matrimony betwixt them without a certificate of the banns being thrice asked from the curate of the other parish. At the day appointed for Solemnization of Matrimony, the persons to be married shall come into the body of the church, with their friends and neighbors. And there the priest shall thus say.

DEARLY beloved friends, we are gathered together here in the sight of God, and in the face of his congregation, to join together this man and this woman in holy matrimony, which is an honorable estate, instituted of God in paradise in the time of man's innocency, signifying unto us the mystical union, that is betwixt Christ and his Church: which holy estate Christ adorned and beautified with his presence and first miracle that he wrought in Cana of Galilee, and is commended of Saint Paul to be honorable among all men, and therefore is not to be enterprised nor taken in hand unadvisedly, lightly, or wantonly, to satisfy men's carnal lusts and appetites, like brute beasts that have no understanding, but reverently, discreetly, advisedly, soberly, and in the fear of God, duly considering the causes for which matrimony was ordained. One was, the procreation of children to be brought up in the fear and nurture of the Lord, and praise of God. Secondly, it was ordained for a remedy against sin, and to avoid fornication, that such persons as have not the gift of continency might marry, and keep themselves undefiled members of Christ's body. Thirdly, for the mutual society, help, and comfort,[1] that the one ought to have of the other, both in prosperity and adversity: into the which holy estate these two persons present come now to be joined. Therefore, if any man can show any just cause why they may not lawfully be joined together, let him now speak, or else hereafter forever hold his peace.

And also speaking to the persons that shall be married, he shall say.

I REQUIRE and charge you (as you will answer at the dreadful day of judgment, when the secrets of all hearts shall be disclosed) that if either of you do know any impediment why ye may not be lawfully joined together in matrimony, that ye confess it. For be ye well assured, that so many as be coupled together otherwise than God's Word doth allow, are not joined together by God, neither is their matrimony lawful.

At which day of marriage, if any man do allege and declare any impediment why they may not be coupled together in matrimony, by God's law or the laws of this realm, and will be bound, and sufficient sureties with him, to the parties, or else put in a caution to the full value of such charges as the persons to be married doth sustain to prove his allegation: then the Solemnization must be deferred unto such time as the truth be tried. If no impediment be alleged, then shall the curate say unto the man.

N . WILT thou have this woman to thy wedded wife, to live together after God's ordinance in the holy estate of matrimony? Wilt thou love her, comfort her, honor and keep her, in sickness, and in health? And forsaking all other, keep thee only to her, so long as you both shall live?

The man shall answer.

    I will.

[1] *Comfort:* strengthening, encouragement.

Then shall the priest say to the woman.

N. WILT thou have this man to thy wedded husband, to live together after God's ordinance in the holy estate of matrimony? Wilt thou obey him and serve him, love, honor, and keep him, in sickness, and in health? And forsaking all other, keep thee only unto him, so long as you both shall live?

The woman shall answer.

I will.

Then shall the minister say.

Who giveth this woman to be married unto this man?

And the minister receiving the woman at her father or friend's hands, shall cause the man to take the woman by the right hand, and so either to give their troth to other. The man first saying.

I N. take thee N. to my wedded wife, to have and to hold from this day forward, for better, for worse, for richer, for poorer, in sickness, and in health, to love and to cherish, till death us depart,[2] according to God's holy ordinance: And thereto I plight thee my troth.

Then shall they loose their hands, and the woman taking again the man by the right hand shall say.

I N. take thee N. to my wedded husband, to have and to hold from this day forward, for better, for worse, for richer, for poorer, in sickness, and in health, to love, cherish, and to obey, till death us depart, according to God's holy ordinance: And thereto I give thee my troth.

Then shall they again loose their hands, and the man shall give unto the woman a ring, laying the same upon the book with the accustomed duty[3] to the priest and clerk. And the priest taking the ring, shall deliver it unto the man, to put it upon the

[2] *Depart:* separate.
[3] *Duty:* oblations or offerings.

fourth finger of the woman's left hand. And the man taught by the priest shall say.

WITH this ring I thee wed: with my body I thee worship: and with all my worldly goods I thee endow. In the name of the Father, and of the Son, and of the Holy Ghost. Amen.

Then the man leaving the ring upon the fourth finger of the woman's left hand, the minister shall say.

O ETERNAL God, creator and preserver of all mankind, giver of all spiritual grace, the author of everlasting life: Send thy blessing upon these thy servants, this man and this woman, whom we bless in thy name, that as Isaac and Rebecca lived faithfully together, so these persons may surely perform and keep the vow and covenant betwixt them made, whereof this ring given and received is a token and pledge, and may ever remain in perfect love and peace together, and live according unto thy laws; through Jesus Christ our Lord. Amen.

Then shall the priest join their right hands together, and say.

Those whom God hath joined together, let no man put asunder.[4]

Then shall the minister speak unto the people.

FORASMUCH as N. and N. have consented together in holy wedlock, and have witnessed the same before God and this company, and thereto have given and pledged their troth either to other, and have declared the same by giving and receiving of a ring, and by joining of hands: I pronounce that they be man and wife together. In the name of the Father, and of the Son, and of the Holy Ghost. Amen.

And the minister shall add this blessing.

GOD the Father, God the Son, God the Holy Ghost, bless, preserve, and keep you; the Lord mercifully with his favor look upon you, and so fill you with all spiritual benediction and

---

[4] *Put asunder:* separate; Matt. 19:6.

grace, that you may so live together in this life, that in the world to come, you may have life everlasting. Amen.

Then the ministers or clerks going to the Lord's Table, shall say or sing this Psalm following.

[*Beati omnes.* Ps. 128

BLESSED are all they that fear the Lord: and walk in his ways.

For thou shalt eat the labor of thy hands: O well is thee, and happy shalt thou be.

Thy wife shall be as the fruitful vine: upon the walls of thy house.

Thy children like the olive branches: round about thy table.

Lo, thus shall the man be blessed: that feareth the Lord.

The Lord from out of Sion, shall bless thee: that thou shalt see Jerusalem[5] in prosperity, all thy life long.

Yea, that thou shalt see thy children's children: and peace upon Israel.

Glory be to the Father, etc.

As it was in the, etc.

Or else this Psalm following.

[*Deus misereatur.* Ps. 67

GOD be merciful unto us and bless us: and show us the light of his countenance, and be merciful unto us.

That thy way may be known upon the earth: thy saving health among all nations.

Let the people praise thee (O God): yea, let all the people praise thee.

O let the nations rejoice and be glad: for thou shalt judge the folk[6] righteously, and govern the nations upon the earth.

[5] "Hierusalem" in text.

[6] Text has "flock," but "folk" in 1549 and 1661 Books. The text seems to copy an error made in the 1552 Book. Cf. Brightman, *English Rite*, II, 808–9.

Let the people praise thee (O God): let all the people praise thee.

Then shall the earth bring forth her increase: and God, even our God, shall give us his blessing.

God shall bless us: and all the ends of the world shall fear him.

Glory be to the Father, etc.

As it was in the, etc.

The Psalm ended, and the man and the woman kneeling afore[7] the Lord's Table: the priest standing at the table, and turning his face toward them, shall say.

> Lord have mercy upon us.
> Answer. Christ have mercy upon us.
> Minister. Lord have mercy upon us.

OUR Father which art in heaven, etc.

And lead us not into temptation.

Answer. But deliver us from evil. Amen.

Minister. O Lord save thy servant, and thy handmaid.

Answer. Which put their trust in thee.

Minister. O Lord send them help from thy holy place.

Answer. And evermore defend them.

Minister. Be unto them a tower of strength.

Answer. From the face of their enemy.

Minister. O Lord hear our prayer.

Answer. And let our cry come unto thee.

The minister.

O GOD of Abraham, God of Isaac, God of Jacob, bless these thy servants, and sow the seed of eternal life in their minds, that whatsoever in thy holy Word they shall profitably learn, they may in deed fulfill the same. Look, O Lord, mercifully upon

---

[7] *Afore:* before.

them from heaven and bless them. And as thou didst send thy blessing upon Abraham and Sarah to their great comfort: so vouchsafe to send thy blessing upon these thy servants, that they obeying thy will, and alway being in safety under thy protection, may abide in thy love unto their lives end; through Jesu Christ our Lord. Amen.

This prayer next following shall be omitted where the woman is past childbirth.

O MERCIFUL Lord and heavenly Father, by whose gracious gift mankind is increased: We beseech thee assist with thy blessing these two persons, that they may both be fruitful in procreation of children, and also live together so long in godly love and honesty, that they may see their children's children, unto the third and fourth generation, unto thy praise and honor; through Jesus Christ our Lord. Amen.

O GOD, which by thy mighty power hast made all things of nought,[8] which also after other things set in order, didst appoint that out of man (created after thine own image and similitude) woman should take her beginning, and knitting them together didst teach that it should never be lawful to put asunder those whom thou by matrimony hadst made one: O God, which hast consecrated the state of matrimony to such an excellent mystery, that in it is signified and represented the spiritual marriage and unity betwixt Christ and his Church, look mercifully upon these thy servants, that both this man may love his wife, according to thy Word (as Christ did love thy spouse the Church, who gave himself for it, loving and cherishing it even as his own flesh), and also that this woman may be loving and amiable to her husband as Rachel, wise as Rebecca, faithful and obedient as Sarah, and in all quietness, sobriety, and peace be a follower of holy and godly matrons. O Lord, bless them both, and grant

---

[8] *Nought:* nothing.

them to inherit thy everlasting kingdom; through Jesus Christ our Lord. Amen.

Then shall the priest say.

ALMIGHTY God, which at the beginning did create our first parents Adam and Eve, and did sanctify and join them together in marriage: Pour upon you the riches of his grace, sanctify and bless you, that ye may please him both in body and soul, and live together in holy love, unto your lives end. Amen.

Then shall begin the Communion, and after the Gospel shall be said a sermon, wherein ordinarily (so oft as there is any marriage) the office of a man and wife shall be declared, according to Holy Scripture; or if there be no sermon, the minister shall read this that followeth.

ALL ye which be married, or which intend to take the holy estate of matrimony upon you, hear what Holy Scripture doth say, as touching the duty of husbands toward their wives, and wives toward their husbands. Saint Paul (in his Epistle to the Ephesians, the fifth chapter) doth give this commandment to all married men.

Ye husbands love your wives, even as Christ loved the Church, and hath given himself for it, to sanctify it, purging it in the fountain of water, through thy Word, that he might make it unto himself a glorious congregation, not having spot or wrinkle, or any such thing, but that it should be holy and blameless. So men are bound to love their own wives as their own bodies. He that loveth his own wife, loveth himself. For never did any man hate his own flesh, but nourisheth and cherisheth it, even as the Lord doth the congregation: for we are members of his body, of his flesh and of his bones.

For this cause shall a man leave father and mother, and shall be joined unto his wife, and they two shall be one flesh. This mystery is great, but I speak of Christ and of the congregation. Nevertheless, let every one of you so love his own wife, even as himself.

Likewise the same Saint Paul (writing to the Colossians) speaketh thus to all men that be married. Ye men love your wives, and be not bitter unto them. [Col. 3 [9]

Hear also what Saint Peter the Apostle of Christ, which was himself a married man, saith unto all men that are married. Ye husbands, dwell with your wives according to knowledge, giving honor unto the wife as unto the weaker vessel, and as heirs together of the grace of life, so that your prayers be not hindered. [1 Pet. 3

Hitherto ye have heard the duty of the husband toward the wife.

Now likewise ye wives hear and learn your duty toward your husbands, even as it is plainly set forth in Holy Scripture.

Saint Paul (in the forenamed Epistle to the Ephesians) teacheth you thus, Ye women submit yourselves unto your own husbands as unto the Lord, for the husband is the wife's head even as Christ is the head of the Church. And he is also the savior of the whole body. Therefore as the church or congregation is subject unto Christ, so likewise let the wives also be in subjection unto their own husbands in all things. And again he saith, Let the wife reverence her husband.[10] And (in his Epistle to the Colossians) Saint Paul giveth you this short lesson, Ye wives submit yourselves unto your own husbands, as it is convenient in the Lord. [Col. 3

Saint Peter also doth instruct you very godly, thus saying, Let wives be subject to their own husbands, so that if any obey not the Word, they may be won without the Word, by the conversation[11] of the wives, while they behold your chaste conversation coupled with fear, whose apparel let it not be outward, with broided[12] hair and trimming about with gold, either in putting on of gorgeous apparel, but let the hid man which is in

---

[9] Text has "Col. 4"; misprint.

[10] Margin note: "Eph. 5."

[11] *Conversation:* behavior.

[12] *Broided:* braided.

the heart, be without all corruption, so that the spirit be mild and quiet, which is a precious thing in the sight of God. For after this manner (in the old time) did the holy women which trusted in God apparel themselves, being subject to their own husbands, as Sarah obeyed Abraham calling him lord; whose daughters ye are made, doing well, and being not dismayed with any fear. [1 Pet. 3

The new married persons (the same day of their marriage) must receive the Holy Communion.

The Order for the
Visitation of the Sick

The priest entering into the sick person's house, shall say.

PEACE be in this house, and to all that dwell in it.

When he cometh into the sick man's presence, he shall say, kneeling down.

REMEMBER not Lord our iniquities, nor the iniquities of our forefathers. Spare us good Lord, spare thy people, whom thou hast redeemed with thy most precious blood, and be not angry with us forever.

Lord have mercy upon us.
Christ have mercy upon us.
Lord have mercy upon us.

OUR Father which art in heaven, etc.

And lead us not into temptation.
Answer. But deliver us from evil. Amen.
Minister. O Lord save thy servant.
Answer. Which putteth his trust in thee.
Minister. Send him help from thy holy place.
Answer. And evermore mightily defend him.
Minister. Let the enemy have none advantage of him.
Answer. Nor the wicked approach to hurt him.
Minister. Be unto him, O Lord, a strong tower.
Answer. From the face of his enemy.
Minister. Lord hear our prayers.
Answer. And let our cry come unto thee.

The minister.

O LORD, look down from heaven, behold, visit and relieve this thy servant. Look upon him with the eyes of thy mercy, give him comfort and sure confidence in thee, defend him from the danger of the enemy, and keep him in perpetual peace and safety; through Jesus Christ our Lord. Amen.

H EAR us, almighty and most merciful God and Savior. Extend thy accustomed goodness to this thy servant, which is grieved with sickness. Visit him, O Lord, as thou didst visit Peter's wife's mother, and the captain's servant. So visit and restore unto this sick person his former health (if it be thy will) or else give him grace so to take thy visitation, that after this painful life ended, he may dwell with thee in life everlasting. Amen.

Then shall the minister exhort the sick person after this form or other like.

D EARLY beloved, know this, that Almighty God is the lord of life and death, and over all things to them pertaining, as youth, strength, health, age, weakness, and sickness. Wherefore, whatsoever your sickness is, know you certainly, that it is God's visitation.

And for what cause soever this sickness is sent unto you, whether it be to try your patience for the example of other and that your faith may be found in the day of the Lord laudable, glorious, and honorable, to the increase of glory and endless felicity, or else it be sent unto you to correct and amend in you whatsoever doth offend the eyes of our heavenly Father: know you certainly, that if you truly repent you of your sins, and bear your sickness patiently, trusting in God's mercy for his dear Son Jesus Christ's sake, and render unto him humble thanks for his fatherly visitation, submitting yourself wholly to his will, it shall turn to your profit, and help you forward in the right way that leadeth unto everlasting life.

If the person visited be very sick, then the curate may end his exhortation in this place.

AKE therefore in good worth the chastisement[1] of the Lord, for whom the Lord loveth, he chastiseth. Yea (as Saint Paul saith)[2] he scourgeth every son which he receiveth. If you endure chastisement, he offereth himself unto you, as unto his own children. What son is he that the father chastiseth not? If ye be not under correction (whereof all true children are partakers) then are ye bastards and not children. Therefore, seeing that when our carnal fathers do correct us, we reverently obey them, shall we not now much rather be obedient to our spiritual father, and so live? And they for a few days do chastise us after their own pleasure, but he doth chastise us for our profit, to the intent he may make us partakers of his holiness. These words, good brother, are God's words, and written in Holy Scripture for our comfort and instruction, that we should patiently and with thanksgiving bear our heavenly Father's correction, whensoever by any manner of adversity it shall please his gracious goodness to visit us. And there should be no greater comfort to Christian persons, than to be made like unto Christ by suffering patiently adversities, troubles, and sicknesses. For he himself went not up to joy, but first he suffered pain; he entered not into his glory, before he was crucified. So truly our way to eternal joy is to suffer here with Christ; and our door to enter into eternal life is gladly to die with Christ, that we may rise again from death, and dwell with him in everlasting life. Now therefore taking your sickness, which is thus profitable for you, patiently, I exhort you, in the name of God, to remember the profession which you made unto God in your Baptism. And forasmuch as after this life, there is account to be given unto the righteous judge, of whom all must be judged without respect of persons: I require you to examine yourself and your state, both toward God and man, so that accusing and condemning yourself for your own faults, you may find mercy at our heavenly Father's hand for Christ's sake, and not be accused and condemned in that fearful

[1] "Text has "chastement."
[2] Heb. 12:6–10.

judgment. Therefore I shall shortly rehearse the articles of our faith, that ye may know whether you do believe, as a Christian man should, or no.

Here the minister shall rehearse the articles of the faith, saying thus.

D OST thou believe in God the Father Almighty?

And so forth as it is in Baptism.

Then shall the minister examine whether he be in charity with all the world, exhorting him to forgive from the bottom of his heart all persons that have offended him, and if he have offended other, to ask them forgiveness. And where he hath done injury or wrong to any man, that he make amends to the uttermost of his power. And if he have not afore[3] disposed his goods, let him then make his will. But men must be oft admonished that they set an order for their temporal goods and lands, when they be in health. And also declare his debts, what he oweth, and what is owing unto him, for discharging of his conscience and quietness of his executors.

These words before rehearsed may be said before the minister begin his prayer, as he shall see cause.

The minister may not forget, nor omit to move the sick person (and that most earnestly) to liberality toward the poor.

Here shall the sick person make a special confession, if he feel his conscience troubled with any weighty matter. After which confession, the priest shall absolve him after this sort.

O UR Lord Jesus Christ, who hath left power to his Church to absolve all sinners, which truly repent and believe in him, of his great mercy forgive thee thine offenses: and by his authority committed to me, I absolve thee from all thy sins, in the name of the Father, and of the Son, and of the Holy Ghost. Amen.

[3] *Afore:* before.

And then the priest shall say the Collect following.

Let us pray.

O MOST merciful God, which according to the multitude of thy mercies, dost so put away the sins of those which truly repent, that thou rememberest them no more: Open thy eye of mercy upon this thy servant, who most earnestly desireth pardon and forgiveness. Renew in him, most loving Father, whatsoever hath been decayed by the fraud and malice of the devil, or by his own carnal will and frailness. Preserve and continue this sick member in the unity of thy Church. Consider his contrition, accept his tears, assuage his pain, as shall be seen to thee most expedient for him. And forasmuch as he putteth his full trust only in thy mercy, impute not unto him his former sins, but take him unto thy favor; through the merits of thy most dearly beloved Son Jesus Christ. Amen.

Then the minister shall say this Psalm.

[*In te, Domine, speravi.* Ps. 71 [4]

I N thee, O Lord, have I put my trust, let me never be put to confusion: but rid me, and deliver me into thy righteousness, incline thine ear unto me, and save me.

Be thou my stronghold, whereunto I may alway resort: thou hast promised to help me, for thou art my house of defense and my castle.

Deliver me (O my God) out of the hand of the ungodly: out of the hand of the unrighteous and cruel man.

For thou (O Lord God) art the thing that I long for: thou art my hope even from my youth.

Through thee have I been holden up ever since I was born: thou art he that took me out of my mother's womb, my praise shall alway be of thee.

---

[4] Text has Ps. 21; misprint.

I am become as it were a monster unto many: but my sure trust is in thee.

Oh let my mouth be filled with thy praise: that I may sing of thy glory and honor all the day long.

Cast me not away in the time of age: forsake me not when my strength faileth me.

For mine enemies speak against me, and they that lay wait for my soul take their counsel together, saying: God hath forsaken him, persecute him, and take him, for there is none to deliver him.

Go not far from me, O God: my God, haste thee to help me.

Let them be confounded and perish, that are against my soul: let them be covered with shame and dishonor that seek to do me evil.

As for me, I will patiently abide alway: and will praise thee more and more.

My mouth shall daily speak of thy righteousness and salvation: for I know no end thereof.

I will go forth in the strength of the Lord God: and will make mention of thy righteousness only.

Thou (O God) hast taught me from my youth up until now: therefore I will tell of thy wondrous works.

Forsake me not (O God) in mine old age, when I am grayheaded: until I have showed thy strength unto this generation, and thy power to all them that are yet for to come.

Thy righteousness (O God) is very high, and great things are they that thou hast done: O God, who is like unto thee.

O what great troubles and adversities hast thou showed me? and yet didst thou turn and refresh me: yea, and broughtest me from the deep of the earth again.

Thou hast brought me to great honor: and comforted me on every side.

Therefore will I praise thee and thy faithfulness (O God),

playing upon an instrument of music: unto thee will I sing upon the harp, O thou holy one of Israel.

My lips will be fain,[5] when I sing unto thee: and so will my soul whom thou hast delivered.

My tongue also shall talk of thy righteousness all the day long: for they are confounded and brought unto shame, that seek to do me evil.

Glory be to the Father, and to the Son, and to the, etc.

As it was in the beginning, is now, and ever shall be: world without end. Amen.

Adding this.

O SAVIOR of the world, save us, which by thy cross and precious blood hast redeemed us, help us we beseech thee, O God.

Then shall the minister say.

THE Almighty Lord, which is a most strong tower to all them that put their trust in him, to whom all things in heaven, in earth, and under earth, do bow and obey: be now and evermore thy defense, and make thee know and feel, that there is no other name under heaven given to man, in whom, and through whom, thou mayest receive health and salvation, but only the name of our Lord Jesus Christ. Amen.

[5] *Be fain:* be glad.

The Communion
of the Sick

Forasmuch as all mortal men be subject to many sudden perils, diseases, and sicknesses, and ever uncertain what time they shall depart out of this life: therefore, to the intent they may be always in a readiness to die whensoever it shall please Almighty God to call them, the curates shall diligently from time to time, but specially in the plague time, exhort their parishioners to the oft receiving in the church of the Holy Communion of the Body and Blood of our Savior Christ. Which if they do, they shall have no cause in their sudden visitation to be unquieted for lack of the same. But if the sick person be not able to come to the church, and yet is desirous to receive the communion in his house, then he must give knowledge overnight, or else early in the morning, to the curate, signifying also how many be appointed to communicate with him. And having a convenient place in the sick man's house where the curate may reverently minister, and a good number to receive the communion with the sick person, with all things necessary for the same, he shall there minister the Holy Communion.

The Collects

ALMIGHTY everliving God, maker of mankind, which dost correct those whom thou dost love, and chastisest every one whom thou dost receive: We beseech thee to have mercy upon this thy servant visited with thy hand, and to grant that he may take his sickness patiently, and recover his bodily health (if it be thy gracious will), and whensoever his soul shall depart from the body, it may be without spot presented unto thee; through Jesus Christ our Lord. Amen.

The Epistle [Heb. 12

M Y son, despise not the correction of the Lord, neither faint when thou art rebuked of him. For whom the Lord loveth, him he correcteth, yea, and he scourgeth every son whom he receiveth.

The Gospel [John 5

V ERILY, verily I say unto you, He that heareth my word, and believeth on him that sent me, hath everlasting life, and shall not come unto damnation, but he passeth from death unto life.

At the time of the distribution of the holy Sacrament, the priest shall first receive the communion himself, and after minister unto them that be appointed to communicate with the sick.

But if any man, either by reason of extremity of sickness, or for lack of warning in due time to the curate, or for lack of company to receive with him, or by any other just impediment, do not receive the Sacrament of Christ's Body and Blood: then the curate shall instruct him, that if he do truly repent him of his sins, and steadfastly believe that Jesus Christ hath suffered death upon the cross for him, and shed his blood for his redemption, earnestly remembering the benefits he hath thereby, and giving him hearty thanks therefore, he doth eat and drink the Body and Blood of our Savior Christ, profitably to his soul's health, although he do not receive the Sacrament with his mouth.

When the sick person is visited, and receiveth the Holy Communion all at one time, then the priest for more expedition shall cut off the form of the visitation at the Psalm, In thee, O Lord, have I put my trust, and go straight to the Communion.

In the time of plague, sweat, or such other like contagious times of sicknesses or diseases, when none of the parish or neighbors can be gotten to communicate with the sick in their houses, for fear of the infection, upon special request of the diseased the minister may alonely[1] communicate with him.

[1] *Alonely:* alone.

The Order for the
Burial of the Dead

The priest meeting the corpse at the church stile, shall say or else the priests and clerks shall sing, and so go either unto the church, or toward the grave.

I AM the the resurrection and the life (saith the Lord): he that believeth in me, yea, though he were dead, yet shall he live. And whosoever liveth and believeth in me, shall not die forever. [John 11

I KNOW that my redeemer liveth, and that I shall rise out of the earth in the last day, and shall be covered again with my skin, and shall see God in my flesh: yea, and I myself shall behold him, not with other, but with these same eyes. [Job 19

WE brought nothing into this world, neither may we carry anything out of this world. The Lord giveth, and the Lord taketh away. Even as it hath pleased the Lord, so cometh things to pass: blessed be the name of the Lord. [1 Tim. 6. Job 1

When they come at the grave, whiles the corpse is made ready to be laid into the earth, the priest shall say, or the priest and clerks shall sing.

MAN that is born of a woman hath but a short time to live, and is full of misery. He cometh up and is cut down like a flower; he flieth as it were a shadow, and never continueth in one stay.[1] In the midst of life we be in death: of whom may we seek for succor but of thee, O Lord, which for our sins justly art displeased. Yet, O Lord God most holy, O Lord most mighty, O holy and most merciful savior, deliver us not into the bitter pains of eternal death. Thou knowest, Lord, the secrets of our

---

[1] Margin note: "Job 11"; a misprint for Job 14.

hearts, shut not up thy merciful eyes to our prayers: but spare us Lord most holy, O God most mighty, O holy and merciful savior, thou most worthy judge eternal, suffer us not at our last hour for any pains of death to fall from thee.

Then while the earth shall be cast upon the body by some standing by, the priest shall say.

FORASMUCH as it hath pleased Almighty God of his great mercy to take unto himself the soul of our dear brother here departed: we therefore commit his body to the ground, earth to earth, ashes to ashes, dust to dust, in sure and certain hope of resurrection to eternal life, through our Lord Jesus Christ, who shall change our vile body that it may be like to his glorious body, according to the mighty working, whereby he is able to subdue all things to himself.

Then shall be said or sung.

I HEARD a voice from heaven saying unto me, Write, From henceforth blessed are the dead which die in the Lord. Even so saith the Spirit, that they rest from their labors.[2]

Then shall follow this Lesson, taken out of the fifteenth chapter to the Corinthians, the first Epistle.

CHRIST is risen from the dead, and become the first fruits of them that slept. For by a man came death, and by a man came the resurrection of the dead. For as by Adam all die, even so by Christ shall all be made alive. But every man in his own order: The first is Christ, then they that are Christ's at his coming. Then cometh the end, when he hath delivered up the kingdom to God the Father; when he hath put down all rule and all authority and power. For he must reign till he have put all his enemies under his feet. The last enemy that shall be destroyed is death. For he hath put all things under his feet. But when he saith all things are put under him, it is manifest that he is ex-

[2] Rev. 14:13.

cepted, which did put all things under him. When all things are
subdued unto him, then shall the Son also himself be subject
unto him that put all things under him, that God may be all in
all. Else what do they which are baptized over the dead, if the
dead rise not at all? Why are they then baptized over them; yea,
and why stand we alway then in jeopardy? By our rejoicing
which I have in Christ Jesu our Lord, I die daily. That I have
fought with beasts at Ephesus after the manner of men, what
advantageth it me, if the dead rise not again? Let us eat and
drink, for tomorrow we shall die. Be not ye deceived, evil words
corrupt good manners. Awake truly out of sleep, and sin not. For
some have not the knowledge of God. I speak this to your shame.

But some man will say, How arise the dead? With what body
shall they come? Thou fool, that which thou sowest, is not quickened except it die. And what sowest thou? Thou sowest not that
body that shall be, but bare corn, as of wheat or some other, but
God giveth it a body at his pleasure, to every seed his own body.
All flesh is not one manner of flesh, but there is one manner of
flesh of men, and other manner of flesh of beasts, and other of
fishes, another of birds. There are also celestial bodies, and there
are bodies terrestrial. But the glory of the celestial is one, and
the glory of the terrestrial is another. There is one manner glory
of the sun, and another glory of the moon, and another glory of
the stars. For one star differeth from another in glory: so is the
resurrection of the dead. It is sown in corruption, it riseth again
in incorruption. It is sown in dishonor, it riseth again in honor.
It is sown in weakness, it riseth again in power. It is sown a natural
body, it riseth a spiritual body. There is a natural body, and there
is a spiritual body. As it is also written, The first man Adam was
made a living soul, and the last Adam was made a quickening
spirit. Howbeit, that is not first which is spiritual, but that which
is natural, and then that which is spiritual. The first man is of
the earth, earthy. The second man is the Lord from heaven,
heavenly. As is the earthy, such are they that be earthy. And as

is the heavenly, such are they that are heavenly. And as we have borne the image of the earthy, so shall we bear the image of the heavenly.

This say I brethren, that flesh and blood cannot inherit the kingdom of God, neither doth corruption inherit uncorruption. Behold, I show you a mystery. We shall not all sleep, but we shall all be changed, and that in a moment, in the twinkling of an eye by the last trump.[3] For the trump shall blow, and the dead shall rise incorruptible, and we shall be changed. For this corruptible must put on incorruption, and this mortal must put on immortality. When this corruptible hath put on incorruption, and this mortal hath put on immortality, then shall be brought to pass the saying that is written, Death is swallowed up in victory. Death where is thy sting? Hell where is thy victory? The sting of death is sin; and the strength of sin is the law. But thanks be unto God, which hath given us victory, through our Lord Jesus Christ. Therefore my dear brethren, be ye steadfast and unmovable, always rich in the work of the Lord, forasmuch as ye know, how that your labor is not in vain in the Lord.

The Lesson ended, the priest shall say.

Lord have mercy upon us.
Christ have mercy upon us.
Lord have mercy upon us.

OUR Father which art in heaven, etc.

And lead us not into temptation.
Answer. But deliver us from evil. Amen.

The Priest.

ALMIGHTY God, with whom do live the spirits of them that depart hence in the Lord, and in whom the souls of them that be elected, after they be delivered from the burden of the flesh, be in joy and felicity: We give thee hearty thanks,

[3] *Trump:* trumpet.

for that it hath pleased thee to deliver this N. our brother out of the miseries of this sinful world; beseeching thee, that it may please thee of thy gracious goodness, shortly to accomplish the number of thine elect, and to haste thy kingdom, that we with this our brother, and all other departed in the true faith of thy holy name, may have our perfect consummation and bliss, both in body and soul, in thy eternal and everlasting glory. Amen.

The Collect

O MERCIFUL God, the Father of our Lord Jesus Christ, who is the resurrection and the life, in whom whosoever believeth, shall live though he die, and whosoever liveth and believeth in him, shall not die eternally; who also taught us (by his holy Apostle Paul) not to be sorry, as men without hope, for them that sleep in him: We meekly beseech thee (O Father) to raise us from the death of sin unto the life of righteousness, that when we shall depart this life, we may rest in him, as our hope is this our brother doth; and that at the general resurrection in the last day, we may be found acceptable in thy sight, and receive that blessing which thy well-beloved Son shall then pronounce to all that love and fear thee, saying, Come ye blessed children of my Father, receive the kingdom prepared for you from the beginning of the world. Grant this we beseech thee, O merciful Father, through Jesus Christ our mediator and redeemer. Amen.

The Thanksgiving
of Women after Childbirth, Commonly Called the Churching of Women

The woman shall come into the church, and there shall kneel down in some convenient place nigh unto the place where the table standeth. And the priest standing by her shall say these words, or such like as the case shall require.

FORASMUCH as it hath pleased Almighty God of his goodness to give you safe deliverance, and hath preserved you in the great danger of childbirth: ye shall therefore give hearty thanks unto God and pray.

Then shall the priest say this Psalm.[1]

I HAVE lifted up mine eyes unto the hills: from whence cometh my help.

My help cometh even from the Lord: which hath made heaven and earth.

He will not suffer thy foot to be moved: and he that keepeth thee will not sleep.

Behold, he that keepeth Israel: shall neither slumber nor sleep.

The Lord himself is thy keeper: the Lord is thy defense upon thy right hand.

So that the sun shall not burn thee by day: neither the moon by night.

The Lord shall preserve thee from all evil: yea it is even he that shall keep thy soul.

[1] The Psalm *Levavi oculos* (Ps. 121) is not identified in the margin in the customary way.

314

The Lord shall preserve thy going out, and thy coming in: from this time forth for evermore.

Glory be to the Father, and to the Son, and to, etc.

As it was in the beginning, is now, and ever, etc.

> Lord have mercy upon us.
> Christ have mercy upon us.
> Lord have mercy upon us.

OUR Father which, etc.

And lead us not into temptation.

Answer. But deliver us from evil. Amen.

Priest. O Lord save this woman thy servant.

Answer. Which putteth her trust in thee.

Priest. Be thou to her a strong tower.

Answer. From the face of her enemy.

Priest. Lord hear our prayer.

Answer. And let my cry come unto thee.

Priest. Let us pray.

O ALMIGHTY God, which hast delivered this woman thy servant from the great pain and peril of childbirth: Grant, we beseech thee (most merciful Father) that she through thy help, may both faithfully live and walk in her vocation, according to thy will in this life present, and also may be partaker of everlasting glory in the life to come; through Jesus Christ our Lord. Amen.

The woman that cometh to give her thanks must offer accustomed offerings. And if there be a Communion, it is convenient that she receive the Holy Communion.

A Commination

against Sinners, with Certain Prayers
to Be Used Divers Times in the Year

After Morning Prayer, the people being called together by the ringing of a bell, and assembled in the church, the English Litany shall be said, after the accustomed manner, which ended, the priest shall go into the pulpit and say thus.

BRETHREN, in the primitive Church there was a godly discipline, that, at the beginning of Lent, such persons as were notorious sinners were put to open penance and punished in this world, that their souls might be saved in the day of the Lord; and that others admonished by their example might be more afraid to offend. In the stead whereof, until the said discipline may be restored again (which thing is much to be wished) it is thought good, that at this time (in your presence) should be read the general sentences of God's cursing against impenitent sinners, gathered out of the twenty-seventh chapter of Deuteronomy, and other places of Scripture; and that ye should answer to every sentence, Amen. To the intent that you, being admonished of the great indignation of God against sinners, may the rather be called to earnest and true repentance, and may walk more warely[1] in these dangerous days, fleeing from such vices, for the which ye affirm with your own mouths, the curse of God to be due.

Cursed is the man that maketh any carved or molten image, an abomination to the Lord, the work of the hands of the craftsman, and putteth it in a secret place to worship it.

And the people shall answer and say.

Amen.

[1] *Warely:* warily.

Minister. Cursed is he that curseth his father and mother.

Answer. Amen.

Minister. Cursed is he that removeth away the mark[2] of his neighbor's land.

Answer. Amen.

Minister. Cursed is he that maketh the blind to go out of his way.

Answer. Amen.

Minister. Cursed is he that letteth[3] in judgment the right of the stranger, of them that be fatherless, and of widows.

Answer. Amen.

Minister. Cursed is he that smiteth his neighbor secretly.

Answer. Amen.

Minister. Cursed is he that lieth with his neighbor's wife.

Answer. Amen.

Minister. Cursed is he that taketh reward to slay the soul of innocent blood.

Answer. Amen.

Minister. Cursed is he that putteth his trust in man, and taketh man for his defense, and in his heart goeth from the Lord.

Answer. Amen.

Minister. Cursed are the unmerciful, the fornicators, and adulterers, and the covetous persons, the worshipers of images, slanderers, drunkards, and extortioners.

Answer. Amen.

The Minister.

NOW seeing that all they be accursed (as the Prophet David beareth witness)[4] which do err and go astray from the commandments of God, let us (remembering the dreadful judgment hanging over our heads, and being always at hand) return unto our Lord God, with all contrition and meekness of heart, bewail-

---

[2] 1661 Book has "land-mark."

[3] *Letteth:* hinders; 1661 Book has "perverteth the."

[4] In the margin: "Ps. 118"; old numbering; cf. Ps. 119:21.

317

ing and lamenting our sinful life, knowledging[5] and confessing our offenses, and seeking to bring forth worthy fruits of penance. For now is the axe put unto the root of the trees, so that every tree which bringeth not forth good fruit, is hewn down and cast into the fire.[6] It is a fearful thing to fall into the hands of the living God;[7] he shall pour down rain upon the sinners, snares, fire, and brimstone, storm and tempest; this shall be their portion to drink.[8] For lo, the Lord is come out of his place, to visit the wickedness of such as dwell upon the earth.[9] But who may abide the day of his coming? Who shall be able to endure when he appeareth?[10] His fan is in his hand, and he will purge his floor, and gather his wheat into the barn, but he will burn the chaff with unquenchable fire.[11] The day of the Lord cometh as a thief upon the night, and when men shall say peace, and all things are safe, then shall suddenly destruction come upon them, as sorrow cometh upon a woman travailing with child, and they shall not escape.[12] Then shall appear the wrath of God in the day of vengeance, which obstinate sinners, through the stubbornness of their heart, have heaped unto themself,[13] which despised the goodness, patience, and long sufferance of God, when he called them continually to repentance. Then shall they call upon me, saith the Lord, but I will not hear. They shall seek me early, but they shall not find me. And that because they hated knowledge and received not the fear of the Lord, but abhorred my counsel, and despised my correction,[14] then shall it be too late to knock,

[5] *Knowledging:* acknowledging.
[6] Margin note: "Matt. 3"; verse 10.
[7] Margin note: "Heb. 10"; verse 31.
[8] Margin note: "Ps. 10"; old numbering; cf. Ps. 11:6.
[9] Margin note: "Isa. 26"; verse 21. Text has "Esa."
[10] Margin note: "Mal. 3"; verse 2.
[11] Margin note: "Matt. 3"; verse 12.
[12] Margin note: "1 Thess. 5"; verses 2–3.
[13] Margin note: "Rom. 2"; verses 4–5.
[14] Margin note: "Prov. 1"; verses 28–30.

when the door shall be shut, and too late to cry for mercy, when it is the time of justice. O terrible voice of most just judgment, which shall be pronounced upon them, when it shall be said unto them: Go ye cursed into the fire everlasting, which is prepared for the devil and his angels.[15] Therefore brethren, take we heed betime,[16] while the day of salvation lasteth,[17] for the night cometh when none can work.[18] But let us while we have the light believe in the light, and walk as the children of the light, that we be not cast into the utter darkness where is weeping and gnashing of teeth.[19] Let us not abuse the goodness of God, which calleth us mercifully to amendment, and of his endless pity promiseth us forgiveness of that which is past, if (with a whole mind and true heart) we return unto him. For though our sins be red as scarlet, they shall be as white as snow, and though they be like purple, yet shall they be as white as wool.[20] Turn you clean (saith the Lord) from all your wickedness, and your sin shall not be your destruction.[21] Cast away from you all your ungodliness that ye have done, make you new hearts and a new spirit: wherefore will you die, O ye house of Israel? Seeing that I have no pleasure in the death of him that dieth (saith the Lord God). Turn you then and you shall live. Although we have sinned, yet have we an advocate with the Father, Jesus Christ the righteous, and he it is that obtaineth grace for our sins,[22] for he was wounded for our offenses, and smitten for our wickedness.[23] Let us therefore return unto him, who is the merciful receiver of all true penitent sinners, assuring ourself that he is ready to receive us, and most

[15] Margin note: "Matt. 25"; verse 41.

[16] *Betime:* in good time.

[17] Margin note: "2 Cor. 6"; verse 2.

[18] Margin note: "John 9"; verse 4.

[19] Margin note: "Matt. 25"; verse 30.

[20] Margin note: "Isa. 1"; verse 18. Text has "Esa."

[21] Margin note: "Ezek. 28"; a misprint (see Ezek. 18:30).

[22] Margin note: "1 John 2"; verses 1–2.

[23] Margin note: "Isa. 53"; verse 5. Text has "Esai."

willing to pardon us, if we come to him with faithful repentance, if we will submit ourselves unto him, and from henceforth walk in his ways; if we will take his easy yoke and light burden upon us,[24] to follow him in lowliness, patience, and charity, and be ordered by the governance of his Holy Spirit, seeking always his glory, and serving him duly in our vocation, with thanksgiving. This if we do, Christ will deliver us from the curse of the law, and from the extreme malediction, which shall light upon them that shall be set on the left hand. And he will set us on his right hand and give us the blessed benediction of his Father, commanding us to take possession of his glorious kingdom,[25] unto the which he vouchsafe to bring us all, for his infinite mercy. Amen.

Then shall they all kneel upon their knees; and the priests and clerks kneeling (where they are accustomed to say the Litany) shall say this Psalm.

[*Miserere mei deus.* Ps. 51

HAVE mercy upon me (O God) after thy great goodness: according to the multitude of thy mercies, do away mine offenses.

Wash me throughly from[26] my wickedness: and cleanse me from my sin.

For I knowledge my faults: and my sin is ever before me.

Against thee only have I sinned, and done this evil in thy sight: that thou mightest be justified in thy saying, and clear when thou art judged.

Behold, I was shapen in wickedness: and in sin hath my mother conceived me.

But lo, thou requirest truth in inward parts:[27] and shalt make me to understand wisdom secretly.

---

[24] Margin note: "Matt. 11"; verses 29–30.
[25] Margin note: "Matt. 25"; verses 33–34.
[26] Text has "fro."
[27] Text has "parties."

Thou shalt purge me with hyssop,[28] and I shall be clean: thou shalt wash me, and I shall be whiter than snow.

Thou shalt make me hear of joy and gladness: that the bones which thou hast broken may rejoice.

Turn thy face from my sins: and put out all my misdeeds.

Make me a clean heart (O God): and renew a right spirit within me.

Cast me not away from thy presence: and take not thy Holy Spirit from me.

O give me the comfort[29] of thy help again: and stablish me with thy free spirit.

Then shall I teach thy ways unto the wicked: and sinners shall be converted unto thee.

Deliver me from bloodguiltiness (O God) thou that art the God of my health: and my tongue shall sing of thy righteousness.

Thou shalt open my lips (O Lord): my mouth shall show thy praise.

For thou desirest no sacrifice, else would I give it thee: but thou delightest not in burnt offering.

The sacrifice of God is a troubled spirit: a broken and a contrite heart (O God) shalt thou not despise.

O be favorable and gracious unto Sion: build thou the walls of Jerusalem.[30]

Then shalt thou be pleased with the sacrifice of righteousness, with the burnt offerings and oblations: then shall they offer young bullocks upon thine altar.

Glory be to the Father, and to the Son, etc.

As it was in the beginning, and is now, etc. Amen.

Lord have mercy upon us.

Christ have mercy upon us.

Lord have mercy upon us.

[28] Text has "isope."

[29] *Comfort:* strength, encouragement.

[30] "Hierusalem" in text.

OUR Father which art in heaven, etc.

And lead us not into temptation.
Answer. But deliver us from evil. Amen.
Minister. O Lord save thy servants.
Answer. Which put their trust in thee.
Minister. Send unto them help from above.
Answer. And evermore mightily defend them.
Minister. Help us, O God our savior.
Answer. And for the glory of thy name's sake deliver us, be merciful unto us sinners, for thy name's sake.
Minister. Lord hear my prayers.
Answer. And let my cry come unto thee.

Let us pray.

O LORD, we beseech thee mercifully hear our prayers, and spare all those which confess their sins to thee: that they (whose consciences by sin are accused) by thy merciful pardon may be absolved, through Christ our Lord. Amen.

O MOST mighty God and merciful Father, which hast compassion of all men, and hatest nothing that thou hast made, which wouldest not the death of a sinner, but that he should rather turn from sin, and be saved: Mercifully forgive us our trespasses, receive and comfort us, which be grieved and wearied with the burden of our sin. Thy property is to have mercy, to thee only it apperteineth to forgive sins: Spare us therefore, good Lord, spare thy people whom thou hast redeemed. Enter not into judgment with thy servants, which be vile earth, and miserable sinners; but so turn thy ire from us, which meekly knowledge our vileness, and truly repent us of our faults, so make haste to help us in this world, that we may ever live with thee, in the world to come; through Jesus Christ our Lord. Amen.

Then shall the people say this that followeth, after the minister.

TURN thou us, O good Lord, and so shall we be turned. Be favorable (O Lord) be favorable to thy people, which turn to thee in weeping, fasting, and praying; for thou art a merciful God, full of compassion, long-suffering, and of a great piety.[31] Thou sparest when we deserve punishment, and in thy wrath thinkest upon mercy. Spare thy people, good Lord, spare them and let not thy heritage be brought to confusion. Hear us (O Lord) for thy mercy is great, and after the multitude of thy mercies, look upon us.

[31] *Piety:* pity.

History of
the 1559 Book of Common Prayer

History of the 1559 Book of Common Prayer

The Book of Common Prayer occupies a place of great importance in the history of the British people. Since 1559 it has been
the book of the Church of England, providing services of worship, a basis for religious education, standards of doctrine, copious
amounts of Holy Scripture, and a use of English which contrib-
uted to the formation of the modern language. Richmond Noble
has provided evidence for the use of the book by Shakespeare.[1]
John Donne, not only as Dean of St. Paul's Cathedral but also
as an Englishman continuously exposed to the weekly sequence
of Matins, Litany, Ante Communion, and Evensong, preached
sermons within the context of the prescribed services and wrote
poems against the background of the liturgy.[2] George Herbert's
works cannot rightly be understood without reference to the Book
of Common Prayer. *The Temple* is largely an exposition of the
worship he knew and valued in the Church of England which
he served.[3] Not every literary figure left notes on the Prayer

---

[1] Richmond Noble, *Shakespeare's Biblical Knowledge and Use of the Book
of Common Prayer* (New York, 1970), pp. 76–86. See also Roland Mushat
Frye, *Shakespeare and Christian Doctrine* (Princeton, 1963), pp. 261–63; and
Stella Brook, *The Language of the Book of Common Prayer* (London, 1965),
pp. 94, 97.

[2] For instance, see James E. Wellington, "The Litany in Cranmer and
Donne," *Studies in Philology* LXVIII, no. 2 (April 1971): 177–99.

[3] The poems of *The Temple* should be read alongside his prose work, *A
Priest to the Temple*, and with the knowledge that Herbert was a working
priest of the Church of England. The printers of *The Temple* wrote: "His
obedience and conformitie to the Church and the discipline thereof was sin-
gularly remarkable. Though he abounded in private devotions, yet went he
every morning and evening with his familie to the Church; and by his example, exhortations, and encouragements drew the greater part of his parishioners

Book, as did Samuel Taylor Coleridge,[4] thus providing direct evidence, but it is common sense to expect that either directly or indirectly the book has had its influence upon virtually all English literature up to the present century. Indeed, without knowing it we may find ourselves using phrases derived from the Book of Common Prayer. "Through fire and water," "outward and visible," "inward and spiritual," "picking and stealing," "pomps and vanity," "earth to earth, ashes to ashes, dust to dust"—these and like words and phrases heard over and over again have become a part of the heritage of English-speaking peoples. It could be argued that the Prayer Book has had a disproportionately high degree of influence when compared with the influence of the Authorized Version of the Bible.[5]

William Ewart Gladstone, the Victorian prime minister, wrote that "the *Book of Common Prayer* supplies the subject-matter of religious worship, and this most vitally enters into the spiritual food of the people, and, in fact, gives them in a very high degree their specific religious tone."[6] It is because vast numbers of people, from 1559 on, lived under the influence of the Book of Common Prayer, whether positively or negatively, as loyal members of the Church of England or as dissenters from that church, that the Prayer Book must be taken seriously as a document of great importance, not simply to detect specific incidents of its influence but also to understand the people, their religion, and

---

to accompanie him dayly in the publick celebration of Divine Service" (F. E. Hutchinson, ed., *The Works of George Herbert* [Oxford, 1941], p. 4).

[4] Samuel Taylor Coleridge, *The Complete Works*, ed. W. G. T. Shedd, 7 vols. (New York, 1884), V, 21–28. See also J. Robert Barth, S.J., *Coleridge and Christian Doctrine* (Cambridge, Mass., 1969), p. 169*n*.

[5] Brook, pp. 192–206. Concerning language and style, see Brook and also Prins, Anton Adriaan, *The Booke of the Common Prayer, 1549: An Enquiry into Its Language* (Amsterdam, 1933); and C. S. Lewis, *English Literature in the Sixteenth Century* (Oxford, 1954), pp. 215–21.

[6] Gladstone to Archbishop Lyaugus of Syra and Tenos, from Hawarden, October 1875, in W. E. Gladstone, *Correspondence on Church and Religion*, ed. D. C. Lathbury, 2 vols. (New York, 1910), II, 66–67.

their culture. A. L. Rowse correctly asserts, concerning Elizabethan England, that "it is impossible to over-estimate the influence of the Church's routine of prayer and good works upon that society: the effect upon imagination and conduct of the liturgy with its piercing and affecting phrases, repeated Sunday by Sunday."[7]

The Elizabethan Prayer Book was chosen for this edition partly because it was the book that did in fact become an integral part of English life. The first two Prayer Books, of 1549 and 1552, lasted but a short while and were not generally accepted. The 1559 Book, a revision of the 1552 Book, was in constant use until 1604, when minor changes were made, none of which affected the general tone of the contents. Indeed, it was not until 1661/62 that further changes occurred, some of which did in fact alter the tone of the book, few of which were of very great importance. The Restoration Book maintained the tradition established in the sixteenth century and represented a defeat both for the High Churchmen, such as John Cosin, and for the Puritans, such as the conciliatory Richard Baxter. The 1662 Book remained the norm until the present day, when the Prayer Book (Alternative and Other Services) Measure of 1965 gives some promise of more drastic revision, indeed, the creation of a new order of worship for the English church.[8]

On the North American continent the 1662 Book was in use among Anglicans until 1789, when, at the founding of the Protestant Episcopal Church as an independent member of the Anglican communion of churches, a new Prayer Book was adopted. It was a revision of the 1662 Book, influenced by the "broadchurch" draft of 1785 and the Scottish Prayer Book of 1764. There were revisions of note in 1892 and 1928, both fundamentally conservative of the tradition, leading up to the promise of something more than a revision. At present the Episcopal Church

---

[7] A. L. Rowse, *The England of Elizabeth* (New York, 1950), p. 433.

[8] See G. J. Cuming, *A History of Anglican Liturgy* (London, 1969), pp. 263, 399–400.

is experimenting with *Services for Trial Use,* as authorized by the General Conventions of 1970 and 1973.[9]

The 1559 Book was chosen for this edition also because in the changes made therein, few in number but of considerable importance, there was the checking of a forceful movement in a Protestant or Genevan direction and a settling down to that *via media* which has become characteristic of Anglicanism. This book is, then, more clearly representative of Anglicanism than either of the earlier books. Furthermore, the 1559 Book was chosen because of the importance of the Elizabethan Age. Shakespeare and Donne, Elizabeth and Essex, Raleigh and Jonson, Coke and Bacon, Hooker and Andrewes all worshiped with the Book of Common Prayer of 1559.

The Advent of the 1559 Prayer Book

The circumstances surrounding the appearance of the 1559 Book were dramatic. The Book of Common Prayer, first produced in the reign of Edward VI, was outlawed during the reign of Queen Mary, so that when Elizabeth came to the throne on November 17, 1558, the Latin Breviary and Missal were in use and there was uncertainty as to what might ensue. As Sir John Neale has reconstructed the story,[1] it would seem that the new Queen was

---

[9] See Edward Lambe Parsons and Bayard Hale Jones, *The American Prayer Book: Its Origins and Principles* (New York, 1950); and Massey Hamilton Shepherd, Jr., *The Oxford American Prayer Book Commentary* (New York, 1950). Concerning the latest work of revision, see *Prayer Book Studies 15: The Problem and Method of Prayer Book Revision,* Standing Liturgical Commission of the Episcopal Church (New York, 1961).

[1] For Neale's reconstruction of events relied upon in this discussion, see his "The Elizabethan Acts of Supremacy and Uniformity," *English Historical Review* LXV, no. 256 (July 1950): 304–32, and *Elizabeth I and Her Parliaments, 1559–1581* (London, 1953). For a brief but serious critique, see C. W. Dugmore, *The Mass and the English Reformers* (London, 1958), pp. 209–12, 214–15.

determined to proceed with circumspection, aware of the delicacy of her own position, concerned first to secure her hold on the throne and thus to reassert the royal supremacy. A uniformity act, accompanied by a Prayer Book of some sort, would be left until the second Parliament or later. She would seem to have been acting in accordance with the advice of Armagil Waad, who, referring to the religious situation, wrote: "This case is to be warily handled, for it requireth great cunning and circumspection, both to reform religion and to make unity between the subjects, being at square for the respect thereof." Waad would have the Queen "proceed to the reformation having respect to quiet at home, the affairs you have in hand with foreign princes, the greatness of the Pope, and how dangerous it is to make alteration in religion, specially in the beginning of a prince's reign." He then made his point in a particularly fascinating statement: "Glasses with small necks, if you pour into them any liquor suddenly or violently, will not be so filled, but refuse to receive that same that you would pour into them. Howbeit, if you instil water into them by a little and little they are soon replenished."[2]

There is no great mystery concerning the Queen's religious predilections. In a speech delivered on December 24, 1586, in connection with the proposal that Mary, Queen of Scots, be executed, Elizabeth said:

When first I took the sceptre, my title made me not forget the giver, and therefore [I] began as it became me, with such religion as both I was born in, bred in, and, I trust, shall die in; although I was not so simple as not to know what danger and peril so great an alteration might procure me—how many great Princes of the contrary opinion would attempt all they might against me, and generally what enmity I should thereby breed unto myself. Which all I regarded not, knowing that He, for whose sake I did it, might and would defend me.[3]

[2] Henry Gee, *The Elizabethan Prayer-Book and Ornaments* (London, 1902), p. 210. The document is reprinted here, pp. 206–15, from State Papers, Domestic, Elizabeth, I, 66.

[3] J. E. Neale, *Elizabeth I and Her Parliaments, 1584–1601* (London,

Here she referred to Protestantism of a particular kind: the Protestantism of her mother, Anne Boleyn, qualified by the faith that her father had professed; the Protestantism of her stepmother, Catherine Parr, a woman imbued with the culture of the Renaissance; and the Protestantism of her teachers—Sir John Cheke, her brother's tutor; William Grindal, who supervised her studies from 1546; and Roger Ascham, who became her tutor on Grindal's death in 1548 and remained her mentor through the first years of her reign.

She was a Protestant-humanist who read Isocrates and Cicero, Saint Cyprian and Philip Melanchthon, and who was well acquainted with the works of Desiderius Erasmus. Ascham said in 1570 that the Queen "readeth here now at Windsor more Greek every day than some prebendary of this church doth read Latin in a whole week."[4] Indeed, she was accustomed to reading some part of Erasmus's Greek New Testament daily. Her religion was not that of the zealous—she could not approve of John Knox and his ways. It was that of the Christian humanist, involving devotion and moderation, and delighting in beauty, the beauty of a perfect literary style, the beauty of orderly religious ceremony. It was a religion linked to national sentiment, with the conviction that God was doing a mighty thing, through his Deborah, for England and, through England, for the world.[5]

Something of the character of her religious nature is revealed in the prayers that she wrote in English, French, Latin, Greek, and Italian. On the one hand they are literary exercises from the pen of a humanist. On the other, they are graceful expressions of a religious person. Her second English prayer begins:

O Lord God Father everlasting, which reignest over the Kingdoms of men, and givest them of thy pleasure: which of thy great mercy hast

---

1957), p. 128. Concerning the public utterances of the Queen, see Neale, *Essays in Elizabethan History* (London, 1958), pp. 85–112.

[4] Roger Ascham, *The Schoolmaster* (1570), ed. Lawrence V. Ryan, Folger Documents of Tudor and Stuart Civilization, 13 (Ithaca, N.Y., 1967), p. 56.

[5] See J. E. Neale, *England's Elizabeth* (Washington, D.C., 1958).

chosen me thy servant and handmaid to feed thy people and thine inheritance: so teach me, I humbly beseech thee, thy word, and so strengthen me with thy grace, that I may feed thy people with a faithful and a true heart; and rule them prudently with power.

Thus far it is the prayer of a self-confident, strong ruler. The tone changes, however, becoming that of a fragile and sinful woman:

O Lord, thou hast set me on high, my flesh is frail and weak. If I therefore at any time forget thee, touch my heart O Lord that I may again remember thee. If I swell against thee, pluck me down in my own conceit.

She asks for the Lord's assistance, acknowledging that it is he upon whom she must rely:

Create therefore in me O Lord a new heart and so renew my spirit within me that thy law may be my study, thy truth my delight: thy church my care: thy people my crown.[6]

Her coronation procession in January, 1559, struck the keynote for the reign. Things foreign were avoided or suppressed. Native Englishry was exalted and the health of the nation related to the Truth as expressed in Scripture. As the Queen moved through London she encountered pageant after pageant and seemed to revel in the words, sights, and drama of it all. At the pageant near the Little Conduit in Cheapside a commonwealth decayed was depicted alongside a commonwealth flourishing. There was old man Time with Truth, the daughter of Time, holding a book in her hands, the Word of Truth. A child, in an oration, declared that for many years no one had dared look into the book, and so the commonwealth had decayed. But now Time had once more brought his daughter Truth, whom the people

---

[6] Queen Elizabeth I, *A Book of Devotions Composed by Her Majesty*, with translations by Adam Fox (Gerrards Cross, Buckinghamshire, 1970), pp. 41–42. Concerning the Queen's prayers, see J. P. Hodges, *The Nature of the Lion* (London, 1962), pp. 126 ff.; and C. F. Tucker Brooke, "Queen Elizabeth's Prayers," *Huntington Library Quarterly* II (1938): 69–77.

were certain the Queen would embrace, thereby bringing prosperity to England. At the conduit in Fleet Street there was a pageant which compared Elizabeth to Deborah, the judge and restorer of Israel. This was an affirmation—over against the judgments of John Knox and Christopher Goodman, who had written against the rule of women—that God had at one time chosen a woman to restore Israel and that he now chose a woman, this new Queen, to restore her native land. Thus it went, with the intermingling of concern for religion and for the nation.[7]

The Parliament began on January 25, 1559, with a sermon at Westminster delivered by Richard Cox, an exile during the past reign, soon to be Bishop of Ely. It was reported by the Mantuan envoy, Il Schifanoya, that the sermon was a long and violent diatribe against the old religion.[8] Whatever Cox may actually have said, it is significant that this moderate Protestant, who had been a faithful servant of both Henry VIII and Edward VI, was chosen to preach at such an auspicious occasion. The opening speech of the Parliament was given by Sir Nicholas Bacon, a Protestant, speaking for the government and outlining the business of the session and, in accordance with tradition, speaking of religion, the commonwealth, and taxation. Concerning religion, he said that the Parliament should have concern for "the well making of laws for . . . uniting of the people of this realm into an uniform order of religion, to the honour and glory of God, the establishment of His Church, and the tranquillity of the realm."[9] Here were generalizations, but he was implying that there would be changes, moderate in tone, and that there would be efforts made to comprehend within the religious uniformity differences insofar as such differences did not endanger the na-

---

[7] *The Quenes Maiesties Passage through the Citie of London to Westminster the Day before Her Coronacion,* ed. James M. Osborn, intro. by J. E. Neale (New Haven, 1960).

[8] Neale, *Elizabeth I and Her Parliaments, 1559–1581,* p. 42.

[9] *Ibid.*

tional well being. It was a carefully measured, reasonable, and flexible speech, saying neither too much nor too little.

This Parliament's work can be divided at March 24, the date of its adjournment. Before that date the government sought to procure a supremacy act, but not an act for religious uniformity. There was seemingly a concern that uniformity, involving a new Book of Common Prayer, might better be dealt with after the conclusion of the war with France in which England was presently engaged, and after the Queen had been able to consolidate her position on the throne. Then, too, to put off a religious settlement until the next Parliament would give the Queen time to deal with the Henrician and Marian bishops still in power and also to fill the numerous sees then vacant with men who could be counted upon to support her. Convocation was solidly devoted to the old religion, a fact that indicated the need for caution.

Two things thwarted the Queen and her councillors. The first was recalcitrance of the bishops and Convocation, who seemingly would never agree to the repudiation of the papacy, although there were those who had so agreed under Henry VIII. Nicholas Heath, archbishop of York and chancellor, had been the Queen's chief hope. He had assisted her at the beginning by proclaiming her accession in the House of Lords. He was known to be a moderate, but he soon made evident his devotion to the old religion and his belief that Elizabeth ought to fulfill the agreement made by her half-sister, Mary, with the papacy. In the House of Lords on March 18, he presented the Roman Catholic case against royal supremacy. There he contested Parliament's right to grant spiritual jurisdiction to the Queen, especially since she was a woman.[10] His behavior was a great disappointment. The speech that Cuthbert Scot, bishop of Chester, made on March 17 was even more alarming.[11] It seemed clear that there was no reasonable hope of securing the support of such men or

[10] *Ibid.*, pp. 65–66.
[11] Contained in Gee, pp. 236–52.

of the vast majority of those in Convocation who recognized them as their leaders. If men such as Heath and Scot could have been Henrician, supporting the royal supremacy as did Stephen Gardiner, bishop of Winchester under Henry VIII, they might have been able to stave off uniformity and the imposition of a new Prayer Book.

On the other hand there were the exiles, Protestants of differing degrees, who, under the leadership of such divines as Cox and such noblemen as the Earl of Bedford, formed a kind of party in the House of Commons. They sought to obtain uniformity according to their own designs by expanding the supremacy bill placed before them by the Crown with uniformity provisions, including a Protestant service as Sir John Neale has suggested.[12] But they did not succeed. The bill that came through in March was most definitely a supremacy bill with but one uniformity provision, that for communion in both kinds, bread and wine, which necessitated the revival of the Order of Communion of 1548, or at least its equivalent. On March 22 a royal proclamation was issued referring to an Act of Supremacy and ordering communion in both kinds at the impending Easter celebrations of the Mass.[13] Here was an indication of intent to proceed gradually, communion in both kinds having been the first step toward religious settlement under Edward VI. It appeared then that Parliament had ended. It had not, however, but had rather adjourned until after Easter.

It became apparent at that time that the Queen desired a uniformity act, intending under the altered circumstances to push on as advised by "The Device for Alteration of Religion."[14] News of settlement of the war with France reached England on

---

[12] See Neale, "Elizabethan Acts of Supremacy and Uniformity," pp. 312–15, and *Elizabeth I and Her Parliaments, 1559–1581*, p. 60.

[13] See Gee, pp. 255–57; and Paul L. Hughes and James F. Larkin, eds., *Tudor Proclamations*, 3 vols. (New Haven and London, 1964–69), II, 109–11.

[14] Gee, pp. 195–202.

Palm Sunday, the nineteenth of March. The devotees of the old religion remained adamant in their position. The Protestant "party," fired by the Marian exiles, was the strongest force in Parliament devoted to the Queen and her supremacy, involving a body of zealous men whose energies could be harnessed for the good of the commonwealth or who, being spurned, could provide a troublesome irritant for growing dissent. She knew their mood and sensed the danger. Yet, giving in to them in part, as she must, she would not give all.

On March 31 a disputation intended to discredit the papists was held at Westminster.[15] Archbishop Heath innocently participated in the arrangements and criticized his own fellows for violating the terms of the dispute. These colleagues were more astute than Heath, for they knew from the outset that the disputation was rigged and was being used against them. Writing to Peter Martyr Vermigli, John Jewel, a former exile and soon to be Bishop of Salisbury, reported that the Protestant contestants were John Scory, Cox, David Whitehead, Edwin Sandys, Grindal, Robert Horne, John Aylmer, Jewel himself, and Edmund Guest (all Marian exiles with the exception of Guest), the papist side being represented by the bishops of Winchester, Lincoln, Coventry and Lichfield, and Chester, along with Henry Cole, dean of St. Paul's, and the archdeacons of Lewes, Canterbury, and Middlesex. These men were to debate three propositions: the first,

that it is contrary to the word of God, and the practice of the primitive church, to use in the public prayers and administration of the sacraments any other language than what is understood by the people. The second is, that every provincial church, even without the bidding of a general council, has power either to establish, or change, or abrogate ceremonies and ecclesiastical rites, wherever it may seem to make for edification.

---

[15] See *The Declaracyon of the procedynge of a conference begon at Westminster the laste of Marche, 1559* (London, [1559]); and Neale, *Elizabeth I and Her Parliaments, 1559–1581*, pp. 71–72.

The third is, that the propitiatory sacrifice, which the papists pretend to be in the mass, cannot be proved by the holy scriptures.[16]

In each instance the propositions were related to liturgical change.

The disputation had barely begun before it was ended, the papists being declared contumacious, Nicholas Bacon pronouncing the verdict. The next day the bishops of Winchester and Lincoln were sent to the Tower and the process of deprivation was begun, by means of which the Church of England was to be reconstituted with Protestant bishops loyal to the Queen. When Parliament reassembled, the way was clear for a uniformity bill incorporating the second Edwardian Book of Common Prayer with certain revisions of a conservative nature.

There has been much discussion concerning the preparations for the Elizabethan Book, but there is little reliable information. Most likely, when the decision was made to go forward with the uniformity bill, a committee was appointed to deal with the Prayer Book, but there need not have been a working committee.[17] Some have felt that the so-called Guest letter indicates the Queen's preference for the 1549 Book, but the letter argues against this, if indeed it is to be dated 1559.[18] It is reasonable to suppose that if the exiles in the House of Commons were proposing the 1552 Book for consideration, they would also have proposed revisions, perhaps some of those made at Frankfurt. It is quite possible that it was such a revised book which the exiles were advocating and urging the Crown to adopt. It was, in fact,

[16] *Zurich Letters*, ed. Hastings Robinson, Parker Society Publications, 50 (Cambridge, 1842), I, 11.

[17] See Francis Procter and Walter Howard Frere, *A New History of the Book of Common Prayer* (London, 1911), p. 98. See also, however, John Strype, *Annals of the Reformation*, 4 vols. (Oxford, 1824), vol. I, pt. 1, 119–22.

[18] On this see Neale, "Elizabethan Acts of Supremacy and Uniformity," pp. 326–27, and for a revision, his *Elizabeth I and Her Parliaments, 1559–1581*, pp. 76–77n. For the letter see Gee, pp. 215–24. The letter does not seem to come from either Guest or Jewel. Perhaps Cox, with his liturgical scholarship and experience, was the actual author.

the 1552 Book that was chosen. But the Queen and her government indicated their independence of the more zealous Protestants, rejecting any revisions that would make the book more Protestant and adopting revisions that could only be interpreted as conservative.[19]

Among the few but significant changes made, the Black Rubric was dropped. This had been a last-minute addition to the 1552 Book, in response to agitation by Bishop Hooper and John Knox, explaining that kneeling at Communion, ordered by another rubric, was a gesture of gratitude, "and to avoyde prophanacion and dysordre," and did not imply adoration of the consecrated bread and wine, or any belief in there being "anye reall and essencial presence . . . of Christ's naturall fleshe and bloude."[20] The Queen needed no defense for kneeling at the Communion. Furthermore, the rubric was altogether too explicit, too detailed on a controversial matter that had best be left alone in a Prayer Book intended for the entire realm.

The phrase in the Litany praying for deliverance from the tyranny of the Pope and all his "detestable enormities" was also dropped, as was the reference to the Pope's "usurped power and authority" in the ordination services. These were too polemical, likely to be embarrassing to those conducting diplomatic affairs among Continental Catholics, and quite unnecessary. The controversial Ornaments Rubric, prescribing the ancient vestments as those were in use during the second year of the reign of Edward VI, was inserted before Morning Prayer.[21] Provision was made for the Queen to take further order in this matter, but, understood as ordering the use of medieval vestments, the rubric caused anxiety and dismay among Protestant subjects. Sensible changes were made in the Lectionary, and in 1561 a large num-

[19] For a contemporary discussion of the difference between the 1552 and 1559 Books, see Gee, pp. 258–60.

[20] *The First and Second Prayer-Books of King Edward the Sixth*, Everyman's Library (London and Toronto, 1910), p. 393.

[21] See Gee, chap. 3; and J. T. Micklethwaite, *The Ornaments of the Rubric*, Alcuin Club Tracts, 1 (London, 1897).

ber of saints' days reappeared in the Calendar. The sentences of administration at communion for the first two books were joined, putting side by side the more conservative references to the Body and Blood of Christ and the more reformed "Take and eat this in remembrance..." and "feed on him in thy heart by faith ...." Clearly, the Queen was still trying to comprehend differing points of view, her own included, and trying to let her more Protestant subjects know that she would not be pushed into an extreme position.

The Marian exiles were disturbed by Elizabeth. They were annoyed by the changes made in the Prayer Book and alarmed that the Queen retained the Mass so long in her chapel, and that she insisted upon the retention of cross (or crucifix) with candles there. Jewel discerned the way things were going and wrote to his friend Peter Martyr:

As to religion, it has been effected, I hope, under good auspices, that it shall be restored to the same state as it was during your latest residence among us, under Edward. But, as far as I can perceive at present, there is not the same alacrity among our friends, as there lately was among the papists. So miserably is it ordered, that falsehood is armed, while truth is not only unarmed, but also frequently offensive. The scenic apparatus of divine worship is now under agitation; and those very things which you and I have so often laughed at, are now seriously and solemnly entertained by certain persons, (for *we* are not consulted,) as if the christian religion could not exist without something tawdry. Our minds indeed are not sufficiently disengaged to make these fooleries of much importance. Others are seeking after a *golden*, or as it rather seems to me, a *leaden* mediocrity; and are crying out, that the half is better than the whole.[22]

The Spirit of the 1559 Prayer Book

In 1559 there did in fact occur a dramatic reversal in the course of the development of the Book of Common Prayer. Up to that point the book had been revised so that it more and more re-

[22] *Zurich Letters*, I, 23.

sembled Lutheran and Reformed orders of worship. Liturgical reform had begun gradually and piecemeal with the Litany of 1544 and continued on to the 1549 Prayer Book, which was basically conservative when compared with later books in England and Continental equivalents. Its major source was the Sarum use, the traditional worship of the Western Church as formulated at the See of Salisbury, but it was influenced by the liturgical reforms of Cardinal Quiñones with respect to the Breviary, by Lutheran Church Orders—mainly in terms of didactic and hortatory content—by the Great Bible of 1539, and to a lesser extent by Cranmer's study of Eastern liturgies, particularly that of St. John Chrysostom. The 1552 Prayer Book involves a more rigorous application of a Protestant, and sometimes Christian humanist, axiom intended to control all liturgical expression. As E. C. Ratcliff has put it: "The axiom is that of Scriptural sanction. What cannot plainly be seen to possess Scriptural sanction should not be found in a Prayer Book. The perfect Prayer Book should provide people and ministers with forms of worship which the Apostles and first believers could acknowledge and approve."[1] Ratcliff regards the application of this axiom as being principally the work of Cranmer, while C. W. Dugmore lays stress upon the importance of the more pronounced Protestant, John Hooper, "the leading 'Anglo-Zuricher.' "[2] This second Prayer Book appears to conform much more closely to the expectations of such Continental divines then resident in England as Martin Bucer and Peter Martyr Vermigli. It was in use for but a short time, however, when Mary came to the throne and supplanted it with the Sarum Missal, Breviary, Manual, and the rest. The 1552 Book was, nevertheless, in use during Mary's

[1] E. C. Ratcliff, "The Liturgical Work of Archbishop Cranmer," in *Thomas Cranmer, 1489–1556, Three Commemorative Lectures Delivered in Lambeth Palace* (Westminster, 1956), p. 40, and also in *The Journal of Ecclesiastical History*, VII (1956):200.

[2] See Dugmore, "The First Ten Years," in Alcuin Club, *The English Prayer Book, 1549–1662* (London, 1963), pp. 6–30.

reign, chiefly among English Protestants in exile who regarded it as official and binding upon them in varying degrees.

To our knowledge, most of the exiles looked upon the 1552 Book as another step along the way toward a more perfect, reformed order of worship. At Frankfurt it was said that before his death Cranmer had "drawen up a booke off praier an hundreth tymes more perfect then this that we now have."[3] There is, however, no other corroboration of this statement. In 1555 attempts were made to displace the Prayer Book at Frankfurt, and in the ensuing battle, with John Knox pushing toward worship patterned after that of Calvin's Geneva, a "Liturgy of Compromise" was produced.[4] It provided for a further revision of the Book of Common Prayer and comprised in the main rubrical directions for the simplification (and thus purification) of the Prayer Book offices and sacraments. In the preface, loyal Protestant Englishmen said that "although in the book of Common prayer last set forth by the authority of King Edward of most famous memory we neither condemn, judge, nor refuse anything as wicked or repugnant to the true sense and meaning of God's word ... yet notwithstanding we have omitted in respect of time, place, and such circumstances, certain rites and ceremonies appointed in the said book, as things of their own nature indifferent."[5] This liturgy did not survive for long. For a time Valerand Pullain's *Liturgia sacra* was used at Frankfurt,[6] and

---

[3] [Thomas Wood], *A Brief Discourse of the Troubles Begun at Frankfort,* repr. from the black-letter edition of 1575 (London, 1846), p. L. Concerning Wood as the supposed author, see Patrick Collinson, "The Authorship of *A Brieff Discours off the Troubles Begonne at Franckford,*" *Journal of Ecclesiastical History* IX (1958): 188–208. Formerly it has been attributed to William Whittingham.

[4] A discussion of this liturgy, along with the text, is found in *The Liturgy of Compromise,* ed. George W. Sprott, bound with *The Second Prayer Book of King Edward the Sixth,* ed. H. J. Witherspoon, Church Service Society (Edinburgh and London, 1905), pp. 205 ff.

[5] *Ibid.,* p. 232.

[6] Cuming, p. 119.

then, under the influence of Richard Cox, who was successful in ousting John Knox, the 1552 Book was revived, howbeit somewhat modified. On April 5, 1555, Cox and others wrote to Calvin:

When the magistrates lately gave us permission to adopt the rites of our native country, we freely relinquished all those ceremonies which were regarded by our brethren as offensive and inconvenient. For we gave up private baptisms, confirmation of children, saints' days, kneeling at the holy communion, the linen surplices of the ministers, crosses, and other things of the like character. And we gave them up, not as being impure and papistical, which certain of our brethren often charged them with being; but whereas they were in their own nature indifferent, and either ordained or allowed by godly fathers for the edification of our people, we notwithstanding chose rather to lay them aside than to offend the minds or alienate the affections of the brethren. We retain however the remainder of the form of prayer and of the administration of the sacraments, which is prescribed in our book, and this with the consent of almost the whole church.[7]

Whatever their own feelings, pressure was on the exiles to further reform their worship in accordance with the practices of the Continental reformed churches. Urged on by the magistrates, even Richard Cox, who defended the Edwardian settlement of religion, showed a willingness to bend in the direction of Zurich, if not Geneva, and would not defend such indifferent matters as surplices, crosses, kneeling at Communion, and the like.

It is with knowledge of the conflict between those who, like Knox with his *Form of Prayers* (1556), regarded *La Forme des prieres* of Calvin's Geneva as a model and those who, like Cox and his friends, resisted the pressures of Knox and Geneva that the 1559 Book should be studied.[8] With this in mind, the Eliza-

---

[7] *Original Letters Relative to the English Reformation*, ed. Hastings Robinson, Parker Society Publications, 53, 2 vols. (Cambridge, 1846–47), II, 753–54.

[8] See Horton Davies, *The Worship of the English Puritans* (Westminster, 1948), pp. 31–32; and William D. Maxwell, *John Knox's Genevan Service Book, 1556* (Edinburgh, 1931).

bethan Book will be seen as relatively conservative, a conclusion strengthened by further knowledge. It is true that in the Advertisements of 1566 Archbishop Parker and others clarified the Ornaments Rubric in such a way that its most conservative implications were denied.[9] Yet the nascent Puritans were still offended by the demand that copes and surplices be worn. Mention has been made of the ornaments in the Royal Chapel, with cross or crucifix and candles, and the addition of saints' days in 1561. One could also mention the articles and injunctions of visitation by which further order was taken. But the most important example of the conservative trend initiated by the 1559 Book is to be found in the Latin translation of the Prayer Book, the *Liber precum publicarum*, which appeared in 1560. Chiefly the work of Walter Haddon, the Queen's Master of Requests and an accomplished Latinist,[10] the *Liber* relies to some extent on the Latin translation of the 1549 Holy Communion made by Alexander Aless for Martin Bucer. The *Liber* professes to be an exact translation of the entire 1559 Book, but it is not. Intended for use in the universities by learned men, it omits such occasional, pastoral offices as Baptism and Holy Matrimony. Of great interest are the indications of a revival of certain medieval practices. For instance, as William Keatinge Clay points out, "In the Communion of the Sick . . . the reservation of a portion of the consecrated elements is ordered, and L'Estrange justifies this, because learned societies, the greater light they enjoyed, the less prone would they be to error and superstition; and he justifies the celebration of the Lord's supper at funerals, because the whole Book was compiled for 'Men of discerning Spirits.' " A further example is provided by the absolution in the Communion service. "In the Book of 1560 Christ is said to have given to the Church his own power (*suam potestatem*) of absolving penitents;

---

[9] See Gee, pp. 271–72.

[10] See Lawrence V. Ryan, "The Haddon-Osorio Controversy (1563–1583)," *Church History* XXII, no. 2 (June 1953): 142–54; and Walter Haddon, *Lucubrationes* (London, 1567).

an expression for which there existed not the slightest ground. This absolution, however, is a transcript from Aless; but not without the transcriber being quite alive to what he was about, for he made additions at the end, sufficient to mark deliberation and design."[11]

One must not infer from this, however, that there was any serious effort made during Elizabeth's reign to revive the 1549 Book. The Queen had achieved a religious settlement, with regard to her own religious convictions and to what was possible and best for the nation, and would not countenance any major adjustment of it. There could be no revival of 1549, nor would she tolerate any movement in Calvin's direction. The Puritans were disillusioned by the Queen's conservatism, but they were not prevented from trying by various means to push further for reform in Convocation, in Parliament, and, if need be, independently. They sought for purer, more scriptural, less papistical worship, and thus struggled to displace the Book of Common Prayer. They objected to its popish ceremonies and forms. In "A View of Popish Abuses," attached to the "Admonition to Parliament" (1572), they protested that the 1559 Book "is an unperfect book, culled and picked out of that popish dunghill, the Mass book full of all abhominations. For some, and many of the contents therein, be such as are against the word of God, as by his grace shall be proved unto you."[12]

These impatient Englishmen would seem to have been intent on carrying Cranmer's principle of scriptural sanction to its logi-

[11] William Keatinge Clay, ed., *Liturgical Services: Liturgies and Occasional Forms of Prayer Set Forth in the Reign of Queen Elizabeth*, Parker Society Publications, 30 (Cambridge, 1847), pp. xxviii–xxix. The *Liber precum publicarum* (1560) is reprinted in this volume, pp. 299–429.

[12] W. H. Frere and C. E. Douglas, eds., *Puritan Manifestoes: A Study of the Origin of the Puritan Revolt*, Church Historical Society Publications, 72 (London, 1907), p. 21. There follows an extensive and detailed indictment worthy of attention. For a discussion of Puritan objections, see Horton Davies, *Worship and Theology in England*, vol. I, *From Cranmer to Hooker, 1534–1603* (Princeton, 1970), pp. 261–68.

cal conclusion. But it was not Cranmer who was directing events, nor were the Puritans: it was the Queen. In reaction to the 1559 Book, some Puritans performed surgery on the lawful Prayer Book, after the example of the "Liturgy of Compromise," beginning with an edition published by Barker in 1578.[13] Sometimes the expurgated editions were attached to the Geneva Bible, thus providing a single volume for use by the Puritan minister responsible for conducting the public worship of the church. This was clearly illegal, and it would be useful to know more about the composition and use of this Puritan Prayer Book. Beyond this, some began to use Knox's order of worship, as eventually adapted and published under the title *A Book of the Form of Common Prayer* by Waldegrave in 1584/5, and then further amended and published at Middelburgh in 1586, 1587, and 1602.[14] This was the book of the "Bill and the Book" seriously introduced in Parliament in the 1580s, where, if the bill had passed and had gained the Queen's assent, it would have ousted the 1559 Prayer Book. The Puritan *Form of Common Prayer* has a dignity and value apparent to anyone who studies it. At times too polemical for a liturgical text, it yet has beautiful and affective prayers, as in the eucharistic prayer where it is acknowledged that it is through Christ and by "him alone we are possessed in our spiritual kingdom, to eat and drink at his table, with whom we have our conversation presently in heaven, and by whom our bodies are raised again from the dust."[15] However, the Puritan Book was not allowed by the Queen, nor can it be imagined that she could ever have read it with any appreciation whatsoever.

The history of the Book of Common Prayer can be viewed as a struggle between those who would further reform English worship after the pattern of Protestant orders of worship and

[13] See Procter and Frere, pp. 133–35; and Clay, pp. xv–xviii.

[14] See Davies, *Worship and Theology*, I, 273–80, and *Worship of the English Puritans*, chap. 6.

[15] Peter Hall, ed., *Fragmenta liturgica*, 7 vols. (Bath, 1848), I, 63–64.

those who would reform it after the pattern of medieval worship. And yet any careful study of the 1559 Book requires that close attention be given to the first two books; for although the 1559 Book has its own uniqueness, it is basically the 1552 Book, which in turn was a revision of the Prayer Book of 1549. A thorough history of the first two Prayer Books is not possible here, yet it is possible and necessary to provide at least a framework of that history.

The 1549 Prayer Book

On September 23, 1548, there was issued from Windsor Castle a royal proclamation concerning religious affairs, in the course of which the government let it be known that it desired "to see very shortly one uniform order" of worship, "for which cause at this time certain bishops and notable learned men, by his highness' commandment, are congregate."[1] This was a reference to the so-called Windsor committee, which is generally regarded as responsible for the final stages involved in producing the first Prayer Book. Cranmer specifically referred to this committee when writing in his own defense to the Queen in September, 1555. The letter, which, among other things, defends worship in the vulgar tongue, indicates that "a good number of the best learned men reputed within this realm, some favouring the old, some the new learning . . . were gathered together at Windsor for the reformation of the service of the church."[2] We know very little about this committee and its procedures.[3] The historian Thomas Fuller provided a list of its members, but his list is

[1] Hughes and Larkin, I, 432–33; and Thomas Fuller, *The Church History of Britain*, ed. J. S. Brewer, 6 vols. (Oxford, 1845), IV, 32–33.

[2] Procter and Frere, p. 47*n*.

[3] For an interesting review of the evidence, see "The First Book of Common Prayer and the Windsor Commission," *Church Quarterly Review* XCVIII, no. 195 (April 1924): 51–64.

suspect. Nevertheless, the names he mentioned can be correlated with the list we have of the group which met at Chertsey Abbey on September 9, 1548, when Cranmer consecrated Robert Ferrar as Bishop of Saint David's, assisted by Bishops Nicholas Ridley and Henry Holbeach. Bishops Thomas Thirlby and Thomas Goodrich were also there, along with Doctors William May, dean of St. Paul's; Simon Haynes, dean of Exeter; Thomas Robertson, afterward dean of Durham; and John Redman, master of Trinity College, Cambridge. In listing the members of the Windsor committee, Fuller also mentioned Bishops George Day and John Skip; John Taylor, dean of Lincoln; and Richard Cox, almoner to the King.[4]

The Grey Friars' Chronicle, referring to the proclamation of September 23, mentions that "at that time divers bishops sat at Chertsey Abbey for some time." It is important to realize that while at Chertsey Abbey these bishops and other learned men assisting them were but two or three miles from Oaklands, where the King and his Court were residing until they all moved back to Windsor the day before the proclamation was issued. Then, too, it was reported that "the holy Eucharist was consecrated," as well as administered, at Ferrar's consecration by Cranmer, "in the vulgar tongue."[5] Most likely the committee was already at work in the beginning of September. It can be argued that the Holy Communion at the consecration was some form of the new service, if not that very service, and that the committee was at Windsor on September 22 and 23, where its progress was reported. The committee, so it is reasonable to assume, must have continued working at Windsor for some time, perhaps through October or even up to the beginning of December, preparing the book that would be presented to Convocation and Parliament.[6]

[4] Fuller, IV, 27. See Procter and Frere, p. 46.

[5] Francis Aidan Gasquet and Edmund Bishop, *Edward VI and the Book of Common Prayer* (London, 1890), pp. 143–44.

[6] *Ibid.*, p. 144n. Miles Coverdale wrote to Paul Fagius from Windsor, October 21, 1548, reporting that he had shown a letter from Fagius to Cranmer the day before.

There is little more that can be said. The men involved were a mixed lot, varying from conservative bishops such as Skip and Day to the more advanced reformers such as Ridley and Cox, with Thirlby and Goodrich somewhere in the middle. When the book was done, presented to the House of Lords, and voted on, January 15, 1549, Day, Skip, and Thirlby voted against it.[7] Considering the members of the committee, it seems evident that of them all only one, Thomas Cranmer, had both the expertise and experience needed for such an extensive liturgical reform. That he did not work entirely alone must be assumed. But we shall probably never know the extent to which the various committee members were engaged in the work. That Cranmer dominated what transpired cannot seriously be doubted.[8]

During the reign of Henry VIII, Cranmer had been engaged in reform affecting the church's worship. He played a role in the authorization of the Great Bible, for which he wrote a preface.[9] This Bible was to be put to liturgical use, by order of Convocation, in 1543. He was also involved in the production of a book of homilies at the request of Convocation in 1542 to provide "official sermons" for use in parish churches and elsewhere, a book which did not appear in print until 1547.[10] Cranmer was working to reform the Breviary, and we have evidence of two schemes, the first dating from 1538 and showing Lutheran influence, natural at a time when the King was negotiating with German Lutheran princes, the second dating from somewhere between 1544 and 1546, during the period of conservative reaction, patterned after reforms instigated by Cardinal Quiñones in Spain.[11] In the manuscripts for these schemes Cranmer's great skill is demonstrated: his ability to think through liturgical problems in

[7] Cuming, p. 67.

[8] Ratcliff, p. 26.

[9] Conveniently found in Thomas Cranmer, *Works*, ed. J. E. Cox, Parker Society Publications, 15–16, 2 vols. (Cambridge, 1844–46), II, 118–25.

[10] Davies, *Worship and Theology*, I, 229.

[11] Thomas Cranmer, *Cranmer's Liturgical Projects*, ed. J. W. Legg, Henry Bradshaw Society, 50 (London, 1915). See also Ratcliff, pp. 32–33.

different ways, his understanding of the basic problems involved in the daily offices, his judgment concerning the ways in which the offices would have to be changed to conform to the principles of the new learning and to be rendered in clear and liturgically effective English, and his knowledge of the ways in which the reform of them would have to be responsive to political, social, and economic events.

Cranmer was also engaged in a reform of the medieval Processional. In 1544 he produced an English Litany in response to the King's request.[12] He then proceeded to prepare further translations. It was in connection with this project that the Archbishop wrote a letter to the King explaining something of the way in which he worked.

It may please your majesty to be advertised, that according to your highness' commandment, sent unto me by your grace's secretary, Mr. Pagett, I have translated into the English tongue, so well as I could in so short time, certain processions, to be used upon festival days, if after due correction and amendment of the same your highness shall think it so convenient. In which translation, forasmuch as many of the processions, in the Latin, were but barren, as meseemed, and little fruitful, I was constrained to use more than the liberty of a translator: for in some processions I have altered divers words; in some I have added part; in some taken part away; some I have left out whole, either for by cause the matter appeared to me to be little to purpose, or by cause the days be not with us festival-days; and some processions I have added whole, because I thought I had better matter for the purpose, than was the procession in Latin: the judgment whereof I refer wholly unto your majesty; and after your highness hath corrected it, if your grace command some devout and solemn note to be made thereunto, (as is to the procession which your majesty hath already set forth in English,) I trust it will much excitate and stir the hearts of all men unto devotion and godliness: but in mine opinion, the song that shall be made thereunto would not be full of notes, but, as near as may be, for every syllable a note; so that it may be sung distinctly and devoutly, as be in the Matins and Evensong, *Venite*, the

---

[12] Conveniently found in F. E. Brightman, *The English Rite*, 2 vols. (London, 1915), I, 174–90.

Hymns, *Te Deum, Benedictus, Magnificat, Nunc dimittis,* and all the Psalms and Versicles; and in the mass *Gloria in Excelsis, Gloria Patri,* the Creed, the Preface, the *Pater noster,* and some of the *Sanctus* and *Agnus.* As concerning the *Salve festa dies,* the Latin note, as I think, is sober and distinct enough; wherefore I have travailed to make the verses in English, and have put the Latin note unto the same. Nevertheless they that be cunning in singing can make a much more solemn note thereto. I made them only for a proof, to see how English would do in song. But by cause mine English verses lack the grace and facility that I would wish they had, your majesty may cause some other to make them again, that can do the same in more pleasant English and phrase. As for the sentence, I suppose will serve well enough. Thus Almighty God preserve your majesty in long and prosperous health and felicity.[13]

We do not have the manuscript that Cranmer sent to the King, nor does it appear that anything came of the work that Cranmer described. Much of his liturgical planning and experimentation during Henry's reign seems to have been frustrated.

Other than the Litany of 1544, the only accomplishments of Cranmer in the reform of worship to find official approval and public use were the reading of the Scripture in the vernacular at church services, a revision of the Sarum Breviary to take account of the breach with Rome, and the revision of the Primers,[14] all of which helped to prepare for what was to come. Behind the scenes, the Archbishop continued working, and, as he did so, he submitted to the influence of the familiar Latin services, the Breviary, the Missal, and the Processional providing him with basic

---

[13] Cranmer, *Works,* II, 412.

[14] See C. C. Butterworth, *The English Primers, 1529–1545* (Philadelphia, 1953); and Procter and Frere, pp. 32–33. For the medieval, see Henry Littlehales, ed., *The Prymer or Prayer-Book of the Lay People in the Middle Ages, in English, Dating about 1400 A.D.* (London, 1891). For a discussion of the medieval Primers, see William Maskell, *Monumenta ritualia ecclesiae Anglicanae,* 2d ed., 3 vols. (Oxford, 1882), III, ii–lxvii. The Primer of 1559 can be found in *Private Prayers, Put Forth by Authority during the Reign of Queen Elizabeth,* ed. William Keatinge Clay, Parker Society Publications, 37 (Cambridge, 1851), pp. 1–114.

structures and content; to the Lutheran Church Orders, such as that of Nuremberg, whence Mrs. Cranmer came; to the work of Quiñones in Spain; and to his studies of the primitive Church, the Fathers, and the Eastern liturgies.

With the death of Henry VIII and the accession of the boy-king, Edward VI, in 1547, the former restrictions inhibiting further reform were seemingly removed. At the opening of the first Parliament of the reign, on November 4, the *Gloria in excelsis*, the Creed, and the *Agnus Dei* were sung in English.[15] Experimentation was rife, and offensive speech concerning the Mass disturbed the government. Parliament responded by passing a bill to put an end to unlawful behavior and to encourage orderly reform. The latter was decided upon in a committee where it was agreed that communion should be in both kinds, bread and wine. The bill was enacted in December, 1547,[16] but it was not until March of the next year that the enabling Order of Communion was produced.[17] This was to be inserted into the Latin Mass, immediately after the priest's communion, and included, in English, an exhortation, confession, absolution, comfortable words, prayer before communion, words of administration, and a blessing. It was an entity unto itself, the communicants' service, and was modeled upon the Cologne Church Order, *Simplex et pia deliberatio*, prepared by Martin Bucer and Philip Melanchthon for Archbishop Hermann von Wied.[18] The entire Order was to find its way into the Book of Common Prayer. Thus the

[15] Davies, *Worship and Theology*, I, 169.

[16] Henry Gee and W. J. Hardy, eds., *Documents Illustrative of English Church History* (London, 1914), pp. 322–28; Hughes and Larkin, I, 410–12, which is the important proclamation issued December 27, 1547.

[17] Henry A. Wilson, ed., *The Order of Communion, 1548*, Henry Bradshaw Society, 34 (London, 1908).

[18] There is an English translation published in 1547, revised in 1548, the latter entitled, *A Simple and Religious Consultation of us Herman, by the grace of God Archbishop of Colone* (London, 1548); see sigs. 2C4 ff. and 2D1 ff.

Litany and the Order of Communion, as well as the English Bible, were installments in what was to be a uniform order of worship.

It was in September and October, 1548, that the Windsor committee was at work drafting a Prayer Book. In December there occurred a debate in the House of Lords which revealed that the bishops were not of one mind.[19] According to the report of the Protector Somerset, George Day, bishop of Chester, alone of the committee members, refused the "book of agreements." Thomas Thirlby, bishop of Westminster, contended that he had subscribed the book only because it was his understanding that the book was to be the basis for discussion and was not the final product.[20] His chief difficulties concerned the Mass and what he viewed as a fatal watering down of eucharistic doctrine. But in spite of such opposition, Parliament passed a uniformity act,[21] to which was appended the Book of Common Prayer, on January 21, 1549, and the first copies were on sale by March 7. The book was to be in use by Whitsunday, June 9, and was to displace all other orders of worship.

In overall structure the Prayer Book of 1549 looks very much like that of 1559. There is a preface derived from Cranmer's first Breviary scheme, dependent upon Quiñones's work in some respects. There follow tables of Psalms and Lessons, and a Calendar, providing for the orderly reading of Scripture and presuming the use of the Great Bible. The daily offices are

[19] See Gasquet and Bishop, app. 5, where the debate is summarized. See also Jasper Ridley, *Thomas Cranmer* (Oxford, 1962), pp. 288–89; and Procter and Frere, pp. 48–49. For Cranmer's important questions respecting the Mass, see his *Works*, II, 150–52.

[20] Gasquet and Bishop, pp. 164–65; and T. F. Shirley, *Thomas Thirlby, Tudor Bishop* (London, 1964), p. 101.

[21] Gee and Hardy, pp. 358–66. The Prayer Book can most readily be obtained in *The First and Second Prayer-Books of King Edward the Sixth*, but the best critical edition is that of Brightman, where the book is printed alongside sources, the 1552 Book, and the 1662 Book.

next, based upon the Breviary: Matins, Lauds, and Prime being combined to form Morning Prayer, Vespers and Compline being formed into Evensong. Terce, Sext, and None were simply discarded. Here, besides the Breviary itself and the work of Quiñones, the influence of the Lutheran Church Orders can be seen. There then follow the Propers, including Collects, Epistles, and Gospels, displacing the medieval Temporale and Sanctorale. Next is that part of the book based upon the Missal, now called "The Supper of the Lord and the Holy Communion, Commonly Called the Mass," the main sources for which, alongside the Sarum Missal, being the Cologne Church Order of Archbishop Hermann and certain Lutheran Church Orders. It is here that most of the discussion concerning the nature of the first Prayer Book is concentrated. Is it more Catholic than Protestant, or more Protestant than Catholic?[22] The question cannot be answered unequivocally, for it would seem that the Prayer Book office of Holy Communion points in both directions. It is conservative to a degree and preserves a recognizable Canon, that which a later generation called a "prayer of consecration." But that very prayer is Protestant in the way in which it redefines the traditional medieval doctrine of sacrifice in the Mass.

After the Holy Communion, which is the sacrament's vernacular name, there follows what was meant to displace the medieval Processional: the Litany of 1544, somewhat altered. The rest of the book is composed of services derived from the medieval Manual, including Baptism, Confirmation, Matrimony, Visitation of the Sick, Burial, and the Churching of Women. Here once more we witness the influence of medieval services and also that of Lutheran Church Orders. Finally, there is the penitential service of Commination, which begins with the rather startling cursings.

---

[22] On this question, see Davies, *Worship and Theology*, I, 178–94. See also James A. Devereux, S.J., "Reformed Doctrine in the Collects of the First *Book of Common Prayer*," *Harvard Theological Review* LVIII (January 1965): 49–68.

Between Baptism and Confirmation there is included a catechism composed by Cranmer, emphasizing the Creed, the Lord's Prayer, and the Ten Commandments, the bases of Christian education. The First Royal Injunctions of Henry VIII (1536) had ordered that Creed, Lord's Prayer, and Ten Commandments be taught by parents to children and servants, and the Second Royal Injunctions (1538) had ordered that they be taught by the clergy to all parishioners.

The Prayer Book concludes with the essay, "Of Ceremonies, Why Some Be Abolished and Some Retained," and with "Certain Notes for the More Plain Explication and Decent Ministration of Things Contained in This Book." The first, based on two of the Thirteen Articles of 1538, is a strong expression of the *via media* concept. The second was designed to fill in gaps in the rubrics or directions for the conduct of the services. Thus the book ends, but Cranmer still had to contend with the medieval Pontifical. The next year, 1550, the Ordinal was published containing services for the ordination of deacons and priests, and for the consecration of bishops.

As constructed, the Book of Common Prayer contained all the services needed for the regular weekday and Sunday worship of the church and occasional services to meet pastoral needs, emphasizing the great events of life: birth, marriage, sickness, and death. The Prayer Book, preserving tradition, thus provided for various understandings of the passage of time: the Church Year of the Propers; secular time in the daily offices; the course of a lifetime in the occasional services; and the dynamic view of time in the Holy Communion with its remembering (*anamnesis*) of events past, in the light of things to come (the messianic banquet), whereby Christ's presence is realized and human existence transformed in the present. The richness revealed here was inherited, but it was made vivid as all the various services were brought together in one book.

The Second Prayer Book

The first Prayer Book was to be short-lived. From the moment of its publication it was under attack both by those who resisted such liturgical reform and by those who wished to have a more thoroughly reformed order of worship. In the West of England rebellion erupted, instigated by persons who objected to the Prayer Book and were distressed by economic and social conditions.[1] Many wanted to worship in the old ways, whether they understood what they saw and heard or not. The Holy Communion was to them a novelty, "a Christmas game." Conservatives, such as Stephen Gardiner, bishop of Winchester, took another line of attack, deeply disturbing Cranmer by suggesting that the new rite could be interpreted in the old ways and could be viewed as supportive of the medieval understanding of the Mass.[2] The more zealous reformers, men such as Nicholas Ridley and John Hooper,[3] signified their discontent, believing that the liturgical reform had not gone far enough. Continental divines then resident in England, such as Martin Bucer, Peter Martyr Vermigli, Valerand Pullain, and John a Lasco, added their criticisms.[4] They all urged a further reform of worship,

[1] See Nicholas Pocock, ed., *Troubles Connected with the Prayer Book of 1549*, Camden Society Publications, n.s., 37 (Westminster, 1884); Frances Rose-Troup, *The Western Rebellion of 1549* (London, 1913); A. L. Rowse, *Tudor Cornwall* (London, 1941); and W. K. Jordan, *Edward VI: The Young King* (Cambridge, Mass., 1968), pp. 453–77.

[2] See, for instance, Cranmer, *Works*, I, 79.

[3] Concerning Ridley's attitude, especially with regard to altars, see his Injunctions for London (1550) in W. H. Frere, *Visitation Articles and Injunctions*, Alcuin Club Collections, 14–16, 3 vols. (London, 1910), II, 241–45; for Hooper, see his *Early Writings*, ed. Samuel Carr, Parker Society Publications, 20 (Cambridge, 1843), p. 479.

[4] The *Censura super libro sacrorum* in Bucer's *Scripta Anglicana*, ed. C. Hubert (Basle, 1577), pp. 456–503. See Constantin Hopf, *Martin Bucer and the English Reformation* (Oxford, 1946), chap. 2; and G. J. Cuming, pp. 100–101. Concerning Peter Martyr, see George Cornelius Gorham, ed., *Gleanings* (London, 1857), pp. 227–31 (Martyr to Bucer, January 10, 1551),

Bucer in his *Censura* submitting some sixty criticisms of the book, almost half of which Cranmer and those working with him adopted in drafting a new book. It is also reasonable to assume that in the midst of much discussion Cranmer was undergoing change within himself, departing more and more from his inherited understanding of the sacraments, moving closer to doctrine associated with the names of Zwingli, Oecolampadius, and Calvin. Throughout this period in his life Cranmer was conducting a far-ranging correspondence with Continental Protestants, seeking an international conference and some basic agreement on important doctrinal issues. He was thus open to their influence and concerned to take seriously criticism made of the Prayer Book by such prominent Continental divines as Bucer and Martyr.

The actual revision of the 1549 Prayer Book must have begun at once.[5] We know very little, however, of the procedures followed. Certainly significant was the removal of the Protector Somerset by the Duke of Northumberland, a man who encouraged the most zealous reformers.[6] It was under the Duke's rule that the second Act of Uniformity was passed on April 14, 1552, accompanied by a second Prayer Book, which was to be in use from All Saints' Day, November 1.

A perusal of the 1552 Prayer Book reveals how much more reformed it was when compared with the 1549 Book. Penitential introductions, resembling the Order of Communion of 1548, were added to the daily offices of Morning and Evening Prayer and changed their spirit, if not their nature. In the Holy Communion, no longer called the Mass, the penitential emphasis was strengthened, the Ten Commandments being added and the

---

391–401 (extracts from the works of Martyr); and J. C. McLelland, *The Visible Words of God* (Edinburgh, 1957). Concerning Valerand Pullain and John a Lasco, see Brightman, I, cxli–cxlvii.

[5] Cuming, pp. 101–2.

[6] Gee and Hardy, pp. 369–72. For editions of the 1552 Prayer Book see p. 353, n. 21, above.

Kyries added to fit. There was no introit, nor was there any mixture of water and wine at the offertory. The new Canon (thanksgiving, consecration prayer) appeared to be truncated, being divided into three parts—the Prayer for the Church Militant (intercessions), the Prayer of Consecration concluding with the recitation of the narrative of the Last Supper, and an alternative post-communion prayer, the Oblation. In the process of breaking up the old Canon, the Invocation of Word and Spirit, which had been added in 1549 by Cranmer, was dropped, as were also the commemoration of the Virgin Mary and thanksgivings for the patriarchs and prophets. The Communion followed immediately after the narrative of the Last Supper, thus emphasizing the "dominical words" as operative in the consecration, in line with Western custom. Yet it is clear that strenuous efforts were made to exclude all reference supportive of the traditional doctrines of Real Presence and Sacrifice in the Mass. This, on the surface, seems to be the chief aim of those engaged in this rearrangement of the Canon.[7]

The emphasis in the Holy Communion now fell, not on the elements of bread and wine miraculously transformed into Christ's body and blood in the consecration, but rather on the communicants, who, approaching the holy Table with penitence, are changed through the indwelling presence of the Spirit, through the sacrifice of praise and thanksgiving. This occurs as they receive the bread and wine from the priest, remembering the sacrifice of Christ upon the cross, thankful for the love shown there and for the many benefits of the cross and passion. The sentences of administration were significantly changed from "The body of our Lorde Jesus Christe whiche was geven for thee, preserve thy bodye and soule unto euerlasting lyfe," "The bloud of our Lorde Jesus Christe which was shed for thee, preserve thy bodye and soule unto euerlastyng lyfe," to "Take and eate this, in remembraunce that Christ dyed for thee, and feede on him in

---

[7] Davies, *Worship and Theology*, I, 201.

thy hearte, by faythe, with thankesgeuing," "Drinke this in remembraunce that Christ's bloude was shed for thee, and be thankefull." The Eucharist as memorial was thus signified with manifold ramifications, some of which we shall note as we proceed. The services of Baptism, Visitation of the Sick, and Burial were all altered, with a reduction of ceremony and further emphasis upon the didactic and hortatory.

This book, the basis of the 1559 Book, lasted officially in England for less than a year, for on July 6, 1553, King Edward died and his half-sister Mary took the throne determined to extirpate the Book of Common Prayer and to restore the Mass of the Roman rite.[8]

Prayer Book Emphases

Difficult although it may be, it is nevertheless helpful to identify and investigate the tendencies and operating principles guiding Archbishop Cranmer and his assistants in the work of liturgical revision. In such a matter there cannot be complete agreement, but prominent among such tendencies and principles as discussed by many are the authority of Scripture, the example of the early Church, reason and the reasonable, the insistence upon continuity where allowable, and the emphasis upon communion. First, the authority of Scripture.

The Prayer Book and the Bible

In defending the first Prayer Book against the Cornish rebels in 1549, Cranmer argued that "in the English service appointed to be read there is nothing else but the eternal word of God: the new and the old Testament is read, that hath power to save your souls; which as Saint Paul saith, 'is the power of God to the sal-

---

[8] Concerning this, see Cuming, p. 117; and Gee and Hardy, pp. 377–415.

vation of all that believe'; the clear light to our eyes, without the which we cannot see; and a lantern unto our feet, without which we should stumble."[1] Echoing the sentiments expressed in the preface that he wrote for the Great Bible and the preface to the first Prayer Book, Cranmer here revealed a basic operating principle: to restore the centrality of the Word of God to the common worship of the Church. He did this by increasing the prominence and the quantity of Scripture in public worship and also through specific reference to the Word of God as equal with the sacraments, as is seen most dramatically in the Ordinal of 1550.

From 1538 on, when he was working on his first scheme for the reform of the Breviary, it was clear that Cranmer desired to simplify the daily offices in order that the Scripture should be properly emphasized. He also increased the amount of Scripture read, deprecating mere snippets and encouraging the reading of entire chapters. In the first Book of Common Prayer it was arranged that through the offices the Psalter should be read through once a month, the Old Testament once a year, except certain parts and passages from several books which were not considered to be edifying, and the New Testament thrice a year, except for the Apocalypse, from which only two chapters were to be read.

Scripture was at the center of attention in all that Cranmer did as he proceeded to reform the inherited liturgy. Discussing the transition from the first book to the second, E. C. Ratcliff argues that there was a more and more rigorously applied axiom of Scriptural sanction, with more and more excluded that could not be shown to warrant that sanction and to be such as "the Apostles and first believers could acknowledge and approve."[2] From a modern point of view the application of such an axiom is fraught with difficulties, and we must realize that Cranmer himself qualified his understanding of the axiom in emphasizing

---

[1] *English Historical Documents, 1485–1558*, ed. C. H. Williams (New York, 1967), pp. 378–79.

[2] Ratcliff, p. 40.

other authoritative matters, such as those contained in the considerations which follow.

The Prayer Book and the Early Church

In the first Act of Uniformity (1549) the statement was made that for the reform of the rites and ceremonies of the Church in England the King appointed certain bishops and other learned men to set to work "having as well eye and respect to the most sincere and pure Christian religion taught by the Scripture as to the usages in the primitive Church."[3] The order of worship designed was to be such that the first believers might be able to recognize and accept it. Behind this aim there was the humanist conviction that the most ancient was best. Cranmer agreed, having read with great interest and appreciation the works of the Fathers coming from the presses of Froben, Aldus, and others, the results of humanist scholarship. Like other reformers, he had observed how different the worship of his youth seemed to be from that of the earliest Christians. Certain things were made apparent by contrast. He learned that early Christian worship was simple, scriptural, intended for edification, and thus in the language of the people and audible. Scholastic quiddities, the use of Latin, the multiplication of ceremonies, the obscuring of the Word of God by such superfluities as responds, legends, and the like, the proliferation of books necessary for the conduct of worship and the difficulties involved in finding one's way in them—all this appeared to be harmful and to represent a decline from a more perfect state of things. For the Protestant reformer, however, there was a limit to the authority of the early Church. That Church was revered not principally because it was ancient but because it was subject to the Word of God and accented the Scriptures in its worship and doctrine. As John Jewel put it, the early Fathers of the Church are to be viewed as "interpreters of

[3] G. R. Elton, *The Tudor Constitution: Documents and Commentary* (Cambridge, 1960), p. 393.

the word of God. They were learned men and learned fathers; the instruments of the mercy of God and vessels full of grace. . . . Yet may they not be compared with the word of God."[4]

The reformers were cautious concerning the authority of the early Church, but this caution was qualified by the Protestant interpretation of history. John Foxe, for instance, taught on the basis of his understanding of the New Testament Apocalypse that the English were living in the last days. After centuries of darkness, ending with the eruption of the Antichrist, Satan, incarnate in the papacy, the end had come. According to this view the long expanse of time from about the year 600 represented a decline into corruption, involving a departure from the simplicity and purity of the primitive times.[5] With such a view of history pervasive among the English reformers from Tyndale on, it is not to be wondered at that Cranmer and those who assisted him in his work looked to the worship of the early Church as a model for reform.

The Prayer Book and Reason

As a man deeply influenced by humanist studies and as one subject to the Word of God, Cranmer was also an eminently reasonable man, and the Book of Common Prayer, contrasted with that which went before, was a book for reasonable persons. First of all, there was purged from common worship a great quantity of what was considered by the reformers to be fantastic and superstitious. In describing to the Cornish rebels what was to be found in the old Latin service, Cranmer wrote that there were many

[4] Cited in S. L. Greenslade, *The English Reformers and the Fathers of the Church* (Oxford, 1960), p. 9. See also, John Booty, *John Jewel as Apologist of the Church of England* (London, 1963), p. 136.

[5] See F. J. Levy, *Tudor Historical Thought* (San Marino, Calif., 1967), pp. 98–105, 123; Glanmor Williams, *Reformation Views of Church History*, Ecumenical Studies in History, 11 (Richmond, 1970), pp. 54–62; and William Haller, *The Elect Nation: The Meaning and Relevance of Foxe's "Book of Martyrs"* (New York and Evanston, 1963), pp. 130–39.

old fables such as this: "The devil entered into a certain person, in whose mouth St. Martin put his finger; and because the devil could not get out at his mouth, the man blew him out behind." "This," wrote Cranmer,

is one of the tales that was wont to be read in the Latin service, that you will needs have again. As though the devil had a body, and that so crass that he could not pass out by the small pores of the flesh, but must needs have a wide hole to go out at. Is this a grave and godly matter to be read in the church, or rather a foolish Christmas tale, or an old wives' fable, worthy to be laughed at and scorned of every man that hath either wit or godly judgment?

He then reported some other things,

most vain fables, some very superstitious, some directly against God's word, and the laws of this realm; and all together be full of error and superstition. But as Christ commonly excused the simple people because of their ignorance, and justly condemned the scribes and Pharisees, which by their crafty persuasions led the people out of the right way; so I think not you so much to be blamed as those Pharisees and papistical priests which, abusing your simplicity, caused you to ask you wist not what, desiring rather to drink of the dregs of corrupt error, which you knew not, than of the pure and sweet wine of God's word.[6]

Thus the reasonable person will not tolerate the existence of error and superstition in common worship. This is a note that prevails in much of the evidence concerning the genesis of the Book of Common Prayer. It was put most crassly by Sir Thomas Smith, principal secretary under Edward VI, at the debate on the Mass in December, 1548. It was reported that during a discussion of the bodily presence of Christ, Smith indulged in "a long process declaring what inconvenience, and how loathsome thing to hear should arise, by description of the natural body in the sacrament. For other Christ must have but a small body, or else his length and thickness cannot be there, which things declare that it cannot be no true body, or else he must want his head or

---

[6] *English Historical Documents, 1485–1558*, pp. 379–80.

his legs or some part of him. And also every part of him must be one as big as another, the hand as much as the head, the nose as much as the whole body, with such innumerable." To this the Bishop of Winchester was heard to retort, "Reason will not serve in matters of faith."[7] But reason was taken quite seriously.

In the doctrine of the presence of Christ in the Holy Communion, the Reformation application of the reasonable results of the Ascension[8] was influential and is echoed in the Prayer Book, the Articles of Religion, and the Homilies. The point was that since Christ ascended bodily into the heavens and sits at the right hand of God, he cannot be bodily present in the Holy Communion, except it be in that body which is constituted by the faithful and worthy receivers. Cranmer expressed it this way:

Figuratively he is in the bread and wine, and spiritually he is in them that worthily eat and drink the bread and wine; but really, carnally, and corporally he is only in heaven, from whence he shall come to judge the quick and dead. This brief answer will suffice for all that the papists can bring for their purpose, if it be aptly applied.[9]

All that love and believe Christ himself, let them not think that Christ is corporally in the bread, but let them lift up their hearts unto heaven and worship him sitting there at the right hand of his Father . . . in no wise let them worship him as being corporally in the bread; for he is not in it, neither spiritually, as he is in man, nor corporally, as he is in heaven; but only sacramentally, as a thing may be said to be in the figure, whereby it is signified.[10]

It has been argued that in such teaching as we find represented in these two brief passages Cranmer was exhibiting his indebtedness to Nominalism.[11] As a Nominalist he viewed things as self-

[7] Gasquet and Bishop, p. 399.

[8] On the importance of this doctrine for Jewel, see Booty, pp. 169–72.

[9] Thomas Cranmer, *Remains*, ed. H. Jenkyns, 4 vols. (Oxford, 1833), II, 401. Also cited in Ridley, p. 323. Compare with the language of the "Black Rubric," *The First and Second Prayer Books*, p. 393.

[10] *Remains*, p. 446.

[11] See Eugene K. McGee, "Cranmer and Nominalism," *Harvard Theological Review* LVII (July 1964): 189–216; and a reply by William J. Courtenay,

enclosed objects, bread and wine being only that which they appear to be except for their symbolic value as associated with the Word of God. Such things cannot be the vehicles of divine grace. Thus Christ is not present in body but only in his divinity. But if Cranmer was a Nominalist, it was only in a popular sense. Cranmer was no philosopher. His emphasis upon common-sense reasonableness was influenced by his attack upon superstition and the humanist teaching concerning reason, as much as by Nominalism. Cyril Richardson correctly says that for Cranmer "it is all a very simple matter—a kind of common-sense British empiricism, which he delights to employ especially in the more earthy moments of his campaign against Gardiner."[12]

We should also note that alongside this common-sense reasonableness there was in Cranmer an insistence on mutual participation. By means of the spiritual feeding in the Supper, with the concomitant exercise of faith in the passion, Christ dwells in us and we in him. This mutual indwelling, with biblical rootage in John 6, is a major theme in the Prayer Book as well as in other of Cranmer's works. Richardson finds this to be irreconcilable with the assertion of Christ's bodily absence and says that "what we have in Cranmer is an unresolved conflict between Nominalist and Realist notions."[13] It is possible that at points such as this, where Cranmer seems to contradict himself, his common-sense reasonableness is qualified by that right-reason to which the humanists and Richard Hooker referred, reason with qualities of heart and soul, conscience as well as mind, the moral law of reason. Which is to say that when Cranmer is most rational, exercising common sense most avidly, he insists upon Christ's bodily absence, but when he is most devotional, when rationality is most qualified by right-reason, he speaks of mutual indwelling.

"Cranmer as a Nominalist. Sed Contra," *Harvard Theological Review* LVII (October 1964): 368–80.

[12] Cyril C. Richardson, "Cranmer and the Analysis of Eucharistic Doctrine," *Journal of Theological Studies*, n.s., XVI, no. 2 (October 1965): 422.

[13] *Ibid.*, p. 429.

In Cranmer, I believe, either we may see operative the endless conflict of mind and heart, reason and piety, striving for a balance, a reasonable adjustment of conflicting elements, or we may behold a reasonable man whose reason expands or contracts in accordance with what the ends demand. Thus, when combating superstition, it is common sense which prevails, but when confronting even the possibility of irreverent rationality, it is devotion, the candle of the Lord, which prevails.[14] This is, however, no place for an adequate exposition of Cranmer's eucharistic theology. It is sufficient here to indicate that for him and for the Prayer Book, the operation of reason is important.

The Prayer Book and Continuity

All of the liturgical reformers, from Cardinal Quiñones to John a Lasco, were concerned to bring about a more scriptural worship through which the Word of God might shine to kindle faith and to guide believers heavenward. They were all looking to the example of the early Church and were all concerned to overcome superstition, and thus, however cautiously, exercised common-sense reasonableness. The English reform of worship differed from reform elsewhere partly through its emphasis upon continuity. Its concern, while purging received orders of worship of error and superstition, was to maintain that from the past which was of genuine value, or at least biblically permissible, not evil. For whatever reason, whether in accordance with conscience or out of political necessity, distinctions were made (for instance, in the Ten Articles of 1536) between necessary doctrine and useful ceremonies, between things expressly commanded by God through Scripture as necessary to salvation, and things not so expressed but enforced for the sake of maintaining a common

---

[14] For other views of Cranmer's position, see Dugmore, *The Mass and the English Reformers*, chap. 8; Peter Brooks, *Thomas Cranmer's Doctrine of the Eucharist* (New York, 1965); and Davies, *Worship and Theology*, vol. I, chap. 3.

order.[15] Cranmer, in the essay "Of Ceremonies, Why Some Be Abolished and Some Retained," annexed to the first Prayer Book and prominently displayed in subsequent books, located an operating principle. He argued that some ceremonies are discarded for good reason while others, not derived from the Word of God, are retained "which although they have been devised by man, yet it is thought good to reserve them still, as well for a decent order in the Church, for the which they were first devised, as because they pertain to edification, whereunto all things done in the Church, as the Apostle teacheth, ought to be referred."[16] Involved here was the conviction that liturgical reform in England did not necessitate the removal of *all* that was traditional. In this respect reform in England was very much like that in the Germanies. As with Luther and Lutheran Church Orders, new forms were not devised, but rather the inherited forms were revised.

Cranmer's concern to preserve continuity can be detected in the very structure of the Prayer Book, which seems to be patterned after the medieval liturgical library in its divisions: the Breviary (Morning and Evening Prayer), the Missal (Collects, Epistles, Gospels, and the Holy Communion), the Processional (the Litany), and the Manual (Baptism through Churching of Women). In addition, it should be noted that unlike all but a couple of minor Lutheran Church Orders, the daily offices of Morning and Evening Prayer do much to preserve the essential tone and spirit of the Breviary. But perhaps Cranmer's conservative nature is most vividly illustrated by the fact that while Luther discarded the Roman Canon of the Mass, the Archbishop retained its order and much of its content. Like the Lutherans, the English used the Latin Mass as an authoritative model, re-

---

[15] For the Ten Articles, see *English Historical Documents, 1485–1558*, pp. 795–805. An interpretation of them is given by F. J. Taylor, "The Anglican Reformation," in F. W. Dillistone et al., *Scripture and Tradition* (Greenwich, Conn., 1955), pp. 65 ff.

[16] See p. 18 of Prayer Book.

forming it by making additions and deletions. The English rite was unique, as Ratcliff rightly claims, in that "it contains a Canon reminiscent, both in name and general arrangement, of the venerable Roman Canon *Missae.*"[17] Cranmer objected to much in the Mass, and in particular to what he understood to be the Roman Catholic doctrine of sacrifice.[18] As his reform progressed, he sought to expunge all references which implied that doctrine, as well as all that might support the doctrines of transubstantiation, purgatory, saint worship, and the like. But he moved cautiously and at least at the beginning must have realized, as Richard Field realized at the beginning of the seventeenth century,[19] that the Roman Canon in and of itself was doctrinally acceptable once certain elements of recent origin were removed from it. In acting to preserve much out of the past, Cranmer was establishing a principle that John Whitgift and Richard Hooker made use of when defending the preservation within the Church of England of things used and abused by the Roman church.

The Prayer Book and the Idea of Communion

Finally, there is the emphasis upon communion in the Book of Common Prayer. The focus of the Book as it was first developed was not only upon God, to whom all worship is directed, but also upon the worshiper. The Prayer Book is in the language spoken by the people; it is to be read audibly; the Word is to be heard, to cultivate faith, to create community, to edify, to engender in all of life the sacrifice of praise and thanksgiving. In the background are the doctrines of justification by faith, the priesthood of all believers, the church as a communion of saints. Worship

[17] Ratcliff, p. 36. But see Davies, *Worship and Theology*, I, 188–90.

[18] That he and others misunderstood the church's teaching is suggested by Francis Clark, S.J., *Eucharistic Sacrifice and the Reformation* (Westminster, Md., and London, 1960), pp. 103–15. See Cyril Richardson's review in *Anglican Theological Review* XLVII, no. 2 (April 1965): 233–35.

[19] *Of the Church, Five Books*, Ecclesiastical History Society, 4 vols. (Cambridge, 1847–52), II, 96 ff.

is meant for the service of God and also for the cultivation of Christian community, the building of a godly nation. When Cranmer set aside the doctrine of transubstantiation, his attention became focused upon the faithful communicants rather than on transformed bread and wine. Thus in his disputation at Oxford at the beginning of Queen Mary's reign, while arguing that Christ's presence in the Holy Communion was actual, he stated that Christ was not present in a natural or corporal body. His opponents replied that Real Presence meant Christ's presence in earthly flesh. Cranmer retorted that this was false and said, "His true body is truly present to them that truly receive Him, but spiritually."[20] Equally illuminating is the way in which he understood sacrifice in the Holy Communion. In the Roman Mass of his time, it was generally understood "that the priest, having (after prayer and by God's grace) duly and legitimately made present the Body and Blood of our Lord, proceeds then and there in the name of the congregation to offer this acceptable sacrifice to God the Father in memory of, and in representation of, Calvary." But, as F. C. Burkitt wrote, in the English Holy Communion the sacrifice is this: "that the congregation, having confessed, been shriven, having 'assisted' at a due consecration of the bread and wine, and finally having received their own portion, do then and there offer unto God themselves, their souls and bodies, to be a reasonable sacrifice."[21] For Cranmer the sacrifice was threefold: It was Christ's sacrifice once for all on the cross; it was the sacrifice of praise and thanksgiving performed as the faithful remember the cross; and it was the offering of the worshipers, their souls and bodies: the people's oblation. The center of attention is focused not on what the priest does, but upon Christ's sacrifice, which inspires the sacrificial service of the faithful.

[20] *Works*, I, 240 ff.
[21] *Eucharist and Sacrifice* (Cambridge, 1921), p. 22. Burkitt views the doctrine as contained in the Prayer Book as "perfectly Augustinian" and cites Augustine, *De civitate dei*, x, 6, and *Epistolae*, 272.

When read with this in mind, it seems clear that the center of attention in the Prayer Book sacrament falls upon the communion, including the self-oblation of the faithful, who by grace participate in Christ, and he in them. This is made evident in the second Prayer Book, where the communion is, as it were, set in the midst of the congregation, with the strong implication that the consecration is completed, or even occurs, in the use.[22] As Hooker stated so clearly in *Of the Laws of Ecclesiastical Polity*, Book V, the purpose and end of the sacrament must determine our understanding of it, its meaning, and how that meaning is exhibited.[23] Thus the communion of the priest and people immediately following the words of institution is central to the action of the liturgy and is appropriately followed by either the Prayer of Oblation or the post-communion thanksgiving (which can be read as a Prayer of Oblation). A logical sequence was thus established: remembrance of Christ's sacrifice, the recitation of the institution of the Supper by Christ himself, a remembrance with thanksgiving, the participation of the faithful, eating the bread and drinking the wine, the Body and Blood of Christ, whereby that mutual indwelling occurs, a participation in his sacrificial life and death, for which the only appropriate response is self-offering with thanksgiving. This interpretation conforms to the mental picture of the Holy Communion as celebrated at the time according to the second Prayer Book (1552): a table standing in place of the altar, the table moved down at the communion time from the sanctuary to the chancel where the people gathered around, the priest presiding at the north end of the table, the prayer of consecration proceeding with the communion an integral part, the prayer flowing without interruption to the

---

[22] For an interesting but debatable statement of this, see F. C. Burkitt, *Christian Worship* (Cambridge, 1930), pp. 97–100.

[23] See Richard Hooker, *Of the Laws of Ecclesiastical Polity*, V.lxvii.5, in *Works*, ed. John Keble, 7th ed., rev. R. W. Church and F. Paget, 3 vols. (Oxford, 1888), II, 352.

Prayer of Oblation or post-communion thanksgiving. The whole was a Holy Communion.

This emphasis upon communion accorded well with contemporary views of society and social reform. It must be remembered that while the first Prayer Book was being readied, the Protector Somerset was developing a program of national reform, with the support of the commonwealth men and the concept of the commonweal which they espoused.[24] This program had as its exponents Sir Thomas Smith, Sir John Hales, and Bishop Hugh Latimer, men whom Cranmer knew well. For a time, while Cranmer was working on the Prayer Book, Latimer was in residence at Lambeth Palace.[25] Furthermore, an investigation of Martin Bucer's *De Regno Christi* reveals how closely related the social and theological goals could be in the sixteenth century.[26] Bucer, who presented his criticism of the first Prayer Book in his *Censura,* stood opposed to Luther's sharp distinction between the *Regnum spirituale* and the *Regnum corporale,* and

[24] See Jordan, chap. 14; Whitney R. D. Jones, *The Tudor Commonwealth, 1529–1559* (London, 1970); and Arthur B. Ferguson, "The Tudor Commonweal and the Sense of Change," *Journal of British Studies* III, no. 1 (November 1963): 11–35.

[25] "I trouble my lord of Canterbury; and being at his house, now and then I walk in the garden looking in my book" (sermon preached before the King, March 1549, in Hugh Latimer, *Works,* ed. George Elwes Corrie, Parker Society Publications, 27–28, 2 vols. [Cambridge, 1844–45], I, 127). It would appear that he changed his view of the Real Presence at the same time and "together with" Cranmer. See *Original Letters,* I, 322. See also, Latimer, *Selected Sermons,* ed. A. Chester, Folger Documents of Tudor and Stuart Civilization, 15 (Charlottesville, Va., 1968), p. xxv; and Richard Edward Barbieri, "Hugh Latimer's Sermons on the Lord's Prayer: A Critical Edition" (Ph.D. diss., Harvard University, 1971), intro.

[26] See Martin Bucer, *Opera,* vol. XV, *De Regno Christi,* ed. Francois Wendel (Paris, 1955), pp. xxxv ff., 6 ff.; Wilhelm Pauck, ed., *Melanchthon and Bucer,* Library of Christian Classics, 19 (Philadelphia, 1969), pp. 166 ff., 179 ff.; and T. F. Torrance, *Kingdom and Church* (Fairlawn, N.J., 1956), pp. 75–89.

spoke fervently of the *Regnum Christi,* the *Communio Christiana* which through Word and Spirit is visibly and actively realized on earth. Such teaching appealed to the English, with their rising national sentiment, and to the preacher Latimer, with his social and prophetic insights. It could not help but be impressive to Cranmer. Communion and commonwealth go together; they are contiguous ideas. And it is possible to regard the Book of Common Prayer as a vital instrument for the creation of a Christian commonwealth in England.

The Use of the Elizabethan Prayer Book

The Elizabethan Prayer Book here reproduced was, like its predecessors, an official book, an instrument of state. The use of and worship according to the Book of Common Prayer was enforced by statute.[1] Royal and local visitations were conducted to see to it that the law was obeyed.[2] Failure to attend Prayer Book worship was punishable by law. Those guilty of offense were presented in ecclesiastical courts where verdicts were rendered and punishments meted out.[3] There were those who objected to this forced uniformity. The Puritans viewed the Prayer Book as popish and ungodly, and sought to displace it. But many of them conformed, and, as we have seen, some made use of the "corrected" Prayer Book attached to the Geneva Bible and felt that by so doing they were obedient to the law. The Roman Catholics

---

[1] See the Act of Uniformity on pp. 5–13 of Prayer Book.

[2] See Frere, I, 147 ff., II, 14–16; and W. P. M. Kennedy, *Elizabethan Episcopal Administration,* Alcuin Club Collections, 25–27, 3 vols. (London, 1924), I, xxxiv–lix.

[3] See Ronald A. Marchant, *The Puritans and the Church Courts in the Diocese of York, 1560–1642* (London, 1960), esp. pp. 1–25, and *The Church under the Law, 1560–1640* (Cambridge, 1969), pp. 218–20, 225–26. For examples, see Sidney A. Peyton, ed., *The Churchwardens' Presentments in the Oxfordshire Peculiars of Dorchester, Thame, and Banbury,* Oxfordshire Record Society, 10 (Reading, 1928).

were evidently torn. Some resisted the laws, paid their fines, and attended the Mass in secret. Others conformed, to the consternation of their priests, attended Prayer Book worship, perhaps with rosaries to occupy the time, and then attended Mass where possible and when it was reasonably safe to do so.[4] Not all were made of the stuff of martyrs. The laws governing recusancy were strengthened after the papal bull *Regnans in excelsis* was promulgated against the Queen in 1570. Nevertheless, even while the government was preparing to fend off the Armada, utilizing repressive measures to control papal forces within England, masses were celebrated. Finally, there were the disgruntled within the Church of England, those in the conservative North and West who maintained traditional customs, kept their altars, and, while using the Book of Common Prayer, interpreted what they heard and saw in accordance with pre–Prayer Book ecclesiastical ways.[5] There were, in addition, the Laodiceans, the seemingly indifferent, who may have been in the majority in Elizabeth's reign, who confessed to being Christians but were immune to religious zeal.

It is, as has been suggested above, an error to believe that the Prayer Book was used in every instance in accordance with what it contained. It assumed that the Holy Communion, with sermon, would be celebrated every Sunday. Cranmer was firm on this, as was Calvin, but he was seemingly ignored by many. In time it proved necessary to command that Holy Communion be celebrated and received three or four times a year, on specific holy days, of which Easter was always one.[6] Prelates such as Thomas Cooper of Lincoln found it necessary to exhort their flocks to come to communion. "We may not," said Cooper, in a

---

[4] See W. R. Trimble, *The Catholic Laity in Elizabethan England* (Cambridge, Mass., 1964); and Davies, *Worship and Theology*, vol. I, chap. 4.

[5] For the kind of conservative priest I have in mind, see the manuscript of Michael Sherbrook, rector of Wickersley in the Diocese of York from 1567 to 1610, in *Tudor Treatises*, ed. A. G. Dickens, Yorkshire Archaeological Society, Record Series, 125 (1959).

[6] See p. 268 of Prayer Book.

homily to be read in all the churches of his diocese, "for our weakness and imperfection despair or refuse the comfort of that heavenly table, but rather let us in all dutiful sort, approach thereunto and pray most heartily (everyone of us all) that we may be fit and worthy guests for the same."[7] It was the opinion of the theologians and preachers that it was a solemn duty for Christians to participate in the Lord's Supper, the Parable of the Great Feast (Luke 14:16–24) being often cited in support.[8] But at the same time, and in line with Cranmer's emphasis on communion, preparation for participation was stressed. The person who would be a worthy receiver must engage in rigorous self-examination. Such examination was to concern his knowledge of the Lord's Supper and of the faith in general, centering upon the Lord's Prayer, the Ten Commandments, and the Creed. In addition, the person must examine his or her life (i.e., conversation) and make amends to those whom the individual has offended, determining all the while to lead a new life. The exhortations, the rubrics, and the penitential sections of the daily offices and of the Holy Communion all emphasized these points.[9] In the Holy Communion, the people were confronted by this awesome invitation to confession:

You that do truly and earnestly repent you of your sins, and be in love and charity with your neighbors, and intend to lead a new life, following the commandments of God, and walking from henceforth in his holy ways: Draw near, and take this holy Sacrament to your comfort; make

[7] Thomas Cooper, *A briefe homily, wherein the most comfortable and right use of the Lord's Supper is very plainly opened and delivered, even to the understanding of the unlearned and ignorant* (London, 1580), sigs. B2ᵛ–4ʳ.

[8] See the first exhortation, p. 255. This is derived from Peter Martyr's *Adhortatio*, of which there is an English translation in his *Loci communes*, ed. A. Marten (London, 1583). See Alan Beesley, "An Unpublished Source of the Book of Common Prayer: Peter Martyr Vermigli's *Adhortatio ad Coenam Domini Mysticam*," *Journal of Ecclesiastical History* XVIII, no. 2 (October 1967): 253–58.

[9] On this see John Booty, "Preparation for the Lord's Supper in Elizabethan England," *Anglican Theological Review* XLIX, no. 2 (April 1967): 131–48.

your humble confession to Almighty God before this congregation here gathered together in his holy name, meekly kneeling upon your knees.

Through this discipline, the community was to be re-created; but it was a demanding discipline if taken seriously, and did not provide the assistance for the weak that was to be found in the medieval sacrament of Penance. Indeed, the rubric stated that if a person were desirous of receiving communion, he or she must first inform the curate (either a day before or after Morning Prayer on the day), who might very well refuse any person concerning whom he had doubts. Infrequent communion was the rule. And in part because of this, the emphasis in public worship fell elsewhere.

Careful attention paid to William Harrison's account of worship in the Church of England reveals the true nature of that worship as experienced by the parishioner. Harrison begins by stressing the use of Scripture and the practice of preaching. The canonical Scriptures are read, the Psalter once a month, the New Testament four times a year, and the Old Testament once a year. The clergyman, if licensed to do so, is permitted "to make some exposition or exhortation in his parish unto amendment of life." And because of the ignorance of many of the clergy, homilies have been provided "to be read by the curates of mean understanding (which homilies do comprehend the principal parts of Christian doctrine, as of original sin, of justification by faith, of charity, and suchlike) upon the Sabbath days unto the congregation."[10] He then describes the course of worship on Sunday in the parish churches:

And after a certain number of Psalms read, which are limited according to the days of the month, for Morning and Evening Prayer we have two lessons, whereof the first is taken out of the Old Testament, the second out of the New; and of these latter, that in the morning is out of the Gospels, the other in the afternoon out of some one of the Epistles. After

---

[10] William Harrison, *The Description of England*, ed. Georges Edelen, Folger Documents of Tudor and Stuart Civilization, 14 (Ithaca, N.Y., 1968), p. 33.

Morning Prayer also we have the Litany and Suffrages, an invocation in mine opinion not devised without the great assistance of the spirit of God, although many curious, mind-sick persons utterly condemn it as superstitious and savoring of conjuration and sorcery.

This being done, we proceed unto the Communion, if any communicants be to receive the Eucharist; if not, we read the Decalogue, Epistle, and Gospel, with the Nicene Creed (of some in derision called the "dry communion"), and then proceed unto an homily or sermon, which hath a Psalm before and after it, and finally unto the baptism of such infants as on every Sabbath day (if occasion so require) are brought unto the churches; and thus is the forenoon bestowed. In the afternoon likewise we meet again, and after the Psalms and lessons ended we have commonly a sermon or at the leastwise our youth catechized by the space of an hour.[11]

To this basic description we must add such additional information as Harrison provides. First of all, he speaks of the services being in "our vulgar tongue" and being rendered in such a way that they are audible and can be understood by the congregation. Here he mentions the singing of the services, now much reduced from previous practice. The singing of the psalms is restricted to cathedral and collegiate churches, "the rest being read (as in common parish churches) by the minister with a loud voice, saving that in the administration of the communion the choir singeth the answers, the Creed, and sundry other things appointed, but in so plain, I say, and distinct manner that each one present may understand what they sing, every word having but one note, though the whole harmony consist of many parts, and those very cunningly set by the skillful in that science."[12] Church music was certainly not ignored during the Elizabethan period, but the church sought to subject it to the principle of edification, virtually ignoring the value of aesthetics to theology and to religious practice.[13]

---

[11] *Ibid.*, pp. 33–34.

[12] *Ibid.*, p. 34.

[13] See Davies, *Worship and Theology*, vol. I, chap. 11; Peter Le Huray,

Next Harrison speaks of the churches themselves: church bells are in use, but the fabric of the parish church is stripped of "all images, shrines, tabernacles, rood lofts, and monuments of idolatry." Stained glass windows (he called them "stories in glass windows") remain in many places, but where it has been possible they have been replaced with windows of "white glass."[14] He does not mention it himself, but we know from other sources that in the sanctuary the altar was replaced by a table, and where the elaborate reredos, or screen, was located on the east wall there were now set up in large letters the Lord's Prayer, the Ten Commandments, and the Creed.[15] Thus the basis of Christian faith in words takes the place of images and pictures. Religion was becoming more and more word-centered and intellectual, a matter of reason and of reasonableness.

Harrison then refers to the removal or diminution of the rood screens that divided the choir or chancel from the nave or body of the church.[16] This partition is not needed, he tells us, "sith the minister saith his service commonly in the body of the church with his face toward the people, in a little tabernacle of wainscot provided for the purpose; by which means the ignorant do not only learn divers of the Psalms and usual prayers by heart, but also such as can read do pray together with him, so that the whole congregation at one instant pour out their petitions unto the living God for the whole estate of His church in most earnest and fervent manner."[17]

Finally he speaks of the way in which "holy and festival days

---

Music and the Reformation in England, 1549–1660 (London and New York, 1967).

[14] Pp. 35–36.

[15] Davies, *Worship and Theology*, I, 371; and G. W. O. Addleshaw and F. Etchells, *The Architectural Setting of Anglican Worship* (London, 1948), pp. 101–7, 158–60.

[16] See Gee, pp. 273–76. This was an order to put an end to wanton destruction.

[17] Harrison, p. 36. But see Kennedy, I, civ–cv, for evidence of great variety in the placing of the minister.

are very well reduced also unto a less number," a fact of which he strongly approves. And he mentions the attire of the clergy, simple and comely when compared with that of the "popish church."[18] We know now that in a cathedral church, the normal attire at service time consisted mainly of copes for the celebrant, epistoler, and gospeler, and in parish churches, for all Prayer Book services, "a comely surplice with sleeves." Their outdoor attire was also to be simple and comely, consisting chiefly of a cloak "with sleeves put on" and a cap.[19]

In all of this, the edification of the faithful was intended: learning by reading and being read to, by means of Scripture, preaching, the recitation of basic formularies, and the formal teaching of the catechism heard recited over and over again at Evening Prayer. Fundamental were the Lord's Prayer, the Ten Commandments, and the Creed, enshrined on the east wall of the church, the basis, along with the Propers (Collects, Epistles, and Gospels) of the Ante Communion, a kind of reformed medieval Prone,[20] the content of the catechism, those things that must be learned before a Christian is confirmed and may worthily receive communion. The tone of this worship, with the Holy Communion only occasionally celebrated, was penitential. As such it was a fundamental and common instrument for the discipline of persons in community, and thus for the re-creation of the community, the commonwealth. It was solemn and impressive in this sense. Indeed, Morning Prayer, Litany, and Ante Communion were the didactic and penitential preparation for the occasional Holy Communion and for the living of the Christian life, the *viva fides*, as exemplified and empowered by that sacrament. This tone was somewhat alleviated, in accordance with the day and the season, by the Scriptures (Psalms and Lessons) recited and the canticles read or sung, the parish clerk

---

[18] Harrison, pp. 36–37.

[19] See the Advertisements of 1566 in Gee, pp. 271–73.

[20] J. A. Thurmer, "Matins and Ante-Communion," *Church Quarterly Review* CLX (April–June 1959): 236.

leading the people. But it was prevalent and provoked a major problem for the Elizabethan church.

Liturgy involves penitence as one of its major elements. The New Testament words translated as worship or liturgy in English refer to bowing down, humbling oneself before the holy God, and to the commitment to serve God and one's neighbor with service such as that of a slave.[21] But this bowing down, this service, is not an oppressive weight or burden. It is rather a grateful expression of the fact that through such humbling and such service there comes salvation, eternal life. The appropriate corollary to penitence is praise. Thus, as Harrison notes, the Holy Communion of the Prayer Book is also the Eucharist,[22] the thanksgiving, where, as in the ancient liturgies, the eucharistic action and presence is effected through the power of the Holy Spirit, as the faithful give thanks for God's mighty act in and through Christ, the sacrifice once-for-all upon the cross. Such, I believe, is evident in what we know of the practice of the Elizabethan church. And in the Prayer Book, the basis of that practice, there is the persistent interplay of penitence and praise, penitence and praise, Cranmer ringing the changes of this essential, interrelated dual response to divine revelation and grace. Viewed from the vantage point of the twentieth century, the prayer seems to be needlessly repetitious and thus overly long and tedious. But Cranmer knew the value of repetition, and he also knew that the rhythm of penitence and praise, penitence rising to praise, praise falling back into penitence and then rising again to praise, was the rhythm of the Christian life. Indeed, all of the Prayer Book can be regarded in terms of this repetition of penitence and praise. It was that fundamental. The problem for the Elizabethan church was that in emphasizing the Ante Communion they were emphasizing penitence and thus one side of the

---

[21] For a discussion of the words, *proskynein* and *latreuein*, see William Nicholls, *Jacob's Ladder: The Meaning of Worship*, Ecumenical Studies in Worship, 4 (Richmond, 1958), p. 15.

[22] Harrison, p. 34.

whole necessary worship experience. Seemingly they seldom appreciated the elation that Bishop Cooper expressed, wishing all to experience in the sacrament of "praise and thanksgiving" a similar elation: "Even as certainly as my taste feeleth the sweetness of bread and wine . . . even so the taste of my faith and sense of my heart doth feel the sweetness of Christ his body and blood broken and shed for me and all mankind upon the cross, and perceiveth it thereby to be the only food of my soul, without which, should perish both soul and body, eternally."[23]

It was left to Richard Hooker, who in the fifth book of his great work, *Of the Laws of Ecclesiastical Polity* (1597), wrote the most extensive and profound commentary on the Book of Common Prayer in the sixteenth century, and to Caroline divines such as Lancelot Andrewes, William Laud, Richard Field, and John Cosin, to make amends, to begin to restore the wholeness of the Prayer Book in practice and in particular the fullness of eucharistic doctrine. Hooker fixed his attention upon the sacraments and especially upon the Holy Communion with his doctrine of participation, whereby he taught: "The bread and cup are his [Christ's] body and blood because they are causes instrumental upon the receipt whereof the *participation* of his body and blood ensueth."[24] This was a strong statement, however much it was qualified by Hooker's "sacramentarian" teachings. And the so-called Laudians of the seventeenth century sought to return to the Prayer Book as it was and away from the practices of the Elizabethan church. This meant placing greater emphasis upon the Eucharist and upon regular communion and led to ceremonial and other additions. In time they began to agitate for the recovery of altars, and the Canons of 1640 testify to their intent. They also began to "tamper" with the Prayer Book Holy Communion itself, the earliest evidence coming from John Overall, who was favorably inclined to private masses and believed in

[23] *A briefe homily*, sig. A3^{r-v}; Booty, "Preparation for the Lord's Supper," pp. 146–47.

[24] Hooker, *Laws*, V.lxvii.5; *Works*, II, 352; see sec. 6 as well.

a traditional doctrine of Real Presence. It is noted that Overall always used the Prayer of Oblation before the communion of priest and people.[25] His model was the 1549 Book, which was becoming for Laudians a kind of liturgical "bible." They strove for the beauty of holiness, the priestly holiness of the sanctuary, and through their efforts, while still stressing preparation for communion, helped some Englishmen to understand the Holy Communion as thanksgiving, Eucharist, once more.

These are judgments made from liturgical and theological points of view. There are, of course, other valid ways of looking at and judging the Book of Common Prayer. The book is a product of the sixteenth century. The language it uses, the service of Commination, the prayers for the Queen, the attitudes expressed concerning God and society, all mark it for what it is, the age and the place where it first appeared.[26] Nothing is more striking in this regard than the appearance in the Almanac of the signs of the Zodiac. There, neatly noted in the proper months, are "Sol in Aquario," "Sol in Piscibus," and the rest. It would be quite surprising to find these signs included in the Prayer Book, particularly in such a book as that prepared by Thomas Cranmer, a person who along with many other Reformers condemned the use of astrology,[27] if we did not remember that Elizabeth not only had an archbishop but also had her Dr. Dee, and that John Jewel, bishop of Salisbury, while arguing against

[25] See G. J. Cuming, "The Making of the Prayer Book of 1662," in Alcuin Club, *The English Prayer Book, 1549–1662* (London, 1963), p. 84.

[26] The fact that the Prayer Book was much influenced by the age in which it appeared and thus has, alongside its permanent values, a dated character is often discussed by persons dealing with the need for liturgical revision, or those dealing with the history of the revision of the Prayer Book. See *Prayer Book Studies 4: The Eucharistic Liturgy*, Standing Liturgical Commission of the Episcopal Church (New York, 1953), pp. 75–132; L. W. Brown, *Relevant Liturgy: Zabriskie Lectures, 1964* (New York, 1965); A. G. Hebert, *Liturgy and Society* (London, 1961); D. E. W. Harrison, *Common Prayer in the Church of England*, rev. ed. (London, 1969), pp. 56–65, 119–24.

[27] Cranmer, *Works*, II, 100.

soothsayers and the like, admitted their power.[28] The presence
of the signs in the Prayer Book should be understood against the
background of the times and in relation to other writings, such
as the *Preces privatae* (1564), wherein the Zodiac is included in
the Calendar, presented in special tables, and explained for the
common reader.[29]

[28] John Jewel, *Certaine Sermons preached before the Queenes Maiestie*
(London, 1583), sig. M6; Jewel, *Works*, Parker Society Publications, 23–26,
4 vols. (Cambridge, 1845–50), II, 1027–28; Richard Deacon, *John Dee:
Scientist, Geographer, Astrologer, and Secret Agent to Elizabeth I* (London,
1968), pp. 49–50.

[29] See *Preces privatae, in studiosorum gratiam collectae, et regia authoritate
appropatae* (London, Gulielmus Seres, 1564), sigs. *1–**4. For a discussion of
all this, see David Siegenthaler's article "Zodiac and Prayer Book," forthcom-
ing in *Journal of Theological Studies*.

Notes

Notes

An Act for the Uniformity of Common Prayer

For a discussion of this Act, see pp. 334–40.

PAGE 5] *Common service . . . and ceremonies:* Common service and prayer would ordinarily refer to Morning Prayer, Evening Prayer, the Holy Communion, and the Litany. Administration of sacraments referred to the Holy Communion and Baptism, the two sacraments recognized as such by the English church. Rites and ceremonies referred to all else in the book. Here the terms are treated as synonymous, whereas in a more exact sense a rite is a liturgical text and ceremony concerns the way in which a liturgy is performed.

The Feast of the Nativity of Saint John Baptist next coming: June 24.

PAGE 6] *Lessons . . . the year:* The 1552 Book had provided "Proper Lessons" for "diverse feasts and days." Now there were to be proper first Lessons for every Sunday, morning and evening. Cf. G. J. Cuming, *A History of Anglican Liturgy* (London, 1969), pp. 122–23.

And the form of the Litany altered and corrected: The prayer for deliverance "from the tyranny of the Bishop of Rome and all his detestable enormities," as found in the 1552 Book, was deleted.

And two sentences . . . communicants: Here were to be combined the sentences of administration of the first two Books: "The body of our Lord Jesus Christ which was given for thee, preserve thy body and soul unto everlasting life" (1549) and "Take and eat this, in remembrance that Christ died for thee, and feed on him in thy heart by faith, with thanksgiving" (1552); "The blood of our Lord Jesus Christ which was shed for thee, preserve thy body and soul unto everlasting life" (1549) and "Drink this in remembrance that Christ's blood was shed for thee, and be thankful" (1552).

PAGE 7] *Bail or mainprise:* Legal methods of obtaining release by finding sureties.

PAGE 8] *And it is ordained . . . in the said book:* For the fuller meaning of this, see, for instance, injunctions 22 and 52 of the Injunctions of 1559, Henry

Gee and W. J. Hardy, eds., *Documents Illustrative of English Church History* (London, 1914), pp. 428, 437.

A hundred marks: At this time a monetary measurement in England, the value of one mark being 13 shillings and fourpence.

PAGE 9] *Shall diligently and faithfully . . . to be kept as holy days:* Cf. injunction 33 of the Injunctions of 1559, in Gee and Hardy, *Documents,* p. 433.

PAGE 10] *Oyer and Determiner:* A variant of oyer and terminer, this concerns a commission directed to the King's judges and/or others, to hear and determine indictments on specified offenses at the assizes. *Assize:* This refers to sessions, or assizes, held periodically in each county for the purpose of administering civil and criminal justice, by judges acting under certain special commissions.

PAGE 12] *Feast of . . . Saint Michael the Archangel:* September 29.

Commissaries . . . ordinaries: Commissaries were officers who represented bishops in parts of their dioceses. The word *ordinary* refers to archbishops, bishops, and their deputies.

Provided always . . . Sixth: See note to the rubric on p. 48.

PAGE 13] *With the advice of her commissioners . . . for causes ecclesiastical:* This is a reference to the Supremacy Act of 1559 (sec. 8), whereby the Queen was empowered to appoint commissioners to exercise ecclesiastical jurisdiction. On this, see R. G. Usher, *The Rise and Fall of the High Commission* (Oxford, 1913); and C. G. Bayne, "The Visitation of the Province of Canterbury, 1559," *English Historical Review* XXVIII (1913); 659 ff.

Metropolitan: A bishop having authority over a province; in England, the archbishops of Canterbury and York.

THE PREFACE

This preface, which deals only with "common prayers" and not with the whole Prayer Book, is based upon the preface to the first recension of Cardinal Quiñones's breviary. Cf. F. E. Brightman, *The English Rite,* 2 vols. (London, 1915), I, lxxxiv, 34–39; and F. A. Gasquet and E. Bishop, *Edward VI and the Book of Common Prayer* (London, 1890), pp. 356–70, where the development of the preface is traced through a comparison of Quiñones's text, Cranmer's early text in MS Reg.7 B. IV., and the 1549 Prayer Book. The preface alone shows Cranmer's debt to Cardinal Quiñones, from whom basic principles were derived.

PAGE 14] *Responds . . . synodals:* "Responds" were short anthems interrupting the Lessons, and longer anthems at the close of the Lessons, bearing upon the Scripture read. "Verses" were the versicles, or short sentences, occurring in the Breviary. "Commemorations" were collects, antiphons, and the like, continued for a day or two, or perhaps an octave, after some festival day. "Synodals" refer to the publication or recital of provincial constitutions in parish churches.

PAGE 15] *The service in this Church of England . . . not been edified thereby:* See Cranmer's defense of the use of English, rather than the traditional Latin, in public worship, in his reply to the Cornish rebels in 1549 in *English Historical Documents, 1485–1558,* ed. C. H. Williams (New York, 1967), pp. 368–71. Also, cf. Nicholas Udall's answer to the rebels, in N. Pocock, *Troubles Connected with the Prayer Book of 1549,* Camden Society Publications, n.s., 37 (Westminster, 1884), pp. 153–54. The subject was debated at the Westminster Disputation at the end of March, 1559. Cf. E. Cardwell, *A History of Conferences,* 3d ed. (Oxford, 1849), pp. 56 ff.

Notwithstanding that the ancient fathers . . . called a nocturn: At nocturnal assemblies for worship psalms were recited. In England night assemblies continued until at least the eighth century. Thus a portion of the Psalms came to be called a "nocturn."

Rules called the pie: The pie was a table indicating which services belonged to each day. It was the same as the *Ordinale of Directorum Sacerdotum.* Cf. W. Maskell, *Monumenta ritualia Ecclesiae Anglicanae,* 2d ed. (Oxford, 1882), I, xlvii–xlviii.

Here is drawn out a calendar: This was normally a list or table of the days of the Christian year, indicating special observances. See the Prayer Book Calendar, pp. 36–47.

Anthems, responds, invitatories: "Anthems" were responses made by the choir or people at the conclusion of Psalms or Lessons, or at other intervals in the service. "Invitatories" were texts of Scripture, chosen for the day, used before and after every second verse of the Venite, itself called the invitatory psalm. For "responds" see note to p. 14.

PAGE 16] *Some following Salisbury use:* The liturgical customs of a particular ecclesiastical center were known as "the use" of that place. There were more uses in England than those mentioned here, but these were the principal ones and that of Salisbury (*Sarum* in Latin) was most prominent. See Cuming, *History of Anglican Liturgy*, chap. 1, esp. pp. 30–31.

PAGE 17] *in any language that they themselves do understand:* Cf. the Letters Patent included in the *Liber precum publicarum*, a Prayer Book intended for scholars and published in 1560, in W. K. Clay, ed., *Liturgical Services: Liturgies and Occasional Forms of Prayer Set Forth in the Reign of Queen Elizabeth*, Parker Society Publications, 30 (Cambridge, 1847), pp. 301–2.

And shall toll a bell . . . to pray with him: Cf. Maskell, *Monumenta*, II, xxxi ff.

Of Ceremonies

In the background of this essay, which first appeared in the 1549 Book, are two sets of Articles, the Ten of 1536 and the Thirteen of 1538. Both sets and the present essay regard ceremonies as of human institution and therefore alterable by proper authority, but the Ten Articles would retain traditional ceremonies and explain them, whereas the Thirteen Articles and this essay would see the ceremonies reduced to a minimum. Cf. Brightman, *English Rite*, I, lxxxiv–lxxxv.

PAGE 18] *Of such ceremonies:* For a discussion of the meaning of the term *ceremonies* in this place, see A. J. Stephens, *The Book of Common Prayer*, 3 vols. (London, 1849–54), I, 137–41. Stephens preferred Johnson's definition, "outward rite, external form in religion," which is more general than some (p. 138).

PAGE 19] *Augustine . . . Jews:* St. Augustine, Epist. 54, ad Jan. Cf. Brightman, *English Rite*, I, 42.

PAGE 20] *But now, as concerning those persons . . . to reform their judgments:* For the Anglican argument on behalf of ceremonies, against Puritan objections, see Richard Hooker, *Of the Laws of Ecclesiastical Polity*, IV.i.1, in *Works*, ed. John Keble, 7th ed., rev. R. W. Church and F. Paget, 3 vols. (Oxford, 1888), I, 417 ff.

For we think it convenient . . . without error or superstition: See the debate on this subject at the Westminster Disputation (1559) in Cardwell, *History of Conferences*, pp. 72 ff.

THE TABLE AND CALENDAR

For a discussion of the Calendar and Lectionary which follow, see F. Procter and W. H. Frere, *A New History of the Book of Common Prayer* (London, 1911), chap. 9; and W. K. Lowther Clarke, ed., *Liturgy and Worship* (New York, 1932), pp. 201–44 (Calendar), 296–301 (Lectionary). For sources and a comparison of different editions, see Brightman, *English Rite*, I, 46–125. On the Church Year in general, see A. A. McArthur, *The Christian Year and Lectionary Reform* (London, 1958); and Noële M. Denis-Boulet, *The Christian Calendar*, trans. P. Hepburne-Scott (New York, 1960), esp. chap. 4. For a theological explanation of time by an Elizabethan, see Hooker, *Laws*, V.lxix, in *Works*, II, 381 ff.

A BRIEF DECLARATION WHEN EVERY TERM BEGINNETH AND ENDETH

This is a table of terms or times when the courts of law sat and conducted their proceedings. Cf. C. R. Cheney, *Handbook of Dates* (London, 1955), pp. 65–69.

AN ALMANAC FOR THIRTY YEARS

The Church Year is based upon the date of Easter, and thus the Almanac is concerned with the establishing of this date for each year. For an explanation of this, see Massey H. Shepherd, *The Oxford American Prayer Book Commentary* (New York, 1950), pp. lii–lvii. And see W. M. Campion and W. J. Beamont, eds., *The Prayer Book Interleaved* (London, 1870), pp. 47–57; and Charles Neil and J. M. Willoughby, eds., *The Tutorial Prayer Book* (London, 1912), pp. 57–75.

JANUARY

The table that follows is composed as follows: In the first column are the Golden Numbers, ranging from 1 to 19, with reference to a cycle of 19 years in which it was thought that the phases of the moon would recur on the same days in the Calendar. In the second column are to be found the letters indicating the day of the week. The third column contains two things, (1) the old Roman Calendar and (2) special notations, including festival days and the signs of the Zodiac. See Cheney, *Handbook of Dates*, p. 75. The fourth column is composed of the days of the month, but is tied to "The Table for the Order of the Psalms to Be Said at Morning and Evening Prayer" (see p. 24), and thus no designation is given for the thirty-first day, the Psalms for the thirtieth day being repeated the day after. Cf. "The Order How the Psalter Is Appointed to Be Read" (pp. 22–23). In the remaining columns the first and second Lessons for Morning and Evening Prayer are indicated. Cf. George Harford, Morley Stevenson, and J. W. Tyrer, eds., *The Prayer Book Dictionary* (London, 1912), p. 117.

PAGE 36] *Sol in Aquario:* Concerning these signs, see pp. 381–82.

PAGE 38] *Easter term:* See "A Brief Declaration when Every Term Beginneth and Endeth" (p. 34).

PAGE 42] *Dog days begin:* This was a period of four to six weeks between July and early September, called "dog days" with reference to the rising of the Dog Star (Sirius), but popularly the sultry part of summer when dogs go mad.

PAGE 43] *Lammas:* The word comes from the Anglo-Saxon and means "Loaf-mass." It is the day on which there was an offering of loaves made from the new wheat. The festival is also that of St. Peter ad Vincula, commemorating the release of St. Peter from his imprisonment at Jerusalem (Acts 12).

PAGE 44] "By 1578 Sept. 7 was marked with 'Nati. of Eliza.,' i.e., Elizabeth's birthday" (Brightman, *English Rite*, I, ccxiii).

THE ORDER WHERE MORNING AND EVENING PRAYER SHALL BE USED AND SAID

Concerning Morning Prayer, Evening Prayer, and the Litany, cf. E. C. Ratcliff, "The Choir Offices," in Clarke, *Liturgy and Worship*, pp. 257–95; Procter and Frere, *New History of the Book of Common Prayer*, pp. 347–429; Brightman, *English Rite*, I, lxxxiv–xciii, 129 ff.; Hamon L'Estrange, *The Alliance of Divine Offices* (2d ed. 1690; 4th ed., Library of Anglo-Catholic Theology, Oxford, 1846), chaps. 3, 4. For the Sarum Breviary, see F. Procter and C. Wordsworth, eds., *Breviarum ad usum insignis ecclesiae Sarum*, 3 vols. (Cambridge, 1879–86). Along with this, see J. W. Legg, *The Second Recension of the Quignon Breviary*, Henry Bradshaw Society Publications, 35, 42, 2 vols. (London, 1908–12). For Cranmer's experiments based upon the Sarum

Breviary, Cardinal Quiñones's reforms, and his observation of Lutheran reforms, cf. J. W. Legg, ed., *Cranmer's Liturgical Projects*, Henry Bradshaw Society Publications, 50 (London, 1915). For Puritan objections, see W. H. Frere and C. E. Douglas, eds., *Puritan Manifestoes*, Church Historical Society Publications, 72 (London, 1907), pp. 29, 144. For an Anglican defense, see Hooker, *Laws*, V.xix–xlix, in *Works*, II, 64–218.

PAGE 48] *In the accustomed place:* By the accustomed place evidently meant the chancel where the offices had long been read, rather than the crossing or nave which the 1552 rubric might be taken to imply. Some interpret this direction as conservative, perhaps influenced by the Queen. Cf. Stephens, *Book of Common Prayer*, I, 325 ff., and Neil and Willoughby, *Tutorial Prayer Book*, pp. 77–78. See p. 377 and n. 17.

And the chancels shall remain as they have done in times past: This is a reference to the fact that some wished to see the screen (*cancelli*) dividing choir or chancel and nave removed for better auditory and visual communication. But the rubric indicates that the Queen, like Cranmer before her, resisted such reform. Cf. Stephens, I, 346–49; and esp. G. W. O. Addleshaw and F. Etchells, *The Architectural Setting of Anglican Worship* (London, 1948), pp. 30–31, where it is said: "The first feature in the Elizabethan arrangement of churches is the continuation of the idea that they are made up of self-contained cells."

And here is to be noted . . . in the beginning of this book: This is commonly called the Ornaments Rubric and was the subject of great controversy from 1559 on, being particularly offensive to the Puritans, for the first *Book of Common Prayer* had retained the use of many of the medieval garments and vestments. This rubric was further defined in the "Interpretations of the Bishops" (1560–61), where it was ordered that the cope be worn at the Lord's Supper and the surplice at all other "ministrations" (W. H. Frere, ed., *Visitation Articles and Injunctions of the Period of the Reformation*, Alcuin Club Collections, 14–16, 3 vols. [London, 1910], I, 70). This was repeated, but modified, in the "Advertisements" (1566), where copes and surplices were ordered worn in cathedrals but surplices only in parish churches (*ibid.*, p. 175). See also J. T. Micklethwaite, *The Ornaments of the Rubric*, Alcuin Club Tracts, 1 (London, 1897).

AN ORDER FOR MORNING PRAYER

PAGE 49] *The minister shall read with a loud voice:* This reflects a reformation principle that worship be in the language spoken by the people and be audible.

Item 53 of the Royal Injunctions of 1559 ordered "that all ministers and readers of public prayers, chapters, and homilies shall be charged to read leisurely, plainly, and distinctly" (Frere, *Visitation Articles*, III, 25).

PAGE 51] *The absolution:* For an interpretation of absolution, or forgiveness of sins, see Hooker, *Laws*, Book VI, in *Works*, III, 1–107. For seventeenth-century interpretations, see L'Estrange, *Alliance*, pp. 108–9, 448–49; and John Cosin, *Works*, V (Oxford, 1855), 47, 163–64, 234, 444–45.

PAGE 53] *Te Deum laudamus:* A nonscriptural hymn generally attributed to Bishop Niceta of Remesiana (d. after 414). Medieval legend attributed it to Saints Ambrose and Augustine. The hymn terminated the office of Matins (nocturns), see Sarum Breviary (Sundays and Festivals). See Shepherd, *Oxford American Prayer Book Commentary*, pp. 10–11; William Palmer, *Origines liturgicae*, 2 vols. (Oxford, 1832), I, 226–30; and on this and other canticles, Vernon Staley, *Liturgical Studies* (London, 1907), chap. 9.

PAGE 54] *Or this canticle:* This canticle, which was a part of Sunday Lauds (the ancient Matins), is an apocryphal addition to the Book of Daniel, inserted between 3:23 and 3:24; cf. *The Oxford Annotated Bible with Apocrypha*, Revised Standard Version, ed. H. G. May and B. M. Metzger (New York, 1965), Apoc. pp. 209–12.

PAGE 57] *Benedictus:* This canticle is derived from Luke 1:68–79 and is otherwise known as the Song of Zacharias. It was a part of daily Lauds. Cf. Shepherd, *Oxford American Prayer Book Commentary*, p. 14.

PAGE 59] *The first of the day . . . at the Communion:* That is, the Collect appointed in the section marked "Collects, Epistles, and Gospels" in this book, beginning on p. 77. The Calendar and Almanac preceding Morning Prayer indicate which Collect is to be read.

AN ORDER FOR EVENING PRAYER

PAGE 63] *Nunc dimittis:* Luke 2:29–32, otherwise known as the Song of Simeon.

PAGE 65] *Quicunque vult:* Popularly, but mistakenly, called the Athanasian Creed. Cf. J. N. D. Kelly, *The Athanasian Creed* (London, 1964). For a theological defense of its use, see Hooker, *Laws*, V.xlii.6–13, in *Works*, II, 181–89.

THE LITANY

The Litany, patterned after the ancient litany form of prayer, was an integral part of Elizabethan formal worship. The English Litany, first drafted by Cranmer in Henry VIII's reign (see p. 350), was used separately or sung in procession. The Edwardian Injunctions (1547) ordered that it be sung or said immediately before High Mass; cf. Frere, *Visitation Articles*, II, 124, and see also pp. 159, 168, 181, 234. Although it was customary, the singing of the Litany in procession was curtailed, and the Litany was read or sung with the "priests and choirs" kneeling "in the midst of the church" (item 18, Injunctions [1559], *ibid.*, III, 14). An exception was made for Rogation days. Cf. item 19, Injunctions (1559), *ibid.*, p. 15; and item [19] 4, of the "Interpretations of the Bishops, 1560–1," *ibid.*, pp. 60, 69. For examples of music for the singing of the Litany, see E. H. Fellowes and S. H. Nicholson, *Four Settings of the Litany: From Early Sources* (London, 1936). In time the Litany became a fixed part of the sequence of Sunday common prayer, being said or sung between Morning Prayer and Holy Communion. Archbishop Grindal's Injunctions for York (1571) directed that Morning Prayer, Litany, and Holy Communion should be said together, without "pause or stay" (Frere, *Visitation Articles*, III, 286). This is the first mention of the three services forming an unbroken whole; cf. Procter and Frere, *New History of the Book of Common Prayer*, p. 424. See also, E. G. C. F. Atchley, *The People's Prayers*, Alcuin Club Tracts, 6 (London, 1906).

PAGE 68] *To be used upon Sundays, Wednesdays, and Fridays:* The Litany was regularly used on Sundays before Holy Communion and was to be recited on Wednesdays and Fridays. Cf. Item 49 of the Royal Injunctions (1559), in Frere, *Visitation Articles*, III, 22.

And at other times, when it shall be commanded by the ordinary: That is, special occasions designated by the bishop or his deputy.

PAGE 69] *And privy conspiracy:* In accordance with the intent of the Act of Uniformity (1559), there was deleted from the Prayer Book at this point the following: "from the tyranny of the bishop of Rome and all his detestable enormities" (Brightman, *English Rite*, I, 176).

PAGE 74] *For Rain:* The prayers which follow, up to the last Collect, are not an integral part of the Litany and in some subsequent Prayer Books are located elsewhere. See Procter and Frere, *New History of the Book of Common Prayer*, pp. 426–28; and Palmer, *Origines liturgicae*, I, 301–7.

THE COLLECTS, EPISTLES, AND GOSPELS

With this section of Propers (Collects, Epistles, and Gospels) the Book of Common Prayer begins to deal with that material which was to be found in the medieval Missal. Using the Calendar, it is here that the Propers appointed for a given celebration of the Holy Communion are to be found. In the background is the Sarum Missal, which can be most conveniently consulted, alongside the texts of the 1549, 1552, and 1661 Prayer Books, in Brightman, *English Rite*, I, 200 ff. For the Sarum Missal alone, as translated, see Frederick E. Warren, *The Sarum Missal in English*, Alcuin Club Collections, 11, 2 vols. (London, 1913), I, 67 ff. For commentary on this section as a whole, see Shepherd, *Oxford American Prayer Book Commentary*, p. 90; Kenneth Donald Mackenzie, "Collects, Epistles, and Gospels," in Clarke, *Liturgy and Worship*, pp. 374–409; Cosin, *Works*, V, 69–83, 247–98, 456, 457; L'Estrange, *Alliance*, chap. 5; and, for an extensive theological commentary, John Boys, *An Exposition of the Dominical Epistles and Gospels used in our English Liturgie throughout the whole yeere* (London, 1610); and Charles Wheatly, *A Rational Illustration of the Book of Common Prayer* (Cambridge, 1858), pp. 190–289. Concerning Collects, Epistles, and Gospels as liturgical forms in particular, see the notes concerning them in the Holy Communion.

PAGE 102] *The Sunday Called Septuagesima:* This is the beginning of the pre-Lenten season, peculiar to the Roman Rite. The Latin titles indicate, roughly, seventy days before Easter (Septuagesima), sixty days before Easter (Sexagesima), and, more accurately, fifty days before Easter (Quinquagesima).

PAGE 164] *The Fifth Sunday:* Otherwise known as Rogation Sunday, because of the three Rogation days following when provisions were made for the offering of intercessions for the fruits of the earth. See Frere, *Visitation Articles*, III, 15, for liturgical directions contained in the 1559 Injunctions.

PAGE 225] *Give us grace so to be established by thy holy gospel:* Keating Clay noted that very early in Elizabeth's reign, perhaps in the 1560s, this Collect was changed to read, "Give us grace so that we be not like children carried away with every blast of vain doctrine, but firmly to be established in the truth of thy holy Gospel" (*Liturgical Services*, p. 167).

HOLY COMMUNION

Concerning the Holy Communion in general see the note to p. 77, and see the notes following.

PAGE 247] The first three rubrics are concerned with ecclesiastical discipline. See S. L. Ollard, G. Crosse, and M. F. Bond, eds. *A Dictionary of English Church History*, 3d ed. (London, 1948), pp. 180–83. More particularly they are concerned to protect the Holy Communion from abuse, and the communicants from damnation. See Article 29 of the Thirty-nine Articles of Religion and the exhortations which follow in the Holy Communion, pp. 254–59. The questions concerning parishioners making their communions was dealt with frequently at the time in the law. See Edmund Gibson, *Codex juris ecclesiastici Anglicani*, 2 vols. (Oxford, 1761), I, 384–87; Frere, *Visitation Articles*, esp. III, 3 (but see the index under "Communion, Admission to the"); and E. Cardwell, *Synodalia* (Oxford, 1842), I, esp. 125 (Canons of 1571), 257–60 (Canons of 1604). Concerning the enforcement of such rubrics and laws, see W. E. Tate, *The Parish Chest* (Cambridge, 1946); and, for example, churchwarden's presentments, such as Sidney A. Peyton, ed., *The Churchwardens' Presentments in the Oxfordshire Peculiars of Dorchester, Thame, and Banbury*, Oxfordshire Record Soc., 10 (Oxford, 1928).

PAGE 248] *The Table having at the Communion time a fair white linen cloth upon it:* The Reformation led in many places to the destruction of altars and the use of tables in their place. In London during the reign of Edward VI, Nicholas Ridley, as Bishop of London, led the way. See his reasons in his *Works*, Parker Society Publications, 39 (Cambridge, 1841), pp. 321–24; and concerning the views of others, see John Hooper, *Later Writings*, Parker Society Publications, 21 (Cambridge, 1852), p. 128; Thomas Cranmer, *Works*, II, Parker Society Publications, 16 (Cambridge, 1846), 524; and James Pilkington, *Works*, Parker Society Publications, 35 (Cambridge, 1842), pp. 544–47. Also of value are G. Burnet, *The History of the Reformation of the Church of England* (London, 1681), II, 158–59, 205; and Lambeth Palace MS 2002, f. 107–9. Two interesting examples of contemporary opinion are the anonymous *Reasons, why the Lordes Boorde shoulde rather be after the forme of a table, than of an aultar*, a printed tract in Corpus Christi College Cambridge MS 113(7), 39; and Bucer on Altars, CCCC MS 113(8), 41. Concerning the altar in Elizabethan times, see Addleshaw and Etchells, *The Architectural Setting of Anglican Worship*, pp. 108–120; Frere, *Visitation Articles*, III, esp. 27–28; and Gibson, *Codex*, I, 390–91.

Concerning the coverings for the Table, see Percy Dearmer, *Linen Ornaments of the Church*, Alcuin Club Tracts, 17 (London, 1929), pp. 9 ff.; and Vernon Staley, ed., *Hierurgia Anglicana* (London, 1902) I, 42 ff.

Shall stand in the body of the church . . . north side of the Table: There is some clarification of what is meant here in W. P. M. Kennedy, *The "Interpretations" of the Bishops*, Alcuin Club Tracts, 8 (London, 1908), p. 31:

"That the table be removed out of the choir [chancel] into the body of the church [nave] before the chancel door, where either the choir seemeth to be too little, or at great feasts of receivings, and at the end of the Communion, to be set up again according to the Injunctions." For the Injunctions, see Frere, *Visitation Articles*, III, 27–28, 61–62, 70–71, 81, 141, 210. See also Staley, *Hierurgia Anglicana*, I, 27–37. The normal place was quite obviously the choir or chancel. For some discussion of both the position of the Table and of the minister at it, see Neil and Willoughby, *Tutorial Prayer Book*, pp. 293–97.

Lord have mercy upon us, and incline our hearts to keep this law: This is an adaptation of the traditional Kyrie eleison of the Mass (Lord, have mercy). See Shepherd, *Oxford American Prayer Book Commentary*, pp. 67–69; and Harford, Stevenson, and Tyrer, *Prayer Book Dictionary*, p. 423.

PAGE 249] *Then shall follow the Collect of the day:* This prayer is found in the collection of Collects, Epistles, and Gospels (the Propers), beginning on p. 77. The correct Collect for a particular day is found by use of the Calendar at the beginning of the book. The Collect, which was a traditional form of prayer reaching back to the Gallican rites, where it gathered up the silent petitions of the people after a preceding litany, has a characteristic form. Normally, it opens with an address to God, with mention of some attribute, usually related to what is to follow. Next there is a petition, often followed by some statement concerning what might be expected once the petition is granted (the "that" clause). Finally there is the pleading or "oblation," praying the preceding "through Jesus Christ our Lord," by whom the prayer is made efficacious. In particular, see Stella Brook, *The Language of the Book of Common Prayer* (New York, 1965), esp. pp. 126–39; Shepherd, *Oxford American Prayer Book Commentary*, p. 70; and Charles Feltoe, in Harford, Stevenson, and Tyrer, *Prayer Book Dictionary*, pp. 210–20. See also W. H. Frere, *A Collection of His Papers on Liturgical and Historical Subjects*, Alcuin Club Collections, 35 (London, 1940), pp. 187–90. On the Collect in the Latin Mass, see Josef A. Jungmann, *The Mass of the Roman Rite*, trans. F. A. Brunner, 2 vols. (New York, 1951–55), I, 359–90.

For the Queen: See Edward O. Smith, Jr., "The Royal Mystique and the Elizabethan Liturgy," *Historical Magazine of the Protestant Episcopal Church* XXXI (1962): 243–54.

PAGE 250] *The priest shall read the Epistle . . . And the Epistle and Gospel being ended:* This is the heart of the Liturgy of the Word, the reading of the Scripture, the Epistle, usually but not always from one of the Epistles of the New Testament, and the Gospel from one of the four New Testament Gospels. The latter has traditionally been considered a high point of the liturgy, involving ceremonial which has been excluded from the 1559 Book. On the liturgical Epistle and Gospel, see the note to p. 77; and see also Harford, Stevenson, and Tyrer, *Prayer Book Dictionary*, pp. 316–17, 371–72; Shepherd, *Oxford American Prayer Book Commentary*, p. 70; Palmer, *Origines liturgicae*, II, 42–53; and, on the Lessons of the Mass, Jungmann, *Mass of the Roman Rite*, I, 391–455.

PAGE 251] *After the Creed . . . by common authority:* The assumption is that the sermon shall be delivered at this point in the Sunday worship of the parish or other church. For an Elizabethan and very Anglican discussion of the sermon and of preaching, over against Puritan views, see Hooker, *Laws*, V.xviii–xxii, in *Works*, II, 61–115. See also Horton Davies, *Worship and Theology in England*, I (Princeton, 1970), chap. 6 (Anglican), chap. 8 (Puritan); J. W. Blench, *Preaching in England in the Late Fifteenth and Sixteenth Centuries* (Oxford, 1964); John Chandos, ed., *In God's Name: Examples of Preaching in England, 1534–1662* (London, 1971). If there should not be a sermon because the clergyman was unlicensed or for some other reason, a homily would be read. The reference in the rubric is to the two authorized books of homilies, the second to be published in 1571, the first appearing by authority of the Privy Council on July 31, 1547. They are listed by title in Article 35 of the Thirty-nine Articles of Religion (cf. Cardwell, *Synodalia*, I, 87), and their use was enforced by this rubric and also by specific direction. Cf. Frere, *Visitation Articles*, III, 10, 18, 70, 99, 157, 254, 258, 278, 298, 305. Concerning the homilies, see John Griffiths, ed., *The Two Books of Homilies* (Oxford, 1859), esp. vii–lxxix; J. T. Tomlinson, *The Prayer Book, Articles and Homilies* (London, 1897), chaps. 9, 10; and Lucius Smith, in Harford, Stevenson, and Tyrer, *Prayer Book Dictionary*, p. 394. On the place of the sermon or homily in the liturgy, see Jungmann, *Mass of the Roman Rite*, I, 456–61. For Puritan objections, see Frere and Douglas, *Puritan Manifestoes*, pp. 23–24; and Horton Davies, *The Worship of the English Puritans* (Westminster, 1948), pp. 64–66.

After such sermon, homily, or exhortation: Not every clergyman was allowed to preach. On licensing, etc., cf. Gibson, *Codex*, I, 306–11; Frere, *Visitation Articles*, I, 148, 196, III, 11, 60, 68, 173, 207; W. P. M. Kennedy, *Elizabethan Episcopal Administration*, Alcuin Club Collections, 25–27, 3 vols. (London, 1924), I, cvi–cvii. If not licensed, he was to use one of the authorized homilies. The exhortation referred to could be one of the homilies specifically called exhortations, or the word could be understood in a general sense. It does not seem to refer to the exhortations following the Prayer for the Whole State of Christ's Church. It could, of course, be a reference to "The form of bidding the prayers to be used generally in this uniform sort," attached to the

Royal Injunctions of 1559, for after the bidding there is the rubric, "And this done, show the Holy-days and fasting days" (Frere, *Visitation Articles*, III, 28–29).

Holy days or fasting days: Richard Hooker presented the case for the retention of feasts and fasts by the Church of England in an exposition beginning with a consideration of the nature of time. Cf. his *Laws*, V.lxix–lxxiii, in *Works*, II, 381–427.

And earnestly exhort them . . . by his discretion: Traditionally, the offertory had involved the offering of bread and wine, among other things; see Jungmann, *Mass of the Roman Rite*, II, 1–70. In the 1549 Book the preparation of the bread and wine was related to the gathering of alms for the poor. By 1552 all mention of the bread and wine was deleted, and no directions were given for placing the elements on the Table. See Brightman, *English Rite*, II, 662–63. This was in line with the efforts of the Reformers to avoid any suggestion that the Holy Communion was a propitiatory sacrifice. See Shepherd, *Oxford American Prayer Book Commentary*, pp. 72–73; and also Francis Clark, S.J., *Eucharistic Sacrifice and the Reformation* (Westminster, Md., and London, 1960). But see also Cyril Richardson's review of Clark's book in *Anglican Theological Review* XLVII, no. 2 (April 1965): 233–35. Concerning offerings for the poor, and alms, see the homily, possibly written by John Jewel, "Alms-Deeds, and Mercifulness toward the Poor and Needy," in *Sermons or Homilies Appointed to Be Read in Churches in the Time of Queen Elizabeth* (London, 1828), pp. 417–36. And see Christopher Hill, *Society and Puritanism*, 2d ed. (New York, 1967); and Whitney R. D. Jones, *The Tudor Commonwealth* (London, 1970), chap. 7.

PAGE 253] *And upon the offering days appointed:* These were Christmas, Easter, the Feast of the Nativity of Saint John the Baptist, and the Feast of Saint Michael. See Clay, *Liturgical Services*, p. 185; Frere, *Visitation Articles*, II, 216, 300, III, 116; Gibson, *Codex*, II, 705.

The due and accustomed offerings: The Latin Prayer Book further defines what is meant here by specifying tithes; see *Liber precum publicarum* (1560), in Clay, *Liturgical Services*, pp. 388, 399. For an Elizabethan explanation of tithes, see Hooker, *Laws*, V.lxxix.7–12, in *Works*, II, 488–92. See also Ollard, Crosse, and Bond, *Dictionary of English Church History*, pp. 607–12; J. Kestell Floyer, *Studies in the History of English Church Endowments* (London, 1917), chap. 8; Christopher Hill, *Economic Problems of the Church: From Archbishop Whitgift to the Long Parliament* (Oxford, 1956).

PAGE 254] *Or any other adversity:* There is no prayer for the dead here, as there had been in the 1549 Book, the Reformers having dropped such petitions because of their convictions concerning purgatory and masses for the dead. See Thomas Becon, *Prayers and Other Pieces,* Parker Society Publications, 4 (Cambridge, 1844), pp. 459–62; John Jewel, *Works,* Parker Society Publications, 23–26, 4 vols. (Cambridge, 1845–50), II, 473–75; Edmund Grindal, *Remains,* Parker Society Publications, 19 (Cambridge, 1843), pp. 23–24. But in the Royal Injunctions of 1559 direction is given in a bidding prayer for praise to God "for all those departed out of this life in the faith of Christ." (See Frere, *Visitation Articles,* III, 29). And the Primer (1559) provides for remembrances of the dead in the *Dirige.* See W. K. Clay, ed., *Private Prayers,* Parker Society Publications, 37 (Cambridge, 1851), p. 67; see also *ibid.,* p. 59*n.*

Then shall follow this exhortation: On the three exhortations which follow, see Shepherd, *Oxford American Prayer Book Commentary,* pp. 85–90; and Booty, "Preparation for the Lord's Supper in Elizabethan England," *Anglican Theological Review* XLIX, no. 2 (April 1967): 136–39. The first exhortation, by Peter Martyr Vermigli (cf. *The Commonplaces of . . . Peter Martyr,* trans. A. Marten [London, 1583], pp. 137–38; and A. Beesley, "An Unpublished Source of the Book of Common Prayer: Peter Martyr Vermigli's Adhortatio ad Coenam Domini Mysticam," *Journal of Ecclesiastical History* XVIII [1967]: 253–58), was prepared in the present form for the 1552 Book. The second and third were derived from the Order of Communion (1548). Cf. Cuming, *History of Anglican Liturgy,* pp. 61 ff., 364–65; H. A. Wilson, ed., *The Order of the Communion, 1548,* Bradshaw Society, 34 (London, 1908).

PAGE 257] *Therefore if there be any of you . . . and avoiding of all scruple and doubtfulness:* This passage has been regarded as a remnant of auricular confession which the Reformers sought to destroy. Cf. Cosin, *Works,* V, 99–100, 326–27. On Anglican attitudes to auricular confession, see P. E. More and F. L. Cross, eds., *Anglicanism* (Milwaukee, 1935), pp. 513–21. See also H. R. McAdoo, *The Structure of Caroline Moral Theology* (London, 1949); and Thomas Wood, *English Casuistical Divinity during the Seventeenth Century* (London, 1952).

Then shall the priest say this exhortation: The rubric indicates that this exhortation was always to be used, whereas the others were to be used on occasion, as needed.

PAGE 259] *Almighty God our heavenly Father . . . through Jesus Christ our Lord:* In this prayer the absolution is pronounced in a way in which it is not in Morning Prayer. It was a sensitive subject in a basically nonclerical society. Concerning the question of absolution, one must consider the *Misereatur* and *Confiteor*. Cf. Jungmann, *Mass of the Roman Rite*, I, 298–311; the Ordinal (1559), in Clay, *Liturgical Services*, p. 292. See also Jewel, *Works*, III, pp. 351 ff.; Hooker, *Laws*, VI, in *Works*, III, 1–107; and the works of McAdoo and Wood mentioned in the note to p. 257.

PAGE 260] *Lift up your hearts:* With this, the Sursum Corda, the consecration, thanksgiving, or canon proper begins. It is the central and most solemn part of the Holy Communion, in the estimation of most Anglican divines of the sixteenth century and after. See Jungmann, *Mass of the Roman Rite*, II, 101 ff., for a discussion of the Canon in the Roman Mass. On Anglican theology with respect to the consecration, see pp. 364–66; and also note especially here E. C. Ratcliff, "The English Usage of Eucharistic Consecration, 1548–1662," *Theology* LX (1957): 229–36, 273–80; C. C. Richardson, "Cranmer and the Analysis of Eucharistic Doctrine," *Journal of Theological Studies*, n.s., XVI (1965): 421–37; Davies, *Worship and Theology*, vol. I, chap. 3; and C. W. Dugmore, *Eucharistic Doctrine in England from Hooker to Waterland* (London, 1942). For an Elizabethan understanding, see Hooker, *Laws*, V.1–lvii, lxvii–lxviii, in *Works*, II, 219–59, 348–80.

PAGE 262] *Therefore with angels . . . O Lord most high:* The Sanctus is derived from Isa. 6:1–3; cf. Rev. 4:8.

PAGE 263] *We do not presume . . . and he in us. Amen:* The Prayer of Humble Access is taken from the Order of Communion (1548). Based upon Matt. 8:5–13 and 15:21–28, and upon John 6:53–56, the prayer, composed by Cranmer, shows the influence of medieval Collects and the Liturgy of Saint Basil. See Shepherd, *Oxford American Prayer Book Commentary*, p. 82.

Remembrance of me. . . . Then shall the minister: The structure of the Canon here deviates markedly from that of the Roman Rite and from the 1549 Book. Here, the communion of priest and people is inserted into the midst of the prayer, as it were, to be followed by either the Oblation or the Thanksgiving. On this, see p. 370; and also *Prayer Book Studies 4: The Eucharistic Liturgy*, Standing Liturgical Commission of the Episcopal Church (New York, 1953), pp. 54–72.

Receive the communion in both kinds: The Reformers insisted that communion be administered in both kinds, bread and wine, and not bread alone as had become customary during the Middle Ages. See Gibson, *Codex*, I, 396–97; Gee and Hardy, *Documents Illustrative of English Church History* (London, 1914), pp. 322–28; and Jewel, *Works*, I, 204–62.

PAGE 264] *In their hands kneeling:* The Puritans objected to kneeling here. See Frere and Douglas, *Puritan Manifestoes*, p. 24; and Davies, *Worship of the English Puritans*, pp. 61–64. Kneeling they saw as related in the popular mind to the medieval practice of adoration of the consecrated Host, and as implying a Real Presence. Earlier concerns had led to the intrusion of a rubric, the Black Rubric, into the 1552 Book (see Editor's Preface, p. vii, and Brightman, *English Rite*, II, 721), which was intended to guard against the misinterpretation of kneeling at communion. This rubric was omitted from the 1559 Book, and the practice of kneeling was defended. See Jewel, *Works*, I, 319; and Hooker, *Laws*, V.lxviii.3, in *Works*, II, 365–66.

The body of our Lord . . . with thanksgiving: Here, as also in the sentences for the administration of the cup, the first sentence is from the 1549 Book and the second from the 1552 Book, in accordance with the 1559 Act of Uniformity. See p. 340.

PAGE 265] *Then shall be said or sung:* For a sixteenth-century setting for the Gloria in excelsis and other parts of the Holy Communion, see, for instance, E. H. Fellowes, *The Office of the Holy Communion as Set by John Merbecke* (Oxford, 1949); and consult, Peter Le Huray, *Music and the Reformation in England, 1549–1660* (London, 1967).

Glory be to God on high: The Gloria in excelsis followed the Kyrie in 1549. On this, the Angelic Hymn, as it is known in the West, see J. F. Keating, in Harford, Stevenson, and Tyrer, *Prayer Book Dictionary*, pp. 394–95; and Shepherd, *Oxford American Prayer Book Commentary*, p. 84.

PAGE 266] *Collects to be said after the offertory when there is no communion:* We have here a direct reference to the Ante Communion which became customary in the Elizabethan church. In order to finish off the sequence of Morning Prayer, Litany, and Ante Communion neatly, the use of the following Collects was suggested. See Frere, *Visitation Articles*, I, 252–53, for specific references indicating attempts to adjust to needs and practices of the time. Concerning these Collects, see Shepherd, *Oxford American Prayer Book Commentary*, pp. 49–50; Palmer, *Origines liturgicae*, II, 162–63; Stephens, *Book of Common Prayer*, II, 1225–27.

PAGE 267] *And if there be not above twenty . . . communicate with the priest:* On this rubric, guarding against private masses, cf. Gibson, *Codex*, I, 388–89; Frere, *Visitation Articles*, II, 237, 274, III, 89, 103, 148, 152; Jewel, *Works*, I, 104 ff. But the Puritans were not satisfied; cf. Frere and Douglas, *Puritan Manifestoes*, p. 25.

And in cathedral and collegiate churches . . . reasonable cause to the contrary: Cf. Frere, *Visitation Articles*, II, 200, 216, 315–16, 317, 421, III, 37, 75, 94, 135, 193, 319, etc. The articles and injunctions indicate some variety in practice. See also Gibson, *Codex*, I, 399.

And to take away the superstition . . . conveniently may be gotten: This rubric was continued from the 1552 Book, but it was ignored when in the Royal Injunctions (1559) order was given "that the same sacramental bread be made and formed plain, without any figure thereupon of the same fineness and fashion round, though somewhat bigger in compass and thickness, as the usual bread and wafer heretofore named singing cakes" (Frere, *Visitation Articles*, III, 28). On all of this, see Reginald M. Woolley, *The Bread of the Eucharist*, Alcuin Club Tracts, 10 (London, 1913), pp. 33 ff.; and Staley, *Hierurgia Anglicana*, II, 129–42.

And if any of the bread . . . to his own use: Cf. Stephens, II, 1237–39.

The bread and wine . . . by order of their houses every Sunday: Cf. the 1549 rubric, in Brightman, *English Rite*, II, 716. Cf. Gibson, *Codex*, I, 392–93; and Frere, *Visitation Articles*, II, 284, III, 283–84.

PAGE 268] *And note, . . . of which Easter to be one:* This was then the recognized rule. Cf. Frere, *Visitation Articles*, III, 275, 287, 307, 337. But in Bentham's Injunctions for Coventry and Lichfield (1565), it was "four times in the year" (*ibid.*, p. 167).

And yearly at Easter . . . at that time to be paid: See note to p. 373; Gibson, *Codex*, II, 705; Stephens, *The Book of Common Prayer*, II, 1241.

THE MINISTRATION OF BAPTISM

The Prayer Book baptismal rite is derived basically from the Sarum Manual, but shows the influence of Lutheran Church Orders and of the *Consultation* of Hermann of Cologne. See in particular, Brightman, *English Rite*, II, 724–61. For the medieval rite, cf. Maskell, *Monumenta*, I, 22–36. For commentary, cf. Shepherd, *Oxford American Prayer Book Commentary*, pp. 271–73; W. K. Lowther Clarke, "Holy Baptism," in Clarke, *Liturgy and Worship*, pp. 410–28; T. Thompson, *The Offices of Baptism and Confirmation* (Cambridge, 1914).

Concerning the English Reformers' understanding of Baptism, see Article 27 of the Thirty-nine Articles of Religion, in Cardwell, *Synodalia*, I, 100; the Catechism that follows Baptism in the Book of Common Prayer; Jewel, *Works*,

III, 460–65; Hooker, *Laws*, V.lix–lxv, in *Works*, II, 262–337; G. W. Bromiley, *Baptism and the Anglican Reformers* (London, 1953). On the broader subject of Baptism among the Reformers, Continental as well as English, cf. J. D. C. Fisher, *Christian Initiation: The Reformation Period*, Alcuin Club Collections, 51 (London, 1970); and P. J. Jagger, *Christian Initiation, 1552–1969*, Alcuin Club Collections, 52 (London, 1970).

PAGE 269] *Easter and Whitsuntide:* Cf. Gibson, *Codex*, I, 361–62; Cranmer, *Works*, II, 56n.

Be ministered but upon Sundays and other holy days: Cf. Frere, *Visitation Articles*, II, 238, 265, III, 89, 98, 103; Shepherd, *Oxford American Prayer Book Commentary*, p. 273.

PUBLIC BAPTISM

Concerning Puritan objections to the Prayer Book Public Baptism, cf. Frere and Douglas, *Puritan Manifestoes*, p. 26; Davies, *Worship of the English Puritans*, pp. 69 ff.

PAGE 270] *And then the godfathers, godmothers:* See Harford, Stevenson, and Tyrer, *Prayer Book Dictionary*, p. 371; and John Whitgift, *Works*, Parker Society Publications, 46–48, 3 vols. (Cambridge, 1851–53), III, 118–22.

Must be ready at the font: On the font and the place it occupied in the church, see Addleshaw and Etchells, *Architectural Setting of Anglican Worship*, pp. 23–24, 64–68; Staley, *Hierurgia Anglicana*, I, 3 ff.; Gibson, *Codex*, I, 360.

Then the priest shall say: The exhortation and much of what follows relies upon the *Consultation* of Hermann. See Brightman, *English Rite*, II, 726 ff.; Fisher, *Christian Initiation*, pp. 54 ff.

PAGE 273] *Dost thou forsake . . . nor be led by them:* In the 1549 Book the renunciation was done in three parts, devil, world, flesh, following the order in the Sarum Baptism, thus making this section more dramatic and definite. Conflated as they are here, the emphasis falls on the confession of faith. See Brightman, *English Rite*, II, 736.

All this I steadfastly believe: In the Sarum Baptism the baptizee answered "Credo" after each section of the Creed concerning Father, Son, and Holy Ghost. This was in accordance with practice in the early Church. The 1549 Book followed Sarum in this respect. The 1552 Book put the three sections together and added "All this" and "steadfastly" to the simple Credo, "I believe." See Brightman, *English Rite*, II, 736–37.

Then shall the priest say: The following four prayers or supplications are survivals, via the 1549 Book, of the elaborate Blessing of the Font. See Shepherd, *Oxford American Prayer Book Commentary*, pp. 278–79. For the Sarum rite of Blessing the Font, see Maskell, *Monumenta*, I, 13–21; and Fisher, *Christian Initiation*, pp. 151–56.

PAGE 274] *Naming the child:* On the name and its significance, see the Catechism, p. 283.

Shall dip it in the water: The dipping of the child approximated the early custom of immersion. Indeed the name *Baptism* for the rite was related to words meaning "to dip" and "to deluge." See C. F. D. Moule, *Worship in the New Testament*, Ecumenical Studies in Worship, 9 (Richmond, 1961), p. 52.

And if the child be weak . . . pour water upon it: This represented a concession for special cases, which became the customary use in Anglican churches.

PAGE 275] *Then the priest shall make a cross upon the child's forehead:* The Puritans strenuously objected to this. Cf. Davies, *Worship of the English Puritans*, p. 63, etc. For a defense of the practice, see Whitgift, *Works*, III, 123–31; Hooker, *Laws*, V.lxv.6–11, in *Works*, II, 321–28. So great was the divergence on this subject that in 1604 a canon was enacted explaining and enforcing the practice. See Gibson, *Codex*, I, 364–65 (Canon 30). See also Ernest Beresford-Cooke, *The Sign of the Cross in the Western Liturgies*, Alcuin Club Tracts, 7 (London, 1907).

This short exhortation following: This exhortation must be understood in terms of Christian education in the Elizabethan parish church. That education was based upon what every Christian was expected to know: the Lord's Prayer, the Ten Commandments, and the Creed. Tools for learning these things consisted of books such as the Primer, the Prayer Book Catechism, and other catechisms, and what was done at service time in the church, in particular at Evening Prayer when the Catechism was rehearsed.

OF THEM THAT BE BAPTIZED IN PRIVATE HOUSES

The Puritans took great exception to private Baptisms, as well as to Baptisms by women. Cf. Frere and Douglas, *Puritan Manifestoes*, p. 26. Because of such objections, great care was taken concerning them, as can be seen in the specifications for the rite given here, and in Gibson, *Codex*, I, 367–70; and Frere, *Visitation Articles*, III, 62, 69, 89, 103. For an explanation and defense, see Hooker, *Laws*, V.lxi.1–5, in *Works*, II, 273–80. See also Fisher, *Christian Initiation*, pp. 135–47. For the peculiarities of the rite itself, the Prayer Book is reliant in large part on the Saxon *Agenda das ist kirchenordnung*. See Brightman, *English Rite*, II, 748–49.

CONFIRMATION

There has been much debate concerning the history and meaning of the Confirmation rite in the Church of England. The literature is extensive; among the best discussions are W. K. Lowther Clarke, et al., *Confirmation*, 2 vols. (London, 1926–27); Dom Gregory Dix, *The Theology of Confirmation in Relation to Baptism* (Westminster, 1946); *Confirmation Today, Being the . . . Interim Reports . . . Presented to the Convocations . . . in October 1944* (London, 1944); E. C. Ratcliff, "The Relation of Confirmation to Baptism in the Early Roman and Byzantine Liturgies, I and II," *Theology* (September and October 1946); A. E. J. Rawlinson, *Christian Initiation* (London, 1947); *The Theology of Christian Initiation, Being the Report of a Theological Commission Appointed by the Archbishops of Canterbury and York to Advise on the Relations between Baptism, Confirmation, and Holy Communion* (London, 1948); Kendig Brubaker Cully, ed., *Confirmation: History, Doctrine, and Practice* (Greenwich, Conn., 1962), esp. "The Anglican Understanding of Confirmation," by Charles U. Harris, pp. 17 ff., and "The Relation of Baptism and Confirmation," by G. W. H. Lampe, pp. 69 ff., both of whom raise objections concerning Dix's theory; and J. D. C. Fisher, "History and Theology," in *Confirmation Crisis* (New York, 1968), pp. 19–42. Of very great importance for understanding all this is J. D. C. Fisher, *Christian Initiation: Baptism in the Medieval West. A Study in the Disintegration of the Primitive Rite of Initiation*, Alcuin Club Collections, 47 (London, 1965). See also E. C. Whitaker, *The New Services, 1967: A Guide and Explanation; Holy Communion, Baptism, and Confirmation* (London, 1967).

PAGE 283] *That Confirmation should be ministered to them that were of perfect age:* Bishop Bentham's Instructions for Coventry and Lichfield (1565) require "presentment of all children being full seven years of age, and not yet confirmed" (Frere, *Visitation Articles*, III, 163). The "Interpretations of the Bishops" (1560–61) state that none may be admitted to the Holy Communion "before the age of twelve or thirteen years, of good discretion and well instructed before"; that is, of age to be confirmed. Cf. Cully, *Confirmation*, pp.

54–55. This latter would seem to be customary, certainly more so than the seven years or earlier specified in "Bishop Bentham's Instructions." At any rate, the rubrics leave the question of the exact age open.

A Catechism: Concerning the Catechism as it is found here, see Morley Stevenson, "Catechism, the Church," in Harford, Stevenson, and Tyrer, *Prayer Book Dictionary*, pp. 160–63, who points to Alexander Nowell, Dean of Saint Paul's Cathedral in Elizabeth's reign, as instrumental in the authorship. Massey Shepherd, *Oxford American Prayer Book Commentary*, pp. 577–83, believes that "Cranmer certainly had a hand in it," and does not mention Nowell as a possible author. Nowell's *Middle Catechism* and *Smaller Catechism* differ very little from that of the Prayer Book. And his *Catechismus* (1570) takes the Prayer Book Catechism as its basis. See A. Nowell, *A Catechism Written in Latin*, ed. G. E. Corrie, Parker Society Publications, 32 (Cambridge, 1853). On catechizing, cf. Hooker, *Laws*, V.xviii, in *Works*, II, 61–64; and L'Estrange, *Alliance*, chap. 4. Concerning the influence of this Catechism and others (such as those on Ponet and Nowell), see Joan Simon, *Education and Society in Tudor England* (Cambridge, 1966), esp. pp. 240–43, 307–8, 316–26.

Page 284] *And all the elect people of God:* Concerning the doctrine of election as held by the English church, see Article 17 of the Thirty-nine Articles, and commentary on it, in Thomas Rogers, *The Catholic Doctrine of the Church of England: An Exposition of the Thirty-nine Articles*, ed. J. J. S. Perowne, Parker Society Publications, 40 (Cambridge, 1854), pp. 142–58. Cf. E. C. S. Gibson, *The Thirty-nine Articles of the Church of England* (London, 1904), pp. 459–87.

Page 287] *Then shall they be brought . . . a witness of his Confirmation:* At this time the godparents were clearly thought of in relation to Confirmation, as well as Baptism; cf. Gibson, *Codex*, I, 363, 376.

Confirmation: Concerning the Confirmation rite itself, it is best to look first at the relevant texts as found in Brightman, *English Rite*, II, 792–99; and in Fisher, *Christian Initiation: The Reformation Period*, pp. 159–260. This latter is particularly valuable. For the Sarum rite, see Maskell, *Monumenta*, I, 34–36. For Puritan objections to the Anglican rite, see Frere and Douglas, *Puritan Manifestoes*, pp. 27–28. For Anglican teaching during the Elizabethan period, see Jewel, *Works*, II, 1125–28; and Hooker, *Laws*, V.lxvi, in *Works*, II, 337–48.

Page 288] *The curate of every parish . . . in some part of this Catechism:* The rubric gives a fair description of what was expected, and the articles and injunctions of visitation suggest that although there was some variation in practice, yet the catechizing before Evening Prayer on Sundays and holy days was ordinarily done. The Royal Injunctions (1559) generally supported this rubric, although "every second Sunday," that is, every other Sunday, was specified (Frere, *Visitation Articles*, III, 22). Parkhurst, bishop of Norwich, and others specified every Sunday (*ibid.*, III, 101), and some required that an hour rather than a half-hour before Evening Prayer be devoted to the catechizing. See *ibid.*, III, 99, 166, 220, 275–76. See also Gibson, *Codex*, I, 374–78, and note canon 59 of the Canons of 1604: "Ministers to Catechise every Sunday." The routine would appear to be that the curate would call each child by name, a certain number each Sunday or holy day, and ask questions, prompting the children in their responses, there being little likelihood that a child would have a copy to read, even if he were able to do so. Cf. Frere, *ibid.*, III, 220, 258, 275–76, 287, 297, 305.

PAGE 289] *And there shall none be admitted to Holy Communion . . . and be confirmed:* On this see James Arthur Muller, *The Confirmation Rubric* (n.p., n.d.), reprinted from *The Southern Churchman*, May 7, 1938; Gibson, *Codex*, I, 378; Frere, *Visitation Articles*, II, 237; and esp. Fisher, *Christian Initiation: Baptism in the Medieval West*, pp. 124, 134–40. It is clear that confirmation prior to being admitted to Communion was a medieval development, dating from the thirteenth century.

MATRIMONY

On the marriage service, see Shepherd, *Oxford American Prayer Book*, p. 300; *Prayer Book Studies, 10: The Solemnization of Matrimony*, Standing Liturgical Commission of the Episcopal Church (New York, 1958), pp. 3 ff.; Brightman, *English Rite*, I, cxxii–cxxiii; H. E. Scott, in Harford, Stevenson, and Tyrer, *Prayer Book Dictionary*. Concerning the teachings of the time, cf. the homily "Of the State of Matrimony," in *Sermons or Homilies* (London, 1828), pp. 551–66; Jewel, *Works*, II, 1128–29; Hooker, *Laws*, V.lxxviii, in *Works*, II, 427–34. The Prayer Book service shows the influence of the Sarum and York uses, Martin Luther, and the *Consultation* of Hermann of Cologne. Cf. Brightman, *English Rite*, II, pp. 800 ff. The Sarum service can be found in Brightman and also in Maskell, *Monumenta*, I, 42–64. Two services are combined to form the one here: the Betrothal, through the promises, and the Espousals, beginning thereafter with the vows.

PAGE 290] *The banns must be asked:* The banns, or the proclamation and announcing of an impending marriage in order that necessary objections might be made, were customary as a preliminary to marriage in sixteenth-century England. It had, indeed, been enjoined by the Synod of Westminster (1200) and the Fourth Lateran Council (1215). There is ample evidence concerning the enforcement of this rubric. Cf. Gibson, *Codex*, I, 424–25; Frere, *Visitation Articles*, III, 6, 64, 89, 93, 103, 107, 110, etc.; Edwin Sandys, *Sermons*, ed. J. Ayre, Parker Society Publications, 41 (Cambridge, 1841), p. 434.

And if the persons . . . the curate of the other parish: Concerning the enforcement of this, cf. Frere, *Visitation Articles*, III, 89, 109, 110, 220.

PAGE 291] *If no impediment be alleged:* The impediments which might be brought to light were various, such as marrying within the prohibited degrees, precontract, lack of consent of parents, especially where a dependent woman was concerned, bigamy, and so forth. See Gibson, *Codex*, I, 408–24, 431; Frere, *Visitation Articles*, III, 5, 72, 85, 92, 96, 106, 157, 178, 214, etc.; Stephens, *Book of Common Prayer*, III, 1558–1604.

PAGE 292] *Who giveth this woman to be married unto this man?:* This signifies the consent of the parents to the betrothal of the woman in accordance with law and custom. See Gibson, *Codex*, I, 418–21. It is derived from the York Manual; see Brightman, *English Rite*, II, 804.

With the accustomed duty to the priest: Seemingly this offering takes the place of the tokens of espousage, such as gold or silver placed on the Prayer Book. See the 1549 Book, in Brightman, *English Rite*, II, 804. See also Hooker, *Laws*, V.lxxiii.6, in *Works*, II, 429–30, and n.

And clerk: This is the first mention of the parish clerk in the Prayer Book. On his office in relation to the Book of Common Prayer, whereat he assisted the priest, making the responses of the congregation and sometimes reading the Scripture, including the Epistle, cf. J. W. Legg, ed., *The Clerk's Book of 1549*, Henry Bradshaw Society, 25 (London, 1903); E. G. C. F. Atchley, *The Parish Clerk, and His Right to Read the Liturgical Epistle*, Alcuin Club Tracts, 4 (London, 1903); A. Tindal Hart, *The Man in the Pew, 1558–1660* (London, 1966), chap. 4; and Kennedy, *Elizabethan Episcopal Administration*, I, cxlii–cxliv.

And the priest taking the ring . . . of the woman's left hand: The ring was strenuously objected to by the Puritans and initiated a vigorous discussion of the ceremony. See Frere and Douglas, *Puritan Manifestoes*, p. 27; Davies, *Worship of the English Puritans*, pp. 61–62; Whitgift, *Works*, III, 353–54; Hooker, *Laws*, V.lxxiii.6, in *Works*, II, 429–31.

PAGE 293] *Those whom God hath joined together, let no man put asunder:*
This ceremony of the proclamation of the marriage, including the following
statement, was derived from Archbishop Hermann's *Consultation* and was in
line with the aims of the Reformers, making explicit the meaning of the ceremony now concluded.

God the Father, God the Son . . . you may have life everlasting. Amen: This
is the first of two formal blessings in the service. It is not the principal or
"operative" one and is derived from the Sarum rite. See Brightman, *English
Rite*, II, 806.

PAGE 297] *Almighty God, which at the beginning . . . unto your lives end.
Amen:* This is the second and the major blessing of this service and is derived
from the Sarum rite.

Then shall begin the Communion: The Puritans objected to the Holy Communion at this place, the nuptial mass being to them a dangerous popish custom.
See Frere and Douglas, *Puritan Manifestoes*, p. 27. For defense of the custom,
see Whitgift, *Works*, III, 356; and Hooker, *Laws*, V.lxxiii.8, in *Works*, II,
433–34.

Or if there be no sermon, the minister shall read this that followeth: The in-
clusion of this homily was clearly as a result of Lutheran influence, and the
text shows some direct reliance upon Hermann's *Consultation*, or a source common to both. See Brightman, *English Rite*, I, cxxiv, II, 814–16.

THE VISITATION OF THE SICK

Concerning this service, which is based on the Sarum Order of Visitation, see
Brightman, *English Rite*, I, cxxv–cxxvi; Maskell, *Monumenta*, I, 66 ff.;
Shepherd, *Oxford American Prayer Book Commentary*, p. 308; *Prayer Book
Studies 3: The Order for the Ministration of the Sick*, Standing Liturgical
Commission of the Episcopal Church (New York, 1951). On the duties of the
clergy with regard to the sick, cf. Gibson, *Codex*, I, 448–49; and Frere, *Visita-
tion Articles*, III, 14 (Royal Injunctions of 1559), 62–63, 71, 260, 341, 378,
etc. Concerning sickness in general, and the visitation of the sick, see Thomas
Becon, *The Sick Man's Salve*, in *Prayers and Other Pieces*, ed. J. Ayre, Parker
Society Publications, 4 (Cambridge, 1844), pp. 97–191.

PAGE 303] *Then shall the minister examine . . . for discharging of his conscience and quietness of his executors:* Whether it was done here, before the

prayers were begun, or at some other time, it was clearly expected that the clergyman would execute this duty. See Frere, *Visitation Articles*, II, 335, 368, 403.

The minister may not forget . . . liberality toward the poor: See *ibid.*, III, 260. This injunction was derived from Hermann's *Consultation*; see Brightman, *English Rite*, II, 828.

PAGE 306] *Almighty Lord, which is a most strong tower . . . the name of our Lord Jesus Christ. Amen:* In the Sarum Manual (see Maskell, *Monumenta*, I, 83 ff.) and in the 1549 Book, provisions were made for Unction, or anointing with sacred oil, after this prayer. This practice was dropped from the 1552 Book and is absent from the present text. For a discussion of such anointing, see Jewel, *Works*, II, 1135–39, III, 178, 243; James Calfhill, *An Answer to John Martiall's Treatise of the Cross*, ed. R. Gibbings, Parker Society Publications, 11 (Cambridge, 1846), pp. 244–48.

THE COMMUNION OF THE SICK

The 1549 Book, relying here in the opening rubric upon the Brandenburg *Kirchenordnung* and following the traditions as received through the medieval Manual, allowed for the use of the reserved sacrament at the communion of the sick. The 1552 Book dropped this permission from the rubric chiefly because of the objection of Peter Martyr (see John Strype, *Memorials of . . . Cranmer*, 2 vols. [Oxford, 1812], II, 899), with the result that the Holy Communion had to be celebrated anew on each occasion at which sick persons were communicated. On Communion of the Sick, and the reserved sacrament in relation to it, see Brightman, *English Rite*, I, cxxv–cxxvi, II, 842–43; Darwell Stone, *The Reserved Sacrament* (London, 1917), esp. chap. 3; David Leslie Murray, *Reservation: Its Purpose and Method*, Alcuin Club Prayer Book Revision Pamphlets, 10 (London, 1923); and Shepherd, *Oxford American Prayer Book Commentary*, pp. 321–22; W. H. Freestone, *The Sacrament Reserved*, Alcuin Club Collections, 21 (London, 1917).

PAGE 308] *In the time of plague, sweat . . . may alonely communicate with him:* On a subject which influenced much of Elizabethan life, including the Prayer Book, see Charles Creighton, *A History of Epidemics in Britain*, 2 vols. (Cambridge, 1891–94); John Caius, *A Boke or Counseill against the Disease Commonly Called the Sweate* (London, 1552); F. P. Wilson, *The Plague in Shakespeare's London* (Oxford, 1927); Edmund Grindal, *A Fourme to be used in Common Prayer . . . during the time of mortalitie* (1563), in Grindal, *Remains*, pp. 75–120; and John Hooper, *An Homelye to be read in the tyme of pestylence* (1553), in Hooper, *Later Writings*, pp. 163–75.

THE BURIAL OF THE DEAD

The basic source for this service is the medieval Burial office, although there is some evidence of the influence of Hermann's *Consultation*. See Brightman, *English Rite*, II, 848–79. For the Sarum rite, see Brightman and also Maskell, *Monumenta*, I, 104 ff. On this service, see Shepherd, *Oxford American Prayer Book Commentary*, p. 324; Brightman, *English Rite*, I, cxxvi–cxxviii; H. E. Scott, in Harford, Stevenson, and Tyrer, *Prayer Book Dictionary*, pp. 115–16; W. Gressell, *A Commentary on the Order for the Burial of the Dead*, 2 vols. (London, 1836). For a contemporary account, see Staley, *Hierurgia Anglicana*, I, 253–55. Concerning Puritan objections, cf. Frere and Douglas, *Puritan Manifestoes*, p. 28; and Davies, *Worship of the English Puritans*, p. 73. For the views of the English Reformers, see the homily entitled "A Fruitful Exhortation against the Fear of Death," in *Sermons or Homilies*, pp. 97–113; Whitgift, *Works*, III, 361–80; and Hooker, *Laws*, V.lxxv, in *Works*, II, 438–44.

PAGE 309] *Church stile:* This was the lich gate at the entrance to the churchyard, the roofed gateway beneath which the coffin was set down to await the arrival of the minister. The gate served as a barrier to keep out cattle, etc.

Or else the priests: See Clay, *Liturgical Services*, p. 233, n. 5.

PAGE 312] *Almighty God, with whom do live . . . everlasting glory. Amen:* This prayer has been altered from that in the 1549 Book, and from the prayer behind that in the Sarum Manual, so that it is a thanksgiving for the deliverance of the departed rather than a prayer that the sins which the departed "committed in this world be not imputed unto him." Brightman, *English Rite*, II, 872–73. Behind this there is the concern to guard against the doctrine of purgatory. See Article 22 of the Thirty-nine Articles, in Cardwell, *Synodalia*, I, 98; Cranmer, *Works*, II, 181–82; Jewel, *Works*, III, 568; and Hooker, *A Learned Sermon of the Nature of Pride* (Oxford, 1612), sec. 5, in *Works*, III, 637–42.

PAGE 313] *The Collect:* This Collect was found in the 1549 Book in "The Celebration of the Holy Communion when there is a Burial of the Dead." See

Brightman, *English Rite*, II, 876. The Requiem Mass was eliminated in the 1552 Book, and the 1559 Book followed suit. But the *Liber precum publicarum* (1560) provided for such a Mass or Communion. See Clay, *Liturgical Services*, pp. 433–34. And it would seem that such Communions took place, at least where there was the sentiment to support the custom. See Frere, *Visitation Articles*, III, 88, 167, and Gibson, *Codex*, I, 451.

THE THANKSGIVING OF WOMEN AFTER CHILDBIRTH

This service is basically a translation of the service found in the Sarum Manual. Cf. Brightman, *English Rite*, I, cxxviii, II, 880–85; and Maskell, *Monumenta*, I, 38–39. Concerning the service, see Shepherd, *Oxford American Prayer Book Commentary*, p. 305; *Prayer Book Studies, 11: A Thanksgiving for the Birth of a Child*, Standing Liturgical Commission of the Episcopal Church (New York, 1958); H. E. Scott, in Harford, Stevenson, and Tyrer, *Prayer Book Dictionary*, pp. 204–5. For sixteenth-century commentary, cf. Whitgift, *Works*, II, 557–64; and Hooker, *Laws*, V.lxxiv, in *Works*, II, 434–38. Whitgift and Hooker write in terms of Puritan objections. Cf. Frere and Douglas, *Puritan Manifestoes*, pp. 28–29; and Davies, *Worship of the English Puritans*, p. 73.

PAGE 315] *The woman that cometh to give her thanks must offer accustomed offerings:* Perhaps offerings made at the Holy Communion, the intention being that this service take place before the Holy Communion begins. Cf. Stephens, *Book of Common Prayer*, III, 1763.

A COMMINATION

This service, intended for use on Ash Wednesday, takes the place of the blessing and distribution of ashes and the ejection of penitents. See Brightman, *English Rite*, I, cxxix, II, 886–901; A. M. Y. Baylay, in Harford, Stevenson, and Tyrer, *Prayer Book Dictionary*, pp. 222–23. For commentary, see Stephens, *The Book of Common Prayer*, III, 1765–85; and L'Estrange, *Alliance*, pp. 477 ff. See also Clarke, *Liturgy and Worship*, pp. 856–57. For Bucer's commendation of this service in the *Book of Common Prayer*, see his *Censura*, in *Scripta Anglicana* (Basel, 1577), pp. 491–92. Archbishop Grindal's Articles and Injunctions for the Province of York (1571) indicate that the service would be used on Ash Wednesday and on three other occasions during the year. See Frere, *Visitation Articles*, III, 254–55, 278. See also Sandys's articles for London (1571), *ibid.*, p. 304. Note also Clay, *Liturgical Services*, p. 239, n. 2.

PAGE 320] *Then shall they all kneel upon their knees:* Up to this point (including heretofore the fixed comminations and the exhortation) all takes the place of the sermon in the Sarum service. From here on, the service is basically a translation of the medieval service.

Selected Bibliography

Selected Bibliography

1. *Texts:* The texts of all the authorized Books of Common Prayer, Primers, and books of private devotion are to be found among the publications of the Parker Society, originally published in Cambridge, 1841–55, and reprinted by the Johnson Reprint Company, New York and London, 1968. The Everyman's Library edition of the *First and Second Prayer-Books of King Edward the Sixth* contains a useful introduction by E. C. S. Gibson and a "Historical and Bibliographic Note" by E. C. Ratcliff (London and Toronto, 1910; repr. 1949). Since 1891 the Henry Bradshaw Society, London, has been publishing liturgical manuscripts, service books, and illustrative documents which have special reference to and importance for the history and development of the Book of Common Prayer.

2. *Documents:* Two important collections of ecclesiastical, political, and social documents which bear on the development of the Church of England and its worship are: *English Historical Documents, 1485–1558,* ed. C. H. Williams (New York, 1967); and Henry Gee and W. J. Hardy, eds., *Documents Illustrative of English Church History* (London, 1914; repr. New York, 1966). The first two chapters of Edward Cardwell, *A History of Conferences . . . Connected with the Revision of the Book of Common Prayer . . . 1558–1690,* 3d ed. (Oxford, 1849; repr. London, 1966), are concerned specifically with the Elizabethan revision; chapter 2 is a collection of parliamentary bills, letters, and other documents.

3. *Sources:* The most comprehensive treatment of the origins of the Book of Common Prayer is: F. E. Brightman, *The English Rite: Being a Synopsis of the Sources and Revisions of the Book of Common Prayer,* 2 vols. (London, 1915; repr. 1970). Brightman's introductory chapters are particularly useful for relating pre-Reformation liturgical forms and service books to those of the reformed Church of England. In respect to the sources and origins of specific parts of the Book of Common Prayer, W. K. Lowther Clarke, ed., *Liturgy and Worship, a Companion to the Prayer Books of the Anglican Communion* (New York, 1932; repr.

London, 1954), examines the sources and rationale of the Prayer Book services in a series of essays from various hands. This volume also contains essays on Judeo-Christian worship in general and on the history and development of the Book of Common Prayer in particular. Although its focus is the Book of Common Prayer of the Episcopal Church in the United States, Massey H. Shepherd, Jr., ed., *The Oxford American Prayer Book Commentary* (New York, 1950), contains a great deal of material relating to the English Prayer Books as antecedents of the American Book.

4. *History:* Henry Gee, *The Elizabethan Prayer-Book and Ornaments* (London, 1902), is concerned specifically with the history of the 1559 Prayer Book and includes an appendix of relevant documents. General histories of the Book of Common Prayer are: Francis Procter and W. H. Frere, *A New History of the Book of Common Prayer* (London, 1911); G. J. Cuming, *A History of Anglican Liturgy* (London, 1969); and D. E. W. Harrison, *Common Prayer in the Church of England,* rev. ed. (London, 1969). E. L. Parsons and B. H. Jones, *The American Prayer Book: Its Origins and Principles* (New York, 1950), includes material relating to the history of the English Prayer Book.

5. *Literary context:* C. S. Lewis, in *English Literature in the Sixteenth Century* (Oxford, 1954), discusses the Book of Common Prayer in the context of literature contemporary with it. Stella Brook, *The Language of the Book of Common Prayer* (New York, 1965), is a literary and linguistic analysis of the Prayer Book, as is W. K. Lowther Clarke's essay "The Prayer Book as Literature," in W. K. Lowther Clarke, ed., *Liturgy and Worship* (London, 1954). Richmond Noble, *Shakespeare's Biblical Knowledge and Use of the Book of Common Prayer* (London, 1935; repr. New York, 1970), provides an insight into the Prayer Book's pervasive influence in English literature.

6. *Political context:* The emergence and development of the Book of Common Prayer took place in the midst of fluid and complicated political situations. W. K. Jordan, *Edward VI: The Young King* (Cambridge, Mass., 1968), illuminates this in respect to the Prayer Books of 1549 and 1552, and J. E. Neale, *Elizabeth I and Her Parliaments, 1559–1581* (London, 1953), illuminates this in respect to the Prayer Book

of 1559. For an overview of the reformation of the English church and its national and international consequences, see: G. R. Elton, "The Reformation in England," in *The New Cambridge Modern History,* II (Cambridge, 1958), 226–50; and R. B. Wenham, "The British Question, 1559–69," in *The New Cambridge Modern History,* III (Cambridge, 1968), 209–33.

7. Two one-volume encyclopedias containing brief, reliable articles relating to English church matters are: S. L. Ollard, Gordon Crosse, and M. F. Bond, eds., *A Dictionary of English Church History,* 3d ed. (London, 1948); and F. L. Cross and E. A. Livinstone, eds., *The Oxford Dictionary of the Christian Church,* 2d ed. (London, 1974). The latter work has especially useful bibliographical notations accompanying its articles.

DAVID SIEGENTHALER

Episcopal Divinity School

Biblical Index

Biblical Index

This index is of quotations from the Bible noted as such in the text of the 1559 Prayer Book or in other editions. It does not include the many quotations and references which are not specifically identified. Nor does it include the Tables and the Almanac (pp. 22–47). References below are to the page numbers of this edition.

Exodus		128	294
20:1–17	248–49, 285	143:2	50

Deuteronomy		Proverbs	
27:15–26	316–17	1:28–30	318
		19:17	253

Job		Isaiah	
1:21	309	1:18	319
14:1–2	309	6:1–3	262
19:25–27	309	7:10–15	224
		26:21	318
Psalms		40:1–11	231
		50:5–11	131–32
2:7	157	53:5	319
11:6	318	55:3	157
16:10	157	63	126–27
41:1	253		
51	320–21	Jeremiah	
51:3	49	10:24	49
51:9	49	23:5–8	214
51:17	49		
67	63–64, 294–95	Ezekiel	
71	304–6		
95	52	18:30	319
98	62		
100	57–58	Daniel	
119:21	317		
121	314–15	9:7	49

423